D1130622

CONSERVATISM IN A DIVIDED AMERICA

CONSERVATISM IN A DIVIDED AMERICA

THE RIGHT AND IDENTITY POLITICS

GEORGE HAWLEY

University of Notre Dame Press
Notre Dame, Indiana

University of Notre Dame Press
Notre Dame, Indiana 46556
undpress.nd.edu

Published in the United States of America

Library of Congress Control Number: 2022935753

ISBN: 978-0-268-20374-0 (Hardback)
ISBN: 978-0-268-20376-4 (WebPDF)
ISBN: 978-0-268-20373-3 (Epub)

For Thomas

CONTENTS

ACKNOWLEDGMENTS

This book would not have been possible without extraordinary support from many generous people. I am grateful to the University of Alabama, where I have taught since 2013. Since my appointment, I have always felt supported as I pursued my various projects. My research agenda has shifted dramatically, more than once, since I began working here. My work today is decidedly different from what it was ten years ago, when I first entered the academic job market, yet I have never been discouraged from examining new topics. Over the last several years, I have written about public opinion, political behavior, immigration, history, and political theory. I even took an intellectual detour a few years ago and wrote a book on religion that had almost no connection at all to political science. This book tries to tie together many different themes I have been thinking about, and I hope my colleagues and superiors are satisfied with the end result, even if they disagree with my conclusions.

I am forever indebted to friends who read earlier drafts of this project, pointing out problems with my arguments, factual mistakes, literature I neglected to cite, and new ways of thinking about the questions I examine here. Special thanks to Leonard Chan, Pedro Zúquete, Richard Marcy, and Nicholas Drummond. I am also thankful for friends and colleagues who discussed the themes of this book with me, asking useful questions and helping to clarify my thinking: Jesse Merriam, Richard Hanania, David Azerrad, and Riley Matheson have my gratitude. I am also indebted to the anonymous peer reviewers at University of Notre Dame Press, and to Editor in Chief Eli Bortz, who has believed in this project since I first pitched the idea at the start of 2020. This book was much improved by all of these people's efforts.

As always, I owe a special thanks to my wife. Over the course of seven books, Kristen has continuously been my most helpful sounding board and diligent copyeditor. For her selflessness, attention to detail, and thoughtful critiques, I will be forever grateful. Thanks also to our children: Henry, Wyatt, Nina, and Thomas. It would be inaccurate to say that they make academic research easier, but they are a valuable source of motivation, and the attention they require forces me to take needed breaks from projects that would otherwise consume most of my time and attention. My entire family is also indebted to Nicole Carter and Hope Hatter, who have always taken such fantastic care of our children. Especially during the long days of the COVID-19 pandemic, they were truly indispensable.

This book is not intended to solve the major problems it considers, but I do hope that it will introduce some useful ideas into an important debate, even if readers reject most of what I have to say in the pages ahead. If you find value in this work, credit must be shared with all of the people named above. Any mistakes belong to me alone.

Introduction

Over the course of its history, the American conservative movement has declared its opposition to several intellectual and political currents it considers antithetical to its vision of ordered liberty. Conservative intellectuals have lambasted socialism, relativism, nominalism, secularism, and hedonism. Some have attacked the very concept of ideology as unhealthy and dangerous. Recently, however, conservatives have focused much of their attention to the purported evils of identity politics. This is not a new subject of concern for conservatives, but the way conservatives have approached questions of identity—and related questions of equality and justice—has evolved over the last seventy years. This book examines this history and the current debates about these issues.

By "identity politics," I mean the tendency to think about politics in terms of groups engaged in a zero-sum struggle for resources. In a sense, it is not entirely dissimilar from class-based politics, such as that described by traditional Marxism. Identity politics, however, is focused on different kind of groups. When we describe identity politics, we typically mean a form of politics built around mostly fixed demographic attributes. That is, politics focused on race, ethnicity, language, gender, sexual identity, religion, and region. This form of politics—alternatively described by conservatives as "tribalism"—is presumably not conducive to compromise and rational discussion. It is qualitatively different from political struggles defined entirely by specific material interests. Conservatives argue that identity politics degrades people, reducing us all to our tribal characteristics, rather than treating us as free-thinking, rational, and unique individuals.

Most American conservative intellectuals look toward the Enlightenment era for arguments in favor of individualism and against collectivism. The modern American conservative's fondness for the Enlightenment and its most important thinkers—John Locke, Adam Smith, and Thomas Jefferson, among others—is one characteristic that sets American conservatives apart from many other conservatives around the world. Classical liberalism, and the individualism it promoted, is a vital part of the American conservative tradition. Conservative arguments are often rooted in claims about the natural rights of individuals.

Despite the impressive intellectual pedigree that many of these conservative arguments possess, the primary conservative claims about identity politics are challenged by our everyday experience. The kind of "individual" that conservatives promote as the ideal—someone not focused on any particular identity group beyond, perhaps, the nation as a whole, and rationally weighing every argument through the use of his or her personal reason—is exceedingly rare. Whatever its origins, tribalism, in some form or another, seems to be an inescapable element of democratic politics.

This implies, of course, that conservatives do not fully understand their own movement. Conservatives promote the narrative that they are the side of ideas, whereas the progressive movement is just a collection of aggrieved identity groups, united by nothing beyond a shared resentment of white, Christian, cisgender, heterosexual men. In terms of how the respective intellectuals, journalists, and activists on the left and right present their arguments, there is some truth to this claim.[1] However, a closer look at the literature on political psychology reveals that self-described conservatives who vote Republican can be just as tribal as their political opponents.

In defense of conservatives, I will note that identity politics can be difficult to understand because identity is complicated, as are the political attitudes that emerge from identity. There are many facets to identity, and different people will find different personal attributes salient to their sense of self. These can further change over time. For most people, identity is not determined by a single variable—be it racial, ethnic, religious, and so on—but some attributes tend to be more politically significant than others.

The latest research has made this subject even more complex. It is well established that our political identities—especially our party identifications—are usually downstream from other forms of social identity. However, in this era of affective partisan polarization, party identification itself has become an important form of social identity. That is, for many of us, identifying as a Republican or a Democrat is not just an indication of which party we vote for. These party identifications have become a meaningful part of our sense of self, as significant as many other forms of identity. The fact that we increasingly, to the extent that we can, reshape other elements of our identity to be consonant with our political loyalties shows that political categories have an incredible emotional hold on us. This is true for both Republicans and Democrats. These findings challenge some of our basic assumptions about how democracies are supposed to function.

In many ways, U.S. politics would be healthier if we followed conservatives' advice. At an individual level, we should strive to think beyond our identity groups when thinking about public policy, and perhaps the conservative call to do so has had some success. Nonetheless, it is important that people across the political spectrum think clearly about these issues, considering the electorate as it actually exists rather than insisting it meet an unrealistic ideal. Nor is it helpful to simply blame identity politics on a liberal conspiracy to divide Americans into antagonistic groups. This argument is incongruent with the facts, and, to borrow conservative firebrand Ben Shapiro's catchphrase, "Facts don't care about your feelings." Scholars of public opinion and political behavior have made important discoveries about identity and partisanship. Any political theory that could prove useful in solving the more intractable problems of twenty-first-century U.S. politics will need to take these findings into account. Accepting that identity politics is here to stay does not mean it should be celebrated. When it comes to the politics of identity, there is much wisdom in Kwame Anthony Appiah's approach: "And so I write neither as identity's friend or foe. . . . As with gravity, you might as well be on good terms with it, but there's no point in buttering it up."[2]

Conservatives are justifiably hesitant to venture into this intellectual territory for several reasons. Most importantly, the relationship between identity and politics is dangerous and potentially explosive. Such a discussion also threatens to undermine many myths that conservatives tell about themselves and their movement, especially the notion that they are somehow above identity politics. As I will note, there was always an identitarian element to conservatism, which arguably became more important (if even less openly acknowledged) as conservatism became a powerful political force. Despite their misgivings about doing so, contemporary conservative intellectuals and journalists must take the subject seriously. Questions of identity, which are disrupting political debates across the globe, in both established and fledgling democracies, and in dictatorships, require answers. The subject of group identity is tied to many of the other most contentious subjects of the day, raising new questions about individualism and democracy. What are we to make of the apparently unexpected resurgence of populist nationalism across the Western world? How do we address the legitimate grievances of historically disadvantaged minority groups without provoking a backlash that leaves them worse off than before? What is the proper response to majority demographic groups expressing anxiety about their forthcoming status as just one more minority among many?

Although conservatives have for years complained of identity politics on the left, recent years have seen an increase in right-wing identity politics. This has been most pronounced in the rise of the so-called Alt-Right, a recent iteration of the American white nationalist movement. What accounts for this movement's rapid rise and fall? If some form of identity politics really is inevitable, why did this effort to bring explicit white racial identity politics out in the open fall apart in such a short amount of time?

In the face of these questions, calling for an end to identity politics will not suffice. One may be correct in stating that the world will be more just and free if we can escape identity politics, if we can base our political loyalties on our individual interests and philosophical beliefs, rather than our group identities and allegiances. The soundness of the argument, unfortunately, may not be important. It is unlikely to prove successful, no matter how many charts conservative pundits and scholars provide. At some point, to use a recurring theme in conservative political philosophy, one must work with human nature as it is.

This is not to say that all conservatives claim identity politics goes against the grain of human nature. Many recognize that some degree of tribalism seems to be innate. They nonetheless also believe it can be transcended. In *Suicide of the West* (2018), conservative author and columnist Jonah Goldberg argues that tribalism—and the identity politics that follow—seems to be hardwired into human beings. However, for several reasons (he does not settle on a single theory), the West, and especially the United States, managed to overcome this aspect of human nature, and it is crucial that Americans safeguard that achievement.[3]

There are a few points where I disagree with Goldberg's book. Most notably, I am not convinced that America's escape from tribalism and embrace of Lockean liberalism, a crucial part of what Goldberg calls "the Miracle," was ever as complete as he suggests. Identity politics was always there, even at the nation's founding, and I am not just referring to the nation's original sin of racial slavery. Identity politics may have taken different forms from what we see today, but at no point has it ever been fully absent. This may be a comforting message. If identity politics in some form or another has always been present, its contemporary versions likely do not signify the end of the republic. Yet it does unquestionably represent a great challenge.

When attempting to explain a large and diverse intellectual and political tradition, especially its approach to controversial subjects, it is very easy for critics, even friendly critics, to oversimplify arguments, attack straw men, exaggerate the influence of irrelevant kooks, or take quotes out of context. This book aspires to avoid that pitfall. I try to fairly and accurately describe conservative arguments about these issues, quoting their words directly when possible, and acknowledging that conservatives have never been monolithic. I will present representative arguments, from respected figures within mainstream conservatism, rather than cherry-pick transparently foolish claims made by obvious intellectual lightweights. I furthermore start from the assumption that the conservatives I discuss in the pages ahead made honest, good-faith arguments. I will mostly take it for granted that, on the occasions that they made incorrect factual statements, they did so out of ignorance rather than a desire to mislead.[4] There are conservatives I do consider patently dishonest about their movement's history, but I will mostly not engage with them here.

Writers working on this subject face other problematic temptations. Several notable authors, including some I admire, have recently published books on the subject of tribalism in modern politics in recent years. Many of them recounted a relevant, famous social science study: the 1954 "Robbers Cave experiment." The social psychologist Mazafer Sharif conducted the experiment as a test of his theory that prejudice results from competition between groups. He gathered two groups of a dozen boys between the ages of eight and eleven and sent them to a state park in rural Oklahoma for about three weeks. The two groups of boys were kept separate except when engaging in competition against each other. The winning side of these games received honors such as trophies and medals, items that may seem symbolically significant but were practically useless. As time went on, the groups became increasingly hostile toward each other. Beginning with verbal insults, tensions intensified, escalating to theft, vandalism, and physical violence.

The results of Sharif's experiment seem to demonstrate something extremely important. They apparently showed that people could develop levels of enmity against total strangers. They further showed that competition is a major catalyst for these feelings of hostility, even when the stakes of the competition are extremely low. From a political science perspective, this finding, if true, could have enormous implications. For example, it helps demonstrate why so many Americans' emotions run so high around Election Day, even if they are almost completely ignorant about issues of public policy and the policy differences between candidates are slight. The mere fact that they personally identify with the Republican or the Democratic Party is enough for them to feel strong negative emotions toward those who identify with the competing party.

I unfortunately do not feel comfortable leaning on Sharif's work to make any kind of case here, as it turns out that the Robbers Cave experiment was so flawed that we may not want to draw any inferences from it. One problem is that we could probably not replicate it today—I doubt any university's Institutional Review Board would approve of such an experiment. A more troublesome concern is that Sharif may not have been honest in his description of what occurred during his experiments.

In her recent book on the subject, Gina Perry examines the Robbers Cave experiment in detail, finding that the story as it is usually told omits many crucial details.[5] For example, before conducting his most famous experiment, Sharif performed a similar study in 1953. This earlier experiment showed very different results, to the point that they undermined his theses. He tried to goad the two sides into conflict, and never succeeded. In his more successful experiment, the researchers took steps to block the boys' efforts to build friendships across group lines. The inferences we can make about human behavior based on Sharif's work are not as clear-cut as we would like.

Although I argue the research on identity, tribalism, and group conflict tells an important story, the story is not always straightforward. Sometimes interesting studies are so flawed that they are ultimately useless, but this may not be understood until after the study has had a great effect. Sometimes researchers examining similar subjects reach very different conclusions, despite all using proper methods. In other cases, results are statistically significant but not substantively important. In the pages ahead, I will try to provide as complete a picture as possible, not relying too heavily on any single set of research and acknowledging the research that contradicts my main arguments. This is a complex topic, and although I argue that identity cannot be extricated from politics, I do not want to overstate my case or oversimplify the subject.

I hope conservatives will view this work as a well-intentioned critique. I hope to start a conversation rather than score partisan or ideological points. The United States benefits from a strong debate between competing ideological visions, even if ideological principles will always be rare in the electorate. This is harder to achieve when different sides fail to understand each other's basic premises or have very different views about the basic nature of democratic politics in a heterogeneous society. Furthermore, I agree with the conservatives who say identity politics can create real problems for American democracy. However, resolving or at least mitigating those problems is not possible until we understand their true nature. I hope this book provides some clarity.

In various passages in this book, I acknowledge that figures on the Far Right and sometimes even the extreme Right have made cogent arguments. This may be a controversial decision, but also one that is necessitated by intellectual honesty. One can recognize that the Radical Right sometimes makes arguments that cannot merely be waved away without agreeing with a radical-right worldview. One can, after all, think that Lenin made some very perceptive arguments without being a Leninist or even a leftist of any sort. As I have argued in the past, the Right should be treated in an intellectually serious manner. Although I take the field of political psychology seriously, I disagree with efforts within that field to pathologize the Right, to treat right-wing views as a sign of some kind of mental disorder. Extremely learned and intelligent people can reach conclusions that many others find abhorrent. The mere fact that a position is discordant with the progressive *Zeitgeist* is not enough to dismiss it. I am sensitive to the concern that discussing extreme views in a dispassionate manner risks normalizing and amplifying these kinds of ideas, perhaps helping them make a breakthrough. In other forms of media, this may be a greater concern. For scholarly texts from a university press, however, I am confident any such effect would be, at most, minuscule.

As I write these words, identity questions are even more salient in U.S. politics than normal. The death of George Floyd, an African American man, at the hands of a white police officer in Minnesota in May 2020 set off a wave of protests across the nation; in rare cases, these protests were followed by rioting and looting. The Black Lives Matter movement has achieved remarkable success in changing how journalists and the general public discuss questions of race and racism. At the same time, conservative activists have recently had great success demonizing critical race theory, leading to acrimonious debates about how race should be discussed in public schools. These developments add an additional level of timeliness to this project, and a greater sense of urgency to the questions I consider here.

Chapter 1 presents definitions and an introduction to key concepts discussed throughout this book. I discuss the concepts of "left" and "right," conservatism as a broad idea, and American conservatism as a unique ideology. My perspectives on these topics, though not unique, are not universally shared among all scholars of this subject, which is why it is important to explain my views and definitions. I do, however, attempt to give a fair hearing to those thinkers whose arguments on this matter deviate from my own. I also explain, as well as I can in short sections, how I define concepts such as "identity politics," "intersectionality," "political correctness," and "cultural relativism." I also try to discuss some of the controversies around these terms.

Chapter 2 examines the various conservative arguments against identity politics. The American conservative tradition is strongly, but not exclusively, influenced by classical liberal thinking. Although intellectuals from this tradition differed in their views, those that most influenced today's conservatives, for the most part, embraced an individualist perspective. Contemporary conservatives mostly share this view, suggesting that group-based political distinctions are at odds with the natural rights tradition. I try, as well as I am able, to describe the conservative critiques of modern identity politics, noting that these arguments are sometimes based on principles and sometimes built upon utilitarian concerns.

Chapter 3 considers how various conservatives have sought to explain the rise of modern identity politics. They do not have a consistent story. Some blame the rise of identity politics on the legacy of the Progressive Era of the late nineteenth and early twentieth century, when the thinking of the American Founders, based on natural rights, gave way to insidious ideas imported from Europe. Other conservatives blame identity politics on new ideas that developed in the post–civil rights era, when demands for equal rights for all people gave way to demands for special recognition for people according to their identities—the Black Power movement, for example. I also discuss those conservatives who have argued that identity politics resulted from other trends, such as the breakdown of the traditional family or the decline of religion.

In Chapter 4, I move to the history of the American conservatism in one of the pivotal periods of the twentieth century: the era of the civil rights movement. In this chapter, I discuss the ways in which an implicit white identity was a key element of conservatism in its early days. I discuss the strange dance between northern conservatives associated with the conservative intellectual movement (working with publications such as *National Review*), who wanted to avoid a reputation for explicit racial prejudice, and southern segregationists who thought the nascent conservative movement could prove a useful long-term ally.

Chapter 5 analyzes the relationship between conservatism and feminism. On this subject, the conservative discussions about identity politics deviate from its other manifestations. Unlike the high-profile opponents of the civil rights movement, who were rarely African Americans, the most notable opponents of modern feminism were often women themselves. Furthermore, when it came to women's rights, conservatives were often more willing than the Left to engage in gender essentialism— the notion that women are fundamentally different from men and thus need to be treated differently by American laws and cultural mores. In the latter decades of the twentieth century, there was a meaningful debate between the Left and the Right as to what represented women's oppression and women's privileges in American life. In their own way, I argue, antifeminists on the right were more explicitly engaged in identity politics than feminists on the left. Recent developments, such as a growing trend among conservative women to describe themselves as feminists, further complicates matters, as do the tense political debates about the status of transgender women in the modern feminist movement.

Chapter 6 looks at the complex issue of immigration and the conservative movement's approach to it. This subject, perhaps more than any other, has raised important recent questions about the meaning of the contemporary American identity. It is also a question that the early conservatives scarcely wrote about at all. Reading early works from leading figures of the postwar conservative movement, one is hard-pressed to find meaningful commentary on the immigration question. These early conservatives furthermore apparently took it for granted that the United States would remain a majority-white country for the indefinite future. As immigration became a more pressing issue in the latter decades of the twentieth century, and it became clear that immigration policies had set the nation on a path that will lead to the end of whites' majority status, conservatives have sought to develop a coherent approach to the immigration question. The conservative movement, however, has always been divided on this issue, with some remaining in favor of generous immigration policies (usually, but not always, for economic reasons), and others maintaining a strong commitment to immigration restriction. I consider conservative approaches to immigration, and discuss the many issues tied to immigration, such as questions about political culture, assimilation, racism, and the partisan consequences of long-term, large-scale immigration.

In chapter 7, I examine the subject of partisan politics and how it disrupts the usual narratives about identity politics. I discuss the most recent research from scholars of public opinion and political behavior, noting the degree to which the typical American voter is not a rational utilitarian or a devotee of abstract principles. Instead, partisan politics increasingly looks like identity politics by another name. Political scientists have made this argument for many years. However, we are increasingly reaching a new, startling conclusion: our party identifications are more than the sum of our various other social identities; for many of us, being a Republican or a Democrat is now a crucial element of our sense of identity. A disturbing number of us view our partisan attachments as a crucial aspect of who we are. Our partisan identities are so strong that they can even influence our other identities, things we long assumed were exogenous to partisan politics: personal attributes such as religion and even race or ethnicity. This is even true of those of us with relatively low levels of political knowledge and little understanding of ideology. Debates about the nature and roots of partisanship and ideology in the electorate are ongoing, and I explain multiple competing theories. However, there is increasingly incontrovertible evidence that partisan politics is both rooted in identity and is itself a form of identity. Conservatives especially should find this unsettling, as it seems to repudiate what many in the conservative movement claim about their own supporters. If conservatives wish to continue to claim that their political philosophy is ultimately rooted in human nature, they will need to update their political theory, incorporating these new findings.

Chapter 8 returns to a subject I examined in detail in two of my previous books: the so-called Alt-Right. At this point, I consider the Alt-Right a defunct movement, and I have begun speaking of it in the past tense. This does not mean that its underlying ideology—white nationalism—has vanished from American life, even though it was always small and punched above its weight when it came to media attention. In this chapter, I discuss the things that we can learn from the Alt-Right's short history. Most readers will find reasons for optimism in this chapter. It is unquestionably true that the Alt-Right was hindered by missteps by its leading figures and dysfunction within its ranks. However, it suffered from a more fundamental problem: very few white Americans actually support white nationalism, especially when offered in a straightforward manner. In a way, the Alt-Right's history seems to further complicate this book's arguments. If most people, at least implicitly, embrace some form of identity politics, it stands to reason that white Americans, especially in a period of extraordinary racial polarization, would support an identitarian movement of their own. Yet, when such a movement was placed before them, and it even seemed to have the endorsement of important political elites, they rejected it.

Despite apparent misgivings with contemporary multiculturalism and high levels of immigration, your typical white American (including your average Republican voter) does not endorse a policy of mass deportation of nonwhite Americans. From the beginning, my approach to the study of white nationalism has always differed from many other academics. I have argued that we should draw a line between white nationalism and American conservatism, even while acknowledging the degree to which conservatives have benefited from, and sometimes contributed to, white racial anxieties. I argue that events of the last few years have substantially vindicated this claim, but I acknowledge problematic exceptions and I recognize that others have a different interpretation of recent events.

In chapter 9, I conclude by discussing how some contemporary conservatives are rethinking some of the movement's assumptions. I have never been an alarmist, and continue to reject some of the apocalyptic scenarios suggested by many people on the left and the right. However, I must acknowledge that this is a precarious moment for the American republic. I hope I have accurately and adequately explained many of the questions that must be resolved if we are to move forward as a tranquil and tolerant liberal democracy. As readers of my earlier writings are aware, I respect and admire much of what the American conservative movement has accomplished, but I have never shied away from naming what I consider its shortcomings. Whatever one thinks of the conservative movement, however, conservatives will play a vital role in determining the future of the United States, and I hope they rise to the extraordinary challenges ahead.

ONE

Conservatism and Other Concepts

I must define some of the terms I use consistently throughout this text. Although this seems like a straightforward task, defining concepts such as "conservatism" can be surprisingly challenging, as the meaning of conservatism can be context-dependent. I must furthermore distinguish modern mainstream American conservatism from other varieties of conservatism, including forms of conservatism found abroad and those self-described American conservatives that reject one or more element of mainstream conservatism in the United States. I similarly must explain what I mean by "identity politics" and some of the concepts associated with it. This also poses challenges, because it is not always clear what we mean by "identity" or how the politics of identity differs from other political contests. Because this book is primarily concerned with the conservative movement's arguments about identity politics, I will attempt to describe "identity politics" as conservatives use the term, and I examine more academic descriptions, noting that they are not always consistent.

WHAT IS LEFT, WHAT IS RIGHT?

Given the frequency that pundits, radio hosts, TV personalities, and politicians use the terms "left-wing" and "right-wing," it is remarkable how rarely we hear coherent definitions of these terms. Most politically savvy Americans have an intuitive grasp on what they mean, and could probably determine whether someone is on the left or the right after learning just a few of their opinions. Yet there is not a clear definition of these terms that all people across the political spectrum agree upon. To the extent that people provide definitions, they are typically self-serving and unfair. An ideologue on the American right may describe a leftist as someone that "hates America."[1] To the Left, a rightist might be defined as nothing more than a reactionary defending his or her unearned privilege.[2] Such definitions coming from partisans on the left or right may even include a few additional epithets: "racist," "elitist," "ethnomasochist," "misogynist," "degenerate," and so on.

When intellectuals and pundits approach this subject, their analysis is often more sophisticated, but almost as self-serving. The Right typically likes to frame the discussion as a divide between liberty and statism. That is, the Right prefers limited government, and the Left prefers expansive government.[3] Conservatives usually temper this a bit out of their belief in moral traditionalism, which many argue requires government intervention, and their typical preference for hawkish foreign policies, which require a powerful military. Libertarians, who prefer a more noninterventionist foreign policy and oppose state-directed efforts to impose moral uniformity, tend to be even fonder of the view that the political spectrum is all about the size of the state. As I argued in *Right-Wing Critics of American Conservatism*, this is a convenient definition for the Right, because it precludes even the possibility of right-wing totalitarianism or even authoritarianism. However much a political party or movement may seem right-wing, once it begins expanding the state it becomes, by definition, left-wing and no longer part of the right-wing camp. Thus, according to this view, the Right has nothing in common with any tyrannical government. I disagree with this definition.

Conservative scholar Thomas Sowell has suggested the critical ideological divide is over beliefs about human nature: Are humans inherently flawed, and thus limited in their ability to be shaped by society, or is human potential limitless, provided we have a proper social order?[4] Libertarian economist Arnold Kling has suggested that different ideological groups view politics through totally different "languages," with each using different moral frameworks.[5] He suggests that conservatives, progressives, and libertarians all use a different axis to examine political questions. Progressives think in terms of "oppressor–oppressed," conservatives communicate along the "civilization–barbarism axis," and libertarians "communicate along the liberty–coercion axis."[6]

Bryan Caplan, also a libertarian economist, provides his own definition of the Left and the Right, which is not flattering to either side. He argues that the Left is defined by its opposition to markets, claiming that "on an emotional level, they're critical of market outcomes."[7] He suggests this is true regardless of how well markets perform. The Right, according to his definition, is arguably even less intellectually impressive. The Right is simply anti-Left, again on an emotional level, rather than a logical one: "No matter how much they agree with leftists on an issue, they can't bear to say, 'The left is totally right, it would be churlish to criticize them.'" This allows all sorts of different ideological categories, both moderate Republicans and fascists, to fall within the Right, without assuming much additional ideological congruence. Paul Gottfried, a scholar associated with the paleoconservative movement,[8] similarly defines the Right by its opposition to the Left.[9]

Intellectuals on the left argue that placement on the left–right scale is based on attitudes toward equality. The Left favors universal equality (however defined) and the Right stands for inequality, particularly inequalities that favor those already privileged. Italian scholar Norberto Bobbio has made the most influential argument for this classification.[10] Political theorist Corey Robin, who agrees with Bobbio, argues this way in *The Reactionary Mind*:

> These ideas, which occupy the right side of the political spectrum, are forged in battle. They have always been, at least since they emerged as formal ideologies during the French Revolution, battles between social groups rather than nations; roughly speaking, between those with more power and those with less. For that is what conservatism is: a meditation on—and theoretical rendition of—the felt experience of having power, seeing it threatened, and trying to win it back.[11]

This comes closer to capturing the essence of the right–left division than the liberty versus government control scale, but it is nonetheless unfair to the Right. Political theorist Patrick Deneen has provided slightly more expansive definitions: "The left is characterized by a preference for change and reform, a commitment to liberty and equality, an orientation toward progress and the future, while the right is the party of order and tradition, hierarchy, and a disposition to valorize the past."[12] I mostly agree with this definition, but it bothers me that it is not immediately obvious which side of the dichotomy one should place libertarianism—libertarians tend to reject both equality and tradition. Americans with a libertarian worldview are unquestionably a small part of the electorate, but libertarian intellectuals have been a crucial element of American political life, especially on the right.

I prefer a definition that accepts the Left's view of itself as the champion of universal equality. Whether their policies always or even usually result in greater overall equality is an empirical question I leave to more qualified scholars. However, the Right is not necessarily always opposed to equality as such. Rather, the Right, in my view, represents all of those different ideological groupings that place something else higher than equality in their hierarchy of political values. This is flexible enough to allow both libertarians (who value personal liberty above all other values) and Nazis (who prioritize racial purity and supremacy) to qualify as right-wing, but it does not imply that Nazis and libertarians share any other important premises. My hope was that people across the political spectrum will find this definition satisfactory.

Since I stated these definitions of the Left and the Right in *Right-Wing Critics of American Conservatism*, conservative friends, students, and correspondents have raised two primary objections. The first is that it downplays conservatives' devotion to equality. That is, conservatives are just as committed to this principle as anyone else; they simply define equality in a different way. I have heard many variants of the following claim: "Progressives are committed to equality of outcome, but conservatives believe in equality of opportunity." In other words, conservatives believe everyone should start from a position of equality, but any subsequent inequalities that emerge based on peoples' virtues or failings are acceptable. Further, this conservative argument goes, mandated equality of outcomes would remove incentives for human striving in economic life. If the fruits of one's labor will be divided up equally among the rest of society, what reason does anyone have to work hard?

There is an important truth to the conservative argument about incentives, but the notion of "equality of opportunity" is problematic, as many on the left have pointed out. We are not born into a position of equality. We are born with varying degrees of privilege, and one does not need to be a leftist to recognize them. Some are born into wealthy families; some enjoy a strong education throughout childhood and early adulthood; some are born genetically disposed to excel at certain pursuits; some are born in places with many economic opportunities for people of all levels of ability, whereas others are born in places where they seem condemned to a life of poverty, despite their personal virtues. As long as this remains the case, the very notion of equality of opportunity is nonsensical. Further, even if it were possible to create a new world with a totally level playing field, it would require a level of social engineering that no conservative would ever endorse.

A more honest conservative approach to equality, which would not require jettisoning the principle entirely, would admit that conservatives desire neither equality of opportunity nor equality of outcome, which is not to say that conservatives necessarily oppose all forms of economic redistribution. Instead, it would be fair to say that American conservatives believe in equality in the sense that all people within a society are entitled to certain negative liberties, such as those liberties protected by the Bill of Rights. Beyond that, other forms of inequality are acceptable.

Some on the right have additionally argued that the Left's calls for universal equality are insincere. That is, few people want genuine equality for all people. Instead, those calling for equality actually desire a new hierarchy, one in which their group is ranked at the top. This is a very old critique of the Left. Vilfredo Pareto, the Italian economist and sociologist, known in part for his theories about elite power, described egalitarian rhetoric as follows:

The sentiment that is very inappropriately named equality is fresh, strong, alert, precisely because it is not, in fact, a sentiment of equality and is not related to any abstraction, as a few naive "intellectuals" still believe; but because it is related to direct interests of individuals who are bent on escaping certain inequalities not in their favour, and setting up new inequalities that will be in their favour, this latter being their chief concern.[13]

It is easy to name examples where this was true. The communist countries around the globe in the twentieth century hardly resembled the utopian, egalitarian societies promised by revolutionary leaders. Whatever their intentions, the Soviet Union and its satellites quickly became oligarchies led by a privileged party elite, overseeing mostly impoverished populations. This phenomenon was parodied by George Orwell in *Animal Farm*.[14]

We might also note that many of the "communist" revolutionary movements of the Cold War were not motivated by a desire to join a worldwide communist crusade that would usher in a new worker's paradise without nations. This was a critical mistake that many conservative cold warriors made during the period. Conservative theorists such as James Burnham, for example, were quite insistent that, whatever fissures existed within the communist bloc, they were ultimately a unified force engaged in a "struggle for the world."[15] In fact, many of these revolutions in the developing world were driven by nationalistic sentiments, ethnic or religious divides within countries, or both. Amy Chua persuasively argues that the United States' failure to understand these forces—instead myopically focusing on the communist ideology—was a crucial element to its defeat in Vietnam.[16]

A variation of Pareto's attack on egalitarian rhetoric has can be employed against proponents of multiculturalism. That is, we can expect groups in a position of weakness to appeal to the majority's sense of fairness, and perhaps its guilty conscience. However, should the roles be truly reversed, and a new dominant power emerges, we can expect the new powerbrokers to be no less domineering than their predecessors. According to sociologist Martin Spencer:

> The analogy can be made here between the political and rhetorical positions of religions. When religions are able to do so they suppress other religions, as competing forms of belief, in the name of the "one true faith." However, when they are politically weak, and are themselves victims of repression, they call for toleration and religious freedom, which is the religious equivalent of multiculturalism. The

rhetoric of multiculturalism, which advances its cause in the name of "diversity" and "inclusiveness," must therefore be suspect.[17]

This may be an accurate description of the multiculturalist view, at least in some cases, but I do not use this approach. To begin with, it is difficult to falsify this argument. How can we definitively say that a person or movement calling for universal equality is insincere? Even if the results of their actions do not ultimately achieve their stated goal, should we infer that their egalitarian rhetoric was always just a cover for something else? I am not comfortable engaging in that kind of psychological analysis.

The more important reason I reject such an approach in my own work is simple consistency. In my studies of right-wing thought, I begin from the assumption that the purveyors of these ideologies mean what they say and write. Once again, this may not be a perfect representation of reality. The left-wing critique of the Right—that all the Right's arguments are merely gloss on defenses of privileges they find advantageous—is also not entirely wrong. It therefore only seems fair that I would examine the egalitarian Left with the same lens I used to study radical libertarians, white supremacists, and other groups on the right.

WHAT IS AMERICAN CONSERVATISM?

Whereas I argue that, in a broad sense, "left" and "right" have fixed meanings, conservatism does not. According to historian Patrick Allitt, "Conservatism is, first of all, an *attitude* to social and political change that looks for support to the ideas, beliefs, and habits of the past and puts more faith in the lessons of history than the abstractions of political philosophy."[18] If we take the simplistic view that conservatism is nothing more than resistance to change, then conservatism will always be context-dependent. A conservative in India will have a different vision for society than a conservative in Finland. In the Soviet Union in 1991, resisting the end of communism was arguably the "conservative" position. For all its talk about "permanent things," the American conservative movement was very much a product of its time.

Mainstream American conservatives describe their movement as a stool with three legs: *limited government, cultural traditionalism,* and *a strong foreign policy.* The stool analogy is used because it implies that each element is necessary and equally important—if you remove one leg from a stool, it collapses. One may understandably find this a curious amalgamation of principles, since the logical connection between them is not obvious. Indeed, before the arrival of modern American conservatism as we know it, many Americans embraced one of these principles without endorsing the others. Indeed, one could make the case that these principles are at odds with each other in important respects. After all, it is the free market, not the state, which provides the cultural products that most traditionalist conservatives find loathsome. Furthermore, throughout most of Western history, and even U.S. history, cultural traditionalists assumed that the state played an important role in maintaining religious and other traditional values. The connection between militarism and limited government is even more tenuous: a country that is always mobilized for war is necessarily a country with a powerful and dangerous government. Wars are also responsible for major cultural and economic upheavals that may make cultural traditionalists uncomfortable; think of all the women who left home and entered the workforce to fill the labor gap in World War II.

Before conservatives began arguing otherwise, it was not obvious that the three legs of American conservatism depended on each other. From a political standpoint, however, the conservative coalition made sense, or it did during the Cold War when the modern American conservative movement was born. Economic libertarians, cultural conservatives, and foreign policy hawks begin from different premises. However, in the mid-twentieth century, they were united by a skepticism, or hostility, toward the Left and the Democratic Party, but for different reasons and with different motives.

Cultural traditionalism, economic libertarianism, and anticommunism were all intellectually relevant in the United States before the modern conservative movement was born. When combined, these three groups had sufficient electoral, financial, and intellectual firepower to challenge the New Deal liberalism that dominated U.S. politics since the early 1930s. First, however, they needed to unite. The creation of a semicoherent movement from these diverse forces was the most important contribution William F. Buckley Jr. and his *National Review* made to American political life. The thinkers associated with this magazine, founded in 1955, played a key role in reconciling these different philosophies.

As I will argue elsewhere in this book, conservatism—and the decisions conservatives often made at critical junctures—can only be fully understood in the context of the Cold War. Indeed, in the absence of the Cold War, American conservatism would likely have developed in very different ways. The Cold War gave the budding movement a sense of urgency it may not have otherwise felt in the seemingly placid 1950s. Fear of Soviet infiltration in the Democratic Party, the educational establishment, and cultural institutions turned the Left into more than a political opponent; it was seen instead as an existential threat to everything moral traditionalists, free-market economists, and foreign policy hawks held dear. Following Whittaker Chambers's revelations about Alger Hiss, an important U.S. State Department official accused of being a communist, anticommunists were convinced that many influential government figures in the Roosevelt administration were not just weak on communism, but that they wanted to facilitate a communist victory. George Nash writes in his history of the conservative movement, "The bare facts of [the Alger Hiss] case, however, cannot begin to suggest its enduring effect on the post-1945 conservative renascence. As much as any other event, the Hiss case forged the anti-Communist element in resurgent conservatism."[19] Paranoia about communist subversion would only increase in the years ahead, reaching a peak during the era of McCarthyism and the zenith of the John Birch Society's influence, when Robert Welch accused the very highest levels of government of actively plotting to bring down the United States and establish a one-world socialist government.

At the very least, cold warriors, cultural traditionalists, and proponents of free-market economics had reason to form an alliance of convenience over the issue of confronting communists at home and abroad. The great achievement of postwar conservative political theorists was their creation of a semicoherent political philosophy that most members of each faction could—more or less—agree upon. Of those making the case for the underlying unity of these different factions, Frank S. Meyer played a particularly important role. He made this argument multiple times in the pages of *National Review*, but his theory was fully developed in *In Defense of Freedom*.[20] M. Stanton Evans, also an early editor at *National Review*, was another key proponent of this view. They argued that virtue is impossible without real freedom; a person must have the ability to make a choice between right and wrong for true virtue to be possible. Those who value freedom from an encroaching state, and consider this the most important political question, should furthermore understand the vital role played by religion and virtue, because freedom cannot long survive in their absence. Stephen Tonsor made this argument in an essay published in a book Meyer edited:

> Religion is important to the democratic state not only because it preserves the fabric of society but also because it acts as the most important power to check the aggressive, centralizing, and totalitarian tendencies of the modern state, without a strong religion, which remains outside and independent of the power of the state, civil liberty is unthinkable. The power of the state is, in part, balanced and neutralized by the power of the church. The freedom of the individual is most certain in that realm which neither church nor state can successfully occupy and dominate.[21]

This combination of libertarian and traditionalist principles we mostly credit Meyer for developing eventually became known as "fusionism," but Meyer did not coin that particular term. Meyer and other like-minded writers at *National Review* were not entirely successful in bringing the competing sides of this debate together. Max Eastman, who was an important free-market economist in the early years of the movement, ultimately broke with *National Review* and conservatism because of its ostentatious religious quality—Eastman was an open atheist. Russell Kirk, author of *The Conservative Mind*, never accepted that libertarians and conservatives were natural allies. Frank Meyer, Richard Weaver, and others rejected Kirk's position that conservatives should look to Edmund Burke as their primary inspiration. A number of important libertarians, most notably Murray Rothbard, wanted nothing to do with the conservative movement, largely because of the movement's hawkish stance on foreign policy. Other leading conservatives, such as Kirk and Robert Nisbet, similarly remained skeptical of the movement's commitment to militarism, but they chose to remain affiliated with the mainstream conservative movement for the rest of their lives.

Despite these disagreements, the conservative movement had, for the most part, agreed upon the basic premises of the ideology by the mid-1960s. Having generated a new ideology, however, the new conservative movement was faced with the task of building a real grassroots movement and, ultimately, capturing political power. Identitarian concerns, especially as they relate to race, played a major role in conservatism's rise. I will discuss this element of conservatism when I talk about conservatism and civil rights in chapter 4.

IS AMERICAN CONSERVATISM AN IDEOLOGY?

Conservatives have long debated among themselves whether they should classify their political philosophy as an ideology. Some of the most important conservative thinkers have argued that it should not, most notably Kirk. Whether or not conservatism meets the definition of ideology depends on how ideology is defined; if ideology has a very limited definition, then Kirk may have been correct. Like conservatism, ideology is a concept that most people intuitively grasp, but often have a hard time describing. How is an ideology different from a set of policy proposals, for example? What distinguishes an ideological way of thinking from a nonideological way of thinking? Like the concept of "conservatism," the concept of ideology can be confusing because there are many competing definitions of the term.

If we rely on Kirk's definition, the conservative is incapable of being an ideologue. That is, if conservatism became an ideology, it would cease to be conservatism as he understood it. To Kirk, an ideologue was a radical, a person with a vision for a future utopia that can be brought into being with a properly instituted government: "The word ideology means political fanaticism, a body of beliefs alleged to point the way to a perfect society."[22] For Kirk, there were few things more dangerous than devotion to an ideology. This is not the same as stating that political principles are not useful or even essential, but to be an ideologue necessarily implies zealous devotion to an inflexible political dogma.

At the time Kirk was writing, his definition of ideology was not unique or even particularly uncommon. The Italian political scientist Giovanni Sartori similarly posited that a political ideology must be theoretically disentangled from a political belief system.[23] Sartori argued that ideological thinking represented a form of closed-mindedness, suggesting that "the ideological mentality represents a typically *dogmatic*, that is, rigid and impermeable, approach to politics."[24] Ideologues can additionally be recognized by their "principled and doctrinaire perception of politics."[25] For them, all political events are viewed through an ideological lens. The true ideologue is typically immune to empirical and other arguments that call into question his or her ideological views.

If we insist ideology requires both fanaticism and intellectual rigidity approaching total closed-mindedness, complete with beliefs that cannot be swayed by empirical evidence, I would not describe most conservatives (or most progressives) as ideologues. Yet, I can understand why one would describe modern American conservatism as an ideology, even if we accept Kirk's definition. Many conservative arguments about U.S. strategy in the global war on terror were premised on an invincible faith in the transformative power of democracy. That is, most influential conservatives at the time were apparently confident that, if we could just provide an appropriate constitution and democratic institutions, stable, prosperous, and peaceful nations could be created from the ashes of the Taliban and Saddam Hussein's Baathist regime, but they ignored all of the religious and ethnic schisms that suggested otherwise. At least during George W. Bush's presidency, when it came to foreign policy, many American conservatives were ideologues in the sense that Kirk used the term.

If we relax the assumption that ideology necessarily implies fanaticism, but continue to define ideologues by inflexible thinking, we can make a stronger case for the ideological nature of both modern American conservatism and contemporary progressivism. Conservatives and liberals have endeavored to build a strong empirical case for political programs; their political platforms are not built entirely on a chain of a priori assumptions. It would be unfair to claim otherwise. But there are certain values that both conservatives and progressives do not consider up for debate, and they have not necessarily come to embrace these values via dispassionate, empirical examination and reflection.

In political science today, most scholars prefer a less rigid view of ideology. According to this view, an ideology requires only a minimal amount of internal consistency. When political scientists consider ideology, they find it useful to rely on this less extreme definition. Or, if they prefer to avoid the semantic headaches that follow any discussion of ideology, they use the term "belief system," which may be a more accurate term.[26] Political scientist Samuel Huntington described ideology as merely "a system of ideas concerned with the distribution of political and social values and acquiesced in by a significant social group."[27] Using this definition, conservatism is of course an ideology.

One prominent conservative scholar, whose esteem in the eyes of contemporary conservatives nearly matches that of Kirk, openly acknowledged that conservatism represented an ideology. In response to the claim that conservatism is not an ideology, sociologist Robert Nisbet wrote the following in *Conservatism: Dream and Reality*:

> But this is to take the narrow and stunted view of the word "ideology." Leaving aside the historical meanings it has had, such as its pejorative reference to a certain class of ideas in Napoleonic times and its use by Marx for the collective consciousness of a social class, the sense of "ideology" in our age is quite clear, and altogether useful. Stated briefly, an ideology is any reasonably coherent body of moral, economic, social and cultural ties that has a solid and well known reference to politics and political power; more specifically a power base to make possible a victory for the body of ideas. An ideology, in contrast to a mere passing configuration of opinion, remains alive for a considerable period of time, has major advocates and spokesmen and a respectable degree of institutionalization. It is likely to have charismatic figures in its history—Burkes, Disrealis, Churchills, etc.—among conservatives and their counterparts in liberalism and socialism.[28]

I do not discount the many criticisms that have been leveled against the use of the word "ideology" to describe conservatism, but I agree with Nisbet. American conservatism meets Nisbet's criterion, and it is entirely appropriate to discuss conservatism as an ideology.

THE CONSERVATIVE CANON AND ITS LIMITATIONS

Given how the United States has changed since modern conservatism was born, it is remarkable how much continuity we have seen in the

American conservative movement. Many things can explain conservatism's impressive ability to maintain ideological continuity over a long period. Funding from generous donors, the creation of respected think tanks, and popular media figures have played an important role. There is another important, sometimes neglected, element to modern American conservatism that we should also consider. Contemporary conservatives have a record of speaking of early conservative journalists and scholars as gurus of "true conservatism." Over time, the leading books from the major figures of the early conservative movement transitioned from being food for thought to being canon, quasi-sacred texts that serve as authorities on political, cultural, and economic questions. The books considered indispensable to conservative thought were written over approximately a two-decade period, beginning with F. A. Hayek's *The Road to Serfdom* (1944) and largely concluding with Milton Friedman's *Capitalism and Freedom* (1962). In between, conservatives released a stack of books that today's voices of intellectual conservatives are expected to absorb and revere: Richard Weaver's thundering assault on modernity, *Ideas Have Consequences* (1948); William F. Buckley Jr.'s first book, *God and Man at Yale* (1951); Whittaker Chambers's gloomy anticommunist memoir, *Witness* (1952); Russell Kirk's case for conservatism's intellectual pedigree, *The Conservative Mind* (1953); Robert Nisbet's classic work of sociology, *The Quest for Community* (1953); Barry Goldwater's manifesto, *The Conscience of a Conservative* (1960); and Frank Meyer's explanation of the fusionist political philosophy, *In Defense of Freedom* (1962).

Scouring the internet, it is easy to find lists of sites explaining which books all conservatives should or even must read. When contemporary conservatives complain about trends within the movement, they rarely suggest that conservatives need to rethink their fundamental premises. Instead, intellectual leaders on the right insist that conservatives can save themselves (and the United States) by returning to their basic principles.[29] Whatever ails the conservative movement, you can always find voices who say conservatives must return to the tradition of Buckley and Kirk. Just reread back issues of *National Review*, the argument goes; they will tell you what you need to know. Likewise, the key to growing the conservative movement (including among racial minorities) is to somehow do a better job teaching the canon. This respect for the conservative canon is not new, but it may seem odd, given that these books are not all in agreement when it comes to important issues of culture, economics, and politics. The role of these books in consolidating conservatism, and maintaining the movement's ideological boundaries, was explained in Michael J. Lee's essay "The Conservative Canon and Its Uses."[30] He argues that the conservative canon is important for conservatives because it helps hold together a movement with many contradictory impulses:

> The canonization of books defending a range of philosophical commitments eased the fusion of dissimilar and contradictory conservatisms both within and beyond the Republican Party: traditionalist and libertarian, populist and elitist, religious and secular, agrarian and corporatist, and principled and adjustable. In addition to furnishing doctrinal and political resources for activists, writers, and politicians, the canon was a resonant symbol of conservative synergy as well as a constituent element of political identity. But in a larger sense, the development of a political identity with a shared history, a trove of insider references, a set of common heroes and enemies, and a repertoire of preferred argumentative forms was aided significantly by an organic process in which conservatism's textual traditions coalesced.[31]

Lee argues that conservatives' obsession with their own canon helps ensure that each new generation develops proper ideological purity and that the movement demonstrates intellectual continuity. Whether they are reading the ostensibly indispensable books because they were recommended by Dinesh D'Souza, they are attending a conference at the Heritage Foundation, or they are being trained at the Leadership Institute, young conservatives entering the movement with an eye on becoming professional journalists or activists are assured of a general familiarity with the canon. Organizations such as the Intercollegiate Studies Institute not only provide support for conservative students and faculty, they provide instruction on proper conservative thought. Knowledge of Hayek and Kirk is considered a hallmark of true conservatives, and absence of such knowledge is ground for suspicion. Although not all important conservatives have personally read the major books in the conservative canon, the books' basic arguments have been repeated so many times, in so many forms, that intellectual conservatives have absorbed the ideas and treat them as fixed tenets.

It is rare that one encounters a successful right-wing talk radio show host or television personality who openly rejects major principles of modern American conservatism. Most of the major voices of the conservative media offer variations on similar themes. One will rarely encounter an antiwar conservative, or a moral traditionalist who is also an economic progressive. Some exceptions are made for libertarians, but libertarians are usually relegated to discussions of economics, where their views are generally congruent with the rest of the conservative movement.

The conservative canon, for all its admirable qualities, may now be a hindrance to a thoughtful, modern conservative movement. The problem has nothing to do with the books themselves; the problem is time. The classic works of the early conservative intellectuals, still revered by the conservative movement, are now all more than fifty years old. Some are more than seventy years old. By pointing out that these books are dated, I am not attacking the authors or the works themselves. The problem is that American conservatism is a political movement facing contemporary issues, and these books do not really speak to these issues.

Much of the conservative canon is dedicating to fighting battles that are long over. In some cases, these are battles that conservatives won decisively. Whether state ownership of the means of production is more or less economically efficient and beneficial for all of society than a system of private property and free enterprise is no longer being debated. The free market proponents won. Conservatives won that victory in part because of theorists such as Hayek and Friedman, and in part because of experience: in the latter decades of the twentieth century, free economies outperformed planned economies. In spite of Bernie Sanders's claim to be a socialist, no serious politician (including Sanders) calls for state ownership of the nation's major industries, with the occasional exception in the case of health care. Conservatives have a right to pat themselves on the back for winning this fight, but the conversation has since moved on.

The Left is no longer fighting to nationalize industries; for the most part, the Left is fighting to increase the social safety net and increase economic equity within a capitalist framework. Mainstream progressives have made peace with free enterprise. When the debate is framed in these terms, a strong knowledge of the errors of socialism is not particularly helpful. If the battle lines have transitioned from ownership of the means of production to questions about the role of government in guaranteeing some minimal level of economic welfare for all, certain aspects of the canon may actually be harmful to the conservative cause. In *The Road to Serfdom*, Hayek expressed a positive attitude toward welfare policies: "There is no reason why in a society which has reached the general level of wealth which ours has attained the first kind of security should not be guaranteed to all without endangering general freedom."[32]

Related to this issue, so much of the conservative canon was single-mindedly focused on the Cold War. Conservatives are right to admire Chambers's writing style. But the case against communism that is laid out in *Witness* is no longer relevant; in spite of Chambers's pessimism, the Soviets lost completely. Again, conservatives can celebrate that they were on the winning side, but to be a ferocious anticommunist in the early twenty-first century is to strike an irrelevant political pose. Conservatives in 2022 who insist their future leaders have a strong knowledge of the horrors of communism would be akin to Republicans in 1893 demanding their young writers and activists study and absorb the arguments against slavery. They are building up an intellectual arsenal for a battle that is already over.

The conservative canon is especially inadequate for contemporary conservatives wrestling with identity issues. When it comes to race, gender, or national identity, the first conservatives were either silent on these subjects or they said things that today's conservatives would rather sweep under the rug. Conservative commentary about the civil rights movement written during the 1950s and 1960s is now mostly forgotten or ignored by conservatives, and only brought up by their opponents to use as a cudgel against them. The postwar conservatives said very little at all about issues related to modern feminism. They similarly have little to offer today's conservatives looking for advice on immigration. Instead, if today's conservatives look to the past for inspiration on these subjects, they tend to extrapolate from certain classical liberal principles or make basic appeals to Burkean prudence.

Although conservatives may wish they could consult old arguments when constructing their responses to contemporary identity politics, the fact that the conservative canon provides so few insights may be a blessing in some ways. Today's conservatives are largely free to develop new ideas about these subjects without worrying about breaking with older conservative dogma.

WHAT IS IDENTITY POLITICS?

Like conservatism, most people can recognize identity politics without necessarily being able to define the term. To define identity politics, we must first define "identity."[33] This may also be trickier than it seems. For this discussion, a person's identity is defined as his or her answer to the question, "Who am I?" One can answer this question with a biological, social, or psychological response. This question is also tied into deeper philosophical questions, such as the meaning of the self, which I will not engage with here. Some elements of identity may be stable throughout the course of life; others can change. The salience of one form of identity rather than another is also contingent on personal and social developments. To further complicate matters, identity has both individual and collective elements. Not all elements of identity are easily politicized.

Although political scientists have long wrestled with questions of identity, our use of the concept is not always clear. I agree with political scientists Scott Weiner and Stone Tatum, who argue that the discipline lacks "congruence across identity frameworks."[34] Our approach to ethnic identities, gender identities, and national identities are often quite different, and this is even true of scholars taking an expressly intersectional approach. I further agree with their definition of the term: "Identity orients a person within a broader social context using a specific set of markers recognized by others."[35] From this broad definition, it is obvious that identity politics can take many forms. For our purposes, it will be helpful to understand what, exactly, conservatives typically mean when they refer to identity politics.

Open proponents of identity politics argue that it represents an effort to push back against oppression. Political scientist Howard J. Wiarda argues, "Identity politics from the beginning was linked to the underlying idea that some groups in society—women, blacks, gays, Indians, etc.—are uniquely oppressed. That one's *identity* as a woman, a minority, an environmentalist, a homosexual, a young person, or any marginalized person made one especially susceptible to violence, ostracism, and oppression."[36] This definition suggests identity politics is not a new development, as identities have proven an inescapable part of American democracy from the beginning, even when only white Christian landowning men were assured access to the democratic process. Different varieties of Protestantism did not always have amicable relationships, for example. In colonial America, Quakers had a very different status in Massachusetts than in Pennsylvania. There was also, from the beginning, a tension between rural communities and urban areas that resulted from perceived cultural differences rather than competing economic interests. We therefore must find some other distinguishing characteristics that make modern identity politics unique.

Conservative scholar David Azerrad writes that modern identity politics is distinct from earlier social movements because of its emphasis on victimhood.[37] This emphasis is so pronounced that the phrase "identity politics" may actually be a misnomer: "Contrary to what the term would seem to indicate, identity politics is first and foremost not a politics of identity, but of oppression."[38] This distinction is important because the use of a victim–oppressor narrative makes compromise more challenging. Compared to Azerrad, political scientist Peter Skerry is far less opposed to identity politics as such, and furthermore argues that most conservative critiques of modern identity politics rely on an ahistorical approach to their own nation's history.[39] Skerry nonetheless concurs that identity politics represents a different form of political struggle: "[There is] an important dimension of contemporary racial and ethnic politics—the fact that minority groups engage in a *special kind of interest group politics*. Because their 'interests' are not ordinary interests but involve grievances against racial discrimination, minority groups can and do make stringent moral demands on the American polity."[40]

Most scholars argue that identity politics as we now understand the term began in the 1960s and 1970s. This requires some explaining, however, as the history of efforts to secure the rights of underprivileged groups extends much further back in American history. In what sense is modern identity politics distinguishable from, say, the fight against slavery or in favor of women's suffrage? Compared to these earlier struggles, identity politics takes a more adversarial approach to the dominant culture and political system.

Older efforts to advance the rights of disadvantaged groups focused on securing access to rights and resources already offered advantaged groups (chiefly, white men). Activists sought the right to assimilate into the dominant American culture. Practitioners of identity politics, however, seek more than the absorption of their group into white, bourgeois

American life. Identity politics asserts that minority cultures have worth and deserve recognition and respect. Put somewhat differently, identity politics seeks more than equal access to the dominant society, it wants to change society in ways that reflect the self-chosen interests, standards, and preferences of diverse peoples. According to historian Linda Nicholson:

> While differences between blacks and whites and women and men had earlier been associated with what was supposedly inferior about the former groups, these younger activists began to associate such differences with what was positive, if not superior, about these groups. This self-conscious attempt to reframe the meaning of these identity categories was reflected in such political slogans as "Black is Beautiful" and "Sisterhood is Powerful." This proud assertion of difference became viewed by these younger activists as linked to a more radical restructuring of the social order than was demanded by the earlier movements, a restructuring that could address the needs of greater numbers of blacks and women.[41]

As with modern conservatism, one could choose a number of plausible dates to mark the birth of contemporary identity politics. Most people agree that identity politics as we now understand the term came from the New Left, which emerged at the end of the 1950s. The New Left was, in part, motivated by the failures of the Old Left and the need to develop a new form of revolutionary politics. Although Marx's utopian vision continued to inspire multitudes across the world, as the twentieth century dragged on, the group Marx predicted would achieve liberation appeared increasingly unreliable. Traditional Marxist theory emphasized the importance of the proletariat; the working people in advanced capitalist societies would inevitably seize the means of production, ushering in a new classless society. This theory first suffered a major setback in 1914. As the great powers mobilized for war, national identities trumped class consciousness. Contra Marx, who declared that "the working men have no country," millions of young working men marched to their doom under their national banners. Their patriotism furthermore remained mostly intact even after the war proved disastrous for all of its primary antagonists. The Great War was not a total loss for Marxism, however, because it did lead to the creation of the Soviet Union, even though, according to Marxist theory, Russia should not have been ripe for a communist revolution because it had not passed through the necessary stages of capitalism. The Left in Western countries nonetheless remained inspired by the Soviet Union in subsequent decades. Its faith in this variety of communism was eventually shaken, however. The Molotov–Ribbentrop Pact, a treaty of nonaggression between Nazi Germany and the Soviet Union, proved disillusioning. Khrushchev's denunciation of Stalin, and his own brutal response to an uprising in Hungary, partly broke the Soviet Union's hold on the Western Left's imagination. Although most did not become cold warriors (some did), they could no longer expect Moscow and its allies to deliver a world free of oppression.

The disillusionment with the Old Left style of politics inspired many on the left to look to the Third World for inspiration. Anticolonial movements suggested a new approach to revolutionary politics, one that did not automatically accept Western hegemony. Maoism became influential among elements of the American Left. The Mau Mau uprising in Kenya against British colonial rule inspired a generation of African American activists. The language of anticolonialism began to seep into American domestic politics. The New Left also took a greater interest in culture than the previous generation's Communist Party activists.[42] Minority groups, especially African Americans, increasingly began asserting their own cultural uniqueness with confidence, rejecting the idea that they needed to conform to white norms—the flamboyant Muhammad Ali was an example of this at the time.[43] Although identity politics is unquestionably the New Left's progeny, perhaps its most significant progeny, it is also distinct from the New Left. Just as the New Left resulted from the failures of the Old Left, much of modern identity politics was driven by perceived problems with the New Left. Although racial equality was part of the New Left's agenda, as a movement it remained dominated by white men.

One key moment, which arguably marked the beginning of modern identity politics, came in 1977, with the publication of the Combahee River Collective Statement. This group of Black feminist lesbians (who took their name from a Civil War raid in which Harriet Tubman and Union soldiers freed a group of slaves) articulated many of the principles that are now considered essential elements of identity politics. In its memorable opening paragraph, the statement reads:

> The most general statement of our politics at the present time would be that we are actively committed to struggling against racial, sexual,

heterosexual, and class oppression, and see as our particular task the development of integrated analysis and practice based upon the fact that the major systems of oppression are interlocking. The synthesis of these oppressions creates the conditions of our lives. As Black women we see Black feminism as the logical political movement to combat the manifold and simultaneous oppressions that all women of color face.[44]

Importantly, the statement explicitly used the term "identity politics" to describe the group's political project:

This focusing upon our own oppression is embodied in the concept of identity politics. We believe that the most profound and potentially most radical politics come directly out of our own identity, as opposed to working to end somebody else's oppression. In the case of Black women this is a particularly repugnant, dangerous, threatening, and therefore revolutionary concept because it is obvious from looking at all the political movements that have preceded us that anyone is more worthy of liberation than ourselves.[45]

Although the practical political effect of the Combahee River Collective Statement was minimal, it did provide a template for future movements making similar demands. This was also a period of significant innovation on the part of left-wing intellectuals. Michel Foucault's arguments about the relationship between discourse and power were becoming increasingly influential on the left, overshadowing more traditional Marxist analysis. The field of critical race theory, established by scholars such as Derrick A. Bell,[46] began calling into question whether the United States was actually making progress on its purported goal of achieving racial equality.

DEMANDING RECOGNITION

At least on the surface, many of the controversies surrounding identity politics seem disconnected from material concerns. Some of the most contentious fights, stirring great emotions on all sides and attracting massive media attention, seem to revolve around controversies such as insensitive Halloween costumes or racist tweets, rather than greater economic equity. These battles seem distinct from older varieties of left-wing politics that had a greater focus on redistribution and class warfare. The logic of these battles is not always obvious to outsiders. Why should anyone care about seemingly trivial "microaggressions"?

Political theorist Charles Taylor provided one of the more influential explanations for why cultural recognition and sensitivity should be treated as serious matters.[47] Taylor argued that society's failure to grant recognition to certain identities, or to favor some identities over others, can cause serious harm.[48] For example, denial of due recognition can lead to self-hatred: "The projection of an inferior or demeaning image on another can actually distort and oppress, to the extent that the image is internalized."[49] This is a key reason much of feminist and antiracist activism is focused on questions of language and tone. Failure to provide recognition to all identities is furthermore at odds with the principle of universal equality.

Contemporary modern conservatives will argue that recognition of cultural differences is not necessary and perhaps even socially detrimental, provided everyone is treated equally as individuals. Society, or at least the state, should be blind to any cultural differences between citizens. The problem, according to Taylor, is that such an approach "negates identity by forcing people into a homogenous mold that is untrue to them." He continues: "The claim is that the supposedly neutral set of difference-blind principles of the politics of equal dignity is in fact a reflection of one hegemonic culture. As it turns out, then, only the minority or suppressed cultures are being forced to take alien form. Consequently, the supposedly fair and difference-blind society is not only inhuman (because suppressing identities) but also, in a subtle and unconscious way, itself highly discriminatory."[50]

Identities are both an individual and a collective phenomenon, which makes these matters additionally complex and challenging. We are all members of multiple identity groups. Furthermore, identity groups wish to survive and maintain their distinctiveness indefinitely, even if material differences across groups dissipate. The challenge in multicultural societies is to create a governing system that treats us all equally and in a manner that is blind to our differences, yet simultaneously recognizes cultural particularities in such a way that minority cultures can survive on their own terms. Taylor approved, for example, of the steps Canada has taken to ensure the survival of French-Canadian culture.

Taylor's ideas are not universally accepted on the left. Kwame Anthony Appiah, for example, has noted that if we concede too much autonomy to collective identities we risk undermining the autonomy of individuals.[51] There is another possibly problematic aspect to Taylor's approach. In his book, he took it for granted that the politics of recognition applied to threatened and marginalized minority groups, those who have long suffered a lack of recognition. His solutions furthermore seem to assume a static demographic profile within a nation. In Taylor's book, it is not clear why the demand for recognition and state protection of an identity is only legitimate when made by disenfranchised minorities. If French Canada has a right to impose laws to protect its culture from the Anglo-Canadian culture dominant in the rest of the country, does that not also imply that Anglo-Canadians have at least some right to safeguard their own culture's future in an increasingly globalized world in which mass immigration is the norm? Are calls for recognition and cultural protection valid only after a group becomes a minority? If so, why?

The contemporary American Left usually takes it for granted that struggles for recognition are only legitimate when practiced by historically oppressed groups. This does not mean that other groups do not make such demands, however. The question of which identities deserve recognition has special urgency in the twenty-first century, especially as it concerns race. At present, it is considered taboo for white Americans to organize explicitly as white Americans and to celebrate an explicit white identity, and those organizations that do so are typically labeled as hate groups. Will this taboo remain when non-Hispanic whites lose their majority status? One argument against this kind of organizing is that white identity is inherently illegitimate because white identity is fundamentally based on oppression of others—according to some theories, this is precisely why the concept of race was invented. Others have argued that white demands for recognition and strong feelings of white identity have been especially destructive, historically speaking, and thus present a unique danger. Shelby Steele, a conservative against all forms of identity politics, makes this very argument: "No group in recent history has more aggressively seized power in the name of its racial superiority than Western whites. This race illustrated for all time—through colonialism, slavery, white racism, Nazism—the extraordinary human evil that follows when great power is joined to an atavistic sense of superiority and destiny. This is why today's whites, the world over, cannot openly have a racial identity."[52]

The problem, however, is that intellectuals declaring, as Shelby has, that white racial identity represents a "grave evil"[53] may be insufficient to keep such identities from developing. The question thus becomes how to manage them. Francis Fukuyama, who is concerned with the rise of identity politics in Western countries, agrees with Taylor that demands for recognition and dignity are at the root of the current debate. Fukuyama further notes that the demand for recognition is a major element to all sides of the dispute—minority and majority. In *Identity* (2018), he argues that "demand for recognition of one's identity is a master concept that unifies much of what is going on in world politics today."[54] Importantly, this demand for recognition does not need to have any connection with economic concerns. He uses the debate about same-sex marriage to make this point. If the question had been purely about ensuring same-sex couples access to the economic arrangements available to heterosexual couples, the problem could have been resolved with a system of civil unions, which, when it comes to things such as property distribution, would have been indistinguishable from the legal privileges of opposite-sex marriages.[55] This could furthermore have probably been accomplished without having to fight a decades-long "culture war."

For some forms of identity, whether our focus should be on material redistribution or cultural recognition is obvious, as feminist philosopher Nancy Fraser has noted.[56] For example, being part of the lower class or, to use an anachronistic term, the proletariat, can form the basis of one's identity. Yet few on the left would argue that providing the proletariat proper cultural recognition is an urgent political goal. Indeed, from a Marxist perspective, abolishing the proletariat by ushering in a classless society is the goal, and economic redistribution is the prescribed method. On the opposite side of the spectrum, we have sexual minorities, a group whose complaints are not, for the most part, rooted in political economy. Rather than economic oppression, "any structural injustices its members suffer will be traceable ultimately to the cultural valuational structure."[57] In this case, cultural recognition, not economic redistribution, is the logical focus for the LGBT community's political activists. The problem gets trickier, according to Fraser, when we begin thinking about identity groups such as gender and race, which have roots in both culture and political economy. In the case of identity groups that face both economic and cultural oppression, determining the proper form of remedy is particularly difficult, because the drives for economic redistribution and cultural recognition may be at odds with each other.

Although we think about identity politics, especially the politics of recognition, as a primarily a phenomenon of the Left and perhaps the Far Right, conservatives often engage in a similar approach, in their own way. Conservatives are more likely, however, to demand respect for their ideological identity, rather than an identity based explicitly on a demographic trait. For example, conservatives complain (often justifiably) about the way they are portrayed in popular media and by academics. They are correct that conservatives, especially white male Christian conservatives, are often treated in movies and film as caricatures, embodying all of the prejudice and other evils of the modern world. Conservative pundits have written entire books seeking to empirically demonstrate that media stereotypes about their group are mistaken.[58]

For the most part, conservatives have not sought to use the state to force more evenhanded depictions of their group in the media, such a push would likely be too at odds with free-market principles. There have been some calls, however, for a kind of affirmative action for conservatives in certain professions that shape the nation's culture. Such arguments have been especially common in discussions about academia. A few years ago, members of the Iowa legislature introduced a bill calling for "consideration of political affiliation and balance in the employment of faculty at institutions of higher education."[59] The bill would have prohibited universities from allowing departments from becoming lopsidedly supportive of one particular party. The bill was never voted upon, and would have been impractical to implement, but the fact that it was introduced at all demonstrates conservative attitudes on these matters. More recently, the Florida legislature passed a bill calling for a survey of the ideological leanings of university and college professors.[60] Such a survey would unquestionably demonstrate that professors typically place themselves on the left, which many conservatives would take as prima facie evidence that conservatives on campus face discrimination. What concrete actions conservative Florida legislators would take once they had that information is not clear at the time of this writing.

INTERSECTIONALITIES LEFT AND RIGHT

"Intersectionality" is not a new concept, but the term itself is just a few decades old. Since legal scholar Kimberly Crenshaw provided an early description of the concept in the late 1980s, however, theories related to intersectionality have became a crucial element of third-wave feminism and identity politics, more broadly. This is an understatement. Intersectionality is one of the most influential ideas to emerge from the social sciences in the last generation. Foundational documents, such as Crenshaw's 1989 article, "Demarginalizing the Intersection of Race and Sex: A Black Feminist Critique of Antidiscrimination Doctrine, Feminist Theory and Anti-Racist Politics,"[61] and her 1991 article, "Mapping the Margins: Intersectionality, Identity Politics, and Violence against Women of Color,"[62] have been cited tens of thousands of times. In her 1990 book, *Black Feminist Thought*,[63] Patricia Hill Collins independently developed many of the same ideas. It has also been cited by tens of thousands of subsequent academic studies. At this point, it is not appropriate to call intersectionality an idea or a method of analysis. It is its own field of study, with its own section at major social science conferences, and the entire subject of global scholarly conferences.

Although its prominence is growing, for most of the concept's history, the term was known mostly within insular academic and activist communities. It has not yet been demonized by the Right to the same extent as identity politics and political correctness, but this is starting to change.[64] The term is starting to become part of the broader national discussion to the extent that it is even appearing in tweets from presidential contenders.[65] *Merriam-Webster* now includes it in the dictionary.

In Crenshaw's groundbreaking work, she notes that feminist and antiracist discourse suffers a blind spot.[66] This literature does not adequately discuss the unique experiences of women of color. Feminism has historically focused on the experiences and interests of middle-class white women. Similarly, antiracist activism was largely led by Black men, who may have been just as invested in patriarchal structures as white men. For this reason, we cannot examine every form of racist or sexist discrimination and oppression as discrete phenomena. People with multiple marginalized identities are at risk of being ignored by discourses on sexism and racism that focus on white women and minority men. As one example, Crenshaw discusses the issue of domestic violence within Black communities, noting that antiracist norms can lead to downplaying this issue in the name of resisting the stereotype that Black men are prone to violence. This left Black women suffering from domestic violence without a voice and their victimization continued. If we think about it from the perspective of quantitative regression models, intersectionality is the notion that interaction terms—which show how the effect of one independent variable on the dependent variable you wish to study is dependent on the value of a different independent variable—are often *extremely* important.[67] For example, the effect of being a woman on an individual outcome will sometimes differ according to race.

To make her argument, Crenshaw pointed to *DeGraffenreid v. General Motors*, a 1976 case argued in U.S. District Court in Missouri.[68] In this case, five Black women sued General Motors for discrimination. They noted that GM had only recently begun to hire Black women, thus when a recession began, and employees were laid off based on seniority, the Black women lost their jobs first. However, although the company had only recently begun to hire Black women, it had hired women for a much longer period. Thus, the district court claimed that there was no evidence of sex discrimination. The court also dismissed the argument about race, saying that the plaintiffs' claims should be consolidated with a separate case that alleged racial discrimination. The court concluded that, although women are a recognized class, as are Blacks, there is not a third category of Black women recognized as separate protected minorities. Crenshaw argued that this was an injustice: "The court's refusal in *DeGraffenreid* to acknowledge that Black women encounter race and sex discrimination implies that the boundaries of sex and race discrimination are defined respectively by white women's and Black men's experiences."[69] At its most simplistic, intersectionality simply means that the social world is complex and that oppression can take many forms. It was furthermore not an entirely novel concept when Crenshaw articulated the idea; it was arguably implicit in the Combahee River Collective Statement, for example.

The Left has predominantly used the language of intersectionality. However, as an analytical tool and a form of argumentation, it can be used by anyone, and it has been used to further conservative ends. Political scientist Keisha Lindsay made this argument well in an article about Black conservative Christians.[70] Her analysis shows that Black opponents of same-sex marriage used the intersectionality framework to build their arguments. These activists argued that the "gay agenda" was not an authentic element of the Black community. Secular and affluent white liberals were the primary proponents of gay rights, and they were motivated by their hatred of Christianity, according to the Black activists. Thus, the logic of intersectionality could be employed to defend a conservative policy. According to Lindsay, "Their ability to do so—to cast themselves as victims of interlocking anti-Christian bias, classism, and heterophobia—is possible because nothing within an intersectional framework compels them to do otherwise."[71]

Although she was primarily focused on conservative Black Christians and their opposition to gay rights, Lindsay noted other ways in which intersectionality had been employed by the Right. White critics of affirmative action often complain that the policy amounts to a form of reverse discrimination, and that in this new system of employment and college admission practices, white men are now the most disadvantaged group. Lindsay did not mention it, but conservative arguments about abortion also now lean heavily on intersectional arguments. The pro-life movement has added another category to the list of victimized and vulnerable groups: the unborn. Borrowing further from the logic of intersectionality, they argue that unborn children of color are a uniquely defenseless and exposed group, because minority women have, on average, higher abortion rates than white women. Some pro-life activists will take this a step further and argue that abortion is being pushed on the Black community for racist reasons, suggesting that the contemporary pro-choice movement retains the pro-eugenics perspective of early twentieth-century progressives.[72]

Because American conservatism remains, at least in theory, an individualist approach to politics, it mostly employs the language of intersectionality haphazardly, when it can score debate points. It has not, at this point, become a key element of conservative thought, even implicitly. However, as we move further to the right on the ideological spectrum, we begin to see a more explicit and well-formed right-wing version of intersectionality. This is political scientist Philip W. Gray's conclusion in his analysis of the Alt-Right.[73]

According to Gray, the Alt-Right and related right-wing identitarian movements have important similarities with the intersectional Left. Specifically, both sides employ a category-based epistemology. Further, both sides view themselves as engaged in a lopsided, Manichean struggle, in which their own identity groups play the underdog in a David-versus-Goliath struggle. Gray further suggests that, although the Alt-Right's rise has many causes, part of its ascension must be attributed to a backlash against the intersectional Left. The degree to which this element of the Left has demonized white males increased the plausibility of the Alt-Right's arguments about their identity group's growing victimization. However, the Alt-Right and the intersectional Left have an enormous difference: the Alt-Right views race as a legitimate biological category, whereas the Left views race as socially constructed. Gray, however, argues that, depending on the degree to which the social construction perspective denies personal agency, this can become a distinction without a difference. That is, if social constructions determine how we understand reality, and this subsequently controls our actions, in practice such a view allows individuals no greater agency than the views of a genetic determinist. Gray puts it this way:

> The alt-right focus on biology reifies contemporary observations as natural "facts," and denies agency in populations through its form of genetic determinism, both in contrast to the methods and concerns of the "intersectional left." The first point is partially correct, as a methodological matter, although this becomes a fundamental dispute between the two views (one reifying biology, the other "construction"). But this difference, and criticism, begins to deteriorate when interrogating what "social construction" means. Authors far outside the sphere of the alt-right have noted the potential difficulties in the intersectional perspective. On the one hand, intersectionality can lead to a type of atomistic specificity, where "Intersectionality, taken to its extreme, would conclude that individuals experience life differently based upon their unique combination of social groupings." On the other hand, it can simply lead to a different form of determinism. If intersectionality is based upon a notion of social

constructivism, and "[s]ocial constructionism maintains that power and knowledge are inextricably linked, such that power is exercised through the construction of knowledge," one must wonder how "far down" construction goes in identity formation.[74]

Gray may overstate his case here. The social construction perspective offers a much easier solution to social problems than the genetic determinism of the Alt-Right and its predecessors. After all, social constructions are, theoretically, more malleable than genes—even the most optimistic eugenicist would acknowledge that it would take multiple generations of draconian policies to force a change in human beings sufficient to alter their average capacities in a meaningful way. In contrast, most social constructions should, theoretically, be changeable within a single generation, if there is sufficient will to do so.

It may not make sense to define the racist Right by its commitment to a genetic basis for racial classifications. From a descriptive standpoint, Gray is correct. The American extreme Right overwhelmingly believes that racial differences are nonnegligible and rooted in genetic differences. But even if that is the case today, and is unlikely to change, I question whether that is *necessarily* the case. That is, can we imagine a scenario in which the racist Right accepts that race is a social construction with negligible connections to biology, yet remains committed to its ideals of racial hierarchy or separation? I think this is plausible. During their early years in power, Italian Fascists were not interested in the kind of biological racialism so prevalent in Nazi Germany. Julius Evola, arguably one of the most right-wing thinkers of the twentieth century, rejected the Nazi approach to racism, which he viewed as too focused on the biological aspect of race, even though he was simultaneously a racist and an anti-Semite. Thus, I am not convinced that arguments seeking to discredit race science will solve the problem of racism, even if they become universally accepted, but I certainly do not think such arguments cause harm. Should we see such a change, and most of the extreme Right abandons its commitment to hard genetic determinism yet maintains its racism, Gray's method of distinguishing the intersectional Right from the intersectional Left will be less useful.

Even those elements of the mainstream right that avoid explicit discussions of identity at times make claims that seem to echo some of intersectionality's essential arguments. Grover Norquist's theory of the major political coalitions in the United States shares certain premises with intersectionality.[75] Norquist, president of the influential conservative nonprofit Americans for Tax Reform, argues that there are two major groups in U.S. politics: the "takings coalition" (made up of groups primarily motivated by what they want from government) and the "leave us alone" coalition (made up of those primarily motivated by what they want to protect from government interference). The takings coalition includes groups such as unions, public-sector employees, trial lawyers, and industries that rely heavily on government subsidies. The leave us alone coalition includes groups such as small business owners, gun owners, homeschooling parents, taxpayers, property owners, and stockholders.

Norquist's insight was that relatively few people are motivated by a passion for limited government as such. Instead, they want to limit government intrusion into something very specific. Every different element of government overreach affects a different element of the electorate. Further, if a person is not directly affected by a government policy, that person is unlikely to actively oppose it. Second Amendment advocates may not care about financial deregulation or property taxes. Homeschoolers may not benefit from changes to the capital gains tax. Further, on their own, no single element of this coalition can constitute an electoral majority. For this reason, government is able to grow in a piecemeal fashion, inconveniencing one small group at a time. Thus, to achieve success, every one of these groups must work together to support each other's interest. That is, gun owners (or at least the organized groups that claim to speak for them) will back up the property rights advocates, who will support antitax organizations, who will advocate for deregulation, who will defend homeschoolers. When combined together, these different interests can become powerful political forces, creating a defensive wall capable of blocking new government interventions into various sectors of the economy and private life.

I must not overstate the degree to which Norquist's theory of U.S. political coalitions resembles progressive theories of intersectionality. After all, Norquist is still operating from an interest-based perspective of political conflict, rather than one grounded in identity, but, especially in the case of gun rights groups, an identitarian undercurrent (especially the rural white identity) is likely lurking beneath high-minded arguments about natural rights and utilitarian defenses of armed societies. Nonetheless, it is worth noting that in both this conservative formulation and in the arguments from left-wing intersectional scholars and activists, there are echoes of Benjamin Franklin's mordant observation: "We must, indeed, all hang together, or assuredly we shall all hang separately."

As is the case with left-wing identity politics, maintaining such a coalition is not a simple task. It requires a high level of coordination and a willingness to put aside potential differences. Norquist has long recognized this challenge, facilitating cooperation across different groups on the American center right. Since the 1990s, his organization has held the weekly "Wednesday Meeting," where representatives from the Republican Party, conservative nonprofit organizations, political candidates, and conservative journalists meet to discuss current events and remain informed on what other elements of the conservative movement are doing.

POLITICAL CORRECTNESS

Political correctness has been the target of conservative scorn for more than three decades. The phenomenon as we currently think of it first became prominent on college campuses in the 1980s, as the dividing lines in racial and gender politics were changing. Broadly speaking, the term usually refers to contemporary efforts to influence language and behavior in ways that promote the well-being of historically disadvantaged groups. It emphasizes the importance of words, and calls on people to refrain from using insulting and prejudicial language. This often leads to the creation of new terms and the abandonment of older words and phrases. To take a recent example, there is growing pressure in academia to refrain from using the gendered word "Latino" and replace it with the gender-neutral neologism "Latinx." For conservatives, the most despised element of political correctness has historically been campus "speech codes," which can sanction students and faculty who deviate from current norms.

According to many conservatives, political correctness has caused changes in language that are absurd or even Orwellian. The phrase itself has unfortunate totalitarian history. We can find the first use of the term in one of Mao Tse-Tung's edicts in 1929, which referred to the *correct* ideological ideas (that is, Maoism as Mao understood it). Other communists, including the leadership of the Soviet Union, adopted this kind of language.[76] The New Left and the Black Power movement first brought the term into the American political lexicon.[77]

People on the right, who claim its practitioners are authoritarian scolds and "snowflakes," now use "political correctness (PC)" as a pejorative term. Political correctness on campus has been the source of endless mockery and derision, but some on the left have sought to reclaim the term.[78] Others on the left have argued that rampant political correctness on campus is a right-wing myth, propagated as part of a wider agenda to weaken higher education and its role in society.

Although we now view political correctness as a phenomenon of the Left, the broad concept is ideologically neutral and has been employed across the political spectrum. As communication scholar Becky Ford correctly notes, "PC does not mean only opposition to racism, sexism, and heterosexism."[79] By creating norms and punishing those that deviate from those norms, it serves as a means of setting limits on acceptable discourse. It is a tool for maintaining coherence and conformity within a group (which is how Mao and other communists used the term), and a tool for intergroup competition, declaring some groups, ideas, and individuals as irredeemably racist, for example, and thus not deserving of a place in mainstream debates. It is not hard to find examples of conservatives pursuing their own forms of political correctness. For example, many conservatives are quick to denounce negative comments about the police, the U.S. military, Christians, or Israel. Conservative groups such as Campus Reform exist largely to name and shame professors that profess radical left-wing views and denigrate groups conservatives value and support. Republican members of the U.S. Congress have sought to use government sanctions to punish corporations that choose not to do business with Israel in protest against Israeli treatment of Palestinians.[80] Such efforts, to the extent that they are meaningful rather than purely symbolic, are clear violations of free speech principles. If these laws do not represent a kind of political correctness, the term has no coherent, consistent meaning.

Conservatives also describe efforts to change college curriculum to be less Eurocentric and increase the visibility of minority views as examples of political correctness. One of the most famous cases, garnering nationwide coverage, occurred at Stanford University in the 1980s. As the result of protests, Stanford abolished the requirement that undergraduate students take a course in Western civilization. The push to de-emphasize the importance of "dead white men" has continued across campuses throughout the country, to the great frustration of many conservatives.

Although the term "political correctness" is relatively new, the phenomenon itself—broadly speaking—is very old. Historian Geoffrey Hughes traces the lineage of political correctness as far back as the Middle Ages, suggesting we can find evidence of "enforced political correctness" and "forms of humorous satire of institutions and even values" in the work of Chaucer.[81] Hughes suggests political correctness was an oppressive force in England after the Reformation, when oaths of religious loyalty became a prerequisite for political power.[82] A conservative form of political correctness also dominated Victorian England, as demonstrated by Oscar Wilde's trial.

Conservatives are not the only critics of political correctness, and even many progressives concur that their side can take cultural sensitivities too far. In fact, some of the most memorable attacks on political correctness have come from the Left. Feminist novelist Dorris Lessing, for example, was a fierce critic of the phenomenon, stating that it represents just a new variation of totalitarian control: "The most powerful mental tyranny in what we call the free world is Political Correctness, which is both immediately evident, and to be seen everywhere, and as invisible as a kind of poison gas, for its influences are often far from the source, manifesting as a general intolerance."[83] Lessing was not optimistic about the future of intellectual freedom, arguing that societies seem always to transition from one form of tyranny to another: "Truly, we cannot stand being free. Mankind—humankind—loves its chains, and hastens to forge new ones if old ones fall away."[84]

Not all on the left simply accept the conservative characterization of political correctness, however. Some deny the phenomenon exists at all, insisting it was invented by the Right as yet another means of attacking higher education. According to this view, conservatives effectively spread the meme, with the assistance of a credulous mainstream media, that universities are hotbeds of ideological intolerance. It has furthermore been used as a tool to discredit the Left, because once an idea has been derided as "politically correct," one may stop taking it seriously.[85]

If we view political correctness as simply a set of taboo words and ideas, taboos enforced either through the law or via social sanctioning, no society has ever been completely free of the phenomenon. The real battle has never been whether or not political correctness in this sense should exist. It will always exist. A more honest discussion of political correctness would ask the following questions: What set of taboos should prevail? How much deviation should be tolerated? How should these norms be enforced? In the United States, the First Amendment provides some guidance when it comes to the law, but when it comes to social sanctioning, there is a great deal of potential variance.

CONSERVATISM, SOCIAL CONSTRUCTIONS, AND RELATIVISM

Conservatives typically mock the concept of social construction. In some ways, elements of the academic Left bring this derision upon themselves. The content of many academic papers in the social sciences and humanities can come across as wordy gibberish, even to educated readers. This was dramatized by the so-called Sokal hoax. In this case, Alan Sokal, a physics professor, sought to demonstrate the lack of scholarly rigor within the fields of cultural studies. To do so, he submitted a paper to an academic journal titled "Transgressing the Boundaries: Toward a Transformative Hermeneutics of Quantum Gravity."[86] Months after the article was published, Sokal admitted that it was a parody, that the entire paper was designed to demonstrate the sloppiness of these fields of scholarship. Sokal explained, "The results of my little experiment demonstrate, at the very least, that some fashionable sectors of the American academic Left have been getting intellectually lazy. The editors of Social Text liked my article because they liked its conclusion: that 'the content and methodology of postmodern science provide powerful intellectual support for the progressive political project.'"[87]

Sokal is not a conservative. In fact, he argued that he conducted this hoax out of concern that the academic Left was discrediting itself.[88] He is correct that some of the more perplexing work from these fields makes it easier for conservatives, such as radio host Glenn Beck, to announce that postmodern left-wing academic thought represents "the biggest pile of horse crap you've ever heard in your life."[89] As is the case with intersectionality, however, the idea of social construction is rather straightforward, but it becomes quite complex when we begin to categorize different kinds of social constructs. The concept of social construction can be misapplied, and people who use that framework can reach wrong conclusions, but dismissing the idea out of hand is a mistake.

In their most extreme form, theories of social construction do seem to imply that there literally is no such thing as an objective reality outside of social practices and the language we use. According to this view, even things that seem transparently "true" or "real" are actually just tools of oppression. Upon hearing this, conservatives can scoff that this statement is at odds with everyday experience and basic common sense. A problematic element of this entire discussion, however, is that there are many different varieties of social construction theories. When we describe something as a social construct, there are many possible things we could mean. Some of these ideas should not be especially controversial, even to conservatives who are committed to a realist perspective, whereas others can and should be contested.

For a short introduction to the classification of different forms of social construction, I recommend philosopher Sally Haslanger's article "Ontology and Social Construction."[90] According to Haslanger, "generic social construction" is the most basic and incontrovertible variety of social construction. In her view, "something is a social construction in the generic sense just in case it is an intended product of social practice."[91] In this instance she uses the concept of marriage as an example of a social construct because "you can't be a wife unless you are part of a social network that provides for an institution of marriage."[92] Some religious conservatives may find this a problematic example, perhaps claiming that marriage has its origin and definition in the Bible, and thus has an independent existence outside of human institutions. I could just as easily make the same point using a different category, however: "college professor" is a category of human that can only exist in a society that recognizes such a category and creates institutions within which it can operate.

Haslanger argues that social construction can take three different forms: causal, constitutive, and pragmatic. An idea or object is causally constructed if social factors were responsible for bringing it about.

It is constitutively constructed if "in defining it we make reference to social factors."[93] To say that a particular distinction is pragmatically constructed, in a broad sense, is to "simply say that our distinction is as much due to contingent historical and cultural influences as to anything else; we inherit vocabularies and classification projects and decide between alternatives based on utility, simplicity, etc."[94] This division of forms of social construction becomes even more complicated when we add in Haslanger's various subcategories.

Despite being one of the more notable intellectual defenders of claim that reality is, at least in a manner, a social construct, Haslanger does not argue that all of existence is simply a human artifact.[95] Instead, she claims that reality is a social construct in a more limited sense: "The distinction we draw between what's real and what's not is weakly constructed, i.e., social factors partly influence our efforts to describe the world."[96] The fact that there are social influences on what we are willing to accept as knowledge challenges the notion that we can fully grasp the nature of an independent reality outside of social context.

Much of the Left, especially the feminist and antiracist Left, has embraced social construction theories because they have revolutionary potential. If gender, race, and sexuality are mere social constructs, and we find those constructs oppressive, we as a society have the power to overturn them, to replace them with new, egalitarian constructs. This is largely why theories of social construction are so controversial on the right. If social construction is true, the thinking seems to be, then conservatism (however defined) must be a force of injustice. Thus, conservatives treat theories of social construction as completely unserious, as worthy of mockery alone.

The idea that social construction theories are mere tools the Left uses in its war on the existing social order, and that they therefore have no redeeming value for nonleftists, is incorrect. In his book *The Social Construction of What?*, philosopher Ian Hacking notes, "One may realize that something, which seems inevitable in the present state of things, was not inevitable, and yet is not thereby a bad thing. But most people who use the social construction idea enthusiastically want to criticize, change, or destroy some X that they dislike in the established order of things."[97] Conservatives could easily concede that something is a social construction and fight in defense of that social construction.

This is not to say that conservatives could seamlessly incorporate the more radical philosophical approaches adopted by the academic Left, which, I should note, is not monolithic and engages in many acrimonious internal debates. For example, I cannot imagine how American conservatism could reconcile itself with, say, philosopher Judith Butler's radical vision of sex and gender. Nor am I suggesting that conservatives should attempt to do so. I argue instead that both the Left and the Right may give too much weight to some of these specific philosophical questions. It is a mistake to assume that, if everyone agreed on some of these basic theories, certain cultural and policy prescriptions would inevitably follow.

The Right could concede many premises to the academic Left, yet make no changes to its preferred cultural norms or policy proposals. Conservatives could state that social constructionist thinkers simultaneously make philosophically sound arguments about the nature of reality, but reject their claim that societal change is necessary. For example, the Right could acknowledge that the bourgeois nuclear family is entirely a social construction. Yet it could nonetheless argue that this particular model of family formation has proven that, from a utilitarian perspective, it represents the best means of human flourishing and should therefore remain the normative ideal. In fact, the social science literature suggests this is the case. Children, on average, have the best outcomes when they are raised in a two-parent household, with a mother and father married to each other. There are obviously exceptions, such as when one of the parents was abusive and things improved for everyone after a divorce. To take a less extreme example, even if neither parent was abusive in any way, but their relationship had become so acrimonious that no one could be happy, perhaps breaking up the family is the best thing for everyone. This does not demonstrate that the traditional norm was wrong, or that life for most people would improve if that norm was abolished. It just means that we, as a society, need to have a way to allow for exceptions.

There is an easy way for conservatives to acquiesce to many of the postmodern Left's premises but still hold fast to their core principles. They could simply state that, yes, many of the things we take for granted in modern American society are social constructions. However, most people are satisfied with these social constructions, and a majority of people would be unhappy if those social constructions were abolished. The fact that something is a social construction, even a social construction that reinforces existing power dynamics, does not mean that it is bad. The real questions are these: How many people find existing social constructions oppressive? How important is a given social construction to the maintenance of a society conducive to widespread human happiness? If we consider a norm vital to a successful society, and can reasonably claim that most people are happy maintaining that norm, but we are also willing to concede that some people feel oppressed by it, are there ways to accommodate such people without throwing the norm out the window? This obviously requires some finesse, but it is clearly possible. We could, for example, find ways to accommodate people who identify as transgendered without abandoning norms about gender entirely. Most biological adult males are genuinely satisfied being what society calls "men," and most biological adult females are happy to be "women." The fact that gender dysphoria exists does not mean abolishing the social construction of gender is a moral imperative. Indeed, if the social construction of gender was completely abolished, the concept of gender dysphoria would cease to be coherent.

One of the major problems conservatives have with theories of social construction is that they raise the specter of another right-wing boogeyman: relativism, be it moral, cultural, or otherwise. If the Left claims that all current standards are human creations, typically enforced to service entrenched powers, the Right charges that the Left would obliterate all standards entirely. In contrast to relativism, however defined, conservatives insist that they stand in defense of eternal truths, or at least objective standards of excellence.

In his most influential work, *Ideas Have Consequences*, Richard Weaver argued that the turning point in the West's history came in the Middle Ages, when William of Ockham's nominalism triumphed over Thomas Aquinas's philosophy. For Weaver, the question of whether universal truths existed outside of human experience was central to human flourishing. With the rise of nominalism and empiricism, the West made a fatal choice, one that explains its slow-motion dissolution: "For four centuries every man has been not only his own priest but his own professor of ethics, and the consequence is an anarchy which threatens even that minimum consensus of value necessary to the political state."[98] From nominalism flowed a skepticism toward social hierarchies, the erosion of chivalry, the rise of contemptable bourgeois values, the triumph of industrialism, the emergence of total war, and the specter of nuclear annihilation.

Conservatives have attacked relativism on other grounds. Harry Jaffa, for example, argued that sincere belief in relativism precludes sincere belief in equality—contra many other conservatives, Jaffa argued that equality was ultimately a conservative value. The problem with relativism, according to Jaffa, was that it removed the intellectual foundation upon which any argument for universal human equality must rest. In the absence of values that have a real existence beyond human institutions, and of a basic human nature that transcends all cultural boundaries, the basis for principled opposition to absolute monarchy or slavery gives way.[99]

In different forms, these arguments were articulated by other important conservatives such as Buckley and Frank Meyer.[100] Russell Kirk called for a defense of the "Permanent Things" (always capitalized). Leo Strauss offered his considerable intellectual influence to the conservative war on relativism.[101] Jaffa similarly lamented the rise of relativism on college campuses.[102] These different conservatives did not always agree on the permanent and universal values they defended (Kirk and Meyer, for example, disagreed on many points), but they agreed that they existed in some form. Conservative intellectuals' arguments about relativism have seeped into the broader political conversation. Former Speaker of the House Paul Ryan (R-WI), for example, stated: "If you ask me what the biggest problem in America is, I'm not going to tell you debt, deficits, statistics, economics—I'll tell you it's moral relativism."[103]

This claim that conservatism and relativism are incompatible should not be accepted without careful consideration. There is another way of being a conservative that is profoundly relativistic, one that furthermore has an important intellectual history. Rather than viewing conservatism as a defense of an absolute and transcendent set of truths dictating a specific social order, a conservative of a different sort is a defender of a *particular* social order, determined by contingent truths specific to a people and a place. This conservatism does not rely on Enlightenment rationalism, but on lived experiences. This variety of conservatism did not come to dominate the American conservative movement, but it was held by one of its important early figures. Kirk's conservatism was, in its own way, highly relativistic. Kirk did believe in a transcendent moral order. In fact, he considered such a belief an essential element to conservatism. However, he rejected the idea that there was a single system of government appropriate for all people and cultures throughout the world as dangerous, ideological nonsense. Although they reach very different conclusions, conservative antirationalist thinkers, going back to Edmund Burke, would accept many postmodernist premises. The French postmodernist Jean-François Lyotard's famous "incredulity toward metanarratives"[104] is shared by many conservative and reactionary thinkers, but not, I should reiterate, by today's mainstream conservative movement.

Attacking relativism requires, at least implicitly, endorsing one or more forms of universalism. Although they do not deny cultural differences, conservative opponents of relativism are nonetheless certain of the existence of universal values that are true in all contexts. This is likely due in large part to American conservatism's connection to Christianity, a faith that proclaims itself the only path to salvation for all people, everywhere—a position starkly at odds with pre-Christian European paganism. We can also find these sentiments in Enlightenment rationalism, which includes the notion that universal truths (such as the existence of natural rights) can be uncovered through the use of human reason.

Most recently we have seen conservatives make this argument in their celebration of governing systems that combine liberal democracy with market economies. Such systems, if embraced universally and across the globe, would purportedly resolve the world's most pressing problems.[105] At President George W. Bush's 2005 inauguration, he emphasized that the Iraq War was justified because, by bringing Western-style democracy to that nation, and eventually the entire Middle East, the problem of terrorism could be permanently resolved.[106] Furthermore, according to this argument, it would be ethnocentric to suggest liberal democracy in some form would not be appropriate for certain cultures—democratic institutions may have different quirks according to the local cultural context, but the broad principles undergirding democracy are everywhere the same. Bush noted in that same speech, "We will persistently clarify the choice before every ruler and every nation: The moral choice between oppression, which is always wrong, and freedom, which is eternally right." Secretary of State Condoleezza Rice was even more pointed, arguing that those who doubted the capability of Iraqis to sustain a liberal democracy were analogous to those who argued Blacks were incapable of responsible citizenship in the United States.[107]

Throughout the George W. Bush years especially, this was the dominant view among American conservatives. However, such a view is at odds with other conservative traditions. There are varieties of conservatism that acknowledge and even celebrate distinct cultural differences and worldviews, some even rejecting the idea of a single human type. We see this perspective best provided by the counterrevolutionary French thinker Joseph de Maistre, who argued that there is no one way to govern a country because all countries are different and these differences must be accounted for: "A constitution that is made for all nations is made for none."[108] As a Christian, Maistre maintained that Christianity was the key to salvation for all humans, yet he fully rejected the idea of a universal humanity: "Now, there is no such thing as 'man' in this world. In my life I have seen Frenchmen, Italians, Russians, and so on. I even know, thanks to Montesquieu, that one can be Persian. But as for man, I declare I've never encountered him."[109] Although one can readily acknowledge that such a view is at odds with contemporary mainstream American conservatism, and some conservatives, notably Jaffa, found it a loathsome view,[110] it is nonetheless a conservative perspective.

Conservatism's defense of unbridled capitalism can also be seen as a kind of relativism, with an important qualification. The free market represents a form of universalism in that it, theoretically, places makes no arbitrary distinctions between people and their preferences. Dollars themselves do not see race, religion, sex, or national origin, and economic actors who allow irrational prejudice to dictate their decisions will be less effective competitors in a free market. Although we have different levels of economic resources of all kinds, we are all free to sell our labor and purchase goods as we see fit. In this sense, capitalism is itself a form of egalitarianism. (I am setting aside the left-wing critiques of capitalism that challenge the amount of real economic freedom that exists in capitalist societies.) However, precisely because the free market represents nothing more than the aggregation of personal preferences, it acknowledges no higher values beyond consumer demand. If the mass public desires cultural products that conservatives find degenerate, the market will provide it for them, nonetheless. As far as capitalism as an ideology is concerned, anything people wish to buy is good, even if it debases them spiritually or physically.

Conservatives may also overstate the degree to which the Left is really motivated by relativism at all. The fact that progressives do not value the same things as conservatives does not mean that progressives make no value distinctions. Indeed, it is hard to imagine how a true relativist could be interested in political or cultural questions at all. If one really believed that one individual preference, cultural institution, set of shared beliefs, or form of government really was just as good as any other, what would be one's justification for challenging the status quo? How could a political ideology stand for nothing and simultaneously employ commissars of political correctness? One of these premises must be false.

Some conservatives have made this argument before, suggesting that relativism has never really been the hallmark of their political opponents. Paul Gottfried has made this point for decades, recently declaring that "moral relativists are no more common than unicorns."[111] Heather Mac Donald of the conservative Manhattan Institute has been even more acerbic in rejecting the notion that progressives are relativists.[112] She notes that the fury of campus protesters is hardly indicative of a nonjudgmental, anything-goes attitude. Instead, the modern Left has simply created a new form of morality based on victimhood status: "They ruthlessly enforce a moral hierarchy of victimhood based on what they know to be the truth: that America is endemically racist and sexist. They are violently intolerant of views that challenge that truth." She further argues that a reasonable conservatism should be relativistic, at least in the sense of understanding humanity's limited ability to know a single and universal "truth."

RIGHT-WING IDENTITY POLITICS

Although most practitioners of identity politics would place themselves on the left side of the political spectrum, we can definitively describe some (and plausibly define other) movements as a form of right-wing identity politics. Viewed in a vacuum, it may not seem obvious whether or how to distinguish between left- and right-wing identity politics. As I suggested in my discussion of intersectionality, the question of whether categories such as race and gender are biological or socially constructed is one major difference, but not necessarily an essential or permanent one.

According to mainstream conservatives, practitioners of identity politics all follow familiar patterns: they define politics as a zero-sum game between groups defined by their immutable characteristics. Whether on the left or the right, conservatives argue, identity politics downplays the importance and efficacy of the individual in favor of the collective. Jonah Goldberg sums up this critique as follows: "This is what I hate about all forms of identity politics. It's an effort to get credit or authority based upon an accident of birth. The whole point of liberalism (the real kind) is the idea that people are supposed to be judged on the basis of their own merits, not as representatives of some class or category."[113]

In describing themselves as opponents of left-wing and right-wing identitarians, conservatives will often appeal to a variant, the "horseshoe theory" of the political spectrum. According to this view, the shape of the ideological spectrum is not linear—that is, the greatest distance on that spectrum is not between the extreme Left and the extreme Right. Instead, the ideological spectrum is curved in such a way that the Left and the Right begin to mirror each other when they reach their far extremes. To take one of the more dramatic examples, Hitler's extreme-right regime and Stalin's extreme-left regime had more in common with each other than with a liberal democracy that respected civil liberties.

Although this conservative perspective has some merit, distinguishing left-wing and right-wing identity politics is straightforward, at least in theory. Identity politics on the left works for the interests of historically marginalized identities, whereas identity politics on the right reinforces the status of historically privileged groups. In keeping with my definition of the Left in preceding pages, the goal of left-wing identity politics is a world with less inequality across groups. Right-wing identity politics, on the other hand, seeks to strengthen existing inequalities. Thus, we can make an ideological distinction between those calling for "Black power" and "white power." This does, however, leave open the theoretical question of what would happen if left-wing identitarian movements fully achieved their goals, and equality, however defined, became real and demonstrable. Would these movements wither away? If not, would they then be classified as right-wing movements? At this point, however, this is a theoretical discussion.

Even if we recognize a stark divide between identity movements on the left and right, there are similarities between them worthy of discussion. Right-wing identity politics often uses the language of victimization, borrowed from the Left. White nationalists, for example, will often state that they merely want to stop the process of "white genocide," the idea that mass immigration and miscegenation will ultimately result in the cultural and biological extinction of the white race. The "men's rights movement," a mostly online phenomenon, focuses much of its attention on the plight of modern men, arguing that misandry, rather than misogyny, is a major problem. In doing so, they often appropriate the language of fairness and equity from modern feminism.

Similarly, not all groups promoting minority interests use the Left's language of fairness and equality. Fringe groups such as the New Black Panther Party use the language of racial separatism and superiority found more frequently on the white nationalist right.[114] Even among members of groups that may seem more traditionally progressive, it is possible to find examples of hateful, exterminationist rhetoric aimed at white people, men, or other privileged groups in society. The fact that there are nuances and gray areas in these categories does not, in my view, undermine the validity of the left–right distinction when it comes to identity politics.

WHERE DOES RELIGION FIT?

Religion is an element of personal identity, but also different from other attributes we often link to identity politics. When social scientists consider religion, we typically discuss three components to the phenomenon: believing, behaving, and belonging.[115] Religion can of course be described as a set of beliefs about the supernatural. What does one believe about the nature of God (or gods) and humanity's place in the universe? These beliefs become entangled in politics. For example, and perhaps most famously in the American context, one's interpretation of scripture can lead one to have very strong beliefs about when human life begins. From the Catholic perspective—a perspective also held by many theologically conservative Protestants—life begins at the moment of conception, and thus fetuses are entitled to the same rights as any other persons, most notably the "right to life." Biblical views on homosexuality and the nature of marriage have similarly played a role in the fight against same-sex marriage in recent decades.

Beyond mere belief, religion is associated with certain behaviors: prayer, scripture reading, tithing, attending worship services, and performing other religious rituals. Although behaviors are linked to beliefs (more fervent believers tend to engage more frequently in religious behaviors), their political consequences are not identical. People who frequently engage in religious practices, especially those practices that are performed in groups such as congregations, are more likely to make their religious beliefs central to their political behaviors.[116] We may also think of the common measures of behaving as representing a person's level of religious commitment, with the caveat that some people may be intensely religious while nonetheless avoiding common religious behaviors, such as belonging to a religious congregation or worshiping in a communal setting.

The final, and perhaps most complex, aspect to religion is religious belonging. It is here that religion can most approximate other manifestations of identity politics. Religion in this sense is more than just a personal set of beliefs and practices. Religion signifies membership in a social group and provides a sense of personal identity. Conservative sociologist Will Herberg made the connection between religion and identity in his classic 1955 work *Catholic–Protestant–Jew.*[117]

Compared to some other elements of identity, however, individuals have a degree of agency when it comes to religion. Unlike racial categories, one can (at least theoretically) easily transition from one religion to another, or to no religion. Yet such a perspective is not a wholly realistic description of religion. Most people are initially socialized into religion at a young age through their family, and are taught to share their parents' religious beliefs. Moreover, religion can be connected to many other elements of culture that are not related to particular theological beliefs. A person may maintain an attachment to a religious identity even if he or she abandons all religious beliefs associated with that religion. That is, one may nonetheless view Catholics, Evangelicals, or Jews as "my people," even after abandoning the religious beliefs of that group. A person can similarly continue to fervently believe in a religion without providing any public indication of that belief. That is, religious belief can be hidden in a way that physical characteristics associated with race cannot.

Religion can also be tied to questions of national identity. Many people continue to believe that the United States is, in some sense, a Christian country. In recent years, some scholars have sounded the alarm about what they call "Christian nationalism." Most notably, Andrew

Whitehead and Samuel Perry made this argument in *Taking America Back for God* (2020).[118] According to their formulation, Christian nationalists are those who believe that Christians—especially white Christians—are the only "true Americans." According to their analysis, about one-quarter of Americans hold this view.

CONCLUSION

The subjects I discuss in this book are not obscure. Ideology, conservatism, identity politics, and the concepts associated with identity politics are all pervasive in the U.S. national discourse. Unfortunately, the terms are often used without clear definitions, and people on different points of the ideological spectrum will use the same words yet mean different things. Many questions about these definitions remain unsettled, and I do not consider my perspective to be the last word on any of these issues. Many books and articles across disciplines have been written on each of the subjects I have discussed so far, and many learned scholars will dispute some of my characterizations. Nonetheless, by explaining my understanding of these issues, I hope readers will be better able to follow my analysis in the chapters ahead. In chapter 2, I will turn to a related subject: the conservative movement's understanding of identity politics and why conservatives claim it is an insidious force in American life.

TWO

Conservative Arguments against
Identity Politics

Conservatives have many scathing critiques of identity politics, but many also offer an alternative: that individualism and ideas, rather than group identities and resentments, should be the basis of political life. I am, by necessity, making some generalizations in this chapter. When I write that "conservatives argue" for a certain point, I am obviously not claiming that all conservatives agree with that argument. Conservatives have never been of one mind on these questions. Indeed, some of the most contentious debates within conservatism have revolved around these issues, but there are some questions where we can find widespread agreement from the mainstream of the movement. In contrast to libertarians, conservatives are willing to consider limitations on individualism. They also tend to recognize the importance of certain group attachments. I will therefore aspire to describe the mainstream conservative view on these subjects but also to acknowledge nuances and disagreements where they are significant.

THE CASE FOR INDIVIDUALISM AND
ITS INTELLECTUAL ORIGINS

In place of identity politics, mainstream American conservatives argue we should maintain our focus on individuals. Conservatives, however, will also concede that this individualistic approach to politics has never been universally accepted, and may in fact be historically rare. Such conservatives argue that individualism as a political principle is founded upon several different sets of ideas, which came together in a salutary union in the United States. These sources include the Enlightenment, ancient Greek philosophy, and Judeo-Christian religion. Elements of these different intellectual traditions are not always compatible with each other, and different conservatives have leaned on different authorities when making their case.

Conservatives have not always fought left-wing identity politics with the politics of individualism. As I will show in chapter 4, this was not conservatives' primary form of argumentation during the early years of the civil rights movement, when conservative opponents of civil rights relied heavily on constitutional arguments, calls for social order, and, in some cases, a form of white identity politics. Nonetheless, today's conservatives have mostly jettisoned those earlier positions, instead offering individualism as an alternative to tribalism and other forms of collectivism. Frank Meyer put it this way: "The fundamental political issue today is that between, on the one hand, collectivism and statism and, on the other, what used to be called liberalism, what we may perhaps call individualism: the principles of the primacy of the individual, the division of power, the limitation of government, the freedom of the economy."[1] Meyer further argued that individualism must be conservatism's bedrock principle: "*all* value resides in the individual; *all* social institutions derive their value and, in fact, their very being from individuals and are justified only to the extent that they serve the needs of individuals."[2]

In yet another example of William F. Buckley Jr.'s status as an indispensable contributor to conservative thought and rhetoric, he explicitly argued against identity politics before the term was in wide circulation. During his quixotic run for mayor of New York City in 1965, Buckley stated the following:

I think it is true that people have become accustomed to thinking that New York voters are merely blocs to be moved around according to sophisticated polls which are supposed accurately to measure the extent to which all of us are affiliated with some bloc or other. We are supposed to be Catholics or Jews or Protestants or bricklayers or non-bricklayers or typists or whatever. . . . A social theorist [Wyndham Lewis] about ten or fifteen years ago said, "You know, if you classify people enough different ways, you deprive them completely of their individuality." If somebody is exclusively moved in virtue of his participation in this bloc or in that bloc, creating enough blocs in which each one of us belongs, in the end we are all treated as categories.[3]

George F. Will is one of the most respected conservative columnists in the United States, with a career spanning decades. After earning a PhD in political science from Princeton, Will worked as an editor for *National Review* and a contributing editor for *Newsweek*. He is the author of more than a dozen books, a syndicated column that is published in hundreds of newspapers, and has won the Pulitzer Prize for commentary. He has taught political philosophy at Harvard University and other prestigious institutions. Since Buckley's death in 2008, Will could arguably be named the most important living thought leader of the conservative movement. He also made it clear in *The Conservative Sensibility* (2019) that he strenuously disagrees with the premise that identity politics is inescapable.

Will is committed to the principle of individualism, and the logic of natural rights informs his worldview. He is an unusual figure in the conservative movement in that he is an atheist, but he was mostly silent about his religious beliefs for most of his career.[4] Will argues that inherited traits should not be critical to one's worldview or his or her moral worth in other people's eyes: "Surely honor should flow to *individuals* because of their attainments of intellectual and moral excellence, not merely because of any membership in any group."[5] Will goes on:

If the premise of identity politics is true, then the idea on which America rests is false. If the premise of identity politics is true, then there are no general standards of intellectual discourse, and no ethic of ennobling disputation, no process of civil persuasion toward friendly consent, no source of legitimacy other than power, and we all live immersed in our tribes, warily watching other tribes across the chasms of "our differences." No sensible person wants to live in such a society.[6]

Will has a reputation for thoughtfulness and nuanced thinking. Yet here there is no room for compromise. Either the premise of identity politics is totally wrong—which implies that identity politics could be jettisoned entirely if there was sufficient will to do so—or the United States was built on a lie and cannot survive.

Political scientist C. Bradley Thompson has also insisted that conservatism must champion individualism against the collectivist ideals of the Left and the Far Right. He argues that antiliberal sentiments on the right have been growing and represent a serious problem, especially at a time when the Left is also denigrating the Founding Fathers and the individualist ideals they promoted. Beyond noting the most extreme right-wing views that seem to have gained ground in recent years, Thompson also warns that skeptics of classical liberalism—such as political theorist Patrick Deneen and *First Things* contributor Sohrab Ahmari—need to be challenged. These more communitarian-minded conservatives were not just wrong, according to Thompson, they were promoting dangerous nonsense: "There is *no such thing* as the 'common good' unless one means the sum of the interests of *all* men and women in a particular society, and the only legitimate 'good' common to all men and women as *rational* beings is freedom, which is the necessary condition from which they pursue all the goods necessary for living and living well."[7]

Many conservative arguments in favor of individualism echo F. A. Hayek's writings from the mid-twentieth century. Hayek insisted that individualism was more than a useful concept developed in the Enlightenment, it was "one of the salient characteristics of Western Civilization as it has grown from the foundations laid by Christianity and the Greeks and Romans."[8] Given his formidable intellectual stature, it makes sense for conservatives to look to Hayek for inspiration. A problem with such a move, however, is that Hayek was not a conservative, and he made this very clear. In Hayek's view, conservatism and classical liberalism (his own ideology) are at odds, and always have been. Conservatives, according to Hayek, are characterized by their lack of belief in spontaneous order, and thus always want "some higher wisdom" to govern society.[9] Hayek acknowledged that, for the time being, conservatives and classical liberals (Hayek never liked the term "libertarian") were allies of convenience, but only because they both feared and loathed socialism, an ideology inimical to both groups. This further raises the question of whether or not modern conservatism, as it was developed by fusionist theorists such as Meyer, can or should be distinguished from classical liberalism.

Libertarian economist Murray Rothbard argued that there was always something disingenuous about Meyer's conservatism.[10] He notes that Meyer started with the same kind of methodological individualism that libertarians favor, rather than using groups as the primary unit of analysis. Fusionism, in Rothbard's view, is really just libertarianism. The only reason Meyer made a distinction between his philosophy and libertarianism was because he mischaracterized libertarianism, unfairly describing libertarians as libertines unconcerned with virtue. Ultimately, fusionism, in Rothbard's estimation, did not really exist as a new and independent political philosophy: "In short, I believe that fusionism is a 'myth' in the Sorelian sense, an organizing principle to hold two very disparate wings of a political movement together and to get them to act in a unified way."[11]

Unless one holds that conservatism and radical libertarianism are literally synonymous, and all forms of collectivism are therefore anticonservative, the question of individualism is always at least somewhat open for conservatives. In contrast to Thompson,[12] most conservatives are not completely dismissive of the concepts of community and the common good, and accept that people have a right to make certain collective decisions. Nonetheless, for most of its history, modern American conservatism—at least theoretically—has preferred to err on the side of greater individualism. For much of the conservative movement's history, the debate about the movement's direction has rarely included open opponents of Lockean liberalism and its emphasis on individual rights. Rather, the movement has been largely divided between those who view classical liberalism as an important aspect of conservative thought and those who would say that all, or almost all, of modern conservatism has its origins in classical liberalism.

As an example of a figure holding the latter position, Jeremy Boering, the founder and chief operating officer for the conservative webzine

Daily Wire, states directly that classical American liberalism is precisely what he wishes to conserve. In fact, preserving this tradition is precisely what conservatism is all about.[13] Will also suggests that modern conservatism and classical liberalism rest on the same foundation.[14] Not all conservatives would go that far, but it is very difficult for an American conservative to fully repudiate classical liberalism without repudiating the United States itself. Jonah Goldberg argues that these ideas represent the only possible way out of our current identity-driven ideological impasse:

> The tragedy here is that liberalism—in the classic Enlightenment sense—is the only system ever created to help people break out of the oppression of identity politics. For thousands of years, nearly every society on earth divided people up into permanent categories of caste, class, peasant, noble, and, of course, male and female. The Lockean principle of treating every human as equal in the eyes of God and government, heedless of who their parents or ancestors were, broke the chains of tyranny more profoundly and lastingly than any other idea.[15]

Beyond Locke, conservatives cite John Stuart Mill as another indispensable theorist who strengthened the intellectual case for individualism. Mill, no conservative himself, nonetheless had a formative influence on the mainstream conservative movement: much of Mill's thought is reflected in Hayek's work, for example.[16] In fact, many contemporary conservative arguments in favor of individualism are indistinguishable from arguments Mill developed. I do not mean this as a criticism. Mill made many trenchant statements that would be difficult to improve. One problem with identity politics that conservatives often note is that it robs individuals of a degree of personal agency, and this was a key point in Mill's work. By allowing ourselves to be defined by our fixed traits, we give up some of our ability to think for ourselves, which means abandoning part of our humanity. Mill put it this way:

> He who lets the world, or his portion of it, choose his plan of life for him, has no need of any other faculty than the ape-like one of imitation. He who chooses his plan for himself, employs all his faculties. He must use observation to see, reasoning and judgment to foresee,

activity to gather materials for decision, discrimination to decide, and when he has decided, firmness and self-control to hold to his deliberate decision. And these qualities he requires and exercises exactly in proportion as the part of his conduct which he determines according to his own judgment and feelings is a large one.[17]

Many American conservatives have also carried on the classical liberal tradition by using natural rights theories to justify the cause of individualism. American conservatives are perhaps in a unique position in that the United States was literally founded on a statement of natural rights. The Declaration of Independence, which announced the new country's birth, relied primarily on theories of natural rights, the notion that there are, in fact, "inalienable rights" that cannot be justly violated. Building the argument from natural rights is useful because it is congruent with several different worldviews. Natural rights can be built upon both a religious and a secular foundation. The existence of natural rights is only founded on the claim that all human beings are entitled to certain rights based on the kind of beings they are, whether their uniqueness is the result of natural selection or a special relationship with God.

Will has been quite emphatic that proper conservative thinking, at least in the American context, is rooted in respect for natural rights. The Founders justified American independence using arguments about natural rights, and questions of natural rights were at the forefront of their minds during debates about the Constitution. The United States has gotten off track, according to Will, because Americans have lost sight of their own natural rights traditions, which provide the means for a diverse nation to flourish: "What is important is to reorient American debate about these questions and by so doing insinuate the Founders' natural rights vocabulary back into our political discourse."[18]

Whether conservatives such as Will are correct about the specific ideological roots of the American Revolution and the early American republic is debatable. It is indisputable that the most memorable lines from the Revolution's marquee names used the language of natural rights. However, some scholars have argued that the degree to which these ideas informed America's political culture has been overstated. Rather than secular Enlightenment thinking, Americans of the colonial period and beyond may have been more heavily influenced by Protestant theology and political thought. Political scientist Barry Alan Shane makes this argument, and further claims that the United States was never as individualist as most contemporary Americans believe. Instead, eighteenth-century Americans believed in "reformed-Protestant, communal theory of the good."[19] Donald Lutz, also a political scientist, has similarly argued that a uniquely Protestant "covenant theology" was responsible for American thinking about constitutions, and this is especially apparent if we look at the individual state constitutions.[20] I am not qualified to answer which side is correct in this dispute, so I will instead simply say that the historical truth may matter very little. The belief that the American Revolution was inspired by natural rights thinking, and that such ideas provide guidance for modern politics, is a significant element of the modern conservative intellectual movement.

Acknowledging the centrality of natural rights logic to conservative thought may raise another challenge, however. Natural rights do not just imply individualism, but also a degree of basic human equality. Indeed, some conservative thinkers have stated plainly that belief in equality is at the heart of the conservative project. Harry Jaffa went so far as to argue that equality is the only reasonable grounds upon which one can argue for limitations on government: "Because man is by nature a rational being, he may not rule over other men as if they were mere brutes."[21]

We should not exaggerate the degree to which modern conservatives are heirs to the classical liberal intellectual tradition. Mill, for example, had no interest in preserving tradition per se,[22] and Russell Kirk was critical of Mill and his contemporary libertarian fans.[23] Yet classical liberalism is an inescapable element of American conservatism, because the United States never possessed the kind of rigid aristocratic hierarchies that motivated a different, throne-and-altar variety of conservatism that was once a powerful force in European politics. Richard Weaver contended that the antebellum South represented a final holdout of the medieval social order, and he thought that was a good thing. Weaver was an outlier, however, and his variety of radical traditionalism has been mostly dormant on the mainstream right for many decades.

The classical liberal tradition is not the only possible source for individualist thinking, of course. Conservatives have also cited ancient Greece as a formative influence. According to the general conservative argument, the Greek's emphasis on reason was their most important contribution to

Western thinking. This was critical to the creation of science, of course, but it also had consequences for government. Ben Shapiro sums up this contribution as follows: "Based on the notion of virtue—use of reason to act in accordance with nature—Plato, Aristotle, and the Stoics developed ethical systems. Those ethical systems didn't merely recommend personal cultivation. They also encompassed the creation of new forms of government. Some of their ideas regarding government were good; others were bad. But they began the process of applying reason to governmental structures—a process that has continued down to our day."[24]

We must not overstate the individualism of ancient Greeks. Aristotle's famous description of human beings as "political animals" suggested that human happiness and development depends on membership in a political community. A people without a *polis* is in fact incapable of achieving its full potential. Thus, community, organized through a government, working toward shared ends, is indispensable to human development. This position further holds that the government has a role in improving the moral lives of its citizens. This is at odds with the hyperindividualism of some libertarians, but not necessarily anathema to most conservatives. Yet even the most communitarian-minded conservatives would likely balk at Aristotle's conviction that people are not true owners of their own lives, but instead belong to their cities—to say nothing of his views on natural slavery. They certainly would not endorse the totalitarian elements of Plato's ideal city. Conservative historian Victor Davis Hanson may have partially resolved this apparent problem by arguing that Greek individualism was real, but not the result of Greek philosophy. Instead, he argues that the individualist tradition was rooted in the unique agrarian culture that developed in classical Greece, a culture dominated by independent small farmers.[25]

When discussing the conservative reliance on classical liberal thought, we should also not overstate the homogeneity of classical liberal philosophers, because the diverse thinkers from this tradition disagreed with each other on many crucial points. Nonetheless, an emphasis on the individual as the unit of analysis (rather than the tribe, state, church, or some other collective grouping) is a common theme among thinkers conservatives. Social contract theories often begin with thought experiments about individual people, living in a state of nature, voluntarily giving up some degree of personal autonomy in exchange for security of some kind.

THE IMPORTANCE OF FREE SPEECH

Questions of free speech are not inherently tied to questions about identity politics. The two are viewed as related because opponents of identity politics claim it hinders freedom of expression via political correctness. Theoretically, a society could simultaneously maintain an absolutist position when it comes to freedom of speech and be interminably embroiled in contentious battles over identity and recognition. Indeed, in the absence of *any* restrictions on the words we use in public discourse, including those restrictions that are maintained solely by a structure of taboos, battles over identity issues might be even more vitriolic and unproductive. Nonetheless, in the current debates about identity politics, especially conservative arguments about identity politics, the issue of free speech and its salutary qualities are omnipresent.

It is difficult to know when a call for untrammeled free speech is sincere or opportunistic. Many conservatives have noted that the ideological successors of the free speech movement at University of California, Berkeley, once a leading element of the American New Left in the 1960s, have, in recent years, been less enthusiastic about the free exchange of ideas. Further, conservatism, broadly understood, has not historically been associated with the libertarian approach to speech.

When it comes to the conservative arguments for free speech, once again, John Stuart Mill's work has had a lasting influence on the discussion. Mill's defense of freedom of speech was mostly utilitarian. According to his theory, the free flow of ideas improves society. This is largely because of human fallibility and the limits of our knowledge and logic. We can never know with absolute certainty that a claim is true. Many times, positions that were once taken for granted as unquestionably true were subsequently shown to be false. Their falsehood could not be demonstrated, however, in the absence of free inquiry. No matter how universally accepted an idea may be in society, dissenters must always be allowed to challenge the consensus: "If all mankind minus one, were of one opinion, and only one person were of the contrary opinion, mankind would be no more justified in silencing that one person, than he, if he had the power, would be justified in silencing mankind."[26]

Even if the people challenging the dominant opinion are incontrovertibly wrong, Mill argued, their freedom to express their opinion free from persecution is nonetheless beneficial to the greater society because they force others to think deeply about their convictions. Iconoclasts keep others from descending into intellectual complacency: "Their conclusion may be true, but it might be false for anything they know: they have never thrown themselves into the mental position of those who think differently from them, and considered what such persons may have to say; and consequently they do not, in any proper sense of the word, know the doctrine which they themselves profess."[27]

Frank Meyer praised Mill for his efforts to advance the principle of free speech. However, he argued that Mill erred by not being sufficiently absolutist in his defense of free speech. Freedom of expression is not justified because it leads to better outcomes in the long run. Instead, freedom of speech must be guaranteed because morality demands it: "I am myself prepared to defend a position more absolute than Mill's, because I assert the right of individual freedom not on the grounds of utility but on the grounds of the very nature of man and the nature and drama of his existence. He lives between good and evil, beauty and ugliness, truth and error, and he fulfills his destiny in the choices he makes. No social institution, not even the conglomerate we call for convenience 'society,' can make the least one of these choices."[28]

If American conservatives universally considered themselves pure disciples of classical liberalism, or if Meyer's libertarianism had quickly triumphed over other conservative approaches, and it was applied consistently by all conservatives, this discussion could probably end here. Conservatism, however, is more complex than that. In their arguments about political correctness, conservatives often do sound like free speech absolutists. However, they have never, as a whole, been consistent on this subject. We can still find conservatives that favor certain kinds of restrictions on freedom of speech and expression. In recent years, for example, some conservatives have revived older arguments about the need to restrict access to pornography.[29] Conservatives have also expressed concerns about the shocking levels of violence in video games.[30]

Even when it comes to purely political speech, however, conservatives have also not been consistent. The most notable exception within living memory was of course McCarthyism. Many conservatives criticized McCarthy's methods, but overall the conservative movement at the time was generally supportive of McCarthy and his goals. Buckley and L. Brent Bozell wrote an entire book providing a qualified defense of McCarthyism.[31] Some of this can be understood as the result of the conservative movement's extreme panic over communism during this period. Leading conservatives genuinely feared a communist victory in the Cold War was not just possible but actually probable.

In contrast to how these issues are today usually discussed, with progressives accused of political censorship and the Right standing (mostly) for free speech, conservative scholar James Burnham argued in 1964 that the Left was *too committed* to free speech. In his view, commitment to freedom of speech is just another instance of the relativism inherent in liberalism. That is, liberals reject the idea of objective truth—or at least are skeptical of our ability to attain it or know with certainty we have attained it—thus, they have no grounds to censor anyone.[32] In the context of the Cold War, which Burnham always viewed as the single most important political issue, the liberal approach to speech was dangerous. The liberals' commitment to abstract concepts such as free expression made them weak and demoralized when faced with genuinely subversive forces that would overthrow the entire liberal order. Many of them would have apparently preferred defeat to the feelings of guilt that would follow betraying their principles. Although Burnham did not explicitly state what form censorship should take, he was clear that some ideologies should not be given free access to the marketplace of ideas: "Common sense, unlike ideology, understands that you can play a game only with those that accept the rules; and that the rules' protection does not cover anyone who does not admit their restrictions and penalties."[33]

Conservatives can argue that their movement's support for McCarthy was a historical aberration. Most contemporary conservatives denounce McCarthyism, but he does still have his defenders.[34] Further, some conservatives at the time opposed McCarthy's tactics. Russell Kirk seemed ambivalent about McCarthy and wrote little about him, but, reading between the lines, Kirk expressed obvious skepticism of McCarthy's methods in a 1953 article.[35] Will Herberg strongly opposed McCarthyism, but turned the subject around, noting that McCarthy's style of politics was only possible because of changes in American political culture stemming from FDR and the New Deal:

"McCarthyism" is the logical outcome of the system of government by rabble-rousing initiated in the first years of the New Deal—only, in "McCarthyism," the rabble-rouser is not a cultured and aristocratic gentleman, but a crude and rather primitive plebeian, not a Pericles but a Cleon. McCarthy, like Roosevelt, wants action and goes directly to the people to get it. McCarthy, like Roosevelt, is impatient with the restraints and limitations of what are called proper constitutional channels. When McCarthy wants a change in the Administration's foreign policy, he does not, as Senator, raise it for deliberation in the Senate; he appeals to the people to swamp the White House with letters and telegrams. He rouses the "rabble" for direct action, in contempt of constitutional channels and procedures. But how far different is that from the mode of operation of the Roosevelt regime in the 1930s?[36]

McCarthy did have a conservative defender whose ideas warrant serious consideration, simply because of his intellectual pedigree. Political theorist Willmoore Kendall is notable in a couple of ways. First, he continued to express support for McCarthy and his methods long after other conservatives had backed away from that position. Second, Kendall was unquestionably one of the most intellectually gifted people to ever join the conservative movement's ranks. Kendall developed his own argument in favor of censorship as a principle, rather than an unfortunate necessity of the Cold War. In doing so, he directly attacked Mill and also Karl Popper, whose defense of "open societies" was enormously influential among American intellectuals at the time.

Kendall provided several critiques of Mill and, by extension, Popper on the subject of free speech. In his view, the goal of untrammeled free speech was always unrealistic. Every society has a set of public orthodoxies, even if they are not publicly acknowledged. In fact, no state can survive without some kind of orthodoxy, widely accepted.[37] He therefore viewed Mill's free speech absolutism as dangerous nonsense: "Not only had no one ever before taught his doctrine concerning freedom of speech. No one had ever taught a doctrine even remotely like his. No one, indeed, had ever discussed such a doctrine even as a matter of speculative fancy."[38]

One wishing to defend, say, contemporary campus speech codes, however, would not lean on Kendall as an authority. Today discussions about freedom of speech focus heavily on the language we should use about marginalized minority groups. Kendall defended censorship on the part of the majority. Compared to most other conservatives of his era, Kendall was a populist, of sorts. Because of his trust in the good sense of ordinary Americans, he was willing to back a populist demagogue such as McCarthy. As historian John Bloxham put it, "To Kendall, McCarthy represented the values of ordinary, orthodox Americans, to whose commonsense opinions the government should give care."[39]

Burnham also offered some qualified support to McCarthy and McCarthyism, declaring himself an "anti-anti-McCarthyite."[40] Although Burnham did not endorse McCarthy's methods, and was often highly critical of the senator, he argued that those who were forcefully against McCarthy were—whether they wanted to be or not—on the same side as the communists. Given Burnham's view of communism's existential threat to the United States, he could not side with communists on any issue, including the issue of McCarthyism. He would not even agree to a compromise position offered by Daniel Bell and Irving Kristol, who suggested it was possible to condemn both McCarthyism and communism.[41]

AGAINST DOUBLE STANDARDS

Leading voices on the political right have noted that identity politics is associated with a growing number of double standards in American life. These separate standards come in two forms: practical advantages set aside for members of minority groups and different approaches to discussions of current events and of world history, depending on the races, ethnicities, and religions involved. By the former, they are usually discussing affirmative action in college admissions and employment. In terms of current events, some on the right claim that the media turns a blind eye to interracial violence when the perpetrators are from minority groups and the victims are white, but it often treats every example of the opposite as a sign of an ominous trend. Conservative author Heather Mac Donald, for example, has argued that "violence committed by non-whites, including Muslims, is minimized, viewed as random and almost never ideological."[42]

Other conservatives have argued that, in academia, expressing even the most vitriolic antiwhite hatred is almost never a hindrance to a scholar's career, whereas a white scholar who made identical comments about Blacks or other minorities would be immediately ruined.[43]

In terms of world history, conservatives complain that contemporary liberal historians provide a distorted view of events. According to conservatives, the common narrative within academia and much of the media is that white Europeans have been a uniquely evil force in the world, perpetually oppressing other cultures and minorities within their borders. One example of this is the way historical slavery is discussed. All mainstream American conservatives would today publicly state and sincerely believe that race slavery practiced by European colonial powers and in the United States was morally contemptible. They will argue, however, that Europeans were never unique in this regard. In the past, Muslim raiders regularly launched attacks into Europe and Africa, capturing and enslaving European and African non-Muslims. Slavery was an important part of the Ottoman Empire. Slaves rowed the empire's ships in the Mediterranean. The elite Ottoman infantry, the Janissaries, began as a group of Christian slaves kidnapped from eastern and central Europe. The Ottomans also practiced sexual slavery. If we look at slavery from a global perspective, the West is not unique for having slavery, but, conservatives argue, it is unique for having abolished it. Ibn Warraq, a notable critic of Islam, argues that the West's (eventual) attitude toward slavery is actually evidence of its cultural *superiority* to other parts of the world: "It was the West that took steps to abolish slavery; the calls for abolition did not resonate even in Africa, where rival tribes sold black prisoners into slavery."[44]

These conservative arguments have remained extraordinarily consistent over time. Although today's conservatives tend to use more sensitive language, the general arguments they use have remained largely unchanged since the 1960s. Burnham, for example, made many of the same arguments we hear from conservatives today. His academic career preceded widespread formal affirmative action in college admissions, but in the mid-1960s he discussed his experiences teaching at New York University, which practiced racial integration much earlier than most other major universities. He noted that, as an unwritten but strongly enforced rule, Blacks should be given better grades than whites for comparable work. This, according to Burnham, was justified because of the

extra challenges that Black students face.[45] Burnham found this irritat-
ing, but admitted that his misgivings were "petty."[46]

Burnham was much more bothered by how liberals treated Western behavior compared to the behavior of peoples elsewhere. Liberals
always, according to Burnham, would excuse and ignore the most atro-
cious behavior of non-Europeans, and Blacks in the United States, while
looking for any excuse to condemn Europeans and white Americans for
acts of barbarism. He noted how the liberal intelligentsia condemned
atrocities performed by the French colonial military during Algeria's war
for independence, but ignored similar, or worse, acts committed by those
fighting for Algeria's liberation, even though the victims of those war
crimes were often indigenous Muslims.[47] He argued that this is part of
the liberal disposition:

> Judging a group of human beings—a race, nation, class or party—
> that he considers to possess less than their due of well-being and
> liberty, the liberal is hard put to condemn that group *morally* for acts
> that he would not hesitate to condemn in his fellows—not to speak
> of reactionaries; his feelings of guilt and his egalitarian principles,
> which incorporate and express that feeling, do not seem to give him
> the *right* to condemnation. Even if, because of an imperious prac-
> tical situation, he finds himself resisting the pretentions of the un-
> derprivileged group, he does so with a divided conscience.[48]

We do see a certain symmetry on the left and right when it comes
to these discussions. Although the terminology is different, both camps
regularly claim to be suffering under unfair disadvantages. Complaints
about affirmative action at times echo complaints about white privilege
and the lingering effects of slavery and discrimination. Both sides claim
that the media and education system inculcates students with a distorted
view of both history and modern society. Narratives of double standards
and victimization cross the political spectrum. There are nonetheless
differences between how the Left and the Right, on average, tend to
approach these issues.

When describing instances of unfairness in American society, the
Left tends to focus directly on the groups most directly affected. That is,
white privilege (however defined) is detrimental to people of color. We

are starting to hear occasional arguments that white privilege is actually detrimental to at least some whites, and that its abolition would actually benefit whites.[49] This style of argument is not yet pervasive on the left, however. In contrast, conservatives regularly attack double standards by claiming that they harm the very people they are supposed to help. That is, affirmative action is not bad because it is bad for whites (though some will say that it is). Instead, many conservatives argue, affirmative action is bad because it is harms Blacks and other supposed beneficiaries of the policy. One such argument is that affirmative action in university admissions leads to a mismatch between student competency and classroom expectations. That is, when minority students are admitted into universities with high standards they are not prepared to meet, they subsequently perform less well than they would at a school to which they were admitted entirely on merit. The end result, according to this logic, is that affirmative action leads to more minority college dropouts saddled with student loan debt they can never repay.[50]

In other instances, conservatives attack affirmative action on the grounds that it is discriminatory toward Asian Americans. They argue that, because Asian Americans tend to outscore other racial groups on standardized tests, they are underrepresented at elite universities in the United States, and this can only be explained by discrimination.[51] There are a number of reasons why conservatives might choose this particular route to attack affirmative action in university admissions. One, of course, is that they are driven by genuine principles, sincerely held. Another is that they hope such an approach might drive a wedge between different minority groups that may have different interests. The more interesting thing to note, in my view, is that today's leading conservative voices are mostly not attacking affirmative action because it is deleterious to whites, but instead feel they must justify their stance on the grounds that their position is, ultimately, better for one or more racial minority groups.

THE WEST AS OBJECTIVELY SUPERIOR

Some on the right openly state that it is right for cultural institutions—especially those associated with education—to give precedence to Western civilization. From this perspective, the West should be studied and celebrated both because the United States' cultural and political inheritance comes largely from Western Europe and because the West is simply better than other regions of the globe according to objective and measurable standards. This, according to some conservatives, is an obvious fact, one that does not go away even if cultural relativists would like to sweep it under the rug in order to safeguard minorities' self-esteem. For an example of this kind of reasoning, we can point to libertarian political scientist Charles Murray's *Human Accomplishment* (2003), which seeks to create an objective measure of contributions to science and the arts, finding that Westerners account for a greater number of significant contributions than members of other groups,[52] a conclusion that was challenged by Murray's critics.[53]

The claim of Western superiority can rest on several different foundations, some more solid than others. Proponents of this view will point out that, when it comes to modern science and medicine, the Western world is responsible for the most significant contributions in recent centuries. Although other civilizations have certainly contributed to humanity's scientific knowledge, and there were periods when the West lagged behind other parts of the world, such as when the Islamic or Chinese civilization was more scientifically advanced than European societies, Westerners have for some time led the way in scientific advances.

Although it is a subjective judgment, and thus potentially more problematic, some conservatives will also declare Western superiority when it comes to literature and other forms of art. As novelist Saul Bellow allegedly once put it, "When the Zulus produce a Tolstoy we will read him." The notion that certain forms of art are superior, or at least socially beneficial, and others are deleterious, was an element of conservative thought from the movement's birth. Weaver, for example, despised jazz, stating that it "shows how the soul of modern man craves orgiastic disorder."[54] Readers may infer some veiled racism in Weaver's attack on jazz. In fairness, Weaver, an extraordinary reactionary, expressed similar contempt for Beethoven, who was, in Weaver's view, largely responsible for the decline of "traditional forms" of music: "The portents of change came with Beethoven, whose sympathy with the French Revolution must not be overlooked. A great architect in music, Beethoven, nevertheless, through the introduction of dynamism and strains of individualism pointed the way which the succeeding century was to take."[55]

In defending their contention that Western civilization is objectively better than its historical and contemporary competitors, conservatives are usually quick to point out that they are explicitly discussing culture, not race. That is, Western civilization is not synonymous with the white race, and they reject the idea that the Western inheritance belongs specifically to white people. Because, today at least, anyone can be Western if they embrace Western values (however defined), promoting the West is not inherently racist. Furthermore, this argument often goes, the glory of the West is chiefly found in its individualism and discovery of natural rights, which again should be enjoyed by all people.

THE CONSERVATIVE WAR ON POLITICAL CORRECTNESS

Before conservatives began emphasizing the evils and dangers of tribalism and identity politics, conservatives attacked political correctness. They are especially focused on political correctness on college campuses, where the phenomenon is most prevalent. Allan Bloom's *The Closing of the American Mind* (1987)[56] was an important early salvo in this new conservative attack on university culture. Bloom decried the rise of cultural relativism. In particular, he was alarmed by the denigration of Western classics. According to Bloom, the push for cultural sensitivity led campuses to abandon important texts, a move to make university curriculum less Eurocentric. Academia's rejection of the very idea of value judgments led to the growth of nihilism.

Reviews for *Closing of the American Mind* were polarized. Influential conservatives loved the book. Many progressives loathed it. The book clearly resonated with the public, however. It was a surprising best seller. More than a million copies were sold. For a dense nonfiction work that covers a tremendous amount of challenging philosophical ground, this was unusual. Bloom played an important role in reigniting the conservative backlash against the culture of college campuses.

Bloom's success inspired a new genre of conservative books. Bloom's jeremiad was followed by a series of commercially successful imitations. Charles Sykes's *ProfScam*,[57] Roger Kimball's *Tenured Radicals*,[58] and Dinesh D'Souza's *Illiberal Education*[59] soon joined the attack on universities. These books and others since then have all promoted the same theme: college professors are anti-American radicals (usually promoting ideas they developed in the 1960s), the intellectual foundation of the American republic is under assault, and students are coddled and never forced to face difficult questions.

Publishers discovered that conservative readers had a massive appetite for these arguments. Rush Limbaugh's 1992 book, *The Way Things Ought to Be*, spent months at the top of the *New York Times* best-seller list. The book repackaged many of Bloom's arguments for a more general audience, with one key difference. Limbaugh, and many who followed, abandoned Bloom's more sophisticated philosophical approach, and instead plainly stated that educators were knowingly promoting lies: "What is being taught under the guise of multiculturalism is worse than historical revisionism; it's worse than a distortion of facts; it's an elimination of facts."[60]

The conservative animosity toward college campuses has only grown more pronounced since the 1990s. The website Campus Reform is constantly on the alert for examples of university professors denigrating white people, men, conservatives, or the United States. The conservative student group Turning Point USA runs the website Professor Watchlist, which seeks to "expose and document college professors who discriminate against conservative students and advance leftist propaganda in the classroom."[61] The site includes a list of hundreds of professors and descriptions of their supposedly outrageous behavior. The conservative attacks on political correctness are closely tied to conservative suspicions of academia more broadly. The American conservative movement has had misgivings with academia since the movement was born. Buckley, after all, launched his career as a public figure with *God and Man at Yale* (1951). However, some scholars have suggested that the major conservative assault on political correctness on campuses began in earnest as the neoconservatives rose in prominence.[62]

These conservative attacks on political correctness have a pragmatic justification. Political correctness, as it is generally understood, is extraordinarily unpopular with the American people. Even many progressives dislike many of the more stifling efforts to police language. The need to stay up to date on the latest requirements of "wokeness" can be exhausting. Matthew Yglesias notes in *Vox*, "What's clear is that in a big country of 310 million people, all of us find some identity-related left-wing claims and practices annoying. (For me it's deploying 'Latinx' as a gender-neutral alternative to 'Latino.')"[63] The conservative arguments against political correctness have not always been consistent. Bloom, for example, was a transparent elitist, defending universities as a place where future leaders will be cultivated. Other conservatives, however, have taken a more populist and even anti-intellectual tone when approaching this subject.

UTILITARIAN ARGUMENTS AGAINST IDENTITY POLITICS

Conservatives often attack identity politics from the standpoint that its very premises are flawed, that approaching politics from the perspective of fixed groups, rather than individuals or interests, is fundamentally wrong on a moral level. Another approach largely accepts that the proponents of identity politics are correct in many ways. One could accept that white privilege is real, for example, or that women have historically been disadvantaged and remain so today. Yet one could at the same time reject the claim that politics, in the sense of using the coercive power of the state to achieve a group's goal, represents the best possible response to these injustices.

According to this argument, racism is a real phenomenon, and minorities, especially African Americans, have been victimized by the state and their fellow citizens. However, the problem in the Jim Crow South, and in other places where Blacks faced systematic discrimination, was that discrimination was enforced by the government. Although race-based discrimination in the private sector was rampant, it could ultimately be undermined by the free market.

Milton Friedman articulated an early form of this argument in *Capitalism and Freedom* (1962). According to Friedman, when the government takes its hand off the scale, personal characteristics that do not affect economic productivity will cease to matter (at least in the economic sphere of life), because businesses that make decisions based on noneconomic traits will be defeated by those that do not engage in this kind of irrational behavior:

> We have already seen how a free market separates economic efficiency from irrelevant characteristics. . . . The purchaser of bread does not know whether it was made by a white man or a Negro, by

a Christian or a Jew. In consequence, the producer of wheat is in a position to use resources as effectively as he can, regardless of what the attitudes of the community may be toward the color, the religion, or other characteristics of the people he hires. Furthermore, and perhaps more important, there is an economic incentive in a free market to separate economic efficiency from other characteristics of the individual. A businessman or entrepreneur who expresses preferences in his business activities that are not related to productive efficiency is at a disadvantage to other individuals who are not. Such an individual is in effect imposing higher costs on himself than are other individuals who do not have such preferences. Hence, in a free market, they will tend to drive him out.[64]

The Civil Rights Act of 1964 made racial discrimination on the part of private businesses illegal. Conservatives and libertarians argued that these laws also effectively nullified the very concept of private property. This alone made these laws lamentable and, according to Friedman's argument, this loss of freedom was ultimately not necessary; free markets would have ameliorated or even resolved the discrimination problem on their own. In fact, some conservatives have argued that this was already starting to occur before the federal government began intervening to end racial discrimination.[65] Conservative economist Thomas Sowell, for example, has argued that "the greatest reduction of poverty among blacks occurred before the civil rights revolutions of the 1960s or the affirmative action policies of the 1970s."[66]

Conservatives have argued that many kinds of efforts to alleviate racial disparities are ultimately self-defeating. Looking at the subject of racial politics in a broad sense, Sowell argues that the very concept of racial leaders has been detrimental to the African American community: "Groups that rose from poverty to prosperity seldom did so by having racial or ethnic leaders. While most Americans can easily name a number of black leaders, current or past, how many can name Asian American ethnic leaders or Jewish ethnic leaders?"[67] He further argues that quixotic political campaigns for slavery reparations are a mistake, because they would never succeed (in part because other minority groups would not stand for it) and they would only serve to turn public opinion further against Blacks.[68]

In *Dictatorship of Virtue* (1994), Richard Bernstein argued that the multicultural ideology could serve as a stumbling block for the disadvantaged groups it seeks to benefit.[69] The problem with denigrating Western norms when it comes to science, work, and culture is that those norms were largely responsible for the West's great economic success. Inculcating those norms is thus essential for future success. Telling our most disadvantaged fellow citizens that they should reject them, with the goal of living authentically according to their own cultural values, will ensure their own future economic stagnation. Bernstein put it this way: "The plain and inescapable fact is that the derived Western European culture of American life produced the highest degree of prosperity in the conditions of the greatest freedom ever known on planet Earth. The rich and advantaged will survive even if they are taught to believe something different. But to teach the poor and disadvantaged that they can ignore the standards and modes of behavior that have always made for success in American life is more than mere silliness. It is a lie."[70]

According to this argument, Western norms about culture and economics should be inculcated among all Americans, perhaps especially among the most disadvantaged, not because they are Western, but because history has shown that they are the most effective means to assure human flourishing. These basic values helped usher in the modern world, for better or worse, and if people wish to thrive in a modern economy, they should embrace them, even if it means breaking with their cultural traditions. The fact that the United States has promoted these values so well is one explanation for the nation's success at allowing so many people to rise from poverty. According to this argument, throwing out these values in the name of multiculturalism will hurt the entire nation, but it will be especially deleterious to those at the bottom of the socioeconomic ladder, those least able to absorb economic and cultural decay.

DOES "WOKENESS" ACTUALLY HARM THE LEFT?

Even people genuinely concerned about social justice issues have expressed frustration with the degree to which political correctness has become puritanical and perhaps even silly. The people eager to demonstrate how "woke" they are on questions of diversity and equity, who denounce others who fail to demonstrate sufficient purity, are at times accused of doing harm to their own cause. Although conservatives remain the primary opponents of left-wing political correctness, it also has its progressive critics. Some progressives dislike political correctness because they are sincerely concerned that it undermines the important liberal value of free speech. Others have a more pragmatic concern: that it is counterproductive. After all, President Trump's explicitly anti-PC campaign resonated with enough voters to secure him a comfortable win in the Electoral College in 2016. After that presidential election, the phrase "this is why Trump won" became a common response to new and extreme examples of political correctness.[71] Some in the political center have worried that the language police have prompted a reactionary backlash, harming the very people political correctness aims to help. Centrist political scientist Yascha Mounk, for example, has repeatedly made this argument.[72] Conservative author Douglas Murray suggests this possibility in his book *The Madness of Crowds*: "We face not just a future of ever-greater atomization, rage and violence, but a future in which the possibility of a backlash against all rights advances—including the good ones—grows more likely. A future in which racism is responded to with racism—denigration based on gender is responded to with denigration based on gender. At some stage of humiliation there is simply no reason for majority groups not to play games back that have worked so well on themselves."[73]

There is some empirical evidence to justify this claim. Scholars Lucian Conway, Meredith Repke, and Shanno Houck conducted a survey experiment during the 2016 election to examine this question.[74] Some of the people in the survey were randomly chosen to receive some additional information about political correctness. The wording of a paragraph emphasized that these social norms can benefit society.[75] Respondents were then asked both how they felt about political correctness and several other political questions. The authors found that priming subjects by reminding them of political correctness increased their support for Trump by a significant margin. Thus, right-wing politicians may benefit if much of the public believes political correctness has gone too far. This is congruent with other research that similarly finds that pressure to conform to egalitarian norms in speech may sometimes result in stronger feelings of prejudice.[76]

On the other hand, the notion that new norms about how we speak about race and gender leads to a significant right-wing backlash is at odds with other empirical evidence. Specifically, scholars have not found evidence that Americans are becoming more reactionary in their views on race, gender, and sexual orientation.[77] In fact, these attitudes continue to move leftward despite (or because of) increased political correctness on college campuses and the media. The rapid change in the public's average views on sexual minorities is especially remarkable, and likely because of pressure from elites.[78] Even attitudes toward Muslims, which have been quite negative, especially among Republicans, seem to have softened in recent years, in spite of Trump's vitriolic 2016 campaign rhetoric.[79]

Another potential problem with identity politics, from a left-wing perspective, is that it focuses on the superficial rather than the substantive. A progressive emphasis on identity issues allows major industries to grant frivolous concessions to the Left without offering any changes that would materially benefit underprivileged groups. Corporate leaders do not mind donating (from their perspective) paltry sums to gay-rights organizations or posting "Black Lives Matter" in their Twitter feeds. They fear meaningful efforts to redistribute wealth. They thus, according to this theory, use the influence they have to keep the Left focused on identity issues that keep the current economic power structure in place.

The most common argument against identity politics from the Left is that it undermines left-wing unity. It keeps the Left from forming a cohesive, class-based populist movement capable of taking on entrenched moneyed interests. Others on the left have responded to this critique, however. They note that there has not been a "turn" toward identity politics on the left. Rather, for the first time, the Left is starting to include other voices that had previously been excluded from efforts to promote economic equality. This was especially true of earlier waves of populism, which was ostentatiously white and male. Daniel Martinez HoSang and Joseph Lowndes provide the following left-wing rejoinder to the populist Left's critique of identity politics:

> For them, the natural political identity of workers and farmers expressed in opposition to monopoly capitalists, bankers, and speculators was relinquished to the right as the moral language of labor was replaced with excessive concern for identity—be it race, nationality,

gender, or sexuality—fragmenting a coherent left identity. Such an understanding fails in two ways. First, identity has always been central to populism insofar as it has expressed whiteness and masculinity as central features of who is included in populist rhetoric. Second, a simple story of rightward shift misses the ways in which, from the Jacksonian era forward, producerist politics have always retained elements of racialized demonization, be it the anti-Black and anti-indigenous politics of the Jacksonians, the anti-immigrant sentiment of the early 20th century, or the exclusion of Black workers from New Deal programs.[80]

CONCLUSION

The conservative movement has deployed many different responses to the rise of identity politics. These different arguments are not always simpatico, which is not surprising as conservatives are not monolithic on these issues. Despite their disagreements about how and why identity politics is harmful, conservatives are all but unanimous in their belief that identity politics is a great evil in American life. In making their case against identity politics, conservatives have leaned on ideas developed by nonconservatives. Conservatives have been quick to praise libertarians and liberals who are willing to ally with conservatives against so-called wokeness. In fact, when attacking identity politics, the mainstream conservative movement in the United States will often rely on arguments that could not be described as right-wing in any meaningful sense. Instead, they argue that progressives would find that their own beliefs and preferences would be better advanced by an identity-neutral political strategy.

Just as there is not a unified conservative argument against identity politics, conservatives have been similarly divided on the reasons identity politics began rising in the first place. Most will argue that this development was not inevitable. In chapter 3 we will describe various conservative theories about these phenomena.

THREE

Conservative Explanations for the Rise of Identity Politics

American conservatives have offered many different critiques of identity politics as it is currently practiced by the Left and the Far Right. They have also provided multiple explanations for why this phenomenon has become so pervasive. When conservatives discuss trends they lament, and seek to explain their origins, some of them will argue that today's problems have ancient roots. Eric Voegelin saw the precursors of today's utopian troublemakers in the ancient Christian heresy of Gnosticism. Richard Weaver thought the rise of nominalism began the West down a path toward dissolution. This is not the case here. When it comes to identity politics, conservatives tend to place the blame on the more recent intellectuals, activists, and social trends.

THE PROGRESSIVE ERA AS THE SOURCE OF OUR PROBLEMS

Most conservatives argue that the Founding Fathers put the United States on solid footing. The Constitution and political principles the founding generation provided could keep the country on the right track, requiring only minor updates over time—aside from the colossal problem of slavery, which required a civil war to resolve. Acknowledging the need for change, conservatives contend that change must be incremental and respectful of tradition. Yet conservatives also often argue that the United Stated has gone off course. The question, then, is when and why did the republic lose its way? For many of America's leading conservative voices, the answer is clear: the American project envisioned by the Founding Fathers was derailed by the Progressives of the late nineteenth and early twentieth century, and many of the ideological currents conservatives consider deleterious have roots in that era.

The Progressive Era (approximately from the 1890s to the 1920s) was a period of massive reform and activism, focused on many projects. Contemporary conservatives have no objection to many of the policies advanced during this period. Few conservatives, for example, would today condemn the push for universal women's suffrage, guaranteed by the Constitution in the Nineteenth Amendment, finally ratified in 1920. Municipal reforms designed to finally end the inefficiency and corruption that plagued America's large cities are similarly uncontroversial.

For many conservatives, however, the Progressive movement represents the moment America lost its way. Some have even suggested that, since the movement began, the major divide in American political life has been between those who believe in the Progressive vision and those that hold fast to the Founding Fathers' principles. Conservative legal scholars have become especially apt to blame the Progressive movement for damaging trends in the United States.[1] This was the era, according to the conservative narrative, that leading American intellectuals turned their back on the nation's natural rights tradition, which allowed for a diverse nation to maintain necessary unity. As Allan Bloom put it, "The old view was that, by recognizing and accepting man's natural rights, men found a fundamental basis of unity and sameness. Class, race, religion, national origin or culture all disappear or become dim when bathed in the light of natural rights, which give men common interests and make them truly brothers."[2] This change had many effects, but one consequence was that it opened doors to a new form of group-based politics. According to Charles Kesler, editor of *The Claremont Review of Books*, the Progressives were some of the first practitioners of identity politics: "The prevailing liberal doctrine of rights traces individual rights to membership in various groups—racial, ethnic, gender, class-based—which are undergoing a continual process of consciousness-raising and empowerment. This was already a prominent feature of Progressivism well over a century ago, though the groups have changed."[3]

There are some problems with the idea that modern identity politics has its roots in the Progressive movement, however. Many of the Progressive movement's initiatives were direct attacks on what we today would call identity politics. For example, like most of today's conservatives, important Progressives called on immigrant groups to abandon their older ethnic attachments and identity simply as Americans. Both Theodore Roosevelt and Woodrow Wilson called for the end of "hyphenated Americans," and the "swat the hyphen" movement had wide support from Progressive circles. According to Roosevelt: "For an American citizen to vote as a German-American, an Irish-American, or an English-American is to be a traitor to American institutions and those hyphenated Americans who terrorize American politicians by threats of the foreign vote are engaged in treason to the American republic."[4]

There were other ways in which Progressives were opposed to the identity politics of their day, pursuing policies today's conservatives would endorse. In their efforts to end the corruption that dominated America's major cities, the Progressives took on the political machines that controlled municipal governments. These machines were often little more than an ethnic spoils system, where local political bosses, dependent on the loyalty of recent immigrant groups, rewarded followers with jobs and access to municipal services—and could deny those goods to their opponents. The Progressives sought to end the system of ethnic patronage with a modern, efficient civil service.

Even more significantly, the Progressives were responsible for the most successful immigration restriction movement in American history, but some of their justifications for that policy would be anathema to modern conservative arguments. Today's mainstream conservatives wholly reject the Progressives' arguments about the superiority of Nordic immigrants and the inferiority of those peoples from southern and eastern Europe. In fact, even today's white nationalists mostly reject this extreme form of Nordicism, preferring a more ecumenical white identity. Nonetheless, reductions in immigration are on the agenda for most modern conservatives, even if they would not want to slam the door as completely as the Progressives did in 1924.

Before concluding that these points represent a major blow to the conservative argument, however, I must note that some conservatives have noted these historical facts and drawn different conclusions. Jonah Goldberg, for example, has suggested that the Progressives' hostility toward hyphenated Americans was itself a form of identity politics.[5] This is a reasonable argument, but it also suggests that antitribal politics is also a kind of tribal politics, which seems to drastically narrow the definition of nontribal politics.

THE FIRST LEFT MODERNISTS

The Progressive movement was ideologically diverse, and there was an element of thought from the Progressive Era that approached cultural diversity from a perspective opposed to TR's assimilationist view. Political scientist Eric Kaufmann argues that early twentieth-century cultural critics laid the foundation for the eventual triumph of multiculturalism, bringing down the once hegemonic WASPs.[6] It was during this period that the concept of cultural relativism first took hold among a minority of cultural and intellectual elites. Liberal Protestantism, calling for greater ecumenism and tolerance for religious minorities, was one source of this trend. Perhaps more important, however, were members of the avant-garde modernist community in Greenwich Village, a group that first articulated many of the ideas now commonly expressed by the multiculturalist Left. In contrast to the Progressives who encouraged assimilation and "Americanism" among immigrants, these "Liberal Progressives viewed American diversity as an embryo of international cooperation and world peace."[7]

According to Kaufmann, these intellectuals from the early twentieth century were the vanguard of contemporary multiculturalism. Philosopher John Dewey was an especially important promoter of cosmopolitan tolerance, as was the writer Randolph Bourne. Kaufmann argues that left-wing Progressives of this period were the first practitioners of what he calls "asymmetrical multiculturalism," an ideology that calls on the WASP majority to abandon its identity while simultaneously encouraging minorities to maintain their cultural distinctiveness.[8] These Progressives foreshadowed the modern left-wing claim that identity politics is legitimate for every group other than the white majority. Many celebrated intellectuals of this period viewed the Anglo-Protestant culture of the United States (which they associated with Prohibition and puritanism) as loathsome. This was even true of some figures we may now reasonably describe as right-wing, notably essayist H. L. Mencken.

The anti-WASP attitude of these cultural elites was not immediately translated into policy. After all, the 1920s witnessed the most sweeping immigration restrictions in American history, which remained mostly in place until the 1960s. This was also the era in which the Ku Klux Klan was at its peak of influence. However, in the long run, the ideas developed by this cultural vanguard in the early twentieth century eventually came to dominate American popular culture. Kaufmann argues: "The Lost Generation's antimajority ethos pervaded the writing of the 1950s 'Beat Generation' left modernist writers like Norman Mailer and Jack Kerouac—who contrasted lively black jazz or Mexican culture with the 'square' puritanical whiteness of Middle America."[9]

If Kaufmann's argument is correct, the roots of contemporary American multiculturalism can be found within the once dominant WASP culture. That is, there were elements of Anglo-Protestant culture that made it uniquely susceptible to feelings of guilt and self-doubt. Other critics of identity politics ascribe its rise to other causes. In recent years, many conservatives have argued that the ideas underpinning modern identity politics were foreign imports.

THE CULTURAL MARXIST INVASION

The term "cultural Marxism" has been pervasive in right-wing discourse about identity politics, but its use may be declining. The specific meaning of the phrase is contested, but the basic premise of the idea is simple. The United States and the West won the Cold War in the realm of economics: central planning of the economy proved inefficient, as early critics of socialism—such as Ludwig von Mises[10]—insisted it would. However, the Left won the "culture war" in the long run, which may ultimately be an even more significant victory. While the Right was focused on partisan elections at home and combating Soviet influence abroad, the Left quietly conquered the means of cultural production, especially universities and the entertainment industries. Rather than focusing solely on economic redistribution, this Left sought to undermine the cultural foundations of bourgeois capitalist society. They attacked, sometimes in subtle ways and sometimes overtly, traditional religion, family structures, and ethnic attachments.

The logic of this emphasis on culture came from the twentieth-century Italian Marxist Antonio Gramsci, who sought to understand why early communist revolutions failed to achieve their stated goals. A key element of Gramsci's thought was that communism was failing to take root, even after a seemingly successful revolution, because political power preceded cultural dominance. As long as more traditional norms were pervasive within a population, the proper mind-set needed for communism to succeed would never take hold. Thus, by first subverting those cultural norms, the Left could clear the path for a more successful revolution.

Many conservatives have blamed cultural Marxism for cultural changes they find detrimental. Paleoconservatives, especially William Lind, Paul Weyrich, and Patrick Buchanan, have played an outsize role in popularizing this narrative. Cultural Marxism was a significant theme in Buchanan's best-selling book *The Death of the West*.[11] Buchanan argues that a small number of European intellectuals deliberately transformed American culture. The scholars associated with the "Frankfurt School" were especially important in this regard. In the 1930s, after the Nazis rose to power in Germany, a group of Marxist scholars affiliated with Frankfurt University fled to the United States, where they began teaching at Columbia University. These scholars included Max Horkheimer, Erick Fromm, Theodor Adorno, and Herbert Marcuse. Using logic similar to Gramsci's, these Marxist academics believed that the revolution they sought first required massive cultural change, and they wanted to systematically deconstruct all cultural mores they considered regressive, including traditional family structures. They also endeavored to pathologize right-wing thinking of all kinds, arguing that ordinary American conservatives were actually incipient fascists.

Buchanan argued that this group was remarkably successful in its efforts, and that its metapolitical war on traditional America began to show signs of success in the 1960s, as the rising counterculture began repeating Marcuse's slogans. Critical theory, developed by these scholars and their successors, eventually became dominant, which helped undermine America's cultural confidence. According to Buchanan: "Critical Theory eventually induces 'cultural pessimism,' a sense of alienation, of hopelessness, of despair where, even though prosperous and free, a people comes to see its society and country as oppressive, evil, and unworthy of its loyalty and love."[12] Buchanan considered the Frankfurt School's war on traditional America especially loathsome, given that the United States had provided a safe haven for its most important theorists when they were driven from their native Germany.

Although his language is acrimonious, Buchanan does accurately describe many of the arguments associated with Frankfurt School scholars. His argument that this group had a significant influence on American intellectual life is widely accepted, but some people claim its influence has been exaggerated.[13] Even among those who do not dispute the central facts he presents, Buchanan's argument has been controversial and widely criticized. To some critics, Buchanan's attack on the Frankfurt School and critical theory is actually an anti-Semitic dog whistle. Many of the intellectuals Buchanan criticized were Jewish, and Buchanan has a history of making remarks that many people (including leading conservatives) have perceived as anti-Semitic.[14] Further strengthening the argument that attacks on "cultural Marxism" is a subtle attack on Jews is the term's similarity to an older term, *Kulturbolshewismus* (cultural Bolshevism), which was often used by the Nazis.

I find it unlikely that most conservatives think of cultural Marxists as a synonym for Jews or cultural Marxism as a synonym for Jewish influence. The fact that the term is often employed by Jewish conservatives, such as Jonah Goldberg,[15] suggests to me that most conservatives are not promoting any hidden agenda when they use the term. Most assuredly have no knowledge of its similarity to the term promoted by Nazis. Generally speaking, when conservatives use this term, they are referring to left-wing movements and intellectuals that place a greater emphasis on cultural issues (such as the issues we associate with identity politics) than with traditional left-wing economic concerns.

Rather than anti-Semitism, there is another reason for conservatives to give an outsize role to cultural Marxism when explaining the West's purported decline. The American conservative intellectual tradition typically ascribes cultural change to nonmaterial causes, declaring that ideas have consequences. There are many plausible economic and technological explanations for the cultural revolutions that occurred over the twentieth century in the United States: increasing urbanization, security threats, faster transportation and communication, economic globalization, oral contraception, among others. But many conservatives look to intellectual trends when seeking to understand cultural change. Given that the culture seemed to be moving in a direction aligned with Marcuse's ideas, it made sense to blame that movement on him.

CHANGING FAMILY STRUCTURES AS A PROPOSED EXPLANATION

Conservative author Mary Eberstadt provides one of the more interesting theories about contemporary identity politics in *Primal Screams* (2019).[16] Eberstadt argues that American society's recent obsession with identity can be blamed, in part, on the decline of the nuclear family. That is, throughout most of human history, our immediate familial bonds mostly determined our identities. Although many people found them stifling or oppressive, an advantage of traditional family structures is that they have provided individuals with a definitive sense of their place in the world. Although those who sought to dismantle those structures intended to liberate individuals, the unintended consequences has been loneliness, social atomization, and identity crises.

In the absence of traditional markers of identity, Eberstadt argues, people seek identities and validation from other sources. New "tribes" take the place of immediate and extended families. In some ways, this is simply another extension of the liberating ideals of liberalism: we are all free to invent our sources of identity and community, rather than simply accept those given to us at birth or formed via a lifelong bourgeois marriage. Many people undoubtedly do find this liberating. According to Eberstadt, however, these new forms of community cannot take the place of traditional families for most people. There is something valuable in having these fixed connections that last a lifetime, and severing them leaves people confused and angry:

It is this loss of givenness that drives the frenzied search for identity these days, whether in the secular scholasticism concerning how to speak about ethnicity or in the belligerent fights over "cultural appropriation." Such phenomena are indeed bizarre if we examine them with the instruments of Aristotelian logic. But if instead we understand them against the existential reality of today—one in which the human family has imploded, and in which many people, no matter how privileged otherwise, have been deprived of the most elementary of human connections—we can grasp in full why identity politics is the headline that just won't go away.[17]

Eberstadt says that this theory applies equally well to left-wing and right-wing variants of identitarianism. Both sides, according to her view, are seeking communities that can explain their place in the world.[18] Left-wing and right-wing identitarians have different grievances, but rank-and-file members of both sides seek something similar.

Some of my own research on the Alt-Right seems to validate her argument. In a report I published for the Institute for Family Studies in 2018, I found that divorced white people were more likely than other whites to support the basic premises of white identity politics.[19] Yet the connection I found between marital status and feelings of white identity, white solidarity, and white grievance was paltry, and even when these variables achieved statistical significance, their substantive importance was questionable. This does not mean Eberstadt's hypothesis is wrong, only that in this particular case (measures of white identity politics) it explains relatively little of the phenomenon.

To bolster her argument, Eberstadt references Alexis de Tocqueville's argument that a nation's political system can shape its family structures, noting his point that families tend to be more egalitarian in democratic societies.[20] There may be an even more relevant passage from *Democracy in America*, however. Tocqueville argued that Americans' religiosity provided important direct and indirect supports for democracy, keeping some of the excesses of individualism in check. One of those indirect effects was the tendency for Americans to form family units at a young age, shortening the period of life in which young men are free from both the benefits and responsibilities of leading a family. He argued that this helped keep radicalism of all sorts in check:

There is certainly no country in the world where the tie of marriage is so much respected as in America, or where conjugal happiness is more highly or worthily appreciated. In Europe almost all disturbances of society arise from the irregularities of domestic life. To despise the natural bonds and legitimate pleasures of home, is to contract a taste for excesses, a restlessness of heart, and the evil of fluctuating desires. Agitated by the tumultuous passions which frequently disturb his dwelling, the European is galled by the obedience which the legislative powers of the State exact. But when the American retires from the turmoil of public life to the bosom of his family, he finds in it the image of order and peace. There his pleasures are simple and natural, his joys are innocent and calm; and he finds that an orderly life is the surest path to happiness, he accustoms himself without difficulty to moderate his opinions as well as his tastes. Whilst the European endeavors to forget his domestic troubles by agitating society, the American derives from his own home that love of order which he afterward carries with him into public affairs.[21]

Although contemporary conservatives like to discuss "American exceptionalism," they are surprisingly quiet about how the United States has deviated from Europe in terms of its family formation patterns. Yet this is arguably one of the most exceptional aspects of America throughout its history.[22] This was something Benjamin Franklin noted as early as 1755, when he pointed out that the extraordinary amount of available land in British North America would allow for easy family formation and an explosive natural population growth.[23]

Other authors have additionally posited that changing norms regarding sexuality and marriage are leading to a rise in identity politics. Angela Nagle, author of *Kill All Normies*, suggests that the losers in the new sexual marketplace are increasingly likely to associate with the extreme Right:

The sexual revolution that started the decline of lifelong marriage has produced great freedom from the shackles of loveless marriage and selfless duty to the family for both men and women. But the ever-extended adolescence has also brought with it the rise of adult childlessness and a steep sexual hierarchy. Sexual patterns that have emerged as a result of the decline of monogamy have seen a greater level of sexual choice for elite men and a growing celibacy among a large male population at the bottom of the pecking order. Their own anxiety and anger about their low-ranking status in this hierarchy is precisely what has produced their hard-line rhetoric about asserting hierarchy in the world politically when it comes to women and non-whites.[24]

Nagle's approach to the study of the Alt-Right differs from my own, as her analysis seems to downplay the importance of race. Her treatment of the Alt-Right as a backlash against the excesses of the Left's extreme "wokeness" seems, to me, at odds with how the Alt-Right has described itself. It is nonetheless an argument that may partially explain the recent growth of far-right attitudes and activism among part of the U.S. population. It is also interesting that, despite describing herself as a cultural critic on the left, her arguments about the rise of right-wing identity politics can be reasonably described as conservative.

Even if one accepts the hypothesis that changing family norms fuel identity politics, it does not immediately follow that cultural progressives have been the sole or even the primary cause of these changes. Economic trends are an important determinant of changes in family formation patterns. Libertarian entrepreneur Peter Thiel emphasizes this in his response to Eberstadt's argument, noting that cultural change must be considered in the context of economic change. Without the economic means to support a family, a person is unlikely to do so: "Every family needs an income to pay for home, school, and hospital: from the bill for giving birth; through monthly payments for a house that combines living space, job proximity, and school access; on top of tuition for a diploma from a more or less dubious college."[25]

Although older conservatives may wish to blame cultural changes and supposed moral deficiencies of younger generations for declining marriage and fertility rates, the economic landscape has changed dramatically for young people in recent generations. Productivity gains since the 1970s have not resulted in higher wages for workers, leading to stagnating living standards and a shocking growth in inequality. For most people, college degrees are now essential for achieving a middle-class lifestyle, and most students defer marriage and family until after they have graduated and found quality jobs. The rising cost of education, far outpacing the rate of inflation, represents another challenge, and is another reason young people put off starting families. Higher student loan debt appears to be a variable associated with later marriage.[26]

Many economic changes in the United States since the 1970s resulted from forces disconnected from public policy, and continued under both Republican and Democratic control of the White House and U.S. Congress. The decline of unions is one of the more important examples. Politicians cannot take all the blame (or the credit, depending on one's perspective) for the decline of organized labor. The decline of important manufacturing industries caused by automation and outsourcing is probably the most significant cause. But policy has played a role, especially policies usually endorsed by conservatives: right-to-work laws. These laws make it unlawful to make union membership a prerequisite of employment, thus creating a collective action problem for union organizers. At the time of this writing, twenty-seven states have some form of right-to-work legislation.

This is relevant to this discussion because there is evidence that union membership is related to family formation.[27] Conservatives have many reasons to dislike unions. Unions call for more regulations, higher minimum wages, more redistribution, and generally encourage their members to vote for Democrats. But unions also provide extraordinary stability for workers. They are especially valuable to workers without college degrees. Conservatives may celebrate the "sharing economy,"[28] but it makes sense for an Uber driver to be more cautious about starting a family than a person with a solid union job with good benefits. Furthermore, unions represent one of those important intermediate institutions between the individual and the government that conservatives, such as Robert Nisbet, have said are vital to democracy. Declining union membership rates also seem to be related to higher rates of drug overdose deaths.[29] If conservatives do really care about families, then they should not be so quick to celebrate the decline of the labor movement.

On the other hand, we should not overstate the importance of economic trends when considering this issue. The economic challenges that young people face today are real, but it would require great ignorance of U.S. history—and of the economic conditions of countries that still have high birthrates—to suggest that American rates of family formation are exceptionally low because today's youth face particularly dire economic and social challenges. Changing cultural norms may not explain all of this phenomenon, but they certainly play a role.

SECULARIZATION AS A SOURCE OF RIGHT-WING IDENTITY POLITICS

Some conservatives have suggested that the decline of religion can help us understand the rise of other forms of identity in the United States and other Western countries. According to this argument, religion (Christianity, in this context) once provided people a strong sense of identity and belonging. In this earlier period, when people considered their most fundamental identities, at least part of their answer was clear: they were Christians. They could furthermore be confident that most of the people in the country shared this identity, even if the United States had a plethora of denominations offering diverse Christian theologies.

As Christianity has waned, this sense of identity and belonging has diminished. Because the need for identity remained, however, people began to search for other identities to fill this void, turning toward other categories, such as race, ethnicity, and political party. In spite of the religious Right's many failings, Christianity is a universal religion capable of transcending racial boundaries. In 2016, Ross Douthat argued in the *New York Times* that, for all their misgivings with the religious Right, the Left will find the postreligious Right to be much more dangerous. He further noted that some elements of the religious Right's agenda were aligned with progressive goals: "When religious conservatives were ascendant, the G.O.P. actually tried minority outreach, it sent billions to fight AIDS in Africa, it pursued criminal justice reform in the states."[30]

The Alt-Right, which was approaching its peak of influence at the time Douthat wrote that column, seemed to provide evidence for this thesis. Many of the most recognizable figures of the Alt-Right were non-Christians or even anti-Christian.[31] In this regard, the Alt-Right was consistent with earlier white nationalist movements. Although never united on this issue, white nationalists in the United States have historically opposed Christianity for several reasons: it is inherently egalitarian, it is universalist, and it has non-European origins.[32] Thus, if whites must have a religion at all, it should take the form of pre-Christian European paganism, or perhaps a form of "Christian identity," a racialized version of Christianity that insists on the racial superiority of whites, a view rejected by all mainstream Christian theologians.

Progressive author Peter Beinart agrees with Douthat.[33] He notes that, in spite of the remaining high levels of segregation in America's churches, they nonetheless help to foster bonds that transcended race. Christianity additionally has represented a stumbling block to those who would prefer that race serve as the foundation of identity and politics. With Christianity playing a diminished role in American life, this hindrance to white identity politics has been largely removed. According to Beinart:

> Secularism is indeed correlated with greater tolerance of gay marriage and pot legalization. But it's also making America's partisan clashes more brutal. And it has contributed to the rise of both Donald Trump and the so-called alt-right movement, whose members see themselves as proponents of white nationalism. As Americans have left organized religion, they haven't stopped viewing politics as a struggle between "us" and "them." Many have come to define us and them in even more primal and irreconcilable ways.[34]

When thinking about Christianity and politics, however, it is important not to overstate the centrality of egalitarianism to the religion. There is, of course, an inescapable egalitarian element to the faith. The New Testament can be interpreted in many different ways. However, the text makes it quite clear that all people are loved by God and are subject to God's judgment. God's love (and wrath) transcends national borders and racial lines—not that the modern concept of race had even been developed when the Bible was written. Christian missionaries have always sought to expand their ranks beyond what used to be called Christendom. Yet the Christian belief that we are all, in some sense, equal before God has not always meant that Christians believe in equality in any meaningful way in this world.

The idea that Christianity is inherently egalitarian and democratic is ahistorical. Constantine was no radical egalitarian. Nor was Charlemagne.

Nor were the Christian slaveholders in the antebellum South. American slaveholders could accurately point out that the condition of slavery was the norm in the Old Testament and accepted in the New Testament. Some passages even seem to validate slavery and call upon slaves to be obedient servants. In the Gospels, Jesus is silent on the question of slavery.

Christianity was unquestionably an indispensable element of the fight against slavery. Even so, in the years leading up to the American Civil War, and throughout that conflict, both sides insisted on their Christian piety. The Southern Baptist Convention, now the largest Protestant denomination in the United States, was founded because of a schism among Baptists over the slavery question. Looking abroad in the twentieth century, Hitler was no Christian, but most Germans in the 1930s and 40s were Christians, and most of them saw no contradiction between their faith and their support for the Nazi regime. Hitler had pious Christian opponents, such as Dietrich Bonhoeffer, who gave their lives to oppose the Nazis, but they were exceptions.

More recent history in the United States has shown that there was a racial element to the rise of the Christian Right. Before abortion became its signature issue, the Christian Right was first motivated by the defense of segregation. After public schools were desegregated, private Christian schools were formed across the South because private schools were allowed to practice racial segregation. Changes to tax policy that would have forced these schools to admit Black students initially motivated Jerry Falwell and other Christian Right leaders. For all of these reasons, it is unlikely Christianity's decline has played a crucial role in the rise of right-wing identity movements, or that a Christian revival would destroy them.

SECULARIZATION AS A SOURCE OF LEFT-WING IDENTITY POLITICS

If we accept, as most conservatives do, that human nature includes a religious impulse, it seems to follow that, as traditional religion declines, people will seek some kind of substitute. Without a transcendent belief system to provide meaning, secularists turn to new ideologies to fill that vacuum. On the left in the twentieth century, communism, which provided life with purpose and promised a future utopia in this world, was especially attractive. This was a major theme in Whittaker Chambers's reflections on life as a communist and his subsequent rejection of communism. Beyond purpose in this life, and hope for a future life, religion also provides a sense of identity and belonging. It used to fulfill a vital social need for most people, and its loss has been painful. Ideologies, and the movements that form around them, can serve a similar psychological and social role.

Since the Cold War's end, communism has lost much of its appeal. The idea that the collective ownership of the means of production would lead to a world of equality and prosperity became increasingly dubious, and is now espoused only by a few radicals. However, given that religiosity in the West only declined further and faster after the Cold War, it follows that some new, noncommunist ideology must take communism's place if one believes the argument that ideology will fill the void left by a retreating religion.

Conservatives have thus suggested that many elements of the contemporary American progressive movement are simply new forms of religion, and this is especially true of identity politics and calls for social justice. In the past, conservatives made a similar argument against contemporary environmentalism. Libertarian economist Paul Rubin, for example, suggests that the modern environmental movement shares many attributes of traditional religion, including a holy day (Earth Day), culinary taboos (against nonorganic foods, for example), and the urge to proselytize.[35] Bruce Thornton of the Hoover Institution adds that environmentalism also shares the common religious trope of a previous golden age, in which the world existed in harmony, which flawed human beings disrupted.[36] In contrast to religious myths about mankind's fall from grace, according to Thornton, the environmentalist points to the Industrial Revolution as the moment when humanity broke its close connection with nature and set us on a path that will ultimately end in destruction—unless, of course, if we repent and change our ways.

Today, it is more common for conservatives to argue that identity politics is the new replacement religion, filling the emptiness left by traditional religious beliefs and institutions. According to this view, multiculturalism shares more in common with a new religion than a traditional secular social movement. Andrew Sullivan has recently made this claim:

For many, especially the young, discovering a new meaning in the midst of the fallen world is thrilling. And social-justice ideology does everything a religion should. It offers an account of the whole: that human life and society and any kind of truth must be seen entirely as a function of social power structures, in which various groups have spent all of human existence oppressing other groups. And it provides a set of practices to resist and reverse this interlocking web of oppression—from regulating the workplace and policing the classroom to checking your own sin and even seeking to control language itself. I think of non-PC gaffes as the equivalent of old swear words. Like the puritans who were agape when someone said "goddamn," the new faithful are scandalized when someone says something "problematic." Another commonality of the zealot then and now: humorlessness.[37]

This story, that a post-Christian society will replace religion with an ideology, even if true, leaves several questions unanswered. Most notably, why would secularists in the United States necessarily gravitate toward the ideology of multiculturalism and minority identity politics? Paul Gottfried argues that we can find the roots of this trend in Christianity itself, especially Protestantism, which continues to have a strong cultural hold on societies, even after belief in Christianity's supernatural claims have dissipated.

According to Gottfried, modern multiculturalist ideology in the West bears many important similarities to Christian thinking. The feeling of guilt and the need for atonement are especially important to both Christian thinking and post-Christian multiculturalism. Like Christianity, modern multiculturalism has its own list of saints and martyrs (such as Martin Luther King Jr. and Matthew Shepard).[38] Progressives in the United States and other Western democracies have abandoned their belief in original sin and replaced it with "white privilege." Moreover, just as the Calvinist Puritans of New England believed they were personally incapable of atoning for their sinful nature, today's progressives suggest that no amount of good works can ever wash away the stain of racism.

Michael Brendan Dougherty, a writer at *National Review*, has argued that the Christian obsession with victimhood (especially Christ's victimization) has survived Christianity's decline and remains a critical part of

Western culture. In modern America, victimhood is associated with righteousness and moral authority. According to Dougherty: "The premise of victim politics is like a mirror image of devotion to the Suffering Servant. Just as in Christianity, so in social-justice politics: The wounds of the primordial victim testify to the broken state of human nature and society at large."[39] Dougherty further argues that we can see religious echoes in the nonrational forms of argumentation often embraced by identity politics practitioners, who respond to reasoned arguments with apparent non sequiturs, such as "you're erasing my existence."[40] In such arguments, the degree to which you can claim victimization by society determines both your moral status and truth of your factual claims. Showing insufficient deference to someone higher in the victimization hierarchy is a great risk, as it opens one up to ritualistic shaming and a loss of social status. After describing an encounter he had with a proponent of identity politics, and the moralizing, puritanical scolding that resulted, Dougherty notes the following: "It sounds like an accusation of atheism, for a good reason: You're being charged with heresy, and if you do not desist, you reveal yourself as morally reprobate, as one who would, with full knowledge, repeat the Crucifixion. Or if you prefer the current academese, you are one who 'reifies the structures of oppression.'"[41]

Conservative scholar James Kurth provided additional arguments for why Protestantism was able to transform into modern secular progressivism with little difficulty.[42] Unlike Roman Catholicism, Protestantism was intensely antihierarchical from the very beginning. When it came to spiritual matters, Protestant thinkers rejected the idea that individual souls needed either a hierarchical institutional intermediary or a community of believers to have a relationship with God. According to Kurth, this led to a radical new individualism that would form the foundation of American political culture: "The elements of the American Creed were free markets and equal opportunity, free elections and liberal democracy, constitutionalism and the rule of law."[43] He argues that this was further universalized, and by the 1970s Americans were speaking of universal human rights, which was the result of taking the American creed to its logical conclusion.

The American Mind, one of the Claremont Institute's online publications, recently published a series of essays examining the connection between religion and identity politics. Joshua Mitchell begins the discussion by noting that identity politics represents a fundamentally different, new form of politics, one that traditional conservatives are not equipped to overcome.[44] The self-described thoughtful conservatives, who "ponder great ideas" and lambasted former President Trump at every opportunity, will never be able to defeat left-wing identity politics through reasoned debate. Identity politics is pursued with a religious fervor. Debate in this new intellectual landscape is largely futile because identity politics entails judging the soundness of an argument according to the demographic attributes of the arguer. The fact that one is a heterosexual white male renders one's positions moot. People can be wrong by virtue of who they are. Mitchell then suggests that, even if heterosexual white males are swamped demographically at the ballot box and knocked from their positions of social and economic power, identity politics will simply expand the category of "unclean transgressors" to serve as a scapegoat. He suggests white women will be next, followed by African Americans who continue to endorse traditional conservative cultural norms.

Spencer Klavan joins the discussion by making an argument similar to Gottfried's earlier suggestion: "The best way to describe what Wokeness has actually become is Christianity without Christ. Progressivism recognizes many of the truths about human nature that Christianity has long taught: we are corrupted down to our bones, we do not have help enough to truly help ourselves, and our best attempts at righteousness are as filthy rags."[45] According to Klavan, "wokeness" was the inevitable result of America's turn away from God.

Not all contributors to this symposium agreed with the claim that identity politics is comparable to religion, or that its rise can be attributed to religion's decline. James Lindsay—who is not religious—agrees that there were some similarities between religion and identity politics.[46] He pushes back, however, against the idea that social justice represents simply a substitution for waning Christian faith. He notes, for example, that many of the ideological trends we see within the secular Left can also be found within the religious Left. That is, there are varieties of Christian theology that are comfortable with identity politics, even in its most extreme manifestations. In fact, even Christian denominations we tend to think of as conservative have become more accepting of the identity politics framework of societal ills. The Southern Baptist Convention, for example, passed a resolution allowing the use of critical race theory and intersectionality as "analytical tools," but it did emphasize that they must be "subordinate to scripture."[47] The existence of people who simultaneously identify as strong Christians and as strong supporters of left-wing identity politics challenges the simple narrative that identity politics is simply a substitution for religion.

To further complicate these matters, we must consider how identity politics has shaped the religious Left. Long before the explosive growth of the Christian Right in the late 1970s, the evangelical Left was organized and active in American politics. In the early twentieth century, progressive Christians focused on social reform efforts were much more interested in politics than more conservative fundamentalists, who were more concerned with individual salvation than questions of national policy. Religious groups played an indispensable role in the civil rights movement, most notably. Historian David R. Swartz has argued that a nascent evangelical Left, on the rise before the Christian Right fully developed, was hindered by identity politics among progressive evangelical Christians.[48] Although there were many progressive voices among evangelicals, they never were able to speak with one voice and were increasingly fractured along "racial, gender, and theological lines."[49] Although we should not overstate the many divisions that existed within the Christian Right (between Catholics and Protestants, cessationists and continuationists, etc.), compared to the Christian Left, it enjoyed a greater level of demographic and political unity, helping it to form a cohesive, sustainable political movement.

CONCLUSION

Conservatives have offered many different explanations for the rise of identity politics. Many argue that it results from the growth of insidious ideas (either homegrown or imported). A few suggest that it results from other demographic or economic trends. In explaining the rise of identity politics, conservatives often turn to their traditional talking points—the United States abandoned the Founding Fathers' vision, traditional family values have declined, we are no longer united in a common religious faith, and so on. They overwhelmingly reject the claim that identity politics represents a reasonable and appropriate response to legitimate grievances.

Identity politics can take many forms, but in the contemporary United States we generally focus on the demographic characteristics: race, gender, and nationality. In the next three chapters, respective, I will discuss how modern American conservatives have approached these three subjects since the movement's birth. These chapters will challenge the claim that conservatives are simply above identity politics, but they will also argue that conservatism is not just a stalking horse for right-wing identitarianism.

FOUR

Conservatism and the Civil Rights Movement

This chapter considers how one facet of identity politics shaped early conservatism, even if that was not the term used at the time. The conservative movement's response to the civil rights movement in the 1950s and 1960s remains a source of some embarrassment for today's conservatives, as most of the leading conservatives of that era made remarks about race that would be considered outrageous in a contemporary setting. For this reason, the temptation for twenty-first-century conservatives to ignore or downplay this history can be difficult to resist. In contrast, some scholars and commentators on the left view almost all of politics through a racial lens. From their perspective, everything conservatives do and have done is driven by a desire to maintain a system of racial oppression.[1] I disagree with both of these positions. Many on the left infer racist intentions where none existed. Conservatives who sweep their own movement's history under the rug, or pretend that race was not an element to the Republican Party's revival in the second half of the twentieth century, should also be critiqued.

THE SOCIAL AND POLITICAL CONTEXT
OF POSTWAR CONSERVATIVES

As I noted in chapter 1, the ideology that we now call American conservatism—the union of free-market economics, moral traditionalism, and hawkish foreign policy—is a relatively new political innovation. There are a number of plausible dates we can choose to mark the birth of modern conservatism. We may choose 1953, because that was the year Russell Kirk published *The Conservative Mind*, the book that gave the conservative movement its name and began the process of rebuilding conservatism's reputation as an intellectually serious political position. Perhaps we could choose 1955, when William F. Buckley Jr. launched *National Review*, the flagship journal of the conservative movement. In any event, conservatism as we now understand it really got off the ground in the 1950s. This was a unique period of American history.

The decade following World War II was unusual in several respects. After the devastation of that conflict, the United States emerged as the only major power mostly unscathed. The great powers of Western Europe were all in ruins. The Soviet Union could still field a massive army, and its industrial capacity was enormous by the end of the conflict, but the Red Army had been bled white by four years of apocalyptic struggle with the Germans. And although the Soviets had proven adept at producing huge numbers of tanks and other weapons and enjoyed abundant natural resources, it never was successful at creating quality consumer goods. This left the United States as an unrivaled economic powerhouse.

The period after the war was thus marked by an extraordinary improvement in living standards in the United States, widely shared. Home ownership and college education became widespread in a way never seen before. The "American dream" of a family, a house, and a pension seemed within reach of anyone willing to work. This new optimism resulted in a remarkable "baby boom." Feelings of national pride were pervasive. Religiosity was also at a peak. Religious conservatives who lament the decline of faith in this country reasonably use the 1950s as their baseline for comparison to the present day. One thing they may not realize is that the 1950s were not just different from today, but also differed from the preceding decades. That is, religious observance was considerably higher in the 1950s than it was in preceding periods of the twentieth century.

The conservative movement was thus created at a moment of remarkable optimism and unity, but leading conservatives did not seem to recognize this at the time. Many of the ethnic divides that had been so contentious in earlier periods had waned. The "culture wars" that would embroil the country in subsequent decades had not really begun. Because it was a period of unusual unity, the early conservative intellectual movement gave little thought to the many questions of identity that later became so central to American political life. Beneath the surface, of course, the country was less united than it appeared, as the conservative movement would realize to its horror in the 1960s. A counterculture, which found the bourgeois uniformity of the period stifling, was gaining strength and would soon disrupt the country's social peace. The subject of civil rights for African Americans was even more important and divisive.

The question of race, however, did not seem to be especially salient to the most important figures of early conservatism. This may be because the life experiences of conservatism's important founders were mostly disconnected from these conflicts. Buckley, arguably the most important conservative journalist and activist of the twentieth century, was the son of an oil developer and raised mostly in Sharon, Connecticut. His upbringing was more like that of a European aristocrat than a middle-class American. Both of his parents were from the South (his father was from Texas and his mother from Louisiana), and he often spent winters in the South, yet he rarely exhibited a meaningful southern identity.[2] He earned a bachelor's degree at Yale University, where he was a member of the infamous Skull and Bones Society. His wife, Patricia, the daughter of an important Canadian industrialist, came from a similar background of privilege. The pair owned residences in Manhattan and Connecticut, and spent winters at a property they leased in Switzerland. Although he had limited personal experience with African Americans in his childhood, Buckley was raised to believe that Blacks were naturally inferior to whites.[3] His father was unquestionably an anti-Semite. Although Buckley idolized his father, as an adult he did not share his views on Jews. His efforts to expunge the respectable American Right of anti-Semitism was clearly based on sincere beliefs, and he was largely successful in this endeavor.

The Midwest was well represented in the early conservative movement. Russell Kirk was the son of a railroad engineer in rural Michigan. He earned his undergraduate degree at Michigan State University. After serving in World War II he earned his doctorate at the University of St. Andrews in Scotland. Although well traveled, Kirk spent most of his time in a small town in Michigan. Even today, Mecosta, where Kirk lived most of his life and is now home to the Russell Kirk Center for Cultural Renewal, has just a few hundred residents and is overwhelmingly white. L. Brent Bozell, a contributor and later a senior editor at *National Review*, and the ghostwriter behind Barry Goldwater's manifesto, *The Conscience of a Conservative*, was born in Nebraska. After serving in the navy in World War II, he also earned a degree from Yale University, where he met Buckley. Willmoore Kendall, also a *National Review* contributor, was born in Oklahoma. Kendall was a political science professor at Yale—both Bozell and Buckley were mentored by Kendall. William Rusher, *National Review*'s publisher and another important conservative activist and strategist, was from Illinois.

Frank Meyer was born to a well-to-do Jewish family in New Jersey. Meyer studied at Princeton, Oxford, the London School of Economics, and the University of Chicago. The Chicago-born James Burnham also studied at Princeton and Oxford, and became a professor at New York University. Whittaker Chambers grew up on Long Island and went to Columbia University, but he did not finish his degree. All three men were communists for much of their lives—Chambers actually served as a Soviet spy. Although not directly involved in espionage, Meyer had been a prominent communist organizer and was very concerned for his life when he broke with the radical Left. He was genuinely worried about an assassination attempt and took steps to mitigate this risk. He moved to isolated Woodstock, New York, and chose to sleep in the day and stay awake at night.[4] Chambers had similar concerns, and after his own break with communism spent time in hiding. Burnham was a well-known leftist intellectual before moving to the right in the 1940s.

These biographical details are worth noting because they demonstrate the demographic disconnect between important early conservative thinkers and the everyday conservative (broadly understood) in the electorate. Although we may think of middle-class white southern Protestants as the prototypical conservative Americans, such people were hard to find in the early years of the conservative intellectual movement. Northerners made up the bulk of the early conservative intelligentsia. It is therefore not surprising that they did not treat civil rights for southern Blacks as a critical issue.

This is not to say southerners were completely absent from the early conservative movement. Richard Weaver was the most significant example. The journalist M. Stanton Evans was born in Texas, and raised, in part, in Tennessee. Gary Wills, for a time considered one of Buckley's brightest protégés, was from Atlanta. Wills did not remain a conservative. In fact, he may have never been a "true conservative" as the movement's leaders understood the term. Wills eventually broke with his former friends and colleagues, in large part because of his liberal attitudes toward civil rights. This break was painful for Buckley, who tried to avoid it as long as possible by giving Wills space in *National Review* to express his more progressive views. Wills, for example, published a piece in the magazine expressing sympathy for the violent left-wing protesters at the Chicago 1968 Democratic Convention. Others at *National Review* urged Buckley not to publish the article, and if it had been written by anyone else, he surely would not have done so.[5] The divide between Wills and the rest of the movement ultimately proved unbridgeable, and he eventually abandoned conservatism entirely.

CHARLES WALLACE COLLINS AND THE SEGREGATIONISTS' CONSERVATIVE STRATEGY

Reading the most important history of the conservative movement— George Nash's classic work *The Conservative Intellectual Movement Since 1945*—one would understandably infer that southerners played relatively little role in the development of modern conservatism. Even the one figure who might be considered a major exception, Weaver, was probably less influential than many conservatives imagine. Although conservatives may recycle the tag "ideas have consequences" from the title of Weaver's best-known book (a title he did not choose and never liked), one will have a hard time finding any of the ideas in the book echoed by today's conservatives. Weaver's quasi-mystical, radical reactionary positions in the 1940s are not embraced by any important contemporary conservatives.

It may thus be challenging to understand how it was that white southerners became the demographic base of the Republican Party and conservative politics more broadly. One plausible argument is that the GOP and conservatism enjoyed a windfall caused by overreach by the Democratic Party and the Left during the 1960s. That is, civil rights crusaders, the Johnson administration, and the counterculture all helped to spark a conservative backlash in that part of the American electorate. The Republican Party was in a position to take advantage of this trend, most famously in Richard Nixon's "Southern Strategy."

This story does not necessarily make conservatives look good, in hindsight. It is quite clear that conservatism became more attractive to white southerners (and to many urban white ethnics in the North) as they became increasingly uncomfortable with the racial progressivism of the Democratic Party. Yet this narrative does seem to downplay the role of conservative intellectuals in the splintering of the Democratic Party's coalition. That is, it suggests conservatives benefited from racial anxieties in the 1960s and 1970s, but race was not a central element of conservative thinking. In the case of the most celebrated and well-remembered conservatives of that period, this is mostly correct. However, this story becomes less tenable when we consider important conservative thinkers who are not today celebrated as crucial figures in the conservative pantheon.

The fact that conservatives do not remember many influential right-wing southern thinkers of the postwar era does not mean that there were no such figures. As the Democratic Party was dividing over the question of civil rights for Blacks, some racial conservatives in the South began to look elsewhere for new coalition partners. As we know, in the late 1940s, the pro-segregationist wing of the Democratic Party did not initially consider defection to the GOP to be their natural move. Instead, they created a new third party, the States' Rights Democratic Party (collo-quially known as the "Dixiecrat Party"), led by Strom Thurmond, who ran on the party's ticket in the presidential election of 1948. President Truman's decision to integrate the U.S. military, along with other signs that the national Democratic Party was adopting a more progressive stance on civil rights, was the catalyst for the party's creation. Thurmond failed to block Truman's victory in 1948, despite winning four states in the Deep South. He further failed to change the Democratic Party's trajectory on civil rights. It was not until several election cycles later, when the GOP nominated Barry Goldwater for president in 1964, that the Deep South began to move decisively toward the Republican Party in presidential elections, and many more years before Republicans began dominating down-ballot elections in that region.

Political scientist Joseph Lowndes has challenged the "backlash" hypothesis of the Republican Party's growth in the South.[6] He argues that much of the language of modern conservatism, albeit since evolved, originally emerged from the South. He notes a few figures that have since been mostly forgotten, but nonetheless played an important role in the development of American conservatism. The Alabama-born Charles Wallace Collins was one such leader. His 1947 book, *Whither Solid South: A Study in Politics and Race Relations,*[7] is a fascinating document because of his predictions about the future of American politics, and it is thus worth examining in some detail.

As Collins was writing in the mid-1940s, he could see the writing on the political wall (in his words, "a Second Reconstruction in the offing"[8]), and he knew that the South's ability to block legislation designed to break down the complex structures of racial segregation was going to eventually fail, given the current electoral alignments. Although southern senators had been adept in their use of the filibuster, this would not be a sufficiently powerful weapon in the long term. Collins was also responding to trends among intellectuals. In particular, he argued against Gunnar Myrdal's influential *An American Dilemma: The Negro Problem and Modern Democracy* (1944), offering his own intellectual justification of the South's social order.

Collins was unquestionably a racist by any definition of the term. Much of the text in his book repeated the ideas promoted by Progressive Era eugenicists and race scientists, arguing, for example, that Africans possess lower levels of natural intelligence than other races, and that this explains Africa's lower level of economic and cultural development.[9] These ideas were already falling out of fashion among American intellectual elites at the time Collins was writing, but they were widely held and advanced by prominent Americans (North and South) just a few years earlier. He did, however, acknowledge the horrors of the African slave trade, describing its "bestial and diabolical cruelty."[10]

What is perhaps more interesting in Collins's book, however, is that he does not rest his argument purely on biological claims about inherent racial differences. Instead, according to Collins, "White supremacy is a political doctrine to enable the white people of the South to live in contact with large numbers of Negroes without the loss of their ancient culture and racial purity."[11] In a surprising passage, Collins concedes many progressive arguments about the social construction of race and racism:

> Public opinion in the South does not permit any question there of the assertion of white supremacy. It is taken for granted and not open for debate. It is not based on a conclusion deliberately derived at that every Negro is inferior in every way to every white man. The fact that individual Negroes have accomplishments and ability does not make any difference. White supremacy is a political doctrine. It is not a question of scientific proof. It will do no good to bring in the phrenologist to measure skulls, the anatomist and the chemist to study brain capacity and brain cells, the psychologist and the social engineer to conduct questions and answers with white and Negro school children or the anthropologist to study racial origins. These activities have their place for various reasons, but they will not have any constructive effect on race relations in the South.[12]

This passage is significant because of the challenge it potentially represents to the cause of racial equality in America. Myrdal's book argued that racial discrimination in the United States never fit well with the American character, which he viewed as inherently liberal and egalitarian. Instead, prejudice in the United States was largely built upon Americans' mistaken ideas about race, which created a vicious circle: whites thought that Blacks were naturally inferior, which led to Black oppression, leading to Black underperformance on many measures, thus reinforcing the initial idea of natural racial hierarchies. It thus followed that, if whites could be persuaded that there is no scientific basis for racial discrimination, they could be persuaded to end racial oppression, which has always been out of sync with other elements of American political culture.

Collins was interesting in this regard because his attitude was different from other defenders of white supremacy, both in his day and our own. The racist Right has usually chosen to fight on Myrdal's chosen ground: Does the science show that there are natural racial distinctions?

The decision to engage in this fight, and make it their hill to die on, suggests American racists, more or less, accept the other aspect of Myrdal's thesis: that if the science is not on the racists' side, racism itself will wither away. Collins rejected this, arguing that science has never been the point: "The doctrine of white supremacy is akin to a religious belief. It is a faith which has become a taboo. It is rooted in the very fibre of the southern soul. It is a well-known fact that no person could be elected to any sort of public office in the South who failed to subscribe to it. An apt description is at hand. The American Red Cross is required to label Negro blood plasma with the racial label. It is thus segregated from the white blood. This, notwithstanding the fact that scientists find no chemical difference in the blood of whites and Negroes."[13]

Collins went on to list all of the ways that the federal government sought to undermine white supremacy in the South. He feared that all of the present tools of southern resistance were beginning to fail. His proposed solution was a new political alliance, in which white southerners would break away from the Democratic Party entirely, and instead work toward "the conversion of the present Republican–Southern Democratic coalition into a new conservative political party."[14] Collins recognized that abandoning the Democratic Party would be painful, as the party had long been a critical element of the southern identity.[15] Nonetheless, out of the more important need to maintain the South's racial order, Collins said that it needed to rethink its party allegiances.

Because southern Democrats in the 1940s created a third party rather than immediately move toward the GOP, one could reasonably infer that the Republican Party at that time remained the party of Abraham Lincoln when it came to racial policy. Collins recognized, however, that the Republican Party was divided between racial liberals and conservatives, just as the Democratic Party was. With older cleavages giving way, Collins thought, it was time for two ideologically homogenous parties, a liberal party and a conservative party.

A problem with this plan, however, was that "conservative" meant seemingly different things in different parts of the country. In the South, conservatism was typically thought of in racial terms, whereas elsewhere it was viewed as a primarily economic division. Collins's insight was that southern conservatism could appeal to conservatives elsewhere, including those conservatives who never really thought about racial questions, if it

framed the question in terms of statism, positive rights, and big government. Collins argued that the liberal push on racial equality was part of
the broader liberal agenda to expand the reach of the federal government.
Although Collins was primarily concerned with race and the maintenance
of the South's system of white supremacy, he sought to connect this to the
larger struggle conservatives were fighting on fronts such as taxation, federalism, bureaucratic red tape, and economic redistribution.[16] By framing
conservatism in this way, and making one of the two major political parties
explicitly conservative in both respects, the South could be the leading
region of a national party capable of winning a majority of the electorate and securing the future of white supremacy: "The Solid South would
naturally fall in with the [conservative] party provided the issue of Negro
equality was left to the Liberal Party. Such a party would be the strongest
in the country because it would attract men of affairs in the East, North,
and West, the rural sections of the Middle West and all the states below
the Mason Dixon line. The failure to draw Negro votes in the North would
be as nothing in comparison to the strength that the South would bring."[17]

To move toward the new party system he envisioned, Collins first
called on conservative southern Democrats to form their own political
party completely separated from the national Democratic Party that
had long enjoyed their loyalty.[18] At that point, Collins, like many other
southern Democrats, did not see the Republican Party as it was consti-
tuted to be a viable vehicle for his political agenda. At the time he was
writing, this view was correct. Many elected Republicans were comparable to northern Democrats on the civil rights questions. In the 1948
election, for example, Truman's Republican opponent, New York governor Thomas Dewey, had a mostly progressive record on race.[19] Thus
Collins believed his vision required the birth of two new parties—one
consistently liberal and another consistently conservative. It turned out
that this was an unnecessary step, because the two parties evolved into
the institutions Collins wanted and predicted: one party mostly committed to the principles of racial and economic liberalism, and another
party mostly committed to racial and economic conservatism. The racial
element of the Republican Party's ideology, however, never did become
as prominent and explicit as Collins would have hoped.

Although today Collins is mostly forgotten, he was influential in
southern politics in the 1940s. He was one of the political strategists

responsible for the Dixiecrat revolt in 1948. He was widely read and discussed among southern political elites.[20] After Thurmond's failed campaign, southern political entrepreneurs continued their effort to gain support for their cause in states outside the former Confederacy, seeking to make common cause with the pro-business conservatives. It is worth reiterating that these efforts took place decades before Kevin Phillips wrote *The Emerging Republican Majority*,[21] which we now think of as the most important articulation of the "Southern Strategy."

Collins was prescient in other ways. Toward the end of *Whither Solid South*, he dedicated a chapter to the subject of Christianity. He was very concerned that the churches would play an important role in the coming battles for civil rights. According to Collins, "Many of [the northern churches] are fanatical in their desire to help the Negro and are not content with what organized Christianity can do through religious and social channels but have entered the political field to urge the Federal Government to wage a holy war against the white people of the South."[22] He thus formulated a series of arguments that he hoped would stymie this approach to advancing civil rights. For example, and from a contemporary perspective this may seem like a strange rhetorical approach for a southern conservative to take, Collins insisted upon the importance of separation of church and state. He argued that even if Christian morality dictates racial integration, Christian morality is not the source of U.S. law. An individual Christian, according to Collins, is "free to exercise all of the Christian virtues in his personal relationships with individual Negroes."[23] However, in his view, this is a private matter, and such Christians do not have the right to dictate these moral decisions to others.

Some discussions of the southern electoral realignment during and after the civil rights movement attribute relatively little agency to southerners. The common view seems to suggest the GOP's Southern Strategy involved a cynical manipulation of white racial prejudices to break the Democratic Party's hold on the region. That is certainly part of the story. We should also remember the southern segregationists' "conservative strategy," which entailed recruiting conservatives across the country to the white southern cause by appealing to the language of federalism and limited government. Connecting the issue to anticommunism was another innovation I will discuss shortly.

One wonders how figures such as Collins would have felt about sub-sequent developments. Some people may reasonably argue that Collins's vision won the day, and the Republican Party resembles the racially and economically conservative party he envisioned. In today's hyperpartisan environment, pundits are quick to claim that the Republican Party (and by implication, the conservative movement that supports it) is "white nationalist."[24] My position is that the southern segregationists' attempt to define conservatism and the Republican Party was, at most, a partial success. To overstate their success one must downplay their racial ambitions.

One may argue that many contemporary public policies hinder the cause of racial equality. However, Collins and those who shared his think-ing were not envisioning a United States with racial divides in the prison population, or politicians using racially coded appeals to undermine sup-port for economic redistribution. In the case of Collins, he wanted even more than to maintain legally enforced segregation. He envisioned that the new and hegemonic conservative political party would not just push back against new civil rights legislation. He wanted Blacks returned to Africa, and thought this was a viable policy.[25] Although today's political coalitions may approximate what Collins had in mind, the substance of politics remains very far removed from his ideas.

NATIONAL REVIEW ON THE CIVIL RIGHTS MOVEMENT

Although there were exceptions, overall the early conservative movement took a reactionary—if muddled—stance on the racial controversies erupt-ing across the United States. In its early issues, *National Review* argued strenuously against *Brown v. Board of Education*.[26] "Why the South Must Prevail,"[27] published in 1957, is arguably the most controversial article ever published in *National Review*. Although unsigned, the essay was almost certainly written by Buckley. The essay directly states that south-erners have the right to deprive Blacks of the right to vote because Blacks were not yet sufficiently "advanced" to be entitled to suffrage: "The central question that emerges—and it is not a parliamentary question, or a ques-tion that is answered by merely consulting a catalogue of the rights of American citizens, born Equal—is whether the White community in the South is entitled to take such measures as necessary to prevail, politically and culturally, in areas in which it does not predominate numerically? The sobering answer is *Yes*—the White community is so entitled because, for the time being, it is the advanced race."[28]

Although this essay would be called racist by all contemporary standards (and Buckley later regretted its publication), it was also not a passionate defense of southern racial policies. It did not argue that Blacks were inherently inferior to whites, and it directly stated that once they became sufficiently "enlightened," they deserved to vote. It further argued that the South must work to prepare Blacks for the responsibilities of democratic citizenship: "The problem in the South is not how to get the vote to the Negro, but how to equip the Negro—and a great many whites—to cast an enlightened and responsible vote."[29] Although the article sought to defend Black disenfranchisement on principled, or at least pragmatic, conservative grounds, it was clearly disingenuous, as legal scholar Carl Bogus argued:

> The editorial suggests that the South's moral claim to disenfranchise black citizens would be extinguished if whites were to engage in that conduct for selfish reasons instead of seeking to advance forward, or at least waiting for, cultural equality between the races. But, of course, everyone conversant with the facts knew that the South was not working for, or even patiently waiting for, cultural equality. It was, for example, notoriously employing sham literacy tests and intimidation to prevent even well-educated blacks from voting while allowing illiterate whites to vote. Moreover, the Southern states were working actively to impede black progress and preserve cultural inequality, and had been doing so since the beginning of the Jim Crow era, some seventy years earlier.[30]

National Review was not united in opposition to progress on civil rights, even in the 1950s. In the following issue, Brent Bozell, who was more sympathetic to the cause of civil rights than Buckley, argued that Blacks should not be disenfranchised simply because they are Black. If the South is to deny the vote to people because of their lack of development, it must apply these rules equally across racial groups. He unambiguously declared, "This magazine has expressed views on the racial question that I consider dead wrong, and capable of doing grave hurt to the promotion of conservative causes."[31] In a reply, Buckley did not back down in his defense of Black disenfranchisement, but merely conceded that "if [the South] determines to disenfranchise the marginal Negro, [it should] do so by enacting laws that apply equally to blacks and whites, this living up to the spirit of the Constitution, and the letter of the 15th Amendment."[32]

Although "Why the South Must Prevail" has achieved justifiable infamy in the history of conservative thought, the emphasis on this particular essay may conceal more than it reveals. This approach to the subject was not an aberration for Buckley or *National Review*. Buckley repeated a nearly identical argument in *Up from Liberalism* (1959).[33] In the magazine's early years, although it was not focused on the issue, it was consistently opposed to the civil rights movement.

Conservative arguments against civil rights took many forms. According to political scientist Nicholas Buccolla, they had four major categories of argument: "constitutionalist, authoritarian, traditionalist, and racial elitist."[34] Of these, the constitutionalist argument is the one remaining argument against civil rights legislation that contemporary mainstream conservatives will sometimes deploy. Broadly speaking, this argument holds that these new civil rights laws, and court decisions such as *Brown*, fundamentally altered the American constitutional order, especially as it relates to the relationship between the states and the federal government and to the right to property and free association. The authoritarian argument was less a defense of principles than a critique of tactics—the civil rights demonstrators sowed chaos and threatened the rule of law. The traditionalist view was also built less on a rational defense of fundamental principles than a Burkean defense of tradition as such. That is, segregation was part of the southern way of life, and could be defended on those grounds alone. Finally, the racial elitist arguments held that, for whatever reason, whites are currently more advanced than Blacks. Until Blacks reached the same level (however defined) as whites, whites had the right, and perhaps the obligation, to maintain the system of racial hierarchy.

Although Buckley and other mainstream conservative voices wished to enforce certain limits on how race would be discussed in major conservative outlets, they published work that would today only be accepted by fringe, openly racist websites. James Jackson Kilpatrick was the most prominent of these figures. He was the editor of the *Richmond News*

Leader, and his ideas for resisting civil rights influenced white leaders throughout the South.[35] To resist federal efforts to dictate policies on racial questions in the South, Kilpatrick sought to revive nineteenth-century states' rights arguments, such as those developed by John C. Calhoun in the late 1820s. Kilpatrick argued in favor of "interposition." Calhoun's basic constitutional argument, later echoed by Kilpatrick, was that states had the power to veto federal legislation. Kilpatrick began writing for *National Review* in 1957, and continued to do so throughout the civil rights era. He laid out his theories of states' rights in *The Sovereign States*, also published in 1957, and released by conservative publisher Henry Regnery.[36] The book was sufficiently successful to warrant a second printing in the early 1960s. He subsequently wrote another book, conceding defeat on the question of school segregation, but nonetheless insisting that the segregationist cause was just and that, in the future, all races would lament the end of segregation.[37]

In the following years, he continued to be a leading conservative voice against the civil rights movement and provided many of the constitutional arguments leading conservative thinkers and politicians employed to combat the Civil Rights Act and similar legislation. Northern conservatives were generally willing to acquiesce to court mandates to end segregation of public schools. Ending segregation by private businesses was another matter. Here, one could argue, there really was a conservative matter of principle at stake. Even if one fully believes the legislation ending discrimination was moral and necessary, it also, unquestionably, undermined property rights and the right to freedom of association. As Frank Meyer, who was not an ardent segregationist, put it, the new civil rights laws were "destroying the foundations of a free constitutional society."[38] When the subject moved away from legal segregation enforced by the state, which conservatives had a difficult time justifying on nonracist grounds, to segregation by private businesses, leading intellectual conservatives felt much less ambivalent about taking an unequivocal hard-line stance.

Other figures associated with *National Review* expressed openly right-wing views on race. Ernest van den Haag was a Holland-born scholar, raised in Italy, and a professor at Fordham University in New York, and thus he had no cultural ties to the South. Like so many leading conservatives of his day, he came from a left-wing background. He was imprisoned by Mussolini's government for his activism.[39] After arriving in the United States, Van den Haag eventually became a conservative (albeit an idiosyncratic one, given his atheism and support for Keynesian economics). When it came to questions of race, however, he was unquestionably right-wing, and he wrote many pieces in support of segregation, including an article in *National Review* that made the case for genetic racial differences in intelligence.[40] In 1965, Van den Haag published an article in *Modern Age* that largely summed up the conservative approach to civil rights questions.[41] As evidence for the article's representativeness, in 1970, Buckley chose to reprint the article in his anthology, *Did You Ever See a Dream Walking? American Conservative Thought in the 20th Century.*[42]

Throughout the piece, Van den Haag makes a number of concessions to the civil rights movement, fully accepting certain key points: "No doubt Negroes suffer grievously by discriminatory exclusion from desirable dwellings, eating places, and educational institutions, solely because they are Negroes."[43] He further sought to fairly explain the civil rights activists' ultimate goals:

> What Negroes want—and nothing could be more understandable—is to be accepted by whites as individuals. This is the true and full meaning of equality, equal rights, etc.—the human and concrete meaning that makes "rights" real, and allows a Negro to feel not as somebody who has human or civil rights but somebody who *is* human—a person in his own right. Negroes want to be loved and hated, respected and disdained as individuals. They don't want to be invisible as persons, blacked out by their all too visible color—black shadows or one dimensional silhouettes.[44]

Despite conceding that African American anger was justified, and that some public remedies for past and present injustices were warranted, Van den Haag insisted that policymakers (and American society more generally) needed to distinguish between "legitimate and illegitimate claims."[45] In order for a claim to be legitimate, and to warrant some form of government intervention, Van den Haag listed a large number of requirements, many ambiguous. According to Van den Haag, state action on behalf of Blacks was only justified if it was in response to "actual hardship," and that it was in response to "rights withheld from Negroes because they are Negroes."[46] Such action is furthermore only justified if it is likely to be effective at achieving a legitimate goal, and will do so in a cost-effective manner without hindering any other rights.[47] One of the rights that must not be hindered, in Van den Haag's estimation, is freedom of association, for both individuals and social organizations, and thus private organizations do have a right to discriminate on the basis of race, provided that current members of that organization favor discrimination. Van den Haag, in this piece, did not argue that such discrimination was justified, only that it was a right.[48]

As he further considered other forms of discrimination and their potential remedies, Van den Haag continued to whittle down the number of situations in which the state might rightfully intervene. Of course, employers should not discriminate against Blacks simply because they are Black, but they can discriminate on the basis of race if it has "some relevance to the customers' feeling of well being, and thus ultimately to the success of the business."[49] Furthermore, we should not forget the "employer's right to follow personal, i.e., social, preferences irrelevant to the job."[50] Additionally, employer discrimination cannot be viewed as a real burden on those discriminated against if there are equivalent jobs available from employers who do not discriminate against Blacks. If we think about how Van den Haag's preferred policies would have worked out in practice, it is clear that they would have a negligible effect on employer discrimination in the real world—all an employer would need to do is state that such discrimination is aligned with customer preferences, his or own social preferences, or that there is similar work available elsewhere, and discrimination would be acceptable.

Despite all of the history mentioned above, we should not overstate the racism of the early conservative movement, or imply that it spoke with one voice on these matters. Chambers expressed open admiration for American Blacks' contribution to American life.[51] In contrast to most prominent conservatives, Kendall expressed support for the 1964 Civil Rights Act, but his reasoning behind that support was complex.[52] Although Burnham always insisted that the United States must approach foreign policy from a harsh and realistic perspective, rather than a moralizing one, he nonetheless deplored the bigotry of white settlers in Rhodesia, and described racism as "in essence evil."[53] Burnham further called for conservatives to take a more evenhanded approach to the subject of Israel and its Arab neighbors, critiquing the anti-Arab racism he witnessed in the United States after the Six-Day War.[54]

Meyer said that Blacks had been terribly wronged by American society, but he also argued that civil rights leaders made many demands that simply could not be conceded.[55] As early as 1954, Meyer was calling for a new political coalition that would include conservative Republicans and southern Democrats.[56] Meyer's argument at the time had nothing to do with race and civil rights, however. He made that argument in the context of expressing his disgust for President Eisenhower's (in his view) ineffectual performance in the Cold War, suggesting that—when it came to standing up to Soviet aggression—southern Democrats were often stronger than northern Republicans. When it came to the civil rights movement, Meyer tried to walk an extremely fine line, one that balanced political principles with political expedience.

For Meyer, and for other leading figures at *National Review*, it was very important that conservatism not be associated with the explicit bigotry of groups such as the Ku Klux Klan. However, the push for civil rights did unquestionably challenge certain political principles Meyer considered nonnegotiable. Meyer, for example, shared Weaver's belief that the sanctity of private property was essential to the maintenance of a free and virtuous society.[57] Meyer's individualist approach meant that he could neither support the state-enforced subordination of Blacks nor the idea that white southerners represented a collective with defined group interests. Yet those same principles meant he could not endorse new federal laws and programs designed to reduce racial disparities. He opposed, for example, Eisenhower's decision to use the military to enforce desegregation of schools in Little Rock, Arkansas, on constitutional grounds.[58]

Although rarely friendly to the civil rights movement, *National Review*'s defenses of the southern system were often qualified and tepid. This was even true of some writers one might have expected to offer vigorous defenses of the southern social order. They preferred not to defend segregation as such and instead focused on the importance of state and local control of government and social norms.

Weaver was surprisingly cagey on civil rights questions. Weaver, born in North Carolina, was influenced by the Southern Agrarian movement, which was prominent in the interwar years. The Agrarians, although not calling for a new secessionist movement, were ardent supporters of southern culture and defended the social order of the antebellum South.[59] Weaver completed his master's thesis under the supervision of one of the most important thinkers of this movement, John Crowe Ransom. Like the other Agrarians, Weaver was a vocal defender of the South and its traditions.[60] He argued that, despite encroachments of bourgeois capitalist thinking, the South maintained many of the best characteristics of feudal Europe.

Nonetheless, Weaver was strangely reticent to talk about race relations directly. He did not defend slavery, and even described it as a "curse," but Weaver suggested that New Englanders, who owned many of the slave ships, were no less responsible for slavery than the southerners who bought the slaves.[61] He was mostly silent on the issue of civil rights for Blacks. His most significant essay on the subject, "Integration Is Communization,"[62] published in *National Review* in 1957, skirted the question of whether racial integration should advance in the South. Instead, he attacked the motives of people making that push. He suggested that racial integration was just one tactic used by communists to abolish private property and erase distinctions of all kinds between people: "'Integration' and 'Communization' are, after all, pretty closely synonymous. In light of what is happening today, the first may be little more than a euphemism for the second. It does not take many steps to get from the 'integrating' of facilities to the 'communizing' of facilities, if the impulse is there."[63]

Although *National Review* remained committed to the principle of states' rights, it was willing to call out white southerners when their uncivil behavior revealed a boorish bigotry rather than a principled political philosophy. In response to whites at the University of Mississippi who rioted upon the entrance of the first African American student, Buckley wrote: "*National Review* is not alone in remarking the cause of principle is never served by jeering mobs."[64]

Conservatives' expressions of disgust toward the more outrageous examples of white southern racism and lawlessness made strategic and moral sense. Few prominent conservatives came out aggressively against the civil rights movement's basic motivating principles. In fact, many publicly stated that they, too, looked forward to the day when racial disparities were gone. Their stated problem, instead, was that the civil rights movement was using improper tactics to pursue its goals. As was the case with the connection between civil rights and communism, the focus on the connection between civil rights and lawlessness was a means of changing the subject to ground where conservatives felt more comfortable. As Black activists and their allies became more militant as the 1960s wore on, *National Review*'s writers took an increasingly hard position against the civil rights movement. Buckley and others feared the violence that occurred in Africa during the transition from colonialism to self-government was coming to the United States.[65] Meyer feared a genuine race war was on the horizon.[66]

CONSERVATIVE RADIO AND CIVIL RIGHTS

When scholars consider conservatism, the Republican Party, and the Southern Strategy during the civil rights era, we tend to focus on those we consider political and intellectual elites. We emphasize, I think reasonably, the role of magazines such as *National Review*. A single-minded focus on one magazine and its contributors may cause us to lose sight of other important developments, however. Conservatism's outreach in the South was not limited to high-brow magazines. In fact, in terms of opening up the South to conservatism (and Republican voting), radio may have had greater influence.

Long before broadcasters such as Rush Limbaugh put a populist spin on conservative ideas and promoted them to an audience of millions, an earlier generation of radio personalities gave its full support to "massive resistance" against civil rights advances. Furthermore, the conservative voices on the airwaves did not equivocate or rely on high-minded principles of federalism and local control.[67] They had massive audiences, reaching millions of people over the airwaves. Historian Nicole Hemmer argues that Clarence Manion, dean of Notre Dame Law School and host of *The Manion Forum*, which began in 1954, a year before the first issue of *National Review* was published, was the real "godfather of modern conservative media."[68]

It is especially important that the most important of these radio programs were not hosted by traditional southern Democratic segregationists.

Many were northern Republicans. The evangelical broadcaster Carl McIntire, for example, was a Republican from New Jersey. His evangelical Christian program, *Twentieth Century Reformation Hour*, which included copious political content, aired on hundreds of radio stations in the South, and reached vastly more homes than *National Review*. Programs such as McIntire's promoted a traditional conservative message, but also offered a full-throated defense of southern mores when it came to race. Although one should be cautious, with the lack of hard evidence, about inferring cynical motivations to explain why media figures take particular positions, there may have been a practical consideration for McIntire to take such a stand: it resulted in a massive audience for his show. The fact that McIntire had shown little interest in racial questions in the early years of his career suggests this was a calculated move.[69] Historian Paul Matzko suggests that these radio hosts played an indispensable role in breaking down the partisan identities of white southern Democrats, clearing the way for their embrace of the GOP: "Broadcasters served a vital function in the partisan transformation of the Deep South. They made it possible for white southern segregationists to imagine that the Republican Party, which many had hated their entire lives, could really be relied upon to be the new home for massive resistance to segregation."[70]

As the battle over civil rights continued, conservative broadcasters such as McIntire and Billy James Hargis, host of the radio program *The Christian Crusade*, proudly promoted segregationist politicians. McIntire gave his enthusiastic support to George Wallace and Strom Thurmond, which was rewarded with high praise from both.[71] Hargis invited Wallace to address one of his gatherings of evangelical Christians.[72] Like the more high-brow conservative print publications, these programs pushed an anticommunist message, but they also embraced the cause of segregation without the careful wording that Buckley and his colleagues used in the 1960s. They, after all, had little interest or need to stay in the good graces of the intellectual elites. This proved to be a mutually beneficial relationship between conservative radio and southern segregationists. Matzko states: "Thumping the pulpit for segregation meant more listeners, more radio stations, and more donations for McIntire. For massive resistors, support from nonsouthern broadcasters was used in the (failed) effort to deflect accusations of racist intent."[73]

CIVIL RIGHTS, CONSERVATIVES, AND THE COLD WAR

As many scholars have noted, the modern American conservative movement must be understood as largely a product of the Cold War. Indeed, in the absence of the Cold War, I doubt the conservative movement that we know today would have come about. Given the communist background of many leading conservatives, it should be no surprise that the Cold War was the movement's overriding obsession. No other issue, including civil rights, had comparable importance. Defeat in the Cold War, which many conservatives considered probable, would be the ultimate disaster, from which the United States—and humanity—would never recover. Avoiding this fate required conservatives, and Americans more broadly, to view all of politics, domestically and abroad, through a Cold War lens. James Burnham put it this way:

> We have entered a period of history in which world politics take precedence over national and internal politics, and in which world politics literally involve the entire world. During this period, now and until this period ends in settlement, one way or another, of the problems which determine the nature of the period, all of world politics, and all of what is most important in the internal politics of each nation, are oriented around the struggle for world power between Soviet-based communism and the United States. This is now the key to the political situation. Everything else is secondary, subordinate.[74]

To Burnham, there was no such thing as a purely domestic issue. Burnham argued that within every nation in every historical era there is a single decisive issue, a question on which all of the future will hinge. Using the United States as an example, he noted that every question—directly or indirectly—revolved around the subject of slavery for much of the nineteenth century, and then shifted to the subject of industrialization.[75] The great statesmen of every age are the ones who recognize the key issue and subordinate all other concerns. After World War II, according to Burnham, the single important issue was the spread of communism, which would dominate the globe unless the United States and its allies mobilized to stop it. Every issue, foreign and domestic, needed to be seen through the lens of the Cold War, which he argued should already be considered World War III, even if the main players were not yet shooting directly at each other. The fact that the Soviets had already adopted this view put them at an advantage: "The communist power moves toward the climax self-consciously, deliberately. Its leaders understand what is at stake. They have made their choice. All their energies, their resources, their determination, are fixed on the goal. But the Western power gropes and lurches. Few of its leaders even want to understand."[76]

The conservative movement was so concerned with Soviet aggression that leading conservatives stated explicitly that there was no other political principle they would not sacrifice in the name of defeating Russia. Although limited government was important to conservatism, Buckley stated that he was comfortable with "totalitarian" measures, provided they were in service to total U.S. victory.[77] In *National Review*'s mission statement, published in its inaugural issue, the subject of race was not mentioned at all. Communism, however, was treated in the most hyperbolic terms: "The century's most blatant force of satanic utopianism is communism. We consider 'coexistence' with communism neither desirable nor possible, nor honorable; we find ourselves irrevocably at war with communism and shall oppose any substitute for victory."[78]

Five years after *National Review*'s founding, the new organization Young Americans for Freedom released its famous "Sharon Statement," which would serve as a foundational document for the growing conservative movement. The statement was drafted at Buckley's residence in Sharon, Connecticut, and was a collaborative effort involving dozens of conservative activists from across the country. In its list of "certain eternal truths," the organization omitted any reference to race or civil rights. The statement's praise for federalism ("That the genius of the Constitution—the division of powers—is summed up in the clause that reserves primacy to the several states, or to the people, in those spheres not specifically delegated to the Federal government") was the only part of the document even tangentially related to civil rights questions. On the other hand, the threat of communism was a pervasive theme in the Sharon Statement: "That the forces of international Communism are, at present, the greatest single threat to these liberties."[79]

The tendency to view all of politics from a Cold War perspective had several—sometimes contradictory—influences on the conservative approach to civil rights. On the one hand, many conservatives tended to look at the civil rights movement as just another communist plot. Weaver argued that the forced integration of facilities was just one step along the way toward the communization of facilities; the former move effectively abolished the principle of private property, thus communization would just complete the process already set in motion.

Other conservatives took these arguments much further. Medford Evans, an English and history professor and father of famed conservative journalist M. Stanton Evans, published *Civil Rights Myths and Communist Realities* in 1965.[80] The book began by attacking various "myths" about the South, notably the claim that Blacks were being mistreated. A majority of the text, however, was dedicated to the claim that communists were largely responsible for creating and sustaining the civil rights movement, and they did so "as a means of destroying the United States and the only civilization you and I have ever known."[81] Much of the text was focused on Martin Luther King Jr.'s communist ties and on evidence of communist support for the National Association for the Advancement of Colored People (NAACP). Evans argued that African Americans in the South were generally content with the system as it existed, and the new problems were entirely the result of outside agitators seeking to foment revolution. We can find similar arguments in *National Review*. In 1959, the magazine published an article by Richard Whalen making this point.[82]

I have no doubt that conservatives were genuinely concerned that there was a connection between civil rights activists and communists. Conservatives saw evidence of communist subversion everywhere. There may nonetheless also have been a strategic element to these arguments. By the 1960s, most mainstream conservatives had abandoned the claim that genetic racial differences justified racial segregation. Many of the movement's leading voices had also publicly expressed their hope and expectation that integration and equality would one day be achieved. In a sense, they had already conceded the moral high ground to the civil rights movement, putting them in an awkward position if they wished to maintain a reactionary position on the subject, something that would be necessary to make further political inroads in the South. One tactic, of course, was to focus entirely on the constitutional issue of states' rights and local control. Another was to avoid the real subject and instead question the motives of civil rights activists. Rather than attempt to justify racial discrimination (a difficult task, given what they had already conceded), changing the subject to the civil rights leaders' communist sympathies was a logical rhetorical strategy. At a time when Martin Luther King Jr. and his allies were winning the debate on the issues, it made sense to try to change the subject, to put them off-kilter by asking, for example, whether Stanley Levison, one of King's advisors and speech writers, was a communist.[83]

The Cold War had other effects on the debate over civil rights. In some ways, the U.S. struggle against the Soviets abroad was a boon to the fight for African American civil rights at home. Burnham had argued that all of politics needed to be examined with the Cold War in mind. This meant that domestic politics also had an international audience. At the time when the two superpowers were seeking to "win the hearts and minds" of the Third World, open, legally sanctioned racism created a propaganda problem, as did Black urban riots. In the postwar era, race relations in the United States were a major theme in the Soviet Union's appeals to developing countries.[84] Legal scholar Mary Dudziak has convincingly argued that American policymakers were thinking about the international implications of domestic debates about civil rights.[85] This was especially true of the executive branch, and Dudziak suggests that the Cold War prompted Truman, Eisenhower, and Kennedy to be much more proactive on civil rights issues than they would have been otherwise.

DID RACIAL CONSERVATISM ORIGINATE AMONG ELITES OR THE ELECTORATE?

Critics of the Republican Party and the conservative movement's approach to race during and after the civil rights era have argued that partisan and ideological elites are largely responsible for America's contemporary racial divide.[86] According to one theory, as the struggle for civil rights was reaching a critical point, Republican leaders (especially Goldwater and his supporters) made a conscious choice to abandon the party's older stances as the party of Lincoln and racial equality, becoming instead the party of racial conservatism. They concluded that entering into a coalition with southern segregationists represented the most straightforward path to power. Outside the South, this theory suggests, there was little grassroots demand for racial conservatism. To the extent that nonsouthern Republicans in the electorate have subsequently exhibited racial conservatism and racial resentment, it is because they took cues from party and ideological leaders. Therefore, if elites had not divided on the racial question, and Republican and Democratic national leaders had united in their support for racial equality, race would not be the partisan, divisive issue it is today. In this scenario, the two parties would have remained distinct and offered the public different ideological visions, but race would not have been one of the critical fault lines.

This theory, if correct, could make conservatives even more uneasy about their movement's history. It suggests that towering figures from their own historical pantheon are largely responsible for today's racial divisions. It is also, however, a hopeful perspective, because it suggests that the public's racial attitudes are quite malleable. If racial attitudes in the mass public were put in place (intentionally or not) by political elites, today's elites can change them.

On the other hand, this theory may overstate the pliability of the electorate when it comes to race. It is also possible that Republicans in the electorate, including those outside the South, wanted their party to promote racial conservatism. If that is the case, given the degree to which parties are directed by their own voters via primary elections, party elites calling for a progressive racial agenda would have been inevitably replaced by leaders pushing racial conservatism. In a sense, we can argue that the 1964 election provides evidence for this. When Republican primary voters were offered the choice between Goldwater and the more racially progressive Nelson Rockefeller, Republican voters chose Goldwater, to the frustration of many GOP party elites. One could reasonably argue that, if Goldwater had not run against new civil rights legislation, someone else eventually would have.

At this point, determining which of these theories has more explanatory power would be extraordinarily difficult. The absence of high-quality longitudinal opinion data makes it hard to understand how attitudes among Republican voters changed (if at all) during the civil rights era. However, as Anthony Chen, Robert Mickey, and Robert Van Houweling recently pointed out, we can point to an example in the postwar era where Republican elites promoted a racially progressive policy.[87] They furthermore note that we can now make sense of how Republican voters responded to those elite cues. According to these scholars, California's Proposition 11 provides a helpful case study.

Proposition 11, called the Fair Employment Practices Act, was on the ballot in California in 1946. The law would have made it illegal for private employers, unions, and employment agencies to discriminate on the basis of race or religion. That is, it would have provided protections similar to those of the Civil Rights Act of 1964. This initiative represents a useful test of the hypothesis that political elites were behind the racial conservatism of northern Republicans in the electorate. At the time of the initiative, Earl Warren was the governor of California and he was also extremely popular among California voters, and by far the most influential Republican in the state. Moreover, he was a well-known racial liberal; he had previously supported similar fair employment legislation that had failed. If California's Republican voters were taking their cues from Republican elites, presumably they would have voted in large numbers for Proposition 11.

When voters were given their say, Proposition 11 was defeated by a huge margin. Less than one-third of voters supported the policy. Although the policy had little support from the public, it was not obvious how support and opposition to the policy broke down along partisan lines. Were white Republicans markedly different from white Democrats? If there was not a major partisan difference, or if Republicans were even more supportive than Democrats, that would indicate that popular partisan elites did have a lot of sway over their party in the electorate. Unfortunately, no exit polls were conducted at the time. However, thanks to the development of ecological inference models, it is now possible to use aggregate data to make plausible inferences about the behavior of smaller groups.[88] This was the methodological strategy Chen, Mickey, and Van Houweling employed. Their statistical evidence indicated that Republicans were far less supportive of Proposition 11 than Democrats. This suggests that, as long ago as 1946, at least in California, Republicans in the electorate were already much more racially conservative than Democrats, despite having a Republican governor well-known for racial progressivism.

Although they do not deny that elites influenced the development of racial politics in American life, Chen, Mickey, and Van Houweling suggest strong opposition to civil rights legislation was definitely present in the Republican grassroots, even outside the South, which would have limited the choices available to Republican leaders: "In a sense, Republican elites were constrained by the racial ideology of Republican voters. Racial liberalism was off limits."[89]

ASSESSING THE RECORD

Many historians and other political observers (including many conservatives) point out that the conservative movement mostly opposed the civil rights movement, and that this fact is a permanent stain on the movement's reputation. On the other hand, one could also imagine a different scenario, in which the conservative movement had taken a much harsher stand on these questions, a scenario in which conservatives had coalesced around the kinds of ideas promoted by ardent segregationists such as Charles Wallace Collins. We know that most leading conservatives, including many who are still celebrated by the movement today, held views that contemporary observers would today immediately describe as white supremacist. Why, then, did they not more aggressively promote an explicitly racist agenda, especially as it became clear that such a move could help the movement make additional inroads in the South? I suspect there were several reasons the conservative intellectual movement sought to maintain its precarious balance between official egalitarianism and mostly tacit support for segregation and discrimination.

The conservative movement was genuinely torn on some of these questions. Even if many conservatives took a cynical approach to these subjects, the issue of civil rights raised real and thorny questions about federalism, property rights, freedom of association, the proper scope of the federal government, individualism, and equality. Furthermore, even if conservatives recognized the need for change, conservatism also holds that social change should come slowly and organically, not via a revolution directed from above. In hindsight, one could argue that most leading conservatives were wrong on all of these subjects during a critical period. It is possible to accept that previous generations really were wrestling with questions they found challenging, and at times reached conclusions that observers, six decades in the future, find repugnant. The fact that more conservatives did not go further in their attacks on civil rights—and rarely directly attacked the principle of racial equality per se—seems to suggest that conservatism always had at least a nascent element of inescapable egalitarianism.

That generous interpretation is certainly not the entire story. At the time of its founding, the conservative movement desperately desired intellectual respectability. Although we may now take the existence of erudite conservative intellectuals for granted, this was not always the case in the postwar years, which is itself interesting, given how conservative American life in that period appears, at least in hindsight. As Lionel Trilling put it in 1950, "There are no conservative or reactionary ideas in general circulation." In fact, Trilling suggested conservative ideas did not even exist, only "irritable mental gestures which seek to resemble ideas."[90] Kirk's *The Conservative Mind* is not really celebrated because it was a great work of scholarship (few claim that it was), but because it provided conservatism with an intellectual pedigree, arguing that the conservative political tradition has a long, noble, and intellectually serious history.

This is one of the seeming paradoxes of the conservative movement. Conservatives never ceased attacking intellectual and media elites, and wore their insults as a kind of badge of honor. Yet they also desired respect and acceptance from those same elites. This seemed especially true of Buckley, whose social circle included some of the most celebrated public intellectuals and literary figures of his day. Maintaining that respectability meant keeping a meaningful distance from the explicitly racist Right. Had *National Review* become viewed as ideologically aligned with groups such as the Ku Klux Klan, it likely would have joined publications such as the anti-Semitic *American Mercury* in obscurity. Indeed, Buckley, perhaps more than any other leading conservative, sought to distance his movement from what he called the "irresponsible right." One of the hallmarks of the irresponsible Right, even in relatively early years for *National Review*, was ostentatious racism—conspiracy theorizing and anti-Semitism were two other qualities he sought to extirpate from the mainstream right.[91]

Although it did not want to be expressly racist, the conservative intellectual movement mostly chose not to support the cause of civil rights. Thus, it tended to tiptoe around the subject, talking about almost anything other than how racial integration and equality can be achieved, despite repeatedly saying it, too, would like to see it happen. Quite often, the conservatives preferred to begin discussions about civil rights as

Kendall did in his most lengthy treatment of the subject: "First, I have no thesis to argue, one way or the other, as to the merits of the Civil Rights Movement as such."[92]

How we judge the conservative intellectual movement's behavior during the civil rights era depends largely on one's perspective, but most contemporaries have good reasons to be critical. The fact that conservatives fought back against civil rights at all is viewed by many modern readers as a problem for the movement. Given that some contemporary conservatives try to downplay that history, or, in some cases, try to rewrite the history entirely, suggests they agree that this was a dark period for the movement. However, mainstream conservatism was also a disappointment to those segregationists who hoped an alliance with conservatives would help them maintain formal white supremacy in the South. Segregationists wanted full-throated, unapologetic white identity politics from the conservative movement. They did not get it. Although the conservative movement did not assist the cause of civil rights, it also did little to stop its progression. Instead, conservatives grumbled about questions of federalism and radicalism, and when it was all over they made little effort to reverse the civil rights movement's greatest successes, even when the Republican Party began to dominate electoral politics. Richard Nixon may have appealed to white southern rage to enter the White House, but once he was there he did not reimpose formal white supremacy. In fact, he dramatically expanded affirmative action in government hiring.

If we judge the conservative movement's performance in terms of what its leading figures wanted to accomplish during the period, we can give it higher marks of success. In terms of electoral politics, the period brought white southerners into the Republican coalition, even though subsequent Republican leaders did not undo the most important civil rights victories. Conservatives also maintained their respectability in elite circles. Conservative intellectual elites were generally not viewed as synonymous with the Ku Klux Klan. Buckley could continue skiing with John Kenneth Galbraith when the dust settled. I am not implying that Buckley and others were entirely cynical and self-serving during the civil rights era. Buckley had a very clear vision of how he wanted to engage with the Left. Although he wanted to defeat the liberal intelligentsia, he wanted to do so on its home turf and by its own rules, as opposed to simply circumventing the Left entirely via appeals to heartland populism, which is what the conservative talk radio hosts were doing. Buckley described his strategy as follows:

> We are very consciously aiming at thoughtful people, at opinion makers . . . we feel that before it is possible to bring the entire nation around politically, we have got to engage the attention of people who for a long time have felt the conservative position is moribund. Once we prove that we can take any comer, once we have engaged in hand-to-hand combat with the best the Liberals can furnish, and bested them, then we can proceed to present a realistic political alternative around which we hope the American right, at present so terribly disintegrated, can close ranks.[93]

As conservative author R. R. Reno points out, this approach to politics meant conceding certain points to liberal opinion-makers before the discussion even began. Most notably, Buckley accepted the major premises of Karl Popper's "open society," which had become hegemonic among American intellectuals.[94] This meant a harder-edged right-wing approach to politics—one that freely embraced crude racism or tribalism, for example—was off the table from the start.

If we evaluate the movement according to its own goals in that very tumultuous period, one can admire its success at walking a very thin rope over a very deep chasm. Conservatives certainly did not always best their political opponents. For example, Buckley's famous debate with James Baldwin at Cambridge University in 1965 on the subject of race in the United States is almost universally recognized as one of Buckley's weakest performances. Nonetheless, conservative intellectuals remained ambiguous enough, and shunned a sufficient number of the most extreme racists, that they could evolve with the times and eventually build up what historian Joshua Tait calls conservatism's "myth of racial innocence."[95] This is not an insignificant accomplishment.

After accepting and even celebrating the results of the civil rights movement, conservatives had to make choices about how they would approach their own history. One approach has been to provide an interpretation of history that suggests conservatives and Republicans had actually been on the side of racial egalitarianism the entire time. In contrast, they argue, Democrats were the real villains throughout the period. Some statements supporting this argument are technically true, but they are not relevant to the contemporary political discussion. It is true, for example, that the members of the first Ku Klux Klan supported the Democratic Party. This is obviously irrelevant today. It is also true that a greater percentage of Republicans in the House of Representatives supported the Civil Rights Act of 1964 than Democrats, but, because of their sizable majority, in total the number of Democrats in favor of the bill was larger than that of Republicans. One must also remember that Democratic opposition to the act came primarily from conservative southern Democrats, a political species that has since become extinct and thus has no influence on the contemporary Democratic Party.

Some conservatives have seemed to solve the conundrum of giving progressive Democrats most of the credit for civil rights by focusing primarily on events that followed the civil rights movement and the passage of landmark legislation. One narrative maintains that there was once a good movement for civil rights, which was aligned with American values and was even, at least in a sense, conservative. With the rise of new identity politics, especially trends such as the Black Power movement, the Left had squandered whatever moral high ground it had gained in the 1950s and 1960s. Because of the Left's change in tone and tactics in subsequent years, their claim to be the true heirs of Martin Luther King Jr. became questionable. Allan Bloom, for example, made this point:

> The civil rights movement provides a good example of this change in thought. In its early days almost all the significant leaders, in spite of tactical and temperamental differences, relied on the Declaration of Independence and the Constitution. They could charge whites not only with the most monstrous injustices but also with contradicting their most sacred principles. The blacks were the true Americans in demanding the equality that belongs to them as human beings and by natural right. . . . By contrast, the Black Power movement that supplanted the older civil rights movement . . . had at its core the view that the Constitutional tradition was always corrupt and was constructed as a defense of slavery. Its demand was for black identity, not universal rights. Not rights but power counted. It insisted on respect for blacks as blacks, not as human beings simply.[96]

Because they could reasonably charge that there had been a philosophical, strategic, and tactical divide between the civil rights leaders of the early 1960s and those that followed, conservatives could simultaneously shower praise on the former figures without feeling obligated to defer to the latter when it came to racial questions. The size and significance of that supposed divide is debatable. Subsequent conservatives have tended to downplay some of King's radicalism, for example, and instead treat his "I have a dream" speech as representing the totality of his thinking.

However, the conservative movement's failure to make a coherent, defensible, and consistent stand on the subject of civil rights proved a hindrance to some future political endeavors. Yes, by maintaining a mostly right-wing position on race, conservatism (or at least support for the GOP) took hold in the South, leading to a major Republican advantage in presidential elections. This more than made up for the GOP's loss of support from African Americans, who had already been moving toward the Democratic Party anyway. In the long run, however, in the face of demographic change, the importance of white southerners is diminishing, and voting trends among nonwhites that took root in the civil rights era remain entrenched. As conservative author William Voegeli noted, "Conservatives have spent half a century trying to overcome the suspicion that they are indifferent to black Americans' legitimate demands, and indulgent towards people who are blatantly hostile to blacks."[97]

Voegeli argued that conservatism's inconsistent response to civil rights questions created additional problems. Because the question of civil rights relates to the broader principles of federalism and local control, the civil rights victories delegitimized those principles in the eyes of many Americans. Today, any calls for states' rights are met by the immediate charge of racism. If conservatives had instead taken a firm stand against the disenfranchisement of Blacks in the South and elsewhere, declaring unambiguously that the "Constitution is color-blind," conservatives would have been in a stronger position to fight back against other racial policies, such as "affirmative action, set-asides, race-normed employment tests, busing, and tortuously drawn 'majority-minority' legislative districts."[98]

CONCLUSION

Few conservatives today, at least among those with significant understanding of the period, take pride in the movement's record during the era of civil rights. Strong support for civil rights from leading conservatives could have made the period much less contentious. Yet proponents of segregation and explicit white identity politics were also disappointed with the conservative record on this subject. Conservatives certainly took advantage of the issue, happy to see growth in their ranks in response to white anxieties, but when they achieved political power via new Republican victories, they did not overturn major civil rights achievements. We can also envision a scenario in which conservatives chose a different strategy, openly rejecting all of the basic premises of the civil rights movement, making an unwavering stand in defense of segregation and prejudice. In the end, the conservative movement chose a path that satisfied almost no one. We cannot know for sure if different decisions by conservatives at critical points could have expedited the process of racial reconciliation in the United States, and we should not overstate the conservative movement's influence over the public in these matters. Nonetheless, as the United States continues to struggle over questions related to race, the writings of the early conservative movement can provide little helpful guidance.

FIVE

Conservatism and Feminism

Whether they were ever especially interested in the issue, William F. Buckley Jr. and his colleagues had no choice but to offer opinions on race and civil rights. *National Review* launched the year after *Brown v. the Board of Education* was decided, and it was not a decision that a political magazine could ignore. The early conservative approach to racial questions was muddled and often contradictory, but conservatives were engaging with the subject. Early conservatism's relationship to feminism is somewhat different, however, in part because second-wave feminism was not yet a highly salient political issue, in their view. In the middle of the culturally conservative 1950s, the subject of greater rights for women was not as high on the agenda as it would later become, and the earlier question of women's suffrage had been settled long enough ago as to no longer be controversial.

Conservatism's relationship with feminism also differed from its relationship with the African American civil rights movement in that women took the lead in organizing for the conservative position. This is not to downplay the diversity of opinion that existed within the African American community—then or now. However, as political battles about civil rights were raging, there were no large, national organizations led by Blacks, with all Black members, dedicated to fighting against civil rights legislation. In contrast, there have been many important women's organizations focused on fighting modern feminism. This has given modern feminism's opponents a degree of credibility that conservative opponents of civil rights legislation always lacked. The most notable antifeminist writers and activists were typically women. Trish Bozell, Buckley's sister and managing editor of the Catholic magazine *Triumph*, for example, expressed far more open loathing for feminism than her brother—she once physically assaulted a feminist speaker while the latter was giving a lecture.[1]

RIGHT-WING WOMEN BEFORE THE CONSERVATIVE MOVEMENT

Women played important roles on both sides of all the most significant disputes related to women's rights. Women's suffrage, for example, had its share of women opponents. The National Association Opposed to Women's Suffrage was led by a woman, Josephine Dodge, and had hundreds of thousands of members across the country.[2] As would be the case later in the twentieth century, antisuffrage women framed many of their arguments on the premise that men and women have separate spheres. This was not an argument about women being unequal to men. Rather, they argued that women had particular gifts that made them best suited for certain kinds of labor, from which they should not be distracted. Dodge put it this way in her 1914 article "Woman Suffrage Opposed to Woman's Rights": "It is woman's right to be exempt from political responsibility that she may be free to render her best service to the state. The state has surrounded her with protective legislation in order that she may attain her highest efficiency in those departments of the world's work for which her nature and her training fit her."[3]

The "world's work" she was referring to was, of course, motherhood, which she argued must be protected so "that future citizens shall have the birth right and the inheritance of a strong and vigorous childhood."[4] Modern readers may be puzzled by Dodge's claim that the right to vote will interfere with women's responsibilities as mothers: How much effort goes into voting? Dodge argued that the right to vote represents an important responsibility, that voters have an obligation to become knowledgeable about a great number of policy issues. She argued that women until that point had been free to ignore these subjects: "Tariff reform, fiscal policies, international relations, those large endeavors which men now determine, are foreign to the concerns and pursuits of the average woman."[5] By giving women new obligations, they would necessarily be distracted from their other tasks. She further suggested that there would be no meaningful political change that would result from women's suffrage, given that the political preferences of women and men are not especially different. Further, given that there were already states with women's suffrage, it was possible to see if legislation was more favorable to women in states where women were allowed to vote. She concluded that there was no evidence of this, and perhaps some evidence for the opposite. Therefore, women's suffrage would double the electorate and create new burdens on women without leading to any substantive political change or other benefit to the women themselves.

Dodge's battle against woman's suffrage ended in failure with the Nineteenth Amendment's passage. Future conservative women, however, employed similar arguments in their struggle against feminists later in the twentieth century. One of Dodge's key arguments was that the push for political equality would ultimately result in the state ceasing to make any distinctions between men and women: "It would be a brutal interpretation of woman's rights to insist that the hard-won body of legislation, which protects woman because she is the potential mother, be abolished and the vote given to woman in exchange. Yet this and this only is *equal* suffrage."[6]

Although gender questions were not initially the primary concern of the first generation of conservatives, they were not ignored entirely. Unsurprisingly, Richard Weaver was opposed to any blurring of social roles for the sexes. As the early conservative movement's most unwavering defender of fixed hierarchies, Weaver believed that the movement of women out of domestic roles and into the workforce was an unfortunate development. From Weaver's perspective, this represented yet another blow to the principles of chivalry, which he argued once provided important protections for women. Weaver noted in the 1940s, echoing Dodge's argument, "No longer protected, the woman now has her career, in which she makes a drab pilgrimage from two-room apartment to job to divorce court."[7]

Whether or not they wanted full inclusion in U.S. politics when they were granted full voting rights throughout the country, conservative women went on to play essential roles in the Republican Party, the conservative movement, and even the extreme Right. The Women of the Ku Klux Klan, for example, formed in the 1920s. Women were furthermore a very important element of the Klan at the time when it enjoyed its greatest successes in mainstream politics.[8] When we think of the isolationist movements of the 1930s and early 1940s, especially those that plainly supported (or at least sympathized with) fascism in Europe, we typically think of men such as Charles Lindbergh or Charles Coughlin. Yet again the historical record shows that women were an indispensable element of the opposition to U.S. entry into World War II. The "mother's movement" promoted isolationism, anti-Semitism, and opposition to the New Deal.[9]

As with most other isolationist movements, the mother's movement collapsed at the start of the war. In the postwar years, however, women would again be important political actors on the right. They were especially significant to the anticommunist movement that grew exponentially as the Cold War took center stage in American political life. Historian Michelle Nickerson argues that the "1950s revival of domesticity had a politically radicalizing effect on many women."[10] Middle-class and upper-class housewives, especially in Southern California, proved to be "important incubators of McCarthyism,"[11] supporting national efforts to root out communists, and personally undertaking local efforts to do the same. Anticommunist women were especially active in PTAs. Nickerson argues it is important to remember conservative women's activism prior to the feminist breakthroughs in the 1960s and beyond. Including them in the narrative indicates that the women who pushed back against causes such as the Equal Rights Amendment (ERA) and formed the pro-life movement were not politicized by a reactionary backlash. In many ways, these women had long been an indispensable part of the American Right, even if they were rarely in the spotlight.[12]

Women were also an essential element of the southern realignment. Women, largely transplants from the North who moved to southern states with their husbands after World War II, built many important grassroots Republican organizations in the region. Majorities of southern white women furthermore began voting for Republican presidential candidates earlier than southern white men. In 1952, Eisenhower performed poorly among white southern men, earning just 41 percent of their votes; he performed very well, however, among white southern women, carrying 59 percent of their votes.[13]

Related to the southern partisan realignment, during one of the key battles for civil rights in the twentieth century—the fight over school segregation—white women were among the most energetic and effective proponents of "massive resistance." As historian Elizabeth Gillespie McRae has argued, "By 1956, white segregationist women had organized effective and widespread resistance to integration. In fact, it was clear that the school integration crisis elevated their positions as the most experienced proponents and sustainers of white supremacist thought in public education."[14] She further notes that their support for segregation was tied directly to their identities as women and, especially, mothers: "In part, they linked the domestic and intimate matters of sex, marriage, childbirth, and childrearing to white supremacist politics."[15]

Throughout the civil rights era and beyond, right-wing women took a leading role in letter-writing campaigns and other forms of activism. They were key players on school boards throughout the South, always looking for means to delay integration. They were essential members of the Citizens' Councils that formed throughout the South, doing much of the essential organizational work and conducting outreach.[16] Women also played important roles in linking the cause of segregation to the fight against communism. Southern women, such as newspaper columnist Florence Sillers Ogden, consistently argued that the fight against segregation was inspired by communism and led by communists, arguments that would help garner additional sympathy from conservatives outside the South.[17]

PHYLLIS SCHLAFLY AND THE ORGANIZING
OF RIGHT-WING WOMEN

No history of American conservatism in the twentieth century would be complete if it neglected Phyllis Schlafly's contributions to the movement. She was arguably the most effective, consequential grassroots organizer the movement ever produced. She is best remembered for her fight against the ERA, an amendment to the Constitution whose ratification was viewed by most observers as a foregone conclusion before Schlafly began her campaign.[18] Feminists had been fighting for the ERA, which would have added language to the Constitution assuring equal rights regardless of sex, since it was first proposed in 1943, but the language was altered slightly over time.[19] By becoming the leader of the anti-ERA movement, Schlafly established herself as the face of antifeminism in the United States, and a champion of traditional gender roles.

There are ironies to Schlafly's public persona in the 1970s and beyond. To begin with, in her early political writings, we see little indication that Schlafly was interested in gender politics. The second curiosity is that, despite being a defender of traditional femininity, Schlafly herself was a trailblazer for women in conservative politics. Beginning as a volunteer for the Republican Party in 1945, Schlafly was persistently engaged in politics—as a grassroots organizer, political candidate, author, radio commentator, and president of Eagle Forum.

Schlafly first emerged as a significant political figure in the context of the 1964 presidential campaign. She was a fervent supporter of Barry Goldwater. In that year, at a time when she was the president of the Illinois Federation of Republican Women, she self-published a book in support for Goldwater's campaign titled *A Choice Not an Echo*. The book opens with the subject that was Schlafly's primary interest at the time: foreign policy. She listed all of the places in the world where the United States and its allies were in retreat and communism was on the march. A majority of the text, however, was focused on the evils of the Republican establishment, those GOP leaders who used every trick at their disposal to promote moderate, milquetoast candidates for the Republican presidential nomination. These were the people responsible for promoting sure losers such as Wendell Willkie and Thomas Dewey. These "kingmakers" had consistently stymied Robert Taft, a consistent and principled conservative, in his efforts to win the Republican presidential nomination. Schlafly argued that the perfidious establishment was again up to its old tricks in 1964, pushing the moderate Nelson Rockefeller and using all of its influence to block Goldwater's path to victory.

A Choice Not an Echo was enormously popular and influential, despite having no institutional support from a publishing house. In less than a year, it went through three printings, selling more than a million copies.[20] Although gauging the book's substantive effect on the GOP primary campaigns is not possible, it is clear that the Goldwater campaign believed that Schlafly's polemical work had helped mobilize thousands of Republicans to vote for him.[21]

After Goldwater's humiliating defeat in the general election, the moderate wing of the Republican Party felt vindicated, and sought to sideline Goldwater's most vociferous promoters, including Schlafly. Party leaders successfully blocked her attempt to become president of the National Federation of Republican Women. Despite being sidelined, Schlafly continued her efforts to influence the Republican Party via a grassroots network. She began distributing a monthly newsletter, the *Phyllis Schlafly Report*, in 1967. The following year she began holding training conferences for Republican women activists.[22] Still, however, she was not especially focused on women's issues, and instead was primarily focused on conventional conservative issues, especially foreign policy.

Schlafly's foray into the arena of gender politics really began in 1972, when she published an issue of the *Phyllis Schlafly Report* focused specifically on the ERA and the reasons women should oppose it.[23] At the start, Schlafly's crusade against the ERA seemed quixotic. The amendment had overwhelming, bipartisan support. Gerald Ford was enthusiastic about the ERA, and even Ronald Reagan supported it.[24] Reagan eventually reversed this position. It had easily passed in Congress, and appeared to be on track to easy ratification by the required number of states (thirty-eight).

According to Schlafly, and in contrast to feminist theorists such as Betty Friedan, American women's ability to stay home and raise children, rather than being forced, or at least encouraged, to take on the drudgery of work, was an important privilege that should not be abandoned lightly. The name of her group, STOP ERA, was actually an acronym. STOP stood for "stop taking our privileges." Schlafly put it this way:

> Why should we trade in our special privileges and honored status for the alleged advantage of working in an office or assembly line? Most women would rather cuddle a baby than a typewriter or factory machine. Most women find that it is easier to get along with a husband than a foreman or office manager. Offices and factories require many more menial and repetitive chores than washing dishes and ironing

shirts. Women's libbers do not speak for the majority of American women. American women do not want to be liberated from husbands and children. We do not want to trade our birthright of the special privileges of American women—for the mess of pottage called the Equal Rights Amendment. Modern technology and opportunity have not discovered any nobler or more satisfying or more creative career for a woman than marriage and motherhood.[25]

Through her anti-ERA campaign, Schlafly demonstrated organizational skills that have yet to be surpassed on the political Right. The activists she led engaged in flier campaigns among the public and aggressively lobbied state legislators. With this cause, Schlafly turned previously apolitical women into dedicated volunteers, and coordinated the efforts of various state and regional groups. Most of the organizational work was done quietly, with little media fanfare. As historian Rick Perlstein put it, "[Schlafly's followers] were invisible—until, that is, a state legislature put the ERA on the docket. Then, her battalions would pounce."[26]

The means by which conservative women challenged the feminist movement in the 1970s and beyond seems in some ways at odds with the usual conservative rhetorical approach to identity politics. Rather than rejecting the idea of an identity-based epistemology, which conservatives tend to do when faced with other forms of identity politics, antifeminists such as Schlafly asserted their own form of gender essentialism. According to Schlafly, women were, by nature, the masters of the domestic realm, and as such they had the right to certain privileges. Policies such as the ERA were a threat to those privileges and gave them nothing of value in return. In contrast, proponents of the ERA and related policies have used the language of individualism, insisting that it is not valid to make legal distinctions between people on account of their demographic group. As future Supreme Court Justice Ruth Bader Ginsberg put it in 1973, "[The ERA] looks toward a legal system in which each person will be judged on the basis of individual merit and not on the basis of an unalterable trait of birth that bears no necessary relationship to need or ability."[27]

Over the course of her fight against the ERA, Schlafly named the many advantages women enjoyed in modern life that would be put at risk if the feminist movement was successful. She provided a comprehensive list of them in a 1981 issue of the *Schlafly Report*.[28] Most notably, and this was a point she made many times throughout her campaign, the ERA would require that women be drafted into the military in the event of a war and be assigned combat duties. She further argued that the ERA would result in essential changes to family patterns, undermining the norm of a two-parent household in which the husband serves as the primary breadwinner and the wife serves as homemaker—the trend instead would be toward both parents working and the government providing childcare. She additionally argued that the logic of the ERA would also lead to the demise of single-sex schools and colleges, and require that fraternities and sororities become gender-integrated.

Schlafly and her allies repeatedly argued that social norms and laws in the United States ensured that men would take financial responsibility for their wives and children. In the event that unmarried sex results in an unplanned pregnancy, a man was expected to marry the woman and take care of his new wife and child. In the case of divorce, a man was expected to provide alimony and child support. The ERA would undermine both the legal and social sanctions against irresponsible husbands and "deadbeat dads." Feminism, this argument went, will free men from the responsibility of family stewardship, and, once so liberated, we can expect men to abandon their responsibilities. As Schlafly put it in *The Power of Positive Women* (1977), it is foolish to expect love alone to keep men bound to their wives and children. The law must keep them in line, and those laws would disappear if the ERA was passed: "Even though love may go out the window, the obligation would remain. ERA would eliminate that obligation."[29] Although she may have overstated her case, progressive author Barbara Ehrenreich was not completely off base when she declared, "In the ideology of American antifeminism, it is almost impossible to separate the distrust of men from the hatred of feminism."[30]

Schlafly provided further evidence that, when mobilized, women are often the most effective organizers and activists on the right. Her leadership skills were critical in another sense. Schlafly was a Catholic, doing her work at a time when conservative evangelical Protestants were still suspicious of Catholicism. In the 1970s, she earned high praise from prominent evangelicals, such as Jerry Falwell and Beverly LaHaye. Historian Gillis Harp notes that "STOP-ERA represents the best early example of a conservative movement that weaved together evangelical, Catholic, and partisan threads."[31] Eventually, Schlafly's fight against the

ERA was successful. After failing to achieve a sufficient number of state ratifications, anti-ERA forces declared victory in 1982. The fight against the ERA resulted in one of the few lasting policy victories at the national level that social conservatives can claim.

DIVISIONS AMONG REPUBLICAN WOMEN

Few people would describe the leading postwar conservatives as feminists in the contemporary sense, but it was not initially obvious how antifeminist the mainstream Right would become. The Republican Party, into the 1970s, maintained a significant feminist component, but these feminist Republicans have largely been overshadowed by their antifeminist opponents, such as Schlafly. Mary Louise Smith, the first woman to serve as the chair of the Republican National Convention, openly embraced second-wave feminism.[32]

As the antifeminists became increasingly prominent in conservative politics, they revealed a significant schism among women on the right, a schism not just about the role of women in society but about greater philosophical concerns about individualism, culture, and the state. Sociologist Rebecca Klatch argued that women on the right, like men on the right, are sharply divided on the question of whether social or economic conservatism should be the dominant force within the broader conservative movement and the Republican Party.[33] This divide has always represented a challenge for conservatism, but this is especially the case when it comes to questions of feminism because social conservatism and laissez-faire conservatism arguably offer incompatible approaches. Whereas social conservatism promotes traditional, biblical approaches to women, especially as it relates to motherhood and the family, economic conservatism emphasizes freedom. The former perspective is communal, noting the essential role women play in their communities and, especially, their families. The latter emphasizes the autonomy of the individual and his or her pursuit of self-interest. Both social conservatives and economic conservatives may deplore the current state of gender politics in the United States, but they offer dissimilar diagnoses and cures.

According to Klatch, the different branches of conservatism offer very different ideas about the nature of women. The social conservative wing argues for clear and distinct gender roles, and further argues that women are, by nature, the more communal sex, that they have a "natural orientation towards others."[34] In contrast, economic conservatives are more likely to reject ideas about natural divisions between men and women, along with any notion of natural hierarchies between them. In fact, economic conservatives are likely to celebrate capitalism precisely because of its emancipatory elements, noting that capitalism has freed women from domination by men.

Although we may consider the economic conservatives more closely associated with progressive feminism than their social conservative counterparts, both wings of conservatism break with progressives when it comes to debates over discrimination against women. The social conservatives, who will argue that men and women have distinct social spheres and naturally possess different interests, do not assume political or economic gender disparities imply discrimination. Economic conservatives, in contrast, may take it for granted that gender discrimination exists and that it is deplorable. In contrast to feminists on the left, however, economic conservatives do not endorse a statist solution to this problem, instead rallying women to relying on their own initiative and the free market to root out unjust and irrational prejudice.[35] Both branches of conservatism came to oppose the ERA, but they had different justifications. The economic conservatives were less concerned about the blurring of gender distinctions than the fact that the ERA would bloat the federal government and create new limitations on individual liberty.[36]

Women engaged in social conservative political activism seem to face a contradiction. They simultaneously affirm the notion of separate realms for separate genders, yet proudly enter the realm of politics, which in some ways seems to be a quintessential masculine sphere. Critics of social conservative women have pointed this out. Social conservative women have offered a coherent explanation for their activism, however. One argument they offer is that women have, in fact, *always* represented a kind of "power behind the throne" and a voice of righteousness in society.[37] This perspective furthermore holds that women have always been the primary guardians of civilization, the family, religion, and morality. Women, for example, played a leading role in the temperance movement. Russell Kirk made this argument in his 1957 book *The Intelligent Woman's Guide to Conservatism*, where he suggested women are political

conservatives by nature.[38] Thus, entering into the political world in
defense of their values represents no contradiction.

The actual irony, according to Klatch, is that, the more vigorously
conservative women reject feminism, the more likely they are to build
their political activism around their gender identity: "Far from suffering from false consciousness, in fact, social conservative women are
well aware of their interests and act to defend their status as women."[39]
Economic conservatives arguably share more premises with progressive
feminists than with social conservatives. However, their individualist
worldview precludes the kind of collective action that progressive feminism tends to embrace. These different approaches to women and feminism further demonstrate the challenge of the conservative fusionist
project—the traditionalist answers and the libertarian answers to these
questions are not always in agreement.

These divisions among conservative women can be seen in the different kinds of organizations they have founded. Conservative women
have, for many decades, organized specifically as women and in the
name of women's interests. Sometimes these were just organizations
that served as auxiliaries for a larger group—such as the Federation of
Republican Women. At other times, these were as part of single-issue
organizations, such as STOP ERA. There are, however, other conservative women's groups that are both formally independent of any larger
organization (and thus are run entirely by women, for women, and without oversight from other groups) and that organize specifically around
what they perceive to be women's interests. Among these groups, however, there is no consensus about what women's interests are or how they
are best achieved.

In her book *Righting Feminism*, political scientist Ronnee Schreiber argues that two groups personify different but sometimes overlap-
ping approaches to organizing conservative women.[40] On the more
traditionalist side of the spectrum, she discusses Concerned Women for
America, founded in 1978. This is a group predominantly made up of
socially conservative evangelical Protestant women. On the other side
(but still part of the broader conservative movement) you find the Independent Women's Forum, founded in 1992, a group that emphasizes
the economic side of conservatism, arguing that the free market is especially good for women. The former group's approach to identity politics

has largely mirrored Schlafly's, defending traditional gender roles and the sanctity of the family. The latter group is different in that its views toward feminism are more aligned with the more common conservative approach to identity politics. Rather than emphasizing the degree to which women are naturally different from men, they argue that limited government is in women's best interests, and furthermore that progressive feminists present a misleading portrait of the world, exaggerating the degree to which women are victimized by men.

IS THERE A CONSERVATIVE FEMINISM?

The history of conservative women activists and organizations raises the question of who should be classified as a feminist. This question became more pressing as prominent conservative women—including some with policy goals that are directly and ostentatiously at odds with the contemporary feminist movement—began using the term as a self-description. In 2008, for example, it was significant that Alaska governor and Republican vice presidential nominee Sarah Palin described herself as a feminist.[41] She continued to describe herself as a feminist after the election was over, and she became a leading figure of the growing Tea Party movement.[42]

In a way, the embrace of the term "feminist" by some conservative women seems to represent an important victory for the feminist movement. It implies that the word is no longer toxic among many conservatives in the way it had been in earlier periods. Yet it also represents a challenge because it raises new questions as to what, exactly, it means to be a feminist and who can reasonably use the word as a self-description. Palin was unquestionably different from the earlier generation of Republican feminists—those who generally supported the feminist movement in terms of substantive policies such as the ERA and other legislation designed to shrink gender disparities. Instead, Palin was a consistent conservative Republican on social issues, rejecting the idea that women need additional state interventions to achieve true equality.

According to communication scholars Katie Gibson and Amy Heyse, Palin promoted a uniquely American version of female identity, one congruent with the premises of conservatism.[43] Drawing on myths of the American frontier, and on her own experiences in Alaska,

Palin coined the term "mama grizzly" to describe her variety of conservative feminism.[44] For Palin, the quintessential American woman is the self-reliant woman on the frontier, one competent with traditionally masculine activities, such as hunting, fishing, and chopping wood, yet still recognizably feminine.[45] Some of Palin's comments echoed those of earlier antifeminists in their valorization of motherhood, and she noted that the frontier woman's ability to raise a family while simultaneously engaging in the aforementioned tasks further demonstrates the discipline, devotion, and work ethic of mama grizzlies. Some conservative women followed Palin in their embrace of feminism as a self-description. Writing in *National Review*, Kathryn Jean Lopez argued that Palin's views, especially as they relate to abortion and the family, are aligned with those of previous feminist leaders, such as Susan B. Anthony and Elizabeth Cady Stanton.[46]

Feminists on the left were split on what to make of women such as Palin using the term "feminist" as a self-description. Jessica Valenti was adamant that Palin's claim was disingenuous: "Palin's 'feminism' isn't just co-opting the language of the feminist movement, it's deliberately misrepresenting real feminism to distract from the fact that she supports policies that limit women's rights."[47] Kate Harding agreed, but noted that feminists should take some comfort in the growing popularity of feminist terminology, even among those that do not promote actual feminist goals, writing in *Jezebel*, "If they're stealing our language to broaden their appeal, then we must have done something right along the way."[48] Meghan Daum, who also rejected Palin's political positions, accepted that Palin had the right to describe herself as a feminist, and argued that it is a good thing if more people use the term to describe themselves.[49]

In some ways, conservative discourse around contemporary feminism mirrors that of conservative talking points about civil rights for Blacks. In both cases, conservatives tend to say that there was a period in which both movements were fighting against genuine injustices, but that, at some point, they went too far, devolving into today's toxic identity politics. For example, today's conservatives will celebrate progressive victories such as the Nineteenth Amendment and the Voting Rights Act of 1965, but argue that new legislation promoting greater equality for women or Blacks is unnecessary or even harmful.

Christina Hoff Sommers, author of *Who Stole Feminism?*, is an important proponent of the view that the feminist movement began with laudable goals but subsequently lost its moral high ground by embracing an unrealistic narrative of female victimhood.[50] According to Sommers, many feminist claims about the oppression of women were simply false, such as the often repeated statement that more than 100,000 women die from anorexia every year, or that a massive percentage of married women are psychologically abused by their husbands. She argued that we need to disaggregate "gender feminism" from "equity feminism." In her view, the modern feminist movement had abandoned the "classically liberal, humanistic feminism that was initiated more than 150 years ago."[51]

RELIGION AND WOMEN'S RIGHTS

Religion operates somewhat differently in disputes over gender than in questions of racial equality. Religion, especially Christianity, was employed on all sides during the debates of slavery and in the battle over civil rights a century later. Foundational Christian texts have little to directly tell us about modern race relations. The modern conception of race did not exist at the time they were written. It is true that both sides of various debates have tried to insist that ancient texts have unambiguous messages when it comes to contemporary political questions. Some Christians justified the enslavement of Africans on the theologically dubious "Curse of Ham."[52] More recently, progressives have sought to reimagine Jesus as a "person of color" who took a stand against the racist, capitalist exploitation of the Roman Empire.[53] Both positions are unconvincing, and represent additional evidence that Christian texts are sufficiently vague to be useful for all kinds of contradictory political positions, especially when it comes to race and economics.

Gender relations are different, however. Although contemporary racial groups did not exist as social categories at the time the Bible was written, ideas about men and women, and their inherent differences, were well established. The notion that men and women have different social responsibilities was explicit in the texts, and it is easy to infer that the Bible sanctions, and perhaps even requires, patriarchy: some passages explicitly call for male leadership of churches and families, for example.

Most mainstream denominations now reject the most aggressive forms of biblical patriarchy. However, many Christian denominations maintain that only men can serve as priests or pastors; this is true, for example, of the largest denominations in the United States, the Roman Catholic Church and the Southern Baptist Convention. In comparison to thinkers who must read between the lines to find biblical messages about modern race relations, especially if one wants to justify racism, it is relatively straightforward to cite the Bible in defense of traditional gender roles.

This is not to say that Christians in the United States have taken a uniform stance on gender relations. There are some Christian writers and even entire denominations that explicitly reject patriarchal institutions, or any kind of social or spiritual inequality between men and women. They further claim that such a stand can be justified according to the original texts. In fact, even Christian conservative women have made such a connection. Claire Booth Luce was a remarkably accomplished writer, politician, and ambassador. She was also a Catholic conservative. In one of her many appearances on Buckley's television program, *Firing Line*, Luce stated, "A Christian man has got to be a feminist. Jesus Christ was the first feminist."[54] In explaining her logic, she suggested that the Old Testament provided a clear sanction for patriarchy, going all the way back to the story of Adam and Eve, in which Eve could be reasonably blamed for bringing sin into the world. She then argued that the Gospels were remarkable precisely because of the degree to which Jesus was concerned with women: he performed many miracles for women or on a woman's request. In her view, the Gospels were fundamentally feminist texts, especially when compared to their predecessors. Nonetheless, Christianity has not been one of the main forces driving contemporary feminist movements, and conservative Christians have been some of feminism's most ardent critics. Luce was furthermore an outlier among leading conservatives in that she was a vocal proponent of the ERA.

CONSERVATISM, FEMINISM, AND THE STRANGE BEDFELLOWS OF TRANSGENDER POLITICS

Gender politics has previously involved occasional cross-cutting political alliances. Although radical feminists such as Andrea

Dworkin unquestionably loathed right-wing women's groups, conservative women's organizations were happy to ally themselves with antipornography feminists such as Dworkin and Cynthia McKinney when discussing that issue and its effects on women. At present, there are new divides and alliances forming around transgenderism. Transgenderism—which refers to a person whose gender identity is not aligned with his or her sex—was not a particularly salient issue in American life until recently, and transgender people remain an extremely small percentage of the U.S. population. It has, however, become one of the more divisive and emotionally charged issues to emerge in recent years. It is also an interesting topic because it touches on so many questions related to identity, feminism, gender essentialism, social construction, and the Left.

The battle over transgender rights and recognition is mostly a culture war battle between the Left and the Right, becoming increasingly intense after the fight over same-sex marriage ended with the *Obergefell v. Hodges* decision in 2015, which legalized same-sex marriage throughout the country. Following that victory, many progressives viewed transgender rights the next logical arena to warrant their attention and resources. Conservatives, for the most part, have been generally dismissive of transgenderism, taking it for granted that gender is synonymous with biological sex. However, the Left is not united on this subject. In particular, an element of the feminist movement rejects the possibility that people that were born male can or should be classified as women, regardless of how they personally identify. This group has subsequently been labeled as TERFs, "trans-exclusionary radical feminists."

The transgender question is significant because it is forcing a debate about biology and social construction. The traditional definition of a woman is simply an "adult human female," and a man is "an adult human male." This suggests that gender is simply an extension of physiology. The truth is, of course, more complicated than that, because the social categories of "man" and "woman" involve many attributes and relationships not driven specifically by biology. Much of the feminist movement has traditionally argued that many of these social relationships are not dictated by biology, but are instead oppressive structures built and maintained by a patriarchy that oppresses women. They reject, for example, the idea that women possess a distinct "female brain" that makes them unqualified for certain kinds of labor and other social roles.

I suspect most feminists would agree with the above characterization of their views, but it is important not to oversimplify complex questions. When it comes to gender and sex, people can reasonably hold different views on the degree to which certain traits and social relationships are, in fact, socially constructed.[55] One could, for example, broadly agree with many basic tenets of feminism without signing onto the notion that all apparent evidence of sexual dimorphism in humans is really just the result of social constructions.[56]

The issue of transgendered people seems to further complicate matters. If someone born male or female can claim to *really* belong to a gender he or she was not assigned at birth, that seems to indicate that there is such a thing as a "man's brain" or a "woman's brain," that gender identity is something innate and unchangeable. This seems at odds with the claim that gender itself is a purely social construct. On the other hand, the notion that gender identity is not necessarily tied to biological sex also seems aligned with the goal of a less gendered, more androgynous society. Thus, some feminists who find certain claims by transgender activists dubious may nonetheless consider the growing visibility of transgendered people a welcome development.

The subject of transgendered people also raises new questions about the nature of homosexuality. Andrew Sullivan, a gay man and political conservative, has argued that the trans movement represents a threat to the gay identity, noting that biology, rather than just the performative aspects of gender, is at the root of homosexual desire. According to Sullivan, "The truth is that many lesbians and gay men are quite attached to the concept of sex as a natural, biological thing."[57] He argues that the "transgenderist ideology" undermined the basis of the gay identity by insisting that anyone—regardless of their anatomy or forms of gender expression—could be a man or a woman. Sullivan suggests that the logical extension of this argument is that a lesbian who does not wish to have sex with a trans woman (even one who still possesses male genitalia) is simply being transphobic: "If it's all a free and fluid nonbinary choice of gender and sexual partners, a choice to have sex exclusively with the same sex would not be an expression of our identity, but a form of sexist bigotry, would it not?"

Conservatives have been overwhelmingly critical of the transgender movement, but some, such as Grover Norquist, have called for a tolerant, libertarian approach to the subject.[58] Many conservatives have treated it as just another example of postmodern folly, and not a subject worthy of intellectually serious treatment. Talk radio host Rush Limbaugh, for example, argued that the transgender movement was just a "fad," a "way to tick off your parents."[59] Some have sought to seriously engage with the various philosophical challenges that surround this subject, focusing on trans activists' seemingly contradictory arguments.

The most interesting development regarding these subjects, in my view, has been an alliance between social conservatives and elements of the feminist movement that oppose the trans movement. Before the rise of transgender issues as an important element of feminism, those two political factions would have likely found few points of agreement. In 2019, for example, the conservative Heritage Foundation hosted a talk by three women associated with the Women's Liberation Front.[60] The panelists were no friends to conservatism, but they claimed that they cooperated with Heritage on this issue because no group was willing to offer them a platform.

CONCLUSION

In some ways, the conservative approach to gender politics has mirrored its approach to racial politics. In both cases, contemporary conservatives, for the most part, accept progressive victories of the last century as legitimate and perhaps even worth celebration. Also, as was the case for racial equality activists, conservatives argue that, at a certain point, the feminist movement went too far. However, in both cases, today's conservatives usually state their belief in equality as an ideal. This seems to preclude serious conservative efforts to undo earlier feminist and antiracist victories. In fact, conservatives will often now insist that they are, in fact, the *real* antiracists and feminists.

There have, however, always been important differences between the conservative approach to gender and the conservative approach to race. In the former case, it was often women themselves that carried the banner of antifeminism. In contrast, there was no large movement of Blacks organizing in opposition to new civil rights legislation—this absence provided evidence against the segregationist claim that most southern Blacks were happy with the Jim Crow system. Although radical Black separatists existed, they did not form a coalition with white segregationists.

Given that many conservative women now declare themselves feminists, one could argue that the feminist movement has been a massive success. At present, however, feminism in the United States has a number of challenges, some resulting from its own internal disputes. The postmodern and intersectional turn of feminism in recent decades has resulted in a deluge of interesting scholarship, but it has also resulted in schisms and an increasing embrace of esoteric language most Americans find perplexing. In place of a simpler perspective, in which women and men were discussed in binary terms of a class of oppressor and a class of the oppressed, the intersectional approach has emphasized that women experience oppression differently depending on their other characteristics. This can result in tensions within the feminist movement, leading, for example, to complaints that mainstream feminism has long been "too white."[61]

The recent #MeToo movement, which has sought to bring new attention to issues of sexual harassment and abuse, especially abusive behavior of powerful men, has arguably been a major success. It is nonetheless criticized for emphasizing the concerns of white women (often elite white women) rather than the experiences of women of color whose voices and concerns receive less attention.[62] These debates and accusations often lead to acrimony within the feminist movement. Most notably, the organization responsible for the "Women's March" movement, which began shortly after Donald Trump was elected president, subsequently fractured over these issues. The overrepresentation of white women in the women's marches was considered problematic. On the other side, a high-profile Black woman associated with the movement was accused of anti-Semitism for her endorsement of Nation of Islam leader Louis Farrakhan.[63] Although conservatives remain divided and inconsistent when it comes to identity issues, the intersectional Left continues to have challenges of its own. Keeping various left-wing identity movements united and focused on common aims is often more difficult than their conservative opponents realize.

SIX

Conservatism, Immigration, and National Identity

Few policies inspire more partisan and ideological acrimony than immigration. Given the economic, partisan, cultural, and demographic stakes of the immigration policy disputes—and the visceral reactions these disputes inspire—it is hard to imagine eras where the issue was not so provocative. Donald Trump's comments about immigration during the 2016 presidential election prompted some of his opponents' angriest reactions. They also inspired some of this most fervent supporters.[1] Throughout his presidency, Trump's rhetoric on immigration continued to enrage his critics, even if, in terms of substance, his policy achievements were relatively modest.

Immigration raises crucial questions about national identity, questions that divide conservatives. What is the American national identity? What does it mean to be an American? Is it just legal status as a U.S. citizen, or is there some other group of attributes that confer "Americanness"? If the latter, what are they? Does changing the nation's demographic profile change the nature of the country? Even if it does, is this a legitimate reason to restrict immigration? How should conservatives react to immigration's effect on the Republican Party's fortunes? What role, if any, should public opinion play in all of these decisions? These questions have divided conservatives for decades, and will continue to do so.

Yet immigration was not always a topic that interested conservatives, in part because of the unusual period in which modern conservatism was born. Conservatism as we know it arrived on the scene when immigration was still low, and the foreign-born population was at a nadir. If modern conservatives wish to look to the movement's canonical early texts for guidance, they will find that their ideological forbearers had little to say about immigration policy.

IMMIGRATION DURING CONSERVATISM'S FORMATIVE YEARS

Because of the Immigration Act of 1924, the explosive levels of immigration that had characterized the late nineteenth and early twentieth century came to an end. After decades of lobbying to end the U.S. policy of loose immigration laws, restrictionists successfully created new policies that closed U.S. borders to most immigrants. It is worth noting that, although this system has been justifiably called racist, it primarily affected potential European immigrants from countries such as Italy and Poland. Immigration from Asia had already slowed to a trickle because of new restrictions on Asian immigration placed several decades earlier.

These immigration policies were driven in part by the eugenicist ideas that were popular among American intellectuals during the Progressive Era. One point worth mentioning about the intellectual climate in this period was that, although these thinkers were unquestionably racist as we understand the term today, they were also very focused on supposed genetic differences between different European groups. This makes them somewhat different from today's white nationalists and scientific racists. Influential thinkers such as Madison Grant, for example, discussed at length the supposed inborn differences between "Nordic," "Alpine," and "Mediterranean" whites,[2] with Nordic Europeans possessing the most admirable qualities, and thus the group the United States should favor in its immigration policies. The new immigration regime was thus intentionally biased in favor of immigrants from northwestern Europe—a region that, by that time, was no longer a major source of immigration. Although the racist Right today praises the immigration restrictions put in place in the 1920s, had those restrictions not been implemented, many millions of additional Europeans (perhaps not primarily "Nordics") may have entered the United States in subsequent decades. The Great Depression provided another blow to immigration, as the United States no longer offered the kinds of economic opportunities that once attracted immigrants by the millions.

Many important political figures were arguing in favor of loosening immigration restrictions in the late 1940s and 1950s, but the quota system remained firmly in place, and its removal and replacement were not high on the national political agenda. Most of the changes to immigration policy involved loosening restrictions in order to admit a greater number of European refugees from communist countries, or making it easier for the foreign wives of American GIs to immigrate. Even these fairly modest policy changes, which had a negligible effect on the country's overall demographic profile, often led to bitter fights in Congress.[3]

THE CATHOLIC AND IMMIGRANT ROOTS
OF THE CONSERVATIVE MOVEMENT

Anti-immigration movements before the restrictions of the 1920s were often openly defensive of WASP culture. These restrictionists wanted to protect the specific culture created by Anglo-Protestant settlers during the colonial era. The Know-Nothing movement of the nineteenth century was explicitly hostile to Catholics. Defending of the Protestant religion against growing numbers of Catholics and Jews, and maintaining the dominance of the white race, was a major part of the Ku Klux Klan's agenda in the early twentieth century.[4] The anti-immigration and eugenicist aspects of the progressive movement were not particularly interested in religion as such, but thinkers such as Grant and Lothrop Stoddard had very low opinions of southern and eastern Europeans—asserting that Nordic whites were objectively superior to other whites.

Given its leading figures' personal traits, the early conservative movement could never fully endorse these earlier anti-immigrant traditions. Among the conservative intellectuals that built the movement, Catholics were massively overrepresented. Furthermore, for many of them, Catholicism was a critical part of their worldview, informing their conservatism. The Catholic-raised William F. Buckley Jr., who wrote at length on his faith, was perhaps the most notable example. Unlike his take on questions of race, on which Buckley tried to maintain a semidispassionate tone, his writings on religion in the 1960s demonstrated his passion for the subject. His critique of Pope John XXIII's 1961 *Mater et magistra* led to a furious intellectual dispute with other leading Catholics.[5] L. Brent Bozell eventually broke with mainstream conservatism entirely, instead calling for a Catholic theocracy.

Like Bozell, Russell Kirk converted to Catholicism as an adult, as did Willmoore Kendall. James Burnham was raised Catholic, but he abandoned the Church as a young adult, only to return to Catholicism on his deathbed to receive last rites.[6] Frank Meyer was raised Jewish, and also spent most of his adult life with no personal religion, but he did have a long fascination with Catholicism (and one reading his conservative writings would have likely inferred he was a believing Christian). Like Burnham, he put off officially joining the Church until the very end, and was finally baptized just hours before he died.[7] Phyllis Schlafly and the political organizer Paul Weyrich were also Catholic. Gary Wills even spent some time in Catholic seminary, but he ultimately decided not to become a priest. The significance of these figures precluded anti-Catholic bigotry from playing any role in the early conservative intellectual movement's view on immigration.

Among the first high-profile figures of the conservative movement, we can find a few Protestants. Whittaker Chambers became a Quaker after his break with communism. Richard Weaver was a Protestant, but he was surprisingly quiet about his personal religious commitments: *Ideas Have Consequences* makes only perfunctory references to Christianity, and, at least while he lived in Chicago, Weaver scarcely attended religious services.[8] Neither figure emphasized the Protestant aspect of the American identity.

The conservative movement also contained many immigrants in its own ranks, and took inspiration from other immigrants who remained aloof from conservatism. Much of the conservative movement's economic platform was developed by immigrants, such as Ludwig von Mises (who was a secular Jew) and Friedrich von Hayek (who was from a Catholic background, but not personally religious). Leo Strauss, who had a profound influence on conservative thought, was an immigrant and ethnically Jewish. The philosopher Eric Voegelin was an immigrant. Even Ernest van den Haag, a figure we may now view as being on the right-wing extreme of mainstream conservatism when it comes to race and immigration (but to the left of other conservatives on economics), was an immigrant. Buckley was not an immigrant, but his family had extensive business ties to Mexico and Venezuela, and he was fluent in Spanish from an early age. Buckley thus never possessed the more crude anti-Hispanic bigotry that has characterized much of the modern immigration restriction movement. The same was true of Bozell, who spent part of his adult life in Franco's Spain, and in some ways thought Latino Catholics were superior to Anglo-Americans because of their more fervent religious beliefs. In fact, he thought Latin American Catholics could revitalize Christianity in North America.[9]

For all of these reasons, the conservative movement was never going to embrace an unthinking nativism, one seeking to perpetuate Anglo-Protestant America for its own sake. At the very least, this meant that one principal component of earlier nativist movements—anti-Catholicism—had no support from the mainstream conservative intellectual movement. This is not to say that conservatives were always pro-immigration. They were not, and *National Review* tended to be on the side of restrictionism during the most heated immigration battles, especially in the 1990s. However, the early conservative movement had personal and intellectual reasons to be at least ambivalent over the subject of immigration. It was never plausible that this movement, at that time, would provide a united nativist front in the political battles over immigration.

IMMIGRATION AND THE COLD WAR

As was the case with civil rights, throughout the Cold War, immigration policy was often viewed as an important foreign policy issue. Regardless of the economic or cultural value new immigrants brought to the United States, a relatively open immigration policy was a useful propaganda tool. The imagery of communist refugees fleeing to a welcoming United States provided evidence that the Soviet Union and its satellites had failed to create the promised workers' paradise. In the early years of the Cold War, U.S. presidents viewed immigration as an important

foreign policy tool, and they were frustrated by the degree restrictionists in Congress limited their use of it. Both Truman and Eisenhower
wanted to admit a greater number of refugees than the quota system
permitted at the time.

Conservative intellectuals similarly viewed the immigration question through a Cold War lens, calling for the United States to accept
refugees from communist countries[10] and condemning the Soviet Union
and its satellites for restricting emigration.[11] Buckley, for example, argued
that the Soviet Union must be denied most-favored-nation trading status until it began allowing Jews in that the country to right to emigrate
to Israel.[12] Burnham similarly condemned the Soviet Union for failing
to recognizing a "right to leave" as a human right.[13]

When framed in the Cold War context, conservatives often argued
that Democrats were *too restrictionist* when it came to immigration, and
that the United States should be even more enthusiastic about accepting immigrants from communist countries. Conservatives criticized
President Carter, for example, for failing to provide more aid to Cubans
fleeing the Castro regime.[14] Throughout this period, mainstream conservatives who addressed the immigration issue at all tended to focus on
the subject of human rights and the degree to which a relatively open
immigration policy provided tangible proof that the United States had
the moral high ground in the Cold War.

The most sweeping changes to U.S. immigration policy came in
1965, when President Johnson signed the Immigration and Nationality Act. This was a time when racially discriminatory policy was under
attack on multiple fronts. The new law ended the old quota system that
prioritized northern European immigrants. It also prioritized family
reunification when selecting immigrants, setting in motion the process
of "chain migration" that has long disturbed immigration restrictionists.

Conservative intellectuals were mostly quiet about the subject
during the debates about these changes to U.S. immigration law. In part,
this was because few people at the time realized the dramatic effect these
changes would have on the nation's demography. The people promoting
the bill incorrectly insisted that it would not result in a new wave of mass
immigration. Many people at the time believed that the emphasis on
family reunification rather than job skills would have favored European
immigrants over immigrants from other sources.

During this period we can find some conservatives who wrote about the potential challenge of high levels of immigration, especially if that immigration did not come from Europe. In 1965, Van den Haag argued for an immigration system that favored the most culturally similar potential immigrants. He further claimed that such as policy was not invariably racist, given that one does not need to believe in any theories of inherent racial, ethnic, or cultural superiority in order to "wish one's country to continue to be made up of the same ethnic strains as before."[15] It is notable that, already by 1965, conservative opinion leaders felt it necessary to insist that opposition to more immigration, even when defended on cultural grounds, was not necessarily racist.

THE PROBLEM OF UNDOCUMENTED IMMIGRATION

Undocumented immigration was also on the rise in the latter decades of the twentieth century. Because such immigration is, by definition, illegal, this trend was not directly connected to the 1965 changes. Given that undocumented immigrants were especially likely to be poor and, at least initially, possess poor English skills, this population generated resentment from many native-born Americans. However, by the 1980s there was a shift in how draconian the government was willing to be to remove undocumented immigrants from the country. In the 1950s, President Eisenhower responded to a growing undocumented population with the notorious "Operation Wetback," a massive effort to round up and deport a huge number of undocumented immigrants throughout the Southwest.[16]

During the Reagan administration, there was a genuine push to permanently resolve the problem of undocumented immigration. Throughout his political career, Reagan had never shown particular interest in the immigration question, but he briefly argued for loosening border restrictions between the United States and Mexico.[17] He also supported the Immigration Reform and Control Act (IRCA), which passed in 1986, a time when Republicans controlled the U.S. Senate. This law included provisions that pleased (and angered) both sides of the immigration divide. On the one hand, it provided a pathway to legalization for unlawful immigrants who had been in the country for several years. At the same time, it hoped to shut down the jobs magnet that attracted so many undocumented immigrants in the first place. New employer sanctions were intended to discourage business from hiring people that were not in the country legally. The amnesty was applied, leading to the rapid legalizing of millions of undocumented immigrants. The new employer sanctions, however, were never implemented in a meaningful way. The flow of undocumented immigrants did not cease or even slow.

Given the experience of IRCA, subsequent Republican skepticism toward comprehensive immigration reform is more understandable. It taught immigration restrictionists to be distrustful of any policy bargain that provides an amnesty today in exchange for future enforcement. There is reason to worry that the amnesty will be provided, but the enforcement measures will be either watered down or killed by the courts. Those Republicans who insisted on an "enforcement first" approach during the heated immigration debates of George W. Bush's time in the White House were reasonably suspicious of the bills being discussed.

CONSERVATIVE RESTRICTIONISM AFTER THE COLD WAR

As the Cold War came to a close, and the foreign-born population in the United States continued to rise, the conservative movement's earlier ambivalence about immigration began to give way to a more consistent nativism. Although the mainstream Right never favored an open-border policy, especially from the developing world, anti-immigration attitudes among leading conservatives arguably reached a peak in the 1990s. We see this in the pages of *National Review* and in a number of influential books that were published in this decade.[18]

Lawrence Auster's short book *The Path to National Suicide*, published in 1990 by The American Immigration Control Foundation, was an important entry to the conservative anti-immigration genre.[19] The book attacked the 1965 changes to the immigration laws, but also the principles of multiculturalism more generally. Auster was disturbed by the lack of serious commentary about the sweeping demographic changes that resulted from immigration. He argued that this was a critical issue, and something that conservatives so single-mindedly focused on the subject of illegal immigration were missing entirely. He noted, correctly, that legal immigration was more responsible for the United States' changing cultural and linguistic landscape than illegal immigration. He further-more argued that the government had set these changes in motion with-out consulting the American people, and it was time for an open and honest debate about whether Americans really wanted their country to be changed:

> There is a need for the information, ideas and arguments that will make it intellectually and morally respectable to question our cur-rent policy and the orthodoxy that upholds it. We need to break free from the paralyzing notion that because "we are all descended from immigrants," we therefore have no right to make such a fateful choice about our nation's future. Let us prove our faith in democ-racy: If the American people truly want to change their historic European-rooted civilization into a Latin-Caribbean-Asian "multi-culture," then let them debate and approve that proposition through an informed political process, as befits a free people. And if Ameri-cans do not want their society to change in such a revolutionary manner, then let them revise their immigration laws accordingly. But let the debate occur.[20]

Another key conservative text from that period was Peter Brimelow's *Alien Nation* (1995).[21] Over his long journalism career, Brimelow had served as an editor at *Forbes* and *National Review.* The book listed many common right-wing critiques of immigration. It provided a generally accurate history of immigration and immigration policy in the United States. It also listed the many ostensibly deleterious economic and cul-tural effects of immigration. It further directly took on the various claims about the supposed immorality of restrictionist immigration policies.

Alien Nation was a national best seller. It was highly praised by con-servative reviewers at the time. The paperback edition listed the many figures that praised Brimelow's work. Conservatives such as Thomas Sowell, David Frum, and R. Emmett Tyrell all provided positive com-ments. This is interesting given Brimelow's subsequent banishment from the mainstream conservative movement. Brimelow is now best known for his website, VDare.com, which he founded in 1999. The site was named for Virginia Dare, the first English child born in North America.

It is arguably the most visited website dedicated entirely to promoting immigration restriction. It has also been listed as a hate group by the Southern Poverty Law Center.[22] Brimelow has not had a byline in *National Review* in many years. *The Daily Caller* is the only mainstream conservative webzine that has published Brimelow in recent years, and it ceased publishing his work in 2017.[23] However, in terms of the substance of his own arguments, Brimelow's own claims about immigration today are not especially different from what they were in 1995, back when he was still considered a member of the mainstream conservative movement in good standing. This suggests that conservatives have moved leftward on the immigration question, or the boundaries of acceptable opinion on immigration and race have narrowed over the last few decades.[24]

National Review also took a strong anti-immigration stance in the 1990s. It was during this period that both Brimelow and John O'Sullivan (also a strong immigration restrictionist) were leading voices at the magazine. In 1992, *National Review* published Brimelow's cover story "Time to Rethink Immigration?"[25] In the piece (as he did in *Alien Nation*), Brimelow explicitly criticized post-1965 immigration policy for changing the "ethnic mix" of the United States. Such arguments are considered mostly taboo among mainstream conservatives today, at least when stated too directly. The norm among mainstream restrictionists today is to avoid complaining about racial or ethnic change as such, and instead insist that, although skin color is not a relevant characteristic for determining immigration, political culture may be a consideration. One could counter that, given that ideological affinities are not distributed evenly across ethnic groups, this is perhaps a distinction without a difference. However, it does demonstrate that, at least in terms of rhetoric, there has been a shift in how conservatives prefer to talk about these issues.

The 1990s was also a period when several immigration restrictionist policies were signed into law, but not all survived court challenges or had their intended effects. The 1990 Immigration Act sought to again solve the problem of undocumented immigration, because it was by then apparent that IRCA had failed. This legislation was focused heavily on border control. In 1994, the Immigration and Naturalization Service announced Operation Gatekeeper, which involved the creation of a steel border fence on the U.S.-Mexico border at the crossing near San Diego, California. Immigration restrictionists also seemed to win some important victories in California in the 1990s. Proposition 187, which would have denied unlawful immigrants access to state-provided services, passed by a large margin in 1994. The policy was politically popular at the time, but it was never implemented. After a long legal battle, the law was voided by the courts.

RETHINKING LEGAL IMMIGRATION?

For decades, we have heard a common refrain from conservatives: they have no problem with immigration, but it must be legal. This seems like a reasonable position: large-scale undocumented immigration is unpopular with the general public. Given that undocumented immigrants are not eligible to vote, they are also a group that one can antagonize with less fear of electoral reprisals, and by making this distinction, restrictionists are presumably not going to alienate those immigrants that did enter the United States via legal channels. It is furthermore reasonable to criticize people that knowingly violate U.S. laws. The conservative focus on undocumented immigration, however, may be less politically astute than it first appears.

To begin with, the focus on undocumented immigration is likely a red herring. Part of the conservative quandary is that conservatives, for the most part, are not critical of the earlier waves of mass immigration to the United States. Thus, expressing frustration with current immigration rates requires finding some means of distinguishing today's immigrants from those of a century ago. And given the taboo against racism, they must find a distinction that does not directly reference race or ethnicity. That being the case, focusing on legality may be the least controversial political approach. For restrictionists, however, I suspect such arguments have limited utility. The notion that conservatives are deeply concerned about the sanctity of our byzantine immigration laws is implausible. It is more likely that they are bothered by the demographic, economic, and cultural changes that result from a rapid influx of immigrants, not the process by which they arrived. If the issue is really just a matter of filling out the correct paperwork, there is a very simple solution: make it easier to legally immigrate to the United States. If the "illegals" that many conservatives complained about could all show that they were, in fact, in the country legally, would conservative complaints about their presence vanish?

An implicit element to discussions about undocumented immigration is that today's undocumented immigrants are qualitatively different from earlier immigrant waves, that the immigrants of the nineteenth and early twentieth century were not illegal immigrants. In a sense, this is true. It is true because, for much of early American history, the country had de facto open borders—at least for Europeans. Eager for the labor, and for people to fill up the frontier, the United States accepted just about anyone willing to move to the country. Even after the process became more bureaucratized—immigrants had to be screened at places such as Ellis Island, for example—it was still a short and straightforward process. The overwhelming majority of the many millions of immigrants that passed through Ellis Island were processed in just hours. There were no passports or visas involved. If legally entering the United States was this simple today, then we could reasonably expect that illegal immigration would come to a virtual halt.

The utility of arguments about undocumented immigration is further weakened by the fact that undocumented immigrants are, overall, just a small percentage of immigrants to the United States. More than 40 million people living in the United States were born abroad. A minority of these (perhaps 12 million) are in the country illegally.[26] Furthermore, undocumented immigration has declined from its peak during the George W. Bush administration, but as of this writing in 2021, it does appear to be increasing again.[27] Although it is more politically problematic to do so, some conservative immigration restrictionists are moving away from exclusive discussions about undocumented immigration (and purported solutions such as border walls) and directly talking about the question of legal immigration.

Mark Krikorian of the restrictionist Center for Immigration Studies has provided the most comprehensive argument in support of major immigration reductions.[28] According to Krikorian, today's potential immigrants are no less worthy than those of a century ago. However, the United States is a fundamentally different country than it was during previous peaks of immigration, and it has changed in ways that make immigrant assimilation much more challenging. Krikorian argues that changes in American culture make mass immigration a greater threat to national cohesion than was once the case. Notably, the United States no longer enjoys a unified national culture. Making matters worse, U.S. elites are increasingly hostile to even the idea of a unified national culture, instead celebrating cosmopolitanism and thinking of themselves as "post-American."[29] Doctrines about multiculturalism, which now permeate the U.S. education system, undermine even the concept of cultural assimilation. Changes in the U.S. economy have also made high levels of immigration problematic.

Although immigrants unquestionably grow the U.S. economy, they may also add to economic inequality. A steady flow of lower-skilled immigrants presumably depresses the wages of American workers, especially those with lower levels of education. Current immigrants furthermore may not enjoy the same levels of upward economic mobility as their predecessors did, and immigrants and the children of immigrants have considerably lower incomes, on average, than those of other native-born Americans.[30] Once again, conservatives can be justifiably accused of being disingenuous on this issue. Conservative politicians and pundits do not typically show great concern about income inequality and higher wages for workers.

Although conservatives rarely do so, one could also argue that the mass European immigration of the nineteenth and early twentieth century was also a mistake—that immigration at a massive scale causes significant problems regardless of the historical context or the countries of origin. Many of the complaints that restrictionists have about contemporary immigrants were true about earlier immigrants. We can argue that, overall, the large-scale immigration from Italy was a net positive for the United States, but it is unquestionably true that Italian immigrants introduced the Mafia to the United States. Immigrants were a key element of Franklin Roosevelt's New Deal coalition, helping to push the United States to the left. During the first red scare after the Russian Revolution, immigrants were overrepresented among the political radicals. Immigrants did contribute to the corruption of political machines in big cities. The arrival of a massive number of Catholics changed the once uniformly Protestant religious landscape of the country, creating new religious tensions. This does not excuse anti-immigrant bigotry, then or now, but one could argue that the challenges associated with contemporary immigration are not qualitatively different from what the United States experienced in the past.

DOES ETHNICITY STILL MATTER FOR WHITE AMERICANS?

When conservatives distinguish the current period of mass immigration from those that occurred before 1924, they tend to note how the earlier immigrant groups abandoned their previous national identities (aside from a few superficial cultural practices) and assimilated into a new American identity. They thus became mostly indistinguishable from Americans who could trace their entire family history back to the colonial era. As conservative scholar Victor Davis Hanson puts it, "After two or three generations, assimilation was mostly complete. Italian Americans were no longer really Italians and were no more likely to prefer pasta over hamburgers than any other Americans. Names such as Cuomo, Pataki, Pelosi, or Giuliani give no more hint to one's politics than did Smith, Jones, and Baker."[31]

In some ways "assimilation" is a subjective assessment, but there are various measures that can be examined empirically. When we talk about the descendants of the earlier immigration waves, we are talking primarily about white Americans (because it would be disingenuous to describe Africans forcibly brought to North America as "immigrants" as we typically use the term). Is there a generic "white American," or do some of these older ethnic distinctions still matter in any real sense?

The U.S. Census Bureau, and many other entities that keep track of demographic trends, including most political surveys, have a peculiar system for categorizing people. When filling out their Census forms, Americans may choose among the following racial groups: White, Black or African American, Asian, American Indian and Alaska Native, Native Hawaiian and Other Pacific Islander, or some other race. "White," incidentally, is not limited to people of European ancestry. Government statistics also classify Americans from the Middle East and North Africa (and their descendants) as white. Some people advocate changing this, possibly coming up with a new label for people from this region. Ultimately, the Census Bureau decided not to make this change for the 2020 Census, so for the time being, this group will be categorized, as far as government statistics are concerned, as "white."[32] Incidentally, if a new category for the Middle East and North Africa (MENA) is added to Census forms, the percentage of Americans considered white will immediately drop, and the estimated date when non-Hispanic whites are officially considered a minority in this country will be much closer. This further demonstrates the slippery nature of race as a concept.

The Census also tracks ethnicity, but only recognizes two ethnic groups: Hispanic and non-Hispanic. Those who classify themselves as Hispanic are expected to list their race, and there are Hispanics from all racial groups. This is why, when social scientists write about whites in the United States, they typically specify that they are referring to "non-Hispanic whites."

The fact that non-Hispanic whites are considered a unified group represents a major change from earlier periods in U.S. history. Although the Census has always treated whites as a single category, it also used to ask respondents their country of birth and their parents' place of birth, distinguishing whites according to which European country they or their family came from. This allowed the government to keep track of the various European ethnicities that were present in the United States.

The large migration of Irish immigrants in the mid-1800s led to a surge in nativism. The Irish spoke English, but they were overwhelmingly Catholic. Fears of these new immigrants prompted the rise of nativist movements, most notably the Know-Nothing Party, which experienced impressive growth during the early 1850s. During this period, however, the more pressing question of slavery eclipsed the question of immigration, and the party enjoyed few major policy successes.

The push for restrictionism was more successful during the Progressive Era. Despite many hurdles to overcome, by the 1920s a confluence of developments (intellectual, political, economic, and in foreign affairs) opened a path for sweeping new restrictions on immigration. For a thorough discussion of this history, I recommend political scientist Daniel Tichenor, *Dividing Lines: The Politics of Immigration Control in America* (2002).[33] Over the next several decades, the significance of white ethnic differences in the United States seemed to wane. With only small amounts of European immigration, high rates of English-language acquisition, the decline of ethnically homogenous neighborhoods, economic and political assimilation,[34] and intermarriage across ethnic lines,[35] these differences became less politically salient and significant. The shared experience of the Great Depression and World War II similarly helped forge a new, shared white American identity. Overtime, the story goes, these groups coalesced into a cohesive entity, just as Angles,

Saxons, Frisians, Jutes, and Celts eventually became simply "English." The election of a Catholic president who strongly identified with his Irish roots, John F. Kennedy, in 1960 seemed to demonstrate that these kinds of divides were no longer significant and important. Stanley Lieberson suggested in the 1980s that white Americans were forming into a new unique ethnic group defined by the following attributes: "There is a recognition of being white, but lack of any clearcut identification with, and/or knowledge of, a specific European origin. Such people recognize that they are not the same as existing ethnic groups in the country such as Greeks, Jews, Italians, Poles, Irish, etc. It is assumed at this point that the vast bulk of persons meeting these conditions are of older Northwestern European origins, but I also assume that there are some persons from newer European sources of immigration shifting into this group."[36]

Three decades after Lieberson first described this phenomenon, we can be confident his description fits an even greater share of white Americans. In fact, there is now a meaningful percentage of whites who, when asked on surveys about their ethnic origins, either give no answer (perhaps because they do not know the answer) or simply describe their ethnicity as "American."[37] At least for Americans of mostly European heritage, one can reasonably argue that the melting pot metaphor of assimilation is reasonably accurate.

On the other hand, there may be another, less innocuous side to the decline of white ethnic identities. In his study of racial politics in Chicago in the mid-twentieth century, Arnold Hirsch suggested that the creation of a new white identity—which supplanted earlier ethnic, religious, and class identifications—resulted from the migration of African Americans from the South.[38] In order to resist this new racial diversity, different white ethnic groups increasingly abandoned their suspicions toward each other in order to form a new, powerful defensive bloc. This process was furthermore both a grassroots phenomenon and the result of actions taken by political elites. A great deal of subsequent research has focused on the formation and maintenance of whiteness as an identity in the United States.[39]

We should also not overstate the degree to which white Americans have abandoned their ethnic attachments, even if very few whites can trace all of their ancestors to a single European country or even region. In the 1970s, whites began showing a renewed interest in ethnic origins. White interest in ethnic roots remains high, as evidenced by the popularity of genetic testing companies such as 23andme, which provide customers with genetic details based on their DNA samples.

There are different ways to interpret the reviving interest among non-Hispanic whites about their ethnic origins. There is little evidence that it results from new antipathies between whites of different ethnic backgrounds. Further, contemporary interest in their ethnic origins seems mostly superficial (taking such forms as celebrating St. Patrick's Day, for example). Sociologist Richard Alba suggested that white Americans' new interest in ethnicity was actually further evidence that ethnic differences were no longer divisive.[40] Sociologist Herbert Gans similarly argued that white ethnicity was increasingly symbolic, rather than substantive:

> As the functions of ethnic cultures and groups diminish and iden-tity becomes the primary way of being ethnic, ethnicity takes on an expressive rather than an instrumental function in people's lives, be-coming more of a leisure-time activity and losing its relevance, say, to earning a living or regulating family life. Expressive behavior can take many forms, but it is often involved in the use of symbols—and symbols as signs rather than myths. Ethnic symbols are frequently individual cultural practices which are taken from the older ethnic culture; they are "abstracted" from that culture and pulled out of its original moorings, so to speak, to become stand-ins for it.[41]

Other scholars have posited that there was a racial element to revived white interest in ethnicity. In his book *Roots Too*, Mathew Fry Jacobson argues that the civil rights movement could explain the sup-posed ethnic revival among whites.[42] Starting in the 1960s, Americans were beginning to acknowledge their nation's history of racial oppres-sion, especially against Blacks and Native Americans. Because of this change, earlier narratives of American history that celebrated pioneers settling the frontier in the spirit of manifest destiny became increasingly problematic. In its place, a new narrative was beginning to take shape. The idea of the United States as a "nation of immigrants" began rising in popularity. This new story, which emphasized Ellis Island rather than Plymouth Rock or Jamestown, allowed many whites to escape the guilt of slavery and genocide. This change in emphasis allowed whites not completely descended from colonial WASPs to deny that they or their ancestors benefited from those earlier historical events. Thus, they were immune from any sense of guilt or obligation to make amends.

This new story served an additional racial purpose. Another aspect of this narrative of the United States as a nation of immigrants was the history of discrimination against newcomers—be they Irish, Italian, or some other European group. The story of plucky immigrants who dealt with discrimination but nonetheless succeeded and enjoyed upward mobility was a useful argument against Black demands for restitution for historical grievances. It allowed whites descended from immigrants (rather than the original English settlers) to claim that their ancestors suffered similar oppression but overcame these challenges through hard work. According to this argument, the fact that Blacks had not been similarly successful suggests that they simply did not work as hard or were deficient in some other way.

In my own research, I have found that whites continue to exhibit ethnic differences in voting, but these differences have declined since the 1970s.[43] Both then and now, whites who described their ethnic background as English or German were much more likely to identify as Republicans than whites that named Ireland or a southern or eastern European country as their family's primary country of origin. These findings were consistent using both individual-level data from the General Social Survey and county-level data from the American Community Survey.

In their more recent analysis, Per Urlaub and David Huenlich argue that German Americans were Donald Trump's strongest supporters in the 2016 presidential election.[44] German Americans are still found in greatest numbers in those parts of the country that were the main destinations for German immigrants in the nineteenth century, especially the Great Lakes region. This region had long been dominated by Democrats in presidential elections, but Trump managed to flip many of these states in 2016.

Making sense of any relationship between white ethnic background and contemporary politics requires overcoming an additional challenge. Given that large-scale immigration from Europe ended in the 1920s, and the high rates of intermarriage among whites across ethnic boundaries, the percentage of whites that can trace all of their ancestors to a single European country is small. As a growing amount of research demonstrates, Americans have a propensity to align their other social identities with their politics. Given that most whites have some discretion regarding which element of their background they wish to identify with, politics may be a consideration. For example, a white conservative may want to identify with her WASP ancestors, taking pride in coming from founding stock Americans. In contrast, a white progressive, with a very similar family tree, may prefer to identify with the part of her family that derives from more recent immigrant waves and experienced discrimination and other forms of oppression.

WHY IS THE PERMANENT DEMOCRATIC MAJORITY PERPETUALLY DELAYED?

In 2004, John Judis and Ruy Teixeira published an important book, *The Emerging Democratic Majority*,[45] a title inspired by Kevin Phillips's 1969 classic *The Emerging Republican Majority*. The book convincingly argues that, just as trends in demographics and voting patterns benefited the Republican Party in the latter decades of the twentieth century, all current signs point toward a new and significant Democratic advantage. Judis and Teixeira's analysis, and that of other scholars considering similar questions, was based on an accurate reading of the data. In fact, it is hard to look at those data and reach any other conclusions.[46] The groups that tend to support the Republican Party are mostly shrinking, and the groups that tend to support the Democratic Party are mostly growing. Thanks largely to post-1965 immigration, the nonwhite population—a majority of which vote for Democrats—has grown dramatically in absolute numbers and as a percentage of the population. Several other trends also seem to benefit the Democrats, such as secularism, which has exploded since the early 1990s.[47] The Democrats have also made gains among unmarried women and professionals with a college degree. The Republicans remain primarily the party of older white married Christians in rural areas and small towns, a group that is insufficiently large to deliver an electoral majority in the long term.

Since 2004, we have seen several examples of massive Democratic victories that seemed to signify the permanent Democratic majority's arrival. The Republicans were crushed in the 2006 midterm elections when Democrats gained control of both houses of Congress and then, in 2008, took the presidency. Yet this dominance was short lived: Republicans came roaring back in 2010 on the strength of the Tea Party movement to win back the House and then take back the Senate in 2014. The unassailable Democratic majority, at least when it comes to the Electoral College, looked like it would arrive in 2016, when most pundits and scholars predicted an easy victory for Hillary Clinton. Trump's victory that year once again delayed the era of Democratic hegemony. The causes of Trump's 2020 loss are too ambiguous to be considered a major signal of renewed Democratic strength. Although Trump lost by a wide margin in the Electoral College and the popular vote, the Republican Party overall performed quite well, maintaining its hold on state legislatures and even making gains in the House of Representatives. Furthermore, Trump's loss was primarily due to his shrinking support from white men—Trump may have increased his share of the vote from women and minorities.[48]

Given its many apparent disadvantages, what accounts for the Republican Party's ability to remain competitive for so long? Some have argued that the GOP has benefited from various unfair and undemocratic practices. Gerrymandering is one obvious explanation. Both sides, of course, engage in this, but after the 2010 election, in which Republicans won big majorities in state legislatures across the country, the GOP was mostly in charge of legislative redistricting, giving them an advantage throughout the decade. Some scholars and commentators have also expressed concern that new laws designed to prevent voter fraud—such as voter ID laws—that have been passed in many states over the last two decades are really designed to suppress turnout among minorities and the poor.[49] Although critics may be right about what these laws are intended to do, the empirical evidence suggests that their effects on turnout are minimal.[50]

I should note that not all of the GOP's advantages in this regard can be ascribed to political dirty tricks. The disproportionate clout smaller states enjoy in the Electoral College, which allows the loser of the popular vote to nonetheless win the presidency, has always been present. The same is true of the U.S. Senate, where smaller, more rural states are also overrepresented based on population. It is furthermore simply harder to effectively gerrymander urban districts. Democratic gerrymandering is also more difficult because of the Voting Rights Act and its requirement that states create majority-minority districts. This does lead to more districts in which minorities have a large majority of the votes, but such districts also tend to be much more Democratic than they need to be to ensure a Democratic candidate's victory. In other words, it would be better, from the Democratic Party's perspective, if some of these minority voters were spread out across multiple districts, rather than packed tightly together.

There is another reason demographic change has not yet led to an unbeatable Democratic majority nationwide: the non-Hispanic white vote has been trending toward Republicans for many decades. According to exit polls, Trump won 57 percent of the non-Hispanic white vote in 2016.[51] This is a slight decrease in the Republican share of the white vote since 2012 when Mitt Romney is estimated to have won 59 percent of those voters.[52] However, Trump made major gains among white voters where it mattered. Winning states such as Michigan, which Obama won with relative ease, thanks to a significant increase in the Republican share of the white vote, especially whites with lower levels of education, was crucial to his victory.

The next question is why the Republican Party has seen an impressive increase in white support. Part of the explanation is, of course, the realignment of the South that began in the civil rights era, as white southerners abandoned the Democratic Party, splitting the New Deal coalition that had once been so dominant in U.S. politics. This is not the entire story, however, given that Trump's 2016 victory was largely the result of gains in the Upper Midwest.

Some scholarship suggests that whites have been moving toward the Republican Party precisely because the country is becoming more diverse. In this sense, greater white support for the GOP is itself a form of backlash against immigration and growing racial, ethnic, and religious diversity. The plausibility of this argument depends largely on how people react to growing diversity. Does increased exposure to people different from ourselves tend to make us more or less tolerant?

There are different theories arguing for both outcomes. The notion that greater exposure to people with different demographic traits leads to greater tolerance is typically called the "group contact" hypothesis. Gordon Allport's *The Nature of Prejudice* (1954) promoted an early variant of this argument.[53] The theory's premise is that groups often have unrealistic negative expectations of each other. These stereotypes result from ignorance, rather than experience. As people begin to interact with each other in meaningful ways, they learn that their earlier views were mistaken and they modify their beliefs.[54]

The "group threat" theory posits a very different outcome to growing diversity. This perspective holds that, as groups come into contact with each other, they become more likely to view themselves as being in direct competition for scarce resources (be they economic or political). V. O. Key's famous *Southern Politics in State and Nation* influenced this theory.[55] In his analysis of the South in the 1940s, he found that anti-Black prejudice was highest in those parts of the South with the largest African American population. These were the places where white supremacy was most precarious, because, if legal roadblocks to Black voting were removed, whites would no longer control the government. Whether a threat is real or imagined, the feeling of threat leads to greater prejudice and hostility across group lines.[56]

Group threat and group contact theories seem like they must necessarily be at odds—if one is correct, the other must be wrong. The two theories can coexist, however, because group contact theory does not state that it is sufficient for two groups merely to be in close proximity to each other to facilitate greater tolerance. Certain additional conditions must be met, conditions that may be hard to create. Allport, for example, argued that contact is most effective if it occurs between social equals, or if it is between people who share common goals. A meta-analysis of studies of group contact seems to confirm that contact can be an effective means of fostering tolerance.[57]

Scholars initially applied group threat theory to relations between Blacks and whites.[58] Researchers have since applied it more broadly, especially as it relates to feelings about immigrants. One common method is to see how native-born white Americans respond to a growing foreign-born population.[59] The results have been mixed: some studies show growing immigrant populations lead to more intolerance, others find the exact opposite. Scholars Yolande Pottie-Sherman and Rima Wilkes argue that the inconsistent findings are probably because different studies use different geographic units in their analysis and rely on different measures of prejudice.[60]

To date, *White Backlash*, by political scientists Marisa Abrajano and Zoltan L. Hajnal, is the most comprehensive argument that immigration has provided—at least in the short term—a boon to conservatism and the Republican Party. The authors argue that this is the case because, as regions become more diverse, whites respond by becoming less tolerant, more supportive of the Republican Party, and more conservative in their policy preferences.[61] In the short term, this means that the Democratic gains from immigration are offset by Republican gains among native-born whites. "Short term" is the key word, however. Eventually, the country will not have enough white voters to provide a victory nationwide, and the GOP will need to perform better among nonwhites in order to maintain viability.

We need to be careful not to overstate and oversimplify the relationship between white voting patterns and diversity. A look at these patterns at the state level does not show a linear relationship between diversity and white support for Republican candidates. West Virginia and Vermont are both overwhelmingly white, yet one consistently elects Republicans in statewide elections, and the other is reliably Democratic. Republicans have maintained power in Texas, despite its rapid demographic change, largely because of the overwhelming support the party receives from Texas Anglos. On the other hand, although non-Hispanic whites ceased to be a majority in California many years ago, exit polls show Trump lost to Clinton even among white Californians.[62]

WHAT EXPLAINS CONSERVATIVE OPPOSITION TO IMMIGRATION?

Although opposition to immigration is found mostly (although not entirely) on the political Right,[63] scholars disagree on the source of that opposition. Xenophobia may be a critical factor; people fear ethnic, religious, racial, or some other form of demographic change, and wish to keep outsiders away. Yet there are other possible reasons people could oppose high levels of immigration. For example, citizens may worry that an unending flow of low-skilled labor will drive down wages and further exacerbate inequalities. Economist George Borjas's research suggests this is a realistic concern.[64] One could also fear that overpopulation

will damage the country's natural environment. Immigration restrictionists of the early twentieth century were also often influential proponents
of environmental conservation.

A growing amount of scholarly literature attempts to explain the
sources of anti-immigration sentiment in the electorate. As always,
people differ in their reasons for holding certain policy preferences, but
some explanations are more common than others. When it comes to
economic anxiety and immigration issues, the evidence is mixed. There
is evidence suggesting economic concerns are a factor. Political scientists
Rafaela Dancygier and Michael Donnelly found that people working in
growing industries tended to be more supportive of immigration than
those in shrinking industries. They further found that this is especially
true during an economic downturn.[65] This finding is congruent with previous research by Kenneth F. Scheve and Matthew J. Slaughter.[66] Judith
Goldstein and Margaret Peters have also concluded that economic anxiety is associated with opposition to high levels of immigration, and that
these attitudes become more prevalent during an economic slump.[67]
Other research suggests the relationship between economics and immigration views is, at most, modest. Jens Hainmueller and Michael Hiscox found that economic self-interest was not an important predictor of
immigration attitudes.[68] This aligns with Peter Burns and James Gimpel's work showing economics has only a minor effect on these views.[69]

Although economic concerns certainly play some role, they cannot
entirely explain the restrictionist sentiments among the U.S. public.
Unsurprisingly, ethnocentrism—the preference of one's own racial or
ethnic group above others—is an important predictor of immigration
views.[70] "Social dominance orientation," a measure of one's acceptance
of inequalities and hierarchies,[71] is also associated with restrictionist attitudes.[72] Among whites, feelings of racial solidarity drive down support
for generous immigration policies.[73] Immigration attitudes can also vary
depending on the degree to which immigration is treated as a racial issue:
attitudes become a bit more restrictionist when it is presented this way.[74]
Reminding whites of their forthcoming loss of majority status in the
United States also apparently leads to greater opposition to immigration.[75]

Religion is another variable that can influence immigration attitudes,
but the relationship is not always straightforward. In part, this is because
religion is both a source of beliefs and a source of identity, and those two

traits sometimes pull people in different directions.[76] Religion may induce compassion for foreigners fleeing persecution or simply seeking a better life, but this sympathy is weaker when those foreigners possess a different religious identity.[77] Members of minority religions tend to be more pro-immigrant that those from the largest religious groups.[78] There is also evidence that prominent religious leaders who promote a pro-immigrant message are able to push public opinion in that direction.[79]

My own contribution to this discussion was to add another variable that had been mostly neglected. Most of the studies considering immigration from a group threat perspective considered "threat" from either an economic, racial, or cultural perspective. I suggested that partisan politics is another possible determinant of these attitudes. Given all of the evidence that partisan affiliation is an important element of personal identity,[80] even among people with relatively little knowledge of politics or public policy,[81] threats to one's party will trigger an emotional response. Thus, Republicans, even if they do not have high levels of racial or ethnic prejudice and they are not economically threatened by immigration, may oppose immigrants simply because they view immigrants as a growing threat to their party.

Similarly, and congruent with group contact theory, Democrats may become more pro-immigration for no other reason than that immigrants tend to vote for Democratic candidates.[82] Recall that group contact theory holds that greater contact between groups is more likely to alleviate prejudice if people view members of the other group as allies with a common goal—in this case, electing Democrats and defeating Republicans. We should therefore expect that, as Democrats realize the partisan benefits of immigration, their attitudes toward immigration and immigrants should become more positive.

In my study examining this question, I looked at how Republican and Democratic attitudes toward immigration varied depending on the local demographic context.[83] Specifically, using the 2004 National Annenberg Election Survey, I used multilevel models in which there was an interaction between individual partisanship and the size of the local immigrant population (counties were the demographic unit of analysis). The results were congruent with my expectations. In counties where the foreign-born population was very small, Republicans and Democrats differed very little in terms of their immigration policy preferences.

However, as the foreign-born population grew, these attitudes increasingly diverged, with Democrats becoming increasingly less likely than Republicans to support new immigration restrictions.

These results seem to suggest that political competition, like economic competition, can influence immigration attitudes. That study had limitations, however. Although the empirical results were aligned with my hypothesis, this phenomenon could have resulted from other causes. For example, perhaps, as the population of immigrants increases, those predisposed to exhibiting hostile feelings toward immigrants become more likely to become Republicans, but would have been Democrats if the immigrant population was small. I do not think this explanation is likely, given the stability of partisanship for most people, but my analysis could not preclude this possibility.

Further bolstering this argument, political scientist Richard Hanania has considered the same question using different methods.[84] In his preregistered survey experiment, he wanted to see how the expected party affiliations of potential refugees affected attitudes toward accepting them into the country. He also wanted to see how the effect of varying the refugees' expected party affiliation compared with varying their race. He expected that conservatives would be more welcoming toward refugees if they were told that those refugees would be likely to support the Republican Party. All respondents to his survey were told about a potential group of refugees. They learned that these refugees would be settled in Florida, and Florida's status as a swing state was emphasized. Some subjects were told that the refugees were coming from Ukraine (and thus would be considered white) and some subjects were informed the refugees would come from Venezuela (and would thus be mostly nonwhite). His survey provided subjects different information about how these refugees would likely vote if they eventually became citizens. To one group of subjects, he said they would likely vote Democratic. Others were informed that they would likely vote Republican. Finally, he allowed the refugees to vary according to skill level. Refugees were presented as either "likely to be low skilled and depend on government assistance or work in lower earning jobs," or "likely to be highly skilled and work in white collar, higher earning jobs." He then asked respondents how strongly they would favor letting in the refugees, on a six-point scale. As expected, he found that conservatives were more likely to favor immigrants if they are told that they are highly skilled. However, varying the country of the origin of the refugee group had no direct effect on conservatives' likelihood to support their admission to the country.

The study's most important finding was that the expected party identification of refugees had an effect on both conservatives and liberals. Whereas conservatives were more supportive of refugees they thought would vote Republican, this same information made liberals less supportive of their admittance. This provides further evidence that partisanship can be a factor in how Americans think about immigration. To say that Republicans tend to be anti-immigration because they are xenophobic, or Democrats favor it because it they are tolerant, does not capture the entire story. Partisan self-interest also seems to be an important variable. That being the case, if the situation were reversed, and immigrants were, on average, more Republican than Democratic, I would expect Democrats to be less pro-immigration. They would, of course, not frame it in explicitly partisan terms, and one could easily come up with a progressive justification for immigration restrictions— the desire to keep wages from falling too low, for example.

ARE MOST IMMIGRANTS DEMOCRATS BECAUSE OF THE IMMIGRATION ISSUE?

I suggested that immigrant voting patterns are one reason (among many) why Republicans are skeptical of large-scale immigration. At a time of widespread affective polarization, any policy that appears to give a major, and seemingly permanent, advantage to one political party will be opposed by supporters of the other party, regardless of that policy's other merits. The subsequent question, then, is why immigrants and their immediate descendants tend to favor Democrats over Republicans.

Although we now mostly take it for granted that post-1965 immigrants and their children tend to lean toward the left, at least when it comes to voting, this was not always the case. Not long ago, Hispanics especially were described as "natural Republicans," who could be persuaded to support the Republican Party in large numbers if the party invested in proper outreach. These arguments were especially common after the 2004 presidential election, when George W. Bush may have earned as much as 40 percent of the Hispanic vote. This relatively impressive showing, however, was not a harbinger of a major realignment. As political scientists Rudolfo de la Garza and Jeronimo Cortina showed, Bush's relatively strong performance in 2004 was not associated with a shift in Hispanic party affiliation: the good feelings many of Bush's new Latino voters had for the president were not, it seems, transferred to the Republican Party overall.[85]

Aside from Bush's relatively strong performance in 2004—the last election in which a Republican presidential candidate won the popular vote since 1988—there were other reasons to think Latinos and other groups we tend to associate with post-1965 immigration could be a swing constituency. For example, we can expect immigrants to have weaker partisan attachments than native-born Americans. Early socialization is one important determinant of party identification.[86] Our initial exposure to politics often comes from parents, who tend to pass on party affiliation to their children. Immigrants who arrive in the United States as adults will not have had this socialization experience, and thus will follow a different process for determining their initial partisan leanings.[87]

Republicans were additionally optimistic about their chances to make gains among immigrants and the children of immigrants because of the purported social conservatism of these groups. Pro-immigration conservatives often praised Hispanic family values,[88] which would translate into support for social conservatism. There is a certain irony to this line of reasoning. The notion that immigrants from majority Catholic countries derive their politics from their faith, taking policy preferences directly from the Vatican, was a major reason nativists *opposed* such immigration in the nineteenth century. Now, this stereotype is cited as a reason conservatives should favor these immigrants.

Despite reasons for optimism, Republicans have not been able to build on the gains they made in 2004. In every presidential election since that time, the GOP has consistently lost among Latinos and Asian Americans (native-born or immigrant) by landslide margins. The question, of course, is why this is the case. The most common answer is that immigrants do not find the Republican Party appealing because they believe, often for good reason, that the Republican Party does not want them in the country. The party that makes earning citizenship more difficult, rather than less, will always be viewed in a less favorable light by recent immigrants.

The children and grandchildren of immigrants will likely have a similar perspective. Although they became U.S. citizens at birth, their family had direct knowledge of the immigrant experience, and they are furthermore more likely to know people at risk of deportation. We may thus reasonably suspect that a large number of immigrants are single-issue voters, who will support whichever party is more pro-immigration.

This of course presents an easy solution to the Republican Party's demographic problem: simply change immigration policies, drop the nativist rhetoric, and the party will soon appeal to these new voters. Leading Republicans such as former Florida governor Jeb Bush have made this argument.[89] Linda Chavez has suggested that a concerted outreach campaign, showing genuine interest in immigrant well-being, could reverse the party's losses in communities containing many immigrants:

> Here's a radical suggestion—but one that wouldn't compromise Republican or conservative principles. Why doesn't the Republican Party launch an aggressive Welcome to America Campaign? The idea would be to set up a network of volunteers to reach out to Hispanic immigrants, and especially their American-born children, to teach English, American history and civics. Estimates are that four in 10 Hispanic voters in this year's election were naturalized citizens—and 75 percent of them cast their votes for President-elect Barack Obama.
>
> But what if those new Americans had been helped to become U.S. citizens by local volunteers from the Federation of Republican Women, the Republican Men's Club or the local Republican central committee? What if Republican volunteers approached employers in their area and offered to set up English classes during lunch breaks or after work for immigrant workers, or distributed DVDs and videos with language and civics instruction? This type of volunteerism has been ceded to Democrat-leaning groups over the years. Is it any wonder that when these new citizens register to vote, their instinct is to support the party that they've come to know firsthand?[90]

There is some polling data suggesting that a more pro-immigrant stance from the Republican Party could result in new voters for the party. In a 2012 study, political scientists Matt Barreto and Gary Segura found that 44 percent of Latino voters said they would be more likely to support a Republican candidate if that candidate supported comprehensive immigration reforms that would provide a pathway to citizenship. The same study showed that 42 percent of Latinos, including 33 percent of Latino Republicans, would be less likely to support the Republican Party if it continued to block immigration reform efforts that provided a way for the undocumented to earn citizenship.[91]

There are reasons to be skeptical of this argument, however. One common narrative, which supposedly demonstrates the disastrous political consequences of Republican nativism, is that Latinos were a swing vote in California before the Republican Party of California took a hard nativist turn in the 1990s, supporting divisive policies such as Proposition 187. If the Republican Party had chosen a different path during those years, it could have remained competitive in that state, even in the face of demographic change. Although this story seems plausible, political scientists Iris Hui and David Sears have published work suggesting it is not quite accurate.[92] Looking at Latino vote choice before and after the struggles over Proposition 187 and similar policies, they could discern only a modest effect on Latino voting patterns. The Republican Party did not make new gains among Latinos in the 1988 election, even though a Republican president, with the help of a Republican majority in the U.S. Senate, passed an immigration law that provided amnesty. All evidence suggests that immigrants and the descendants of immigrants are not all single-issue voters on immigration, and it is likely that a majority of these voters will continue to support the Democratic Party even if Republicans become more pro-immigrant.

IMMIGRATION AND STRANGE POLITICAL BEDFELLOWS

The political coalitions around immigration have been consistent for some time, which is why many people may forget that different interest groups have previously held very different views on the subject. Immigration policy debates have always involved coalitions that cut across partisan divides. For now, however, the political coalition in favor of generous immigration policies has certain key advantages over their restrictionist opponents, making sweeping restrictionist policies difficult to implement.

In the past, a number of groups we traditionally think of as part of the Left were strongly in favor of tight immigration restrictions. Labor unions in the mid-twentieth century mostly favored maintaining strict limitations on immigration. From the standpoint of supply and demand, it seems intuitive that lower levels of immigration would lead to higher wages for workers, as businesses would need to compete with each other for labor. Unions feared immigrants could serve as strikebreakers. For the first half of the century, the American Federation of Labor (AFL) was strongly opposed to loosening U.S. immigration laws.

The labor movement did not maintain its restrictionist stance for long in the postwar years, however. A particularly important moment came when the restrictionist AFL merged with the more progressive Council of Industrial Organizations (CIO), creating the AFL-CIO in 1955.[93] The CIO had long supported dismantling the quota system that had limited immigration since the 1920s. This new, larger organization was strongly pro-immigrant, creating a powerful new member of the political coalition in favor of liberalizing reforms. Unions have both principled and practical purposes for supporting generous immigration policies. On the principled front, this fits with the broader progressive agenda of the modern labor movement. Practically speaking, immigrants represent a new potential source of members (and dues) for many unions, which is important given the long-term, steady decline in union membership over the last several decades.

Leaders and organizations focused on African American rights and economic uplift have also, at times, been divided on the immigration question. On average, African Americans have had higher levels of economic insecurity and lower levels of educational attainment, leading some to argue that high levels of immigration have had a negative effect on Black American workers.[94] For a time, groups such as the National Association for the Advancement of Colored People (NAACP) favored new legislation to curb undocumented immigrants, especially sanctions on employers that took advantage of illegal labor.[95] Leading African American civil rights groups have not subsequently maintained this position, however, and instead have focused on building alliances with Hispanic groups over their shared interests.

Environmental groups have also been inconsistent on this issue over time. Several decades ago, organizations such as the Sierra Club favored immigration restrictions to slow population growth in the United States and thus better safeguard natural resources and open spaces.[96] The Sierra Club has since abandoned this position and is now an actively pro-immigrant organization.[97] One can still find a few environmental groups that remain skeptical of large-scale immigration, but they are small and marginalized.

The pro-immigration camp also benefits from support from groups more typically found on the political Right. Business interests have strong reasons to maintain a steady flow of immigrants, for the same reasons important labor unions once opposed such a policy.[98] The leadership of the Roman Catholic Church in the United States has also always been pro-immigration. Major Protestant organizations have similarly expressed support for generous immigration policies. Even the leadership of the Southern Baptist Convention, still considered the quintessential conservative evangelical denomination in the United States, has offered unequivocal support for a "pathway to legal status" for undocumented immigrants and has stated that "any form of nativism, mistreatment, or exploitation is inconsistent with the gospel of Jesus Christ."[99]

Reflecting the diverse attitudes of their own political coalition, the Republican Party and the conservative movement have also been historically divided on the immigration question. The pro-business wing of the conservative intellectual movement has been consistent in its enthusiasm for immigrants since the 1980s.[100] The neoconservative wing of the conservative intellectual movement has also historically been pro-immigrant, or, if that wording is too strong, it has been generally opposed to transparent nativism.

As a result of this, there are comparatively few organized groups pursuing nativist immigration policies. There are nonprofit groups that support restrictionist policies, such as the Center for Immigration Studies and NumbersUSA, but, in terms of their resources, they are dwarfed by pro-immigration groups and lobbyists when it comes to funding and organization. This disconnect extends from the national to the local level. In the latter case, pro-immigrant groups tend to be more organized and effective than local anti-immigrant groups—in the rare cases when nativists form real-world local groups at all.[101]

Nativists have had one important advantage in the immigration debate: public opinion. Historically, immigration policy has been much more expansionist than majorities of the public would prefer.[102] These voters are occasionally able to make waves, such as when a restrictionist immigration policy or candidate is on the ballot. Given the basic logic of democracy, there should be a connection between public preferences and policy outcomes. This has generally not been the case with immigration, however, for many reasons. First, public opinion is important, but in U.S.-style representative democracy, organized groups are critical.[103] For many years, pro-immigrant groups have been much better organized than their opponents. Some of the pro-immigration advantage can be explained by money—there are few powerful, wealthy interests eager to fund the cause of immigration restrictions. However, aside from that advantage, the pro-immigration side of the divide clearly enjoys more motivated and energetic grassroots activists committed to their cause. In contrast, although a large number of Americans may think immigration numbers are too high, comparatively few are willing to march in the streets or call their U.S. senators or representatives to demand immigration cuts. Nor do we see large numbers of native-born Americans organizing boycotts of industries that rely on undocumented immigrant labor or those that lay off native-born workers in favor of cheaper workers in the country on H1B visas. Many Americans may bristle at large-scale immigration, but few make a concerted, organized effort to force political elites to listen to their concerns.

DOES POLITICAL CULTURE SURVIVE DEMOGRAPHIC CHANGE?

The mainstream conservative position on demographic change is that the changing ethnic or racial makeup of the country ultimately does not matter, as long as the transition is orderly and new arrivals assimilate. But assimilate into what? Again, the general conservative response is that they should adopt the English language and, importantly, the nation's political norms. Ben Shapiro has stated this in very straightforward language: "I don't give a good damn about the so-called 'browning of America.' Color doesn't matter. Ideology does."[104] Shapiro has additionally stated that "conservatives must indeed root out and destroy any elements of race-driven policy from its midst."[105] Even if one accepts that Shapiro is being completely honest in this statement, and he is genuinely indifferent to demographic change as such, one might still have a problem with this argument. It seems to imply an ideological litmus test to immigration, one that will only accept immigrants that are at least receptive to his brand of conservatism.

There is an additional problem to considering ideology an important variable when thinking about immigrants. Ideological constraints are relatively rare in the electorate. Most people simply do not possess an internally coherent political worldview. But perhaps there is a way to think about this subject that will get at the same subject, yet keep us grounded on relevant scholarship. Perhaps, instead of thinking about ideology, we can focus on "political culture," which is an established concept in political science, albeit a sometimes controversial one.[106] We can define political culture as follows: "[Political culture is] the set of attitudes, beliefs and sentiments which give order and meaning to a political process and which provide the underlying assumptions and rules that govern behavior in the political system. It encompasses both the political ideals and operating norms of a polity. Political culture is thus the manifestation in aggregate form of the psychological and subjective dimensions of politics."[107]

When working with this concept, it is possible to have a coherent discussion about immigration and assimilation that does not inevitably devolve into racialism. That is, one could reasonably argue that if immigration rates are sufficiently large, and the immigrants come from a sufficiently different political culture, a nation's political culture could change in dramatic ways that native-born citizens oppose. This could apply to immigrants sharing the same racial categorization as the receiving country.

Nonetheless, we should not simply take it for granted that immigrants will fundamentally change a nation's political culture. Several influential scholars have argued that a region's political culture tends to persist, even in the face of demographic change. Wilbur Zelinsky made this argument in *The Cultural Geography of the United States* (1973).[108] Zelinsky developed the "doctrine of first effective settlement." According to this argument, "variations in the cultures of the people that dominated the first settlement and the cultural traits developed by people in the formative period" can explain a region's political culture over time, even as it absorbs newcomers who initially possessed different cultural traits.[109]

From this literature scholars developed another key point: the United States does not have a single political culture. It has always had many different political cultures, all with deep roots, which are at times in tension with one another. Political scientist Daniel Elazar, for example, applied these ideas to the United States.[110] Elazar argued that there are three distinct political cultures in the United States: individualistic, moralistic, and traditional. The individualistic political culture dominates in the mid-Atlantic states, the region that initially had a strong Quaker influence, and also comparatively high levels of religious and ethnic diversity. This political culture tends to view society mostly as an economic market, and thus supports a more limited role for the government. The moralistic political culture is centered on New England, and it was developed by the initial Puritan settlers to the region. This political culture is more inclined to believe in a "common good" that can be promoted by an active government. The traditionalistic political culture, centered in the South, believes that the government should help protect established hierarchies.

The roots of these political cultures extend to the other side of the Atlantic Ocean. That is, many of the cultural and political norms that took root in colonial America can be traced back to specific regions of England. This was David Hackett Fischer's argument in *Albion's Seed* (1989).[111] Fischer argued that the mores of New England, many of which still exist today, were transplants from the East Anglia region of England. Similarly, the culture established by the Scots-Irish in Appalachia and elsewhere was already developed among the people on English-Scottish border and in Northern Ireland where these migrants initially came from. Although their environment changed, their culture remained intact in important ways. Collin Woodard expanded on these ideas in *American Nations* (2011).[112]

As is often the case, there are several different ways we could interpret this scholarship. We could note that United States has never had a single, unified political culture. We have managed to get by as a society with many regional political cultures in a federal system. Thus, adding people with different views does not change things very much. Furthermore, the theory of first effective settlement suggests that newcomers to various regions will not ultimately change the nation's culture beyond recognition. However, the theory that the first settlers to a region determine its culture indefinitely seems at odds with the recent historical record. In the postwar years, Southern California was the center of the rising conservative movement. That is no longer the case, and changing demographics are certainly part of the explanation. We can and should make a distinction between partisan leanings and political culture, but even with that caveat, we can reasonably say that California was changed by the newcomers.

Some influential scholars have argued that immigration represents a threat to American political culture. The most recent famous example of this is the late Samuel Huntington, whose final book, *Who Are We?* (2004), argued that the United States does have a distinct and mostly unified political culture, and large-scale, long-lasting immigration—especially from Latin America—threatens that culture.[113] Waves of immigration have added diversity to American life, yet a recognizable culture has remained intact throughout U.S. history. According to Huntington, "the central elements of that culture can be defined in a variety of ways but include the Christian religion, Protestant values and moralism, a strong work ethic, the English language, British traditions of law, justice, and the limits of government power, and a legacy of European art, literature, philosophy, and music."[114] One reason these cultural attributes have remained intact despite widespread immigration is that, until recently, "it was Anglo-Protestant culture and the political liberties and economic opportunities it produced that attracted them to America."[115]

The problem, in Huntington's view, was that contemporary immigration to the United States is qualitatively different from previous periods of large-scale immigration. Although the United States had successfully incorporated large waves of immigrants, this was only possible because "immigrants were subjected to intense programs of Americanization to assimilate them into American society."[116] Today, elites have not just abandoned efforts to assimilate newcomers, they actively seek to undermine what remains of the nation's cultural unity. These elites, whom Huntington labeled "deconstructionists," had many reasons to justify these efforts, but broadly speaking they believed that America's Eurocentric culture was oppressive and responsible for historical atrocities. This effort to deconstruct the nation's national identity was, in Huntington's view, so successful because it was backed by so many of the nation's most important elites—in media, government, academia, and big business.[117]

There are additional arguments that U.S. political culture is more threatened by contemporary immigration than it was in earlier periods. There is, of course, the ethnocentric argument that Europeans have always been easier to incorporate into mainstream American life. Such arguments are often built on crude racism. There are other means by which one could reach a similar conclusion, however. To return to Huntington, he argued that immigration from Latin America was uniquely challenging for several reasons. For example, the fact that Mexico and the United States share a border is a significant difference.[118] Although we should not downplay the many hardships immigrants, especially undocumented immigrants, endure to enter the United States, crossing the Rio Grande today is a less daunting challenge than crossing the Atlantic Ocean in the nineteenth century. Greater geographic distances furthermore made it harder for earlier immigrant groups to remain culturally connected to the countries of their birth. The persistence and the scale of the immigration from a single region is also a way in which today's immigration differs from that of earlier periods. Large-scale immigration from Latin America, especially Mexico, has been consistent for many decades. Huntington worried that this remarkable movement of people would inevitably and fundamentally alter American culture: "Important portions of the country become predominantly Hispanic in language and culture, and the nation as a whole becomes bilingual and bicultural."[119]

THE CONTESTED MEANING OF AMERICA

Discussions of American political culture and its resilience in the face of demographic change have an additional challenge. There is no consensus in the United States about what the American political culture is or whether it deserves defending. Even conservatives are split on the meaning of the United States. This question has special urgency. The United States is currently engaged in a contentious debate about statues honoring elements of its history many view as shameful. At first, this was primarily focused on statues dedicated to Confederate leaders and to Christopher Columbus, but this recently shifted to the Founding Fathers, especially those who owned slaves—Washington and Jefferson being two prominent examples. Even statues of Abraham Lincoln have come down in the name of racial sensitivity.[120]

In a previous book, I noted that the Left and the extreme Right often approach the U.S. founding in a similar manner.[121] Both tend to argue that the United States was tainted by racism from the beginning. This view holds that, whatever high-minded rhetoric we see in the Declaration of Independence, the inescapable fact is that the slaveowning Jefferson did not really believe that "all men are created equal," nor did most of the men who singed their names to his document. The Left and the extreme Right disagree, of course, on how we should interpret this fact. The racist Right would say that the Founding Fathers got it right the first time (but few on the extreme Right today endorse slavery), whereas the Left argues that the men who created the United States as a political entity do not deserve the veneration they have received.

Parts of the Left now push this narrative about America more aggressively than ever. In 2019, in recognition of the 400th anniversary of slavery's introduction into North America, the New York Times launched the 1619 Project, which "aims to reframe the country's history by placing the consequences of slavery and the contributions of Black Americans at the very center of our national narrative."[122] According to this view, few institutions or historical developments in American history are not connected in some way to slavery and related forms of racial oppression. This project has been lauded by many on the left, who argue that Americans have downplayed the historical significance of slavery and its contemporary consequences. Some historians, including progressive historians, have challenged the project, however. Gordon Wood, for example, argues that many of the essays associated with the project make dubious claims about slavery and its role in the American Revolution.[123]

Conservatives typically hold a laudatory view of the American Revolution and the men who led it, with a few important caveats. Most notably, conservatives today acknowledge the problem that slavery poses to a straightforward narrative about the Revolution representing a triumph of enlightened, egalitarian values. They nonetheless hold that America's successful war for independence represented an important step forward for these values, and that the most important Founding Fathers sincerely believed in them. Slavery was allowed to continue, according to this argument, because of pragmatic concerns: the states most dependent on slave labor would not remain in the national union if their "peculiar institution" was threatened. Furthermore, at the end of the eighteenth century, most Americans assumed that slavery was going to die as an institution anyway, thus it made little sense to threaten the national project over the issue.

CONCLUSION

The conservative movement has never had a shared and consistent approach to immigration. These divisions have hindered the ability of conservative intellectuals and conservative elected officials to present a coherent approach to this subject. The free market and the traditionalist elements of conservatism have typically been at odds on this question. The elites that provide critical funding to election campaigns and conservative institutions are also often at odds with conservatives in the electorate, who tend to support restrictionist policies.

The 2020 election provided surprisingly few hints about the future of the immigration policy or the conservative approach to immigration. Although it was arguably Trump's signature issue when he ran in 2016, he said relatively little about it during his reelection campaign. Joe Biden similarly did not make immigration a central element of his successful campaign. Supporters of less restrictive policies had hoped Trump's defeat would signal the decline of Republican nativism, yet the results have been ambiguous. It is conventional wisdom that Republicans performed poorly among Hispanic voters because of the party's reputation for nativism. Yet, according to exit polls, Trump performed unusually well among Hispanic voters in 2020. The idea that Hispanics are all single-issue immigration voters is clearly mistaken. Even so, future Republicans will likely want to expand on the gains the party seemed to make among Latino voters in the 2020 elections. This may discourage future candidates from pursuing the same aggressive nativist platform that Trump relied upon in 2016.

In any event, immigration, at least from Latin America, is unlikely to remain the hot-button issue it has been for many decades simply because immigration from that region is likely to decrease. Latin America's long-term demographic trajectory does not suggest it will continue to be a source of future immigration the way it was in the last years of the twentieth century. Birthrates in most countries in the Western Hemisphere have been on a long-term decline. Countries neighboring the United States are undergoing demographic transition, with aging populations; older people are less likely to emigrate than younger people. The concerns expressed by restrictionists such as Huntington about revanchist Mexican immigrants eager to reconquer the U.S. Southwest appear less plausible than ever. Indeed, at present they seem ridiculous.

Current debates about the nature of American identity will likely continue. Now that Trump is out of office, will much of the Left continue to push the narrative of the United States as an irredeemably racist country? If they do, will that message resonate with many voters? As the twenty-first century progresses, will a recognizable American political culture survive? Does it matter? Will elections become demographic headcounts? These are among the most pressing political questions of the coming years. Their answers will determine the likelihood of future conservative political success.

SEVEN

Partisan Politics as Identity Politics by Another Name

Modern American conservatives declare that their commitments are to principles, not to group identities. Ramesh Ponnuru wrote in the pages of *National Review*: "Conservatives tend to place a lot of emphasis, maybe too much, on the idea that ideas have consequences. They hoist their ideas up a flagpole and see who salutes."[1] These ideas are not set in stone, but, broadly speaking, mainstream American conservatives are united behind the principles of limited government intervention in the economy, traditional values, and a strong national defense. Creating a coherent philosophy out of these disparate ideas was a difficult task, but it has worked reasonably well to keep the centrifugal forces on the right in check for several decades. Beyond the basic premises of fusionism, conservatives also emphasize the importance of constitutional government, federalism, and a Burkean approach to political and cultural change. That is, change over time is necessary, but it must occur at an incremental pace, and with respect for tradition.

Yet the notion that conservatism is about abstract ideas has been challenged in recent years, at least if we are talking about conservatives in the electorate. The notion that conservatives, in contrast to the Left and the Far Right, are united by ideals rather than tribalism became increasingly untenable during the 2016 presidential election and the years of the Trump administration. It turned out that most Republican voters were not deeply committed to conservative values per se, and were willing to provide unwavering support to a Republican president personally indifferent to those values. Some conservatives have acknowledged this, noting with concern that many self-described conservatives seem to be following the siren song of identity politics.

As we've seen in previous chapters, identity politics on the right is not a new phenomenon. Self-described conservatives have engaged in it for decades. Many on the left make this point, suggesting that conservatives engage in their own forms of identity politics, but with perhaps a bit more subtlety. That is, they use coded language to activate racial or other anxieties among white voters—so-called dog whistle politics. I do not ascribe that much cynicism to the typical political professional working in the Republican Party or one of the major organs of the conservative movement. Some of the things called racist dog whistles are genuinely not viewed as racial by many conservatives.

This chapter considers the question of identity politics and conservatism from a different perspective. I will discuss the latest research on the nature of partisan politics, noting the increasingly compelling evidence that Americans' party preferences have become a kind of tribal identity, often disconnected from public policy outcomes. Put another way, some of the people conservatives view as immune to identity politics—people who define themselves politically according to their party or ideology—are simply practicing identity politics under another guise. This new form of identity politics furthermore may represent a unique challenge to American democracy.

OTHER MODELS OF PARTY IDENTIFICATION AND IDEOLOGY

There is not a formal "conservative theory of party identification." Not all conservatives subscribe to identical theories on this subject, and many have probably not given it much thought. Nonetheless, because many conservatives have made similar arguments, we can make some generalizations. Leading conservatives such as Ben Shapiro consistently emphasize the importance of dispassionate reasoning when it comes to politics. According to this view, political attitudes should result from a clear-eyed, rational examination of the world. If everyone used this kind of utilitarian calculus, this thinking goes, conservatism would immediately dominate American political life. The fact that conservatism is not dominant, despite the (supposedly) strong empirical evidence of its superiority to progressivism, is evidence that many people fail to live up to this standard. Or, if they are living up to that standard, liberal voters are taking a short-sighted or selfish view. That is, progressive voters support the party of economic redistribution because it will lead them to personally enjoy new government largess, at the expense of the economic dynamism needed to keep the country strong. According to conservatives, such voters are sacrificing long-term opportunity, and thus their own long-term economic prospects, for the sake of immediate, unearned gains. Although conservatives disagree with voters who endorse these kinds of progressive policies, the theory nonetheless contends that policy preferences are the root of vote choice.

From this perspective, voters behave in a manner analogous to Anthony Downs's model in *An Economic Theory of Democracy* (1957).[2] In this model of voting, policy is the only thing that matters to the electorate; indeed, to base a vote on anything other than policy is irrational and thus not considered in Downs's model. According to this model, every individual has expectations about how changes in public policy will influence his or her life. We survey the array of policies that could be influenced by an election result and determine our preferred bundle of policies. We look at the available candidates and discern which candidate will enact the policies most aligned with our own preferences.

This model does not seem to leave much room for ideologies and political parties. However, it also recognizes that rational people may not spend very much time thinking about politics. Given the low likelihood that any single individual's vote will change an election outcome, it makes little sense to invest a huge amount of time and cognitive effort into studying the many issues at stake in any given election. We instead can turn to political parties as a useful heuristic. We have a general sense of where each party stands on the political spectrum and can predict how any candidate representing a party on the ballot will behave once in office. This perspective allows politics to remain entirely about policy outcomes, while still allowing for a population that has relatively little knowledge of or interest in politics—a model that assumed high levels of political sophistication from the electorate could be immediately dismissed, given the strong empirical evidence suggesting otherwise.

This idea, which suggests politics is (or should be) a process of rational efforts to enhance personal utility through public policy, has supporters on the right, even if few put it in such blunt terms. This is not the only lens that conservatives have used to examine politics, however. Some conservatives make the case that political divides really are about fundamentally different views of the world. As I mentioned in chapter 1, Thomas Sowell has argued that the political divide is characterized by different attitudes toward human nature. Those who have an unconstrained view of human potential (progressives), perhaps even believing in human perfectibility, fall on one side, whereas those who accept that there is a fixed and fallible human nature (conservatives), which must be managed via prudent checks on human weaknesses, fall on the other.

Other scholars have advanced a related argument. This perspective is more fully developed by James Davison Hunter in *Culture War* (1992).[3] According to Hunter's view, political disputes in the contemporary United States represent, at their root, a religious divide. That is, modern liberalism and modern conservatism are built upon fundamentally different and opposed views about the nature of reality. In one camp you find those described as "progressive" by Hunter. In this formulation, progressives are people that believe that values are human creations, and as such they can change. In contrast to progressives, Hunter describes the "orthodox." These are people that believe that values are not mere social constructions because they have a religious dimension and are not subject to human manipulation.

According to Hunter's view, most of U.S. political history has been defined by disagreements among various factions of orthodoxy. That is, most people held an orthodox view of the world, but they disagreed on the specifics—Catholics had different views from all Protestants, different Protestant groups disagreed with each other. In the twentieth century, however, this began to change. The progressive worldview was gaining ground. By the 1990s, the political battle lines were primarily between the progressive and the orthodox camp. In the face of growing progressive strength, the different varieties of orthodoxy formed a new coalition. Catholics and Protestants put their differences aside to focus on their shared opposition to secular progressives.

Both the rational choice perspective, which holds voters are rational utility calculators focused on policies, and the theory that political struggle is, at its core, a struggle between different worldviews, can appeal to conservatives of various sensibilities. Although different from each other, both views are individualistic in nature. Both views also assume a certain level of intellectual sophistication on the part of voters. I am not arguing that all conservatives believe one of the above models perfectly describes the electorate, but neither theory challenges important aspects of center-right thinking.

Although not part of the original models, the rational choice perspective on party identification is not rendered moot by identity politics. Identitarian considerations can be incorporated into such models, it just requires relaxing some of Downs's restrictions. Stephen Ansolabehere and M. Socorro Puy, for example, have developed a "general model that accommodates identity as well as positional issues."[4] They note that this leads to different outcomes than one would expect in a model that is focused entirely on policy preferences. They then conducted an empirical analysis using results from elections among Basques (an ethnic minority) in Spain, finding that "Euskera speakers and others who identify with the culture, vote in line with that identity, above and beyond their preferences about regional autonomy, and quite apart from the usual left–right division common to most European political systems."[5]

Political scientists have also convincingly argued that the actual performance of political parties can influence vote choice. In *Retrospective Voting in American National Elections* (1981), Morris Fiorina suggested a model that could incorporate various perspectives.[6] Although party identification holds mostly steady for most people during normal periods, it is not set in stone. People notice when their lives improve or get worse, and notice which party is in control. In Fiorina's words, they maintain a "running tally" of party performance. As they absorb new information over time, they reevaluate their partisan loyalties. Nonetheless, it is important to contemplate why party identification has such a strong hold on us, even in the absence of evidence that our parties successfully better our lives when they are in power.

PARTISANSHIP AS DOWNSTREAM FROM SOCIAL IDENTITY

Angus Campbell and coauthors, in *The American Voter* (1960), among the most influential books on political behavior ever written, suggested that parental influence and other forms of early socialization play key roles in the formation of partisan identities.[7] Our parents and other important authority figures introduce us to politics and have a formative influence on our political identities. This of course does not entirely explain partisan affiliation. In their important book on this subject, *Partisan Hearts and Minds*, Donald Green, Bradley Palmquist, and Eric Schickler argued for the centrality of social identities to party identification.[8] This model is useful because it allows for people to have very strong partisan identities without also having well-formed opinions about public policy. In fact, this perspective allows people to have strong opinions about political parties while being almost entirely ignorant of what politicians are doing.

The political science literature arguing this viewpoint was influenced by Henri Tajfel and his colleagues. Tajfel is best remembered for his theories about social identities and group behavior. Our self-esteem is tied to our group memberships, and we seek to maintain this self-esteem by comparing our in-group to out-groups.[9] One of this theory's innovations was that it allowed for group conflict and hostility even in the absence of competition over scarce resources. Group status can be its own reward, even when nothing material or substantive is at stake.

According to this perspective, as we begin to think about politics, we note the kind of people we are (or the kind of people we aspire to be). We all already have racial, ethnic, linguistic, gender, sexual, generational, class, educational, occupational, and regional identities. Each of us places different values on these different elements of our identities. Some may place a higher value on their religion than their class. For some, race overrules all other considerations. Others may primarily think of themselves as upper class, regardless of their objective economic circumstances, and some may identify with the poor, even if they are not personally poor. Having unconsciously taken this survey of ourselves, we discern which political party is typically associated with "people like us." A middle-class, white, heterosexual, married, evangelical man without a college degree in the rural South from the Baby Boom generation has little difficulty discerning that, of the two major parties, the Republican Party is most closely aligned with people like him. In contrast, a young, secular, urban, gay, unmarried Latina, with a graduate degree but not a high income in California will be similarly aware that the Democratic Party is associated with her major group identities. These are obviously extreme examples, in which every major element of their identities are associated with a particular party. Many people have aspects of self-identification that are not consistently associated with a single political party. However, in such cases we individually know which elements of our personal identity we consider preeminent to our sense of self. These are likely to be the definitive characteristics when it comes to choosing a party. The authors of *Partisan Hearts and Minds* put it this way:

> Our thesis is that partisan identities reflect a blend of cognition and affect. People know who they are and where they fit in the matrix of prominent social groups. Citizens' group attachments shape the way that they evaluate political candidates and the policies they espouse. These evaluations change as new information becomes available, but seldom does the political environment change in ways that alter how people think of themselves or their relationship to significant social groups. For this reason, voters' attachments may remain firm even as their voting preferences shift. Thus, the basic structure of electoral competition remains intact even as the personae and policies that dominate politics change.[10]

Having established a partisan identity, our next step as politically interested citizens is discerning which ideology is associated with our party. Because one identifies as a Democrat or Republican, one subsequently identifies ideologically with progressivism or conservatism. A person may do this even if he or she has no idea what those terms mean in a philosophical sense and has no clue what policies are downstream from either ideological position. If people continue to learn about politics, they discover which policies are associated with their ideologies and political party, and adopt those preferences. It's worth noting that many people do not take that last step, and despite having very strong attachments to political parties, and even describing themselves in ideological terms, their stated public policy preferences indicate very limited ideological thinking.

We further now know that partisans' policy preferences can be swayed with relative ease by informing them of their party's stance on issues. Geoffrey Cohen demonstrated this with a series of experiments. He showed that, when subjects were shown information about a public policy, their attitudes toward it were shaped by which party favored it. When they were given no information about where their political parties stood on the issue, they used their own judgment to determine their view of the policy. However, when the subjects were informed of their party's view on the policy, "participants assumed that position as their own, regardless of the content of the policy."[11] Subsequent research has only reinforced this conclusion.[12]

Other research has provided additional evidence that Americans' policy preferences are often downstream from partisan loyalties. Gabriel Lenz, for example, has shown that voters will, at times, shift their policy views to align them with those of a party leader.[13] In a recent experiment, Michael Barber and Jeremy Pope found evidence for something observers of the 2016 presidential election already suspected: Donald Trump's supporters took policy cues from Trump.[14] When told that the president had adopted a policy position—including a position that is generally considered liberal—Trump supporters adopted that position as their own. Beyond suggesting that partisans can shift their policy preferences according to partisan cues, this research further suggests that we should be even more suspicious of voters' claims to have a coherent ideology. According to Barber and Pope, "Self-described ideological conservatives were very quick to respond to the treatment of liberal Trump cues, moving an average of 12 points in a liberal direction across the issues."[15]

One might raise a reasonable objection at this point. Assuming this is true, why is the electorate now more ideologically sorted into political parties than in the past? That is, why is it that most people who call themselves conservatives now identify with the Republican Party, and most people who call themselves liberal or progressives identify with the Democratic Party, when just a few decades ago you could find plenty of conservative Democrats and liberal Republicans? One answer is that political and cultural elites are now giving more consistent cues to average Americans. The old conservative Democrats in the South and the liberal Republicans in New England have mostly left the political scene.[16] As political scientist Matthew Levendusky put it, "Elite Democrats are now almost all liberals and elite Republicans are almost all conservatives, with very little ideological overlap between the parties."[17] It is now therefore easier for ordinary people to align their ideology with their parties.

PARTISANSHIP AS AN IDENTITY

For more than a decade, one of the most well-known disputes in U.S. politics has been over whether the American public actually is polarized when it comes to politics. Scholars such as Fiorina have argued that polarization in the electorate is a myth. In fact, according to Fiorina and his colleagues, claims about a polarized public "range from simple exaggeration to sheer nonsense."[18] In *Culture War? The Myth of a Polarized America* (2005), they provided public opinion information across a wide variety of issues. They found that even on the most contentious issues of policy, Americans tend toward moderate views, and the gap between Republicans and Democrats is not wide. Nor are there massive opinion gaps between "Red States" and "Blue States." To the extent that polarization exists, it is primarily an elite phenomenon. However, since elites are the ones on television, on the radio, and on the internet opining on politics to a large audience, they provide the picture of political life. Fiorina's arguments have been challenged, most forcefully by Alan Abramowitz.[19] According to his interpretation of similar data, there are deep divisions between Republicans and Democrats in the electorate when it comes to policy preferences, and this is not limited to a relatively small number of activists.[20]

I mostly agree with Fiorina's view, especially as I think about Republicans. In my own examination of the data, I found that few Republican voters express consistent conservative opinions.[21] Yet, in some ways, this only makes political life even more confusing. We may be able to convince ourselves that the public is not polarized on questions such as tax rates, foreign policy, or even abortion. It is simultaneously clear, however, that Americans have extraordinary emotional investments in politics. The relationship between politics and identity provides the best explanation for this apparent contradiction.

Although partisanship tends to follow other forms of identity, once it is established, it becomes its own form of identity. That is, for many of us, a party is not simply a label attached to a group of politicians that we tend to prefer over a different group of politicians. For much of the electorate, being a Republican or a Democrat is itself an important part of self-identity. We care deeply about our parties and want to see them succeed; we similarly loath the opposing party and are happy to see them lose. These feelings are not necessarily tied to the real-world stakes of a particular political battle. Whatever the initial cause of our party identification, once it is established, for many of us, being a Republican or a Democrat is an important part of our sense of self.

Political scientist Lilliana Mason has done important work bringing this issue to light. She has emphasized the important point that researchers need to disentangle different forms of polarization.[22] The failure to properly define polarization, and acknowledge that it takes different forms, has led to debates in which the various camps seem to be talking past each other. When we make this distinction we can see that different forms of polarization are following different trends. Americans are becoming angrier about politics (what we may call "affective" or "emotional" polarization), even as their level of issue-based polarization, which was never that high to begin with, has held steady. Mason argued that partisan identity, rather than policy issues, explains the negativity in American politics:

> Even as we agree on most issues, we are becoming increasingly uncivil in our approach to politics. This increasing vitriol is all the more troubling because it is unconnected from issue attitudes. It is not that we are angry because we disagree so strongly about important issues; instead, we are angry, at least partially, because of team spirit. Regardless of how the other team feels about the issues, we don't like them because they are the other team. This changes the view of American political conflict from one of reasoned disagreement to one closer to ethnic discord. The "other" is inferior, infuriating, and must be stopped, simply because of its increasing "other-ness."[23]

This explanation for polarization seems unsatisfying because it leaves several questions unanswered. Most notably, Why now? Partisan politics has always existed, yet the kind of polarization we are currently facing seems new. What has changed? One possible answer is that nothing has actually changed. Perhaps this was always how party politics has operated, it is just now more noticeable because politics is increasingly nationalized. Mason and other scholars, however, have suggested that there is a new phenomenon at work, driving these trends and shifting the nature of the nation's politics. Once again, identity issues are at work.

The rise of affective polarization is in part driven by social polarization. Although, as a nation, we are becoming more diverse on many measures, within our major political parties certain kinds of diversity seem to be on the decline. Mason states, "Social sorting involves increasing social homogeneity within each party, such that religious, racial, and ideological divides tend to line up along partisan lines."[24] A growing number of us find ourselves in a situation where most of our various forms of personal social identity are aligned with a single political party, and we have fewer cross-cutting cleavages—that is, possessing some social identities that are strongly associated with the Republicans and others typically associated with the Democrats. Some of this has resulted from growing demographic splits in party affiliation and vote choice. Since the civil rights era, the racial gap in vote choice has grown increasingly prominent, with overwhelming majorities of African Americans and other minorities voting for the Democratic Party, and large majorities of non-Hispanic white voters supporting the Republican Party (at least in presidential elections).[25] The rise of the Christian Right and the politicization of evangelical Christianity has also played a role. There was once a time when knowing one's religious identity provided relatively little information about how one voted. Although there was always a partisan divide between Catholics and Protestants, not long ago religious congregations were often politically diverse places. This has become less common.

ALIGNING RELIGION WITH PARTY

Scholars of political attitudes and behaviors long took it for granted that religion was a quintessential exogenous variable. Although religious identity, religious behaviors, and religious beliefs are not fixed and unchanging, we could reasonably assume that people did not change their religion because of partisan politics. Thus, we could assume that the relationship between religion and politics (at least on an individual level) only goes one way. This is beginning to change. Increasingly, religion has become yet another element of personal identity that people bring into alignment with their political identities.

For generations, many observers took it for granted that the United States was an exceptional nation when it came to religion. Alexis de Tocqueville, for example, remarked on the unique and intense religiosity of the American people. More recently, many religious Americans have taken pride in the fact that the United States was not experiencing the same explosive growth in secularism that was occurring in other countries, especially in Western Europe. To the extent that religion in the United States was on the decline, it was largely confined to the mainline Protestant denominations, those denominations often associated with liberal politics.[26] This is no longer the case. Although their decline began later than it did for mainline Protestants, evangelical Protestants are also losing adherents. Roman Catholicism has also suffered a period of long-term decline, but this was masked for some time by recent immigrants filling Catholic pews.

Robert Putnam and David Campbell described the decline of religion in the United States as a "shock and two aftershocks."[27] Following the 1950s, which represented a high point of conventional religious identification and activity in American life, the 1960s counterculture, which challenged authority and traditions of all kinds, was a major shock. For a growing swath of the population, "sex, drugs, and rock 'n' roll" replaced traditional religious morality. This revolution began to stall, however, as religious conservatives began to push back—the first aftershock. Evangelical Christians engaged in vigorous outreach efforts during the 1970s and 1980s, continuing to grow even as mainline Protestant churches declined. Political religious groups such as the Moral Majority became major players in Republican politics.

By the 1990s, however, there was a backlash to the backlash—the second aftershock—that began showing up in the aggregate data of Americans' religious practices and identities. The number of Americans that told pollsters that their religion was "none" began to creep upward. There are of course many reasons why people abandon a religious identity. Every person is different and has personal justifications. Some stories are more common than others are, however.

In an influential 2002 article, sociologists Michael Hout and Claude Fischer sought to understand why Americans were losing their religious identities at a remarkable pace.[28] They found that demographic changes could explain some of this trend—delayed marriage, for example, is associated with declining religiosity. They found little evidence that changing religious beliefs are the source of this change. It turns out people with no formal religious affiliation (and hence would tell a pollster their religion is "none") nonetheless tend to hold religious beliefs. This remains the case. As I showed in my analysis of data from 2014, a majority of them continue to believe in the afterlife, for example.[29]

In their data, Hout and Fischer found that there were political correlates to religious decline. The decline occurred most rapidly among political liberals and moderates, rather than conservatives. They suggested the phenomenon was driven, in part, by people's misgivings with the religious Right. The 1990s was a period when "culture war" issues were front and center. Groups such as the Christian Coalition were growing in strength and influence, becoming major power brokers in conservative politics. Ralph Reed, Pat Robertson, and Jerry Falwell, for example, were household names. For many people, conservative politics became associated with Christianity itself. Once they made such an association, many liberals and moderates determined that they no longer wished to be affiliated with Christianity.

Hout and Fischer made a compelling argument, but at the time they were writing, they were unable to demonstrate the causal relationship they proposed. Since that time, a growing amount of literature has provided additional evidence. Nicholas Vargas looked at longitudinal data and found that religious people who supported same-sex marriage in the past were more likely to leave their religion in the future, compared to be people that did not support this policy.[30]

More recently, Paul Djupe, Jacob Neiheisel, and Anand Sokhey have considered the question from a somewhat different perspective.[31] Rather than look at individual affiliation with religion, they consider affiliation with a specific congregation. Congregational affiliation may be a more important variable (from a societal perspective) than personal religious identity. One can wonder, after all, how much it really matters if a person who previously engaged in no religious activity simply stopped telling pollsters that he or she is a Christian, but otherwise changed nothing. In their data, they found that disagreeing with the religious Right had a meaningful effect on the probability that a person would leave his or her congregation. Related research has found that, at the state level, a higher level of political activity on the part of the religious Right was associated with rising rates of secularization.[32]

If these findings are accurate, they represent a devastating rebuke of the Christian Right. Far from reclaiming America for Christ, this movement may have inadvertently expedited Christianity's decline in the United States. This should be especially demoralizing, given how few lasting victories the Christian Right achieved in the policy arena. Same-sex marriage is not just legal but enjoys overwhelming support from the public. Abortion remains legal, and, at the time of this writing, *Roe v. Wade* remains in place, but its long-term future may be in doubt. Stopping the ERA was perhaps the religious Right's most significant accomplishment, but that occurred *before* many of the well-known religious Right organizations we know today even existed.

The religious Right's opponents may take satisfaction in the idea that the movement undermined its own institutions by driving people away from organized religion. However, there is a significant problem with this narrative. If the religious Right is to blame for Christianity's recent decline in the United States, how do we explain that Christianity has declined farther and faster in other countries? Is it plausible to believe that American evangelical leaders, such as John Hagee, are to blame for Catholicism's free fall in Ireland, or empty Anglican churches in the U.K.? There must be additional explanations for rising secularism in the United States.

In *From Politics to the Pews* (2018), Michelle Margolis fills in some crucial details in the story of American secularization.[33] It is true that, as the two parties took consistent, opposite positions on cultural issues, Democrats began moving away from religion. However, for the same reason, partisanship has further entrenched the religious identities of Republicans. The idea that our religious identities could be downstream from our partisan identities may seem implausible, but Margolis provides an impressive amount of data to make her case. The fact that our political identities tend to congeal at a time in our lives when our religious identities are especially malleable is a critical aspect of this process.

For most of us, young adulthood is when we develop strong political identities. Young adulthood is also when people who were raised with a religion are most likely to drift away from religious institutions—they stop attending worship services with any frequency, for example. This drop-off in religiosity cuts across party lines. However, members of the major parties differ in their likelihood of returning to religion. Republicans are much more likely than Democrats to return.

This research suggests that the United States does remain exceptional when it comes to religion, but that exceptionalism has not meant that the country is immune to secularization. Rather, the country is exceptional in that its path toward secularization is unique. In the United States, the decline of religion primarily occurs on the left, whereas the Right remains highly religious.

The implications of this finding are disturbing in a number of ways. It is problematic that religiosity is increasingly tied to partisanship. It is better for society if there are spaces that are not dominated by partisan politics. Churches and other places of worship should be places where people with different political preferences and identities can come together in a social setting.

In the end, this process of asymmetrical secularization will only further worsen the religious/political divide. At present, most living Americans—even if they currently have no religion—were raised with a religious identity. Although there are adult converts, most people raised by parents with no religion never come to identify with a religion.[34] The growing population of secular Democrats is likely to be self-perpetuating into the future. The addition of religious identity to the list of attributes on which Americans are polarized along party lines will only further exacerbate tensions between Republicans and Democrats. Regardless of whether Christianity is true in a literal sense, it once provided Americans with a widely shared moral framework that transcended class, regional, and political boundaries.

These findings also have unnerving implications about the nature of religion itself. Religion presumably is about our search for the answer to life's deepest questions. The idea that people place their partisan identities above their religious identities, and would abandon the former for the sake of the latter, seems at odds with our basic intuitions. From a religious person's perspective, the idea that people would abandon their faith (and presumably put their souls in jeopardy) because they prefer to vote Democratic rather than Republican seems foolhardy—if not crazy. This does not paint religious Republicans in a particularly favorable light either, as it seems to suggest that religion is just another way to signal partisan loyalty, as though identifying as a Christian is analogous to displaying a partisan bumper sticker.

ALIGNING RACIAL IDENTITY WITH PARTY

If we accept that religious politics can be a form of identity politics, we may at least acknowledge that religion represents a different kind of identity. It is true that most of us do not come to our religion (or lack of religion) through a purely rational process in which we independently examine religious texts and determine which, if any, we view most concordant with reality. These identities are shaped by parental influences and other forms of socialization, geography, and ethnic background. Abandoning religion can also be very difficult, especially when a person's base of social support is mostly or entirely connected to a religious group. Yet, even when there are challenges in doing so, for most people it is at least theoretically possible to drop a religious identity instantaneously. Adopting a religious identity can be similarly easy, but this will vary according to the religion—it is much easier for anyone to become a Baptist than a Jew, for example. Nonetheless, we can still think of religion as being, ultimately, a matter of personal choice.

Race is presumably different, however, and we may be tempted to think of race as truly outside of an individual's control, especially in a country such as the United States, which has so long followed the "one drop" rule of racial identification. Further, unlike religions, racial groups are mostly not out seeking "converts." White supremacists are not trying to grow their ranks by convincing people not currently identified as white to change their racial affiliation, but the definition of who qualifies as white has unquestionably evolved over time. Similarly, although members of minority groups may be happy to have white allies eager to assist them in their political struggles, provided those allies have the correct motives and proper humility, they are not calling for whites to literally identify as members of a different demographic group. The controversy surrounding Rachel Dolezal seems to demonstrate this. Dolezal publicly identified as an African American woman. She further made her purported blackness an essential element of her identity. She served as an NAACP chapter president, and taught courses on African American history, culture, and politics. Dolezal faced extraordinary criticism, however, when local journalists revealed that she had no African American ancestry and was passing as Black by altering her appearance.

Dolezal's case seems to indicate that race (even if it is, at bottom, a social construct) remains tied to ancestry, and is not subject to change or personal preference. However, this is a rare and unusual example. Although it may remain taboo for a person with an exclusively European family tree to identity as African American, there are other cases where the boundaries are less clear. In fact, it is not uncommon for Americans to change their racial or ethnic identity over the course of their lives. This is especially true for people from a mixed racial or ethnic background.

Early work on the subject of racial change focused on social status. However, new research indicates a political element to this phenomenon. Political scientists Alexander Agadjanian and Dean Lacy have examined longitudinal data on racial identification change that also included data on presidential vote choice.[35] They had data for both 2012 and 2016. Like other scholars, they found that a certain percentage of Americans change their racial identities over a short time period. Specifically, they found that 4.64 percent of their sample changed from a nonwhite identity to a white identity between 2011 and 2016; over that same period, 3.58 percent changed from a white to a nonwhite identity. The transition to white mostly occurred among people who previously identified as mixed race, other race, Native American, or Hispanic in the previous period. The shift from white to nonwhite occurred mostly among people that later identified as mixed-race, other race, or Hispanic. African Americans and Asian Americans were the most stable groups over time.

Beyond presenting evidence of racial switching, the authors also found that changes in racial self-identification are associated with changes in partisan identification. People who changed their race from nonwhite to white were *much* more likely to have also changed their vote from non-Republican to Republican over this period—that is, voted for Obama, a third-party candidate, or no one in 2012, but for Trump in 2016. The percentages may seem small, but when applied to the very large U.S. electorate, the total numbers are quite impressive: "Extrapolating to the 136,639,786 votes cast in the 2016 presidential election implies that 5.3 million American voters changed their racial identities between 2011 and 2016, and over 276,000 specifically changed their vote from non-Republican to Republican and their race from non-white to white."[36]

Longitudinal data can be an excellent tool for determining causal relationships, but they also have limits. These data show a correlation between political change and racial change, but do not demonstrate the direction of the causal arrow (or even establish that there is a causal relationship). Nonetheless, the authors make a strong case that many people have some discretion about their racial identities and are choosing to align their race with their politics, and that this was especially true of people who changed to a Republican partisan identity.

RACE AND WELFARE ATTITUDES

I disagree with many scholars of critical race theory on the degree to which race is central to all or most elements of American politics. It is not my position that racism and capitalism are inextricably linked. Nor am I convinced that the latter is dependent on the former. I furthermore argue that most economic conservative and libertarian scholars and journalists make their arguments in good faith, and are not trying to hide an underlying oppressive agenda. Nonetheless, there is strong evidence that racial attitudes are tied to feelings toward the welfare state.

American conservatives have taken great pride in their nation's economic system and have contrasted it favorably with most Western European countries, where the regulatory burden is greater, tax rates are higher, and the social safety net is more generous. Conservatives argue that the more limited U.S. government accounts for the nation's greater economic dynamism and prosperity. The smaller welfare state has furthermore strengthened American character, whereas extravagant or poorly executed welfare states reward dysfunctional behavior. They further viewed the more modest welfare state in the United States as evidence for a commitment to rugged individualism, personal responsibility, and preference for economic dynamism over material security.

Martin Gilens, in *Why Americans Hate Welfare* (1999), argued that Americans' opposition to a greater welfare state has other roots.[37] In particular, according to Gilens, white Americans are hostile to the idea of a generous welfare state because they view it through a racial lens. In the United States, where poverty is not distributed evenly across racial populations, the white majority views welfare as a form of racial redistribution. Examining many different public opinion surveys, Gilens demonstrated that racial attitudes were an important predictor of attitudes toward welfare, and further argued that this resulted from how the media portrays poverty in the United States, treating it as a predominantly Black problem. Other research has since reinforced the idea that racial diversity is associated with diminished support for generous welfare policies.[38]

This does not mean that the intellectual conservative movement's opposition to the welfare state is rooted in conscious or unconscious attitudes toward race. William F. Buckley Jr. and his colleagues, after all, were intense opponents of New Deal policies that were implemented before welfare policy was heavily racialized. However, as the public increasingly came to view welfare from a racial perspective, conservative arguments against these policies apparently became more compelling to a significant portion of the electorate.

ALIGNING RACIAL ATTITUDES WITH PARTY AFFILIATION

The political science literature has demonstrated, again and again, that racial attitudes are correlated with partisan identification.[39] Among whites, more progressive racial attitudes are associated with greater support for the Democratic Party. For the most part, the literature on this subject has assumed that this was a simple, unidirectional relationship: how a white person feels about racial issues determines, in part, which party (if any) he or she will gravitate toward. The racial realignment that occurred in the South during and after the civil rights era seems to provide strong evidence for this.[40] As the parties began to give different messages to voters about racial issues, voters began to shift their partisan loyalties accordingly.

Although racial attitudes are relatively rigid, they are not permanently fixed. We furthermore know that all kinds of attitudes, and even identities, can shift in response to partisan pressures.[41] As cues about racial attitudes from party leaders change, we can expect some partisans in the electorate to change with them. Political scientist Andrew Engelhardt argues that this occurs.[42] Using panel data, he shows that whites do sometimes engage in party switching because of their racial attitudes, but this is less common now than it was several decades ago. However, he has found that more recently it has been increasingly common for whites to change their racial attitudes (specifically, their attitudes toward Blacks) to align with their party. His results further indicate that attitude change among partisans on racial issues, rather than a partisan sorting among whites according to their racial attitudes, accounts for much of the difference between white Republicans and white Democrats in their racial views.

In the main text of the article, Engelhardt does not focus on how this effect has differed between Republicans and Democrats. He simply suggests that partisans on both sides have come to align their racial attitudes with the norm of their parties. In an appendix, however, he notes that, after 2012, we see a more substantial shift in racial attitudes among Democrats. This would be congruent with other research indicating that the parties have become more polarized on racial issues in the Obama and Trump eras, but the movement in attitudes has been asymmetrical. White Democrats have become much more progressive on these subjects over the last decade, but, in the aggregate, Republicans have changed relatively little.[43] This means that, in the United States overall, white prejudice is actually on the decline, but the decline is driven largely by new antiracist sentiments among Democrats.[44]

WE MAY NOT LOVE OUR PARTIES, BUT WE DO HATE THE OTHER SIDE

There is an important possible objection to the ideas I am discussing in this chapter. As we survey the political landscape, we may see little evidence that people are extraordinarily fond of their political parties. This is especially true of Republicans, who on average tend to give the Republican Party a very low level of favorability. As we consider events of the last several years, much of the populist energy on the right and on the left in the United States has been directed at the "party establishments." So what is going on here? Once again, I think it will be useful to disaggregate partisan affiliation as a marker of personal identity from party identity as an expression of support for a set of policies or even politicians. Dissatisfaction with current party leaders can, but often does not, lead to a weakening of our partisan identities.[45] In fact, our intense frustration with our parties may, perhaps paradoxically, be leading to rising feelings of partisan anger.

Political scientist Eric Groenendyk has published provocative research making the case for this possibility.[46] He suggests that the psychology of party affiliation often leads us to have conflicted feelings about our political parties. Because party identification is an important part of personal identity, we want to be good and loyal partisans. We feel good when our team wins. On the other hand, we like to imagine ourselves as rational beings, forming political opinions and loyalties according to our analysis of what is happening in the world. When our parties are performing well, there is no psychological conflict between these desires. Ideally, when our political party wins, it implements policies that we like, with results we find beneficial. When our parties disappoint us, however, our different motivations conflict with each other. From a rational perspective, if our parties disappoint us, we should reevaluate our loyalty to our parties. But, for many people, party loyalties are not easily abandoned.

Groenendyk argues that we can resolve the tension between our party identifications and our frustration with our parties by increasing our antipathy toward our parties' opponents. In other words, we can justify our vote choice if we believe the opposing party is worse. This allows us to acknowledge our disgust with our parties without betraying them. The end result is an unusual type of polarization. Although relatively few of us may feel fondness for the policies or leading figures of our parties, we absolutely loath the alternative and view their victories in almost apocalyptic terms. We see additional evidence for this in the increase in apparent "negative voting"—voting out of dislike for the other party's candidate, rather than out of love for the candidate they actually choose.[47]

If correct, this argument has other important consequences. Notably, it provides further evidence that American partisans, even strong partisans, may not be especially committed to a particular political platform. As long as our party defeats the other side, we are willing to give our party leaders quite a bit of ideological leeway. This gives some insight into the GOP electorate's support for Trump in the 2016 presidential primaries. His expressed support for political principles (conservative or

otherwise) were mostly perfunctory. He did, however, promise his supporters that he would win. As Groenendyk put it, "If partisans' identities
are increasingly anchored to hatred of the outparty than affection for
their inparty, electoral dynamics are likely much more fluid than many
accounts suggest. Thus, insurgent candidates with questionable ideological credentials (e.g., Donald Trump) may be more appealing than
one might expect in the age of ideologically sorted parties."[48]

CONCLUSION

As we better understand the psychology of partisan affiliation, and its
consequences for ideological commitments, policy preferences, and vote
choice, many essential conservative claims about the nature of American
politics become increasingly untenable. Conservatives in the electorate
are not immune to identity politics. To a meaningful extent, the claim
that "all politics is identity politics" is insightful. However, partisan politics in the United States represents a special kind of identity politics.
Americans tend to launder other forms of identity through political parties, which in theory are driven by ideas and interests, not identities. Furthermore, identity politics seems to lie beneath some of the core policy
initiatives supported by the conservative movement and advanced by the
Republican Party. Most notably, there has likely been a racial element,
perhaps mostly unconscious, to Americans' traditional hostility toward
expansion of the welfare state. "Self-reliance" has become a part of white
America's self-conception, which has policy implications.

At the same time, certain progressive critiques of conservatives and
the Republican Party are also incorrect. The idea that people adopt conservatism and support for the GOP as a cover for their support for white
supremacy is wrong. The political science literature strongly suggests
that party identification is downstream from other forms of identity,
but identity is a complex phenomenon and rarely determined by a single
personal characteristic. The fact that, once established, party identity
itself becomes an important aspect of personal identity further complicates matters. The finding that people are willing to change their religion
and even, when possible, their racial identity in order to be better aligned
with a political party demonstrates the shocking power of partisanship

in the United States. It further explains why efforts to foster under-standing and tolerance across party lines are so rarely successful, and why efforts to promote third-party candidacies are so quixotic, even when voters are dissatisfied with their parties' candidates.

Building relationships and understanding across partisan lines is additionally challenging when new media forms allow us to live in information bubbles, in which we are able to curate news and opinions in ways that flatter and reinforce our existing prejudices.[49] Although dif-ferent media venues may be talking about roughly the same subjects, they present them in a very different manner. Sean Hannity and National Public Radio, for example, provide dissimilar pictures of politics. Further, despite all the recent concerns about "fake news," one or both sides does not even need to be willfully dishonest to provide these different visions. The United States is a massive country. It is easy to find information that will reinforce just about any narrative.

EIGHT

Lessons from the Alt-Right's Rise and Fall

The Alt-Right, short for "alternative right," and the label used for the most recent manifestation of the U.S. white nationalist movement, scarcely exists anymore. Very few people still describe themselves as Alt-Right. The Alt-Right did not build lasting institutions. Vigorous organizing by the movement's opponents hindered the Alt-Right's ability to hold public events. Lawsuits from people harmed in Charlottesville have consumed massive amounts of the Alt-Right's time and resources. Doxings have created social and economic problems for people involved in the movement, and discouraged others from getting involved. Charlottesville also changed the public's perception of the Alt-Right. When the public thinks of the Alt-Right, they think of that event, not the smirking cartoon frog that had previously served as the movement's mascot.

For these reasons, I now mostly use the term "Alt-Right" in the past tense. Few people continue to identify as Alt-Right, even if they have not fundamentally changed their ideology in recent years. It will likely be some time before an analogous movement will be able to emerge and enjoy as much success as the Alt-Right experienced during its peak.

Although the subject may be somewhat less urgent, the Alt-Right still requires attention. In some ways, its story seems to challenge the argument I put forth in this book. That is, I have argued that identity politics in some form is likely inevitable. However, with the Alt-Right, white Americans were offered racial identity politics in an unadulterated form. Yet most declined to buy what the Alt-Right was selling. Why was this the case? Does this mean that explicit white racial identity politics has no future as a major player in American life?

THE ALT-RIGHT'S RISE

The term "alternative right" was first introduced toward the end of George W. Bush's second term of office. This was a low point for mainstream conservatism. The Iraq War had become a quagmire, the economy was on the verge of collapse, conservative politicians across the country were ensnared in scandals of all kinds. Conservatism seemed to be losing credibility. It was during this period that Richard Spencer, then the editor of a webzine called *Taki's Magazine* (named for its founder, the paleoconservative Taki Theodoracopulos), began to use the term "alternative right." The term itself had been inspired by a speech given by a paleoconservative scholar named Paul Gottfried, who called for a new right-wing movement to dethrone the neoconservatives from their position as the dominant force in the mainstream Right.[1]

Over time, especially after Spencer left *Taki's Magazine* to form his own webzine, *Alternative Right*, the term became increasingly associated with racism and anti-Semitism. During this time a growing racist subculture was emerging on the internet, building online discussion forums, hosting podcasts, writing articles, and trolling social media. They took advantage of racial controversies that occurred during the Obama administration (the shooting of Trayvon Martin, for example) to promote a narrative of white racial grievance. The movement eventually adopted the shorter term "Alt-Right" as its label.

In early 2015, the Alt-Right was already a growing presence online, but the 2016 presidential election provided it an opportunity to enter the national discussion. Most figures in the Far Right were genuinely enthusiastic about Donald Trump, but not about recent Republican candidates, such as Bob Dole (1996), George W. Bush (2000/2004), John McCain (2008), and Mitt Romney (2012). There were two main reasons for this. This first is quite obvious: Trump used rhetoric about immigrants and Islam unlike any other major Republican leader, rhetoric much more aligned with a far-right worldview. He began his campaign by calling Mexican immigrants criminals. He called for a total ban on Muslim immigration. These positions are in sharp contrast to those of George W. Bush or McCain, both of whom were generally pro-immigration. Trump's message on the campaign trail was also much more extreme than anything uttered by Romney during his campaign, making Romney's call for undocumented immigrants to "self-deport" seem moderate.

In other recent presidential elections, the white nationalist movement was mostly apathetic. In those years, neither the Republican nor the Democratic candidate was viewed as useful for the racist Right's agenda. Some even viewed Barack Obama's election in 2008 as a positive development, as they hoped an African American president would be a catalyst for greater feelings of white identity and racial polarization. More importantly, some hoped it represented the forthcoming demise of the Republican Party, which white nationalists have long accused of failing to support the interests of white Americans while simultaneously using racial dog whistles to attract white support. Louis Andrews, who led the white nationalist think tank the National Policy Institute until his death in 2010, explained his vote for Obama as follows: "I want to see the Republican Party destroyed, so it can be reborn as a party representing the interests of white people, and not entrenched corporate elites."[2]

The Alt-Right appreciated the chaos Trump caused within the Republican Party and the conservative movement. Although mainstream conservatives are typically to the right of liberals on issues related to race, and conservative Republicans have unquestionably used both explicit and implicit racial appeals to white voters, it is also true that the conservative movement has (with varying levels of success) sought to drive open racists and anti-Semites from its ranks. Since the conservative movement was founded, it has periodically shunned groups and individuals that crossed certain boundaries. In other words, the conservative movement and the Republican Party had for some time served as gatekeeper, keeping the openly racist Right out of the mainstream discussion.

The Alt-Right was therefore delighted that Trump was causing the leading voices of the conservative movement such consternation. Persistent attacks from the conservative intelligentsia seemed to have no discernible effect on Trump's support in the electorate. *National Review* dedicated an entire issue to opposing Trump in the GOP primaries, explaining why conservatives needed to oppose his nomination. This attack, and persistent critiques from popular conservative radio hosts such as Glenn Beck, did not halt Trump's momentum in the primaries. This suggested to the radical Right that new possibilities were opening in American political life. Many believed, not without justification, that Trump gave the racist Right a new level of breathing space. At the very least, it suggested that the Republican base was disconnected from the party elite, suggesting these voters were willing to consider right-wing alternatives.

One of the Alt-Right's assets at this time was an ironic sensibility that spread white nationalist ideas largely via racist and anti-Semitic jokes. Its tone and messaging strategy was well suited to attract white millennials who wanted to push back against political correctness. The Alt-Right attacked both the Left and the mainstream Right—the latter it viewed as spineless "cuckservatives." It attracted genuine white nationalist ideologues but also brought in nihilistic trolls, who simply enjoyed sowing discord online.

As an online movement, it was mostly anonymous. Relatively few people associated with the movement used their real names. Instead, unknown figures using pseudonyms were posting essays, tweets, podcasts, and comments without fear of any consequences. The ease of anonymous communication online opened up space for people to post racist, sexist, and misogynistic material that few would share using their real-world identities. The ability of people on the Alt-Right to create multiple social media accounts with different names also made it easier to create the illusion that the movement was larger than it really was.

The Alt-Right benefited when Trump's opponents in the 2016 election sought to connect the Alt-Right to Trump's larger right-wing populist movement in the public eye. The most dramatic example of this came in August 2016, when Hillary Clinton focused an entire speech on the Alt-Right and its affiliation with the Trump campaign. The speech was likely intended to drive a wedge between Trump and many traditional Republican voters who were uncomfortable with his rhetoric about women and minorities.

Whether or not Clinton's speech hindered Trump is impossible to know. Perhaps he lost some votes as a result, but obviously not enough to change the result. It is clear, however, that Clinton's speech benefited the Alt-Right, which received an unprecedented amount of attention. Traffic to its most visible websites surged. Further, given the extreme levels of negative partisanship in the United States, the fact that Clinton disliked the Alt-Right may have nudged some Republicans otherwise ignorant of the movement to assume the Alt-Right was their ally.

Finally, by arguing that the Alt-Right and the Trump campaign were synonymous, Clinton and others were in a way making the 2016 election a referendum on the Alt-Right. Should Trump win, the Alt-Right could plausibly argue it had massive support from the American people. After Trump's victory, this is exactly what many of them inferred.

. . . AND ITS FALL

The Alt-Right's elation after Trump's victory did not last long. The first major real-world Alt-Right event after the election was a National Policy Institute conference in Washington, DC. With cameras from mainstream media outlets capturing the entire event, Richard Spencer concluded his speech at the event with "Hail Trump. Hail our people. Hail victory." At this point, multiple people in the audience responded with Nazi salutes. This event resulted in Trump disavowing and condemning the Alt-Right for the first time. It also led to a schism within the Alt-Right, with the less radical voices (a group that came to be known as the "Alt-Lite" or "Alt-Light") distancing itself from the explicit white nationalists increasingly dominant in the Alt-Right. The event was subsequently described within the Alt-Right as "Heilgate."

The Alt-Right soon faced new disappointments, especially when it became clear that the Trump White House was being staffed primarily with longtime Republican insiders, including many who had opposed Trump throughout the campaign. If personnel is policy, Trump was clearly signaling that his administration would be less disruptive than many mainstream Republicans feared. There were a handful of prominent figures in the White House with a reputation for nativism and right-wing populist attitudes. Steve Bannon, formerly of Breitbart, was the most significant example. Stephen Miller, a speech writer for Trump and former staffer for Alabama senator Jeff Sessions (who for a time served at Trump's attorney general) is another. Otherwise, however, the Trump White House was mostly filled with conventional figures, such as White House Chief of Staff Reince Priebus, former head of the Republican National Committee.

Trump further disappointed the extreme Right when he chose not to aggressively pursue a far-right policy agenda. Aside from a ham-fisted policy banning people from several majority-Muslim countries from entering the United States, the Trump administration did not achieve many meaningful policy victories for immigration restrictionists. For the first two years of Trump's time in office, the president largely outsourced domestic policy to House Speaker Paul Ryan and Senate Majority Leader Mitch McConnell, Republican leaders in their respective chambers.[3] These Republicans used their majorities these years to pursue traditional Republican policies, such as tax cuts and an (unsuccessful) effort to repeal the Affordable Care Act, also known as Obamacare. Trump did not insist that congressional Republicans fulfill his campaign promises, such as the creation of a border wall between the United States and Mexico. When the Republicans lost their majority in the House of Representatives in 2018, the window in which Trump could have made significant changes to U.S. immigration policy closed.

Although denied meaningful direct political influence, many primary figures of the Alt-Right nonetheless spent much of early 2017 attempting to transition the Alt-Right from a loose, online subculture into a real-world phenomenon, complete with real institutions, professional activists, and public events. Right-wing groups conducted a number of small events that year in Washington, DC, and in smaller cities, such as Pikeville, Tennessee. The new "Alt-Right Corporation," and its website, Altright.com, were intended to further institutionalize the Alt-Right.

In mid-2017, leading figures of the Alt-Right decided to hold a rally in the city of Charlottesville, Virginia, home to the University of Virginia. The catalyst was the decision by city officials to remove statues dedicated to Confederate leaders. It is worth noting that, up until that point, the main voices within the Alt-Right had shown relatively little interest in Confederate heritage. The event was called "Unite the Right." It was initially billed as a rally that would attract widespread support and attendance from across the right-of-center spectrum. Instead, more moderate right-wing figures stayed away from the event, and it attracted the most extreme right-wing elements, including groups such as the Ku Klux Klan and the National Socialist Movement.

The event occurred over two days. The evening before the scheduled rally, a group of white nationalists arrived in Charlottesville and conducted a torchlight rally. Attendees initially chanted the words, "You will not replace us." They soon changed the wording to, "Jews will not replace us," making their anti-Semitic views clear. Although the event involved some minor scuffles with counterprotesters, the leaders of the event viewed the march a success.

The following day was different. The City of Charlottesville initially tried to keep the event from happening at all, but the organizers convinced the courts to allow Unite the Right to go forward. On the day of the event, counterprotesters were out in force and outnumbered Alt-Right attendees by a large margin. In comparison to earlier Alt-Right public gatherings, the police in attendance took fewer efforts to make sure that the right-wing rallygoers were separated from counterprotesters.[4] Before any speeches could begin, Alt-Right attendees brawled in the streets with their opponents. The Virginia governor quickly declared a state of emergency, and the police declared the event an unlawful assembly. When the police cleared the park where the rally was scheduled to occur, the Alt-Right attendees again clashed with counterprotesters. While the Alt-Right was dispersing, a white nationalist named James Fields drove his car through a crowd of antiracist protesters, injuring dozens and killing one. He was subsequently arrested, tried, and convicted of murder.

Unite the Right was a major news story across the globe. It brought the Alt-Right unprecedented attention. World leaders denounced the event, as did U.S. politicians across the political spectrum. The one positive, from the Alt-Right's perspective, was President Trump's equivocating response, in which he said blame for the mayhem was shared "on both sides." Beyond that small victory, however, Unite the Right was an unmitigated public relations disaster for the Alt-Right.

In the months following Unite the Right, the Alt-Right fractured. Some insisted that the event should, despite the bad publicity, be viewed as a success. Others said that the event permanently tarnished the move-ment. The various sides of this debate fought furiously over the question of "optics"—how the movement should present itself to the world. For his part, Spencer continued to push for new real-world events, attempt-ing a new speaking tour on college campuses.

Spencer eventually abandoned his college speaking tour. After an unsuccessful event at Michigan State University, which very few people attended, in large part because counterprotesters blocked access to the venue, he stopped trying to gain access to universities. At that point, the Alt-Right largely disengaged from real-world events. It was also at this time that many real-world right-wing organizations fell apart. The Traditionalist Worker Party disbanded, in part because of a personal dis-pute among the group's leadership. The National Socialist Movement also collapsed around this time. Spencer's new website, Altright.com, stopped posting new material.

By the end of 2017, the Alt-Right lost whatever unity it previ-ously enjoyed. Having mostly broken ties with more moderate voices the previous year, the radicals that remained in the movement began to turn on each other. Different cliques began blaming each other for the movement's disarray. Individuals that, months earlier, seemed to have amicable relationships were denouncing each other. The Alt-Right seemed to become a circular firing squad, more focused on infighting than spreading a message beyond its ranks.

The Unite the Right rally led to a new and unprecedented wave of online deplatforming, as a large number of extreme-right accounts were purged from Twitter and payment processors stopped working for Alt-Right publications and organizations. In the most extreme case, the neo-Nazi website The Daily Stormer was, for a time, pushed off of the internet entirely, being only available on the "dark web" via Tor.

Unite the Right also opened the major leaders and organizations up to lawsuits. Historically, lawsuits have been one of the most effective tools against the extreme Right. Violence committed by extremist group members have typically led to successful lawsuits that wiped out their small amounts of capital. Even when not ultimately successful, defend-ing lawsuits requires a massive amount of time and money, diverging capital away from organizing new events.

More importantly, the Alt-Right lost whatever credibility it had among ordinary conservatives. From that point on, the Alt-Right was viewed by most Americans as a violent extremist movement.[5] It was then treated as no different from the other marginalized movements of the extreme Right.

MAJOR TAKEAWAYS

Deplatforming and Censorship Was an Effective Tool against the Far Right

In my 2017 book on the Alt-Right, I note that new efforts to kick the Alt-Right off of major platforms could create major problems for the movement. The Alt-Right had more success than its immediate ideological predecessors because it was able to interact with the mainstream in ways previously impossible for explicit white nationalist activists.[6]

Subsequent events have borne out this argument. If anything, I did not realize just how disastrous deplatforming would be for the Alt-Right. In that same chapter, I also say that new efforts to deny the Alt-Right access to online venues "do not at this point pose the movement any kind of existential threat."[7] Although this was a reasonable claim to make at the time I was writing, it is mistaken in hindsight. In part, this is because of the extraordinary scope of the deplatforming that occurred after Charlottesville. At the time I was writing about deplatforming, I was primarily focused on Twitter's efforts to crack down on hate speech or on Reddit deleting right-wing subreddits. The Twitter bans were significant, as that platform was the Alt-Right's most effective online space for the Alt-Right to break out of isolation and into the larger discussion. Unlike Facebook, Twitter allows anonymous accounts, and most people spreading Alt-Right propaganda preferred to be anonymous. It is true that people can get around bans. One just needs to create a new account with a different e-mail address. However, rebuilding a lost audience takes time, and once it becomes clear that a new account belongs to a previously banned person (or that account does something to warrant a new ban), it is shut down again. The extreme Right still has a presence on Twitter, but it is nothing like it was in 2015.

There have been other developments that I had not foreseen when I was first researching this subject, however. I was not considering new efforts to cripple the Alt-Right's ability to raise money or how extensive they would be. Throughout 2017, PayPal deleted accounts associated with the Alt-Right. Amazon stopped allowing certain far-right groups to use their affiliate program to raise money, and banned certain racist books. The loss of PayPal and other means to accept payments online was a huge blow to the Alt-Right, which had always existed on a shoestring budget. Some sites have attempted to raise money via Bitcoin, which cannot be blocked by banks or any other financial institution, but cryptocurrencies are incredibly volatile, and relatively few people actually use them. At this point, they cannot fully take the place of more conventional ways to transfer funds.

The question, of course, is whether the disease warranted this cure. Very few people are mourning the loss of the most vile, hate-filled voices on social media. But we should think carefully about the precedent set here. There is still a free speech issue that we should consider, even if we as a society ultimately decide that these kinds of crackdowns are necessary. Conservatives and libertarians accurately point out that this is not really a First Amendment issue: social media platforms are private entities and thus have a right to exclude anyone for any reason. There is furthermore a precedent for shutting open racists out of the mainstream debate. Mainstream conservative leaders have, in the past, shunned certain figures, cutting them off from right-wing venues and effectively rendering them mostly invisible to mainstream society.

The internet in general, and social media in particular, are a bit different, however. It is true that, like magazines and other publications, the companies that regulate online activity are owned by private entities. They are, however, much more like a public space than print publications. For a growing number of Americans, they are the primary means of gathering and sharing information. In the late twentieth century, one could reasonably say, "If you do not like *National Review*'s perspective on the correct orientation of American conservatism, start your own conservative magazine." It is quite different to say, "If you are mad about being kicked off the internet, start your own internet." I am certainly not decrying the existence of reasonable restrictions on what gets posted online. It is a very good thing, for example, that illegal materials are not just a Google search away. However, we are in a new era in which the primary means of disseminating information is controlled by a handful of large tech corporations with unprecedented power. We are thus in an unfamiliar situation, and we should think very carefully about what this means.

"Reverse Dog Whistles" Were Some of the Alt-Right's Most Effective Propaganda Tools—and We Still Do Not Know the Best Way to Combat Them

Critics of conservative politicians and media figures are frequently—and often with justification—accused of employing racial "dog whistles."[8] This involves making comments that, if taken literally and at face value, have no racial content. However, these comments are intended to send a coded racial message to followers. This message activates racial prejudices and anxieties while allowing the speaker to maintain a degree of plausible deniability regarding his or her intentions. Ronald Reagan's attack on "welfare queens" is viewed by many observers as an example of this. Comments by Republican strategist Lee Atwater from that era indicate that Republican leaders understood perfectly well what they were doing.[9] When this strategy is employed, racists hear the message they want, while the rest of society remains oblivious.

Elements of the Alt-Right adopted a variation of this strategy. In their case, however, they were not targeting the racial prejudice of mass publics. They were targeting the racial paranoia of antiracist activists, researchers, and journalists. Their goal was to provoke progressives into a furious response, and do so via a message that seemed completely innocuous to most other observers. The goal of this exercise was to make the Left appear unhinged and full of hatred for white people.

Over the last few years, we have seen a few successful Alt-Right propaganda pushes in this regard. One of the more bizarre, but successful, extreme-right memes was the idea that the "okay" hand gesture is actually a secret symbol of white supremacy. This was promoted on the anonymous online image board 4chan. The claim was that when one makes such a gesture, the fingers and forearm in combination look a bit like a W and a P, which stands for "white power." The idea that this common gesture was a secret symbol white supremacists used to signal each other struck most people as ridiculous.

Perhaps the Alt-Right's most successful propaganda effort in recent years was the "It's okay to be white" poster and sticker campaign. Once again, this idea was also apparently born on 4chan. The campaign was extraordinarily simple. People supportive of the movement hung up stickers and pieces of paper containing just the slogan "It's okay to be white," but a few also listed the name of a white nationalist organization. College campuses across the country, and even around the world, were especially likely to be targeted for these efforts. The goal was to provoke an overreaction from the media and campus activists and administrators. A writer at The Daily Stormer explained the logic of the campaign this way: "The point of the exercise is precisely to have this kind of reaction. Then some normies might read the article and briefly wonder 'if the flyer said "it's okay to be Black," would the police be trying to find the perpetrator and question him about his intentions?'"[10]

The campaign was a success. Where they appeared, these signs, stickers, and fliers prompted massive controversy and denunciations. In some cases, universities called for FBI assistance in investigating the posters.[11] At least one student was expelled for hanging one up.[12] That is probably not what that student was hoping for, but it nonetheless served the movement's larger propaganda purposes. Mainstream conservatives began to defend the slogan and attack the Left for its hypersensitivity and hostility toward whites. Tucker Carlson of Fox News, for example, weighed in on the controversy on his popular evening program. At the conservative website Redstate, Brandon Morse wrote: "Today's society is pretty filled to the brim with anti-white sentiment thanks to the media, activists, and politicians. . . . The racism against white people is pretty blatant but never acknowledged, especially by the very people who shout 'racism' whenever a white person so much as smirks."[13]

This campaign was successful in part because there is a disconnect in American life about how race is defined and understood. For many Americans, especially white Americans, race is just skin color, and racism is just prejudice against people according to their skin color. This of course is in sharp contrast to how these concepts are discussed and defined by antiracist activists and intellectuals, who view whiteness as an oppressive set of societal structures. For people with the former view, nothing could be more innocuous than the claim "It's okay to be white." Taken literally, the slogan denigrates no one and does not say or even imply that whites are superior to others. In fact, holding any contrary opinion would itself literally be racism. Carlson put it this way in his segment on the controversy: "Being white by the way is not something you can control. Like any ethnicity, you're born with it. Which is why you shouldn't attack people for it, and yet the left does it constantly—in case you haven't noticed."[14] Among people who hold the position that whiteness itself is a tool of oppression, of course, the statement "It's okay to be white" is an insidious defense of white supremacy, and an implicit endorsement of racism, colonialism, and genocide.

There has yet to be an effective counter to Alt-Right campaigns of this kind. I disagree with the idea that all efforts to crack down on hateful rhetoric are inevitably self-defeating. We have seen how increased censorship online hamstrung the Alt-Right. In this case, however, it seems true that attacking these fliers and the people that post them only reinforces their core message. Yet, doing nothing at all in response also seems problematic, given that the campaign is mostly pushed by white nationalist groups. On the other hand, we should not infer from the occasional success of memes such as "It's okay to be white" that the Alt-Right was led by masters of political propaganda. For every success, there were innumerable failures—memes and slogans that never caught on. Furthermore, the long-term consequences of these kinds of "meme wars" may not be as significant as many people fear.

The Conservative Movement and Republican Establishment Was More Resilient Than I Expected

Donald Trump's successes in the 2016 GOP primaries, and the Alt-Right's apparent appeal to lots of young people on the right, seemed to demonstrate the conservative movement's growing weaknesses. The conservative movement seemed increasingly anachronistic, with a worldview that seems stuck in the early Cold War. The conservative talking points did not seem to move on from that period, and their arguments remain permanently rooted in discussions about capitalism versus socialism, or individualism versus collectivism, or some variant of this.

At the end of 2016, one might have reasonably argued that the conservative movement was on its last legs.[15] It is unquestionably true that, when the conservative intelligentsia declared war on Trump in 2015 and

2016, the Republican electorate shrugged its shoulders and voted for him anyway. At the time I took it as a signal that the direction of the Republican Party was going to change in a fundamental way. Yet, as of this writing, it is clear that this has not happened.

At least when it comes to policy, the Republican Party largely tamed Trump. Most of his campaign's populist promises were neglected during the period when Republicans controlled both chambers of the U.S. Congress. Congress gave no significant new funds to a border wall. The Republicans' major policy victories, such as the confirmation of conservative Supreme Court justices and new tax cuts, would have occurred under any Republican president.

Some of Trump's populist policies, such as infrastructure investments, could have been viable even with a Democratic majority in the House of Representatives. In fact, such policies could have been even more likely in such a scenario, as Democrats should not have had ideological objections to such a policy. This was not to be, however, likely because intense partisan polarization in Washington precluded major bipartisan initiatives. Both sides would apparently prefer gridlock to conceding anything to their opponents.

In terms of foreign policy, Trump's record was mixed. I suspect that, had any of the other major Republican candidates won the presidency—with the notable exception of the (quasi-) libertarian noninterventionist Rand Paul—the United States would have had an even more belligerent foreign policy. The United States may have even instigated a ground war in Syria. On the other hand, Trump has also been more aligned with the Christian Zionist wing of the GOP than previous Republicans. His decision to move the U.S. embassy in Israel to Jerusalem, for example, was a bold move that even George W. Bush did not seriously pursue.

In any event, contrary to some of the hyperbolic claims from the media, Washington under Trump was much less disruptive than many feared or hoped. The policies coming from the White House and the U.S. Congress were what one would have anticipated, given the partisan makeup of those bodies. If we disregard his contentious style (the tweets, the insults, etc.), the actual policies were what one would have expected had any of the other major Republican candidates won in 2016. Despite their opposition to Trump during the 2016 presidential election, the leading voices of the conservative movement mostly made peace with the Trump presidency, for good reason—he largely gave them what they wanted.

Institutions and Money Matter

Why did conservatives enjoy so much success during the Trump administration? Trump won the Republican nomination in the face of strong conservative opposition. Even after securing his spot at the top of the GOP ticket, support from most of the conservative intelligentsia ranged from tepid to nonexistent. He certainly did not owe his general election victory over Hillary Clinton to the main organs of the conservative movement. Following his victory, he seemed in a strong position to fundamentally reshape the Republican Party, turning it in a more explicit right-wing populist direction. Had he done so, the conservative movement could have either gotten on board or become largely irrelevant. Yet that is not what happened.

One problem for Trump's variety of right-wing politics was that it followed a very different trajectory from mainstream conservatism as we understand it. We can briefly describe conservatism's rise as a series of logical steps, beginning as a mostly intellectual movement of journalists and academics in the early 1950s. It then built a grassroots activist network with organizations such as Young Americans for Freedom. In the 1964 election, conservatives established themselves as the dominant force within the Republican Party. Following Goldwater's defeat, conservatives continued to raise money, largely thanks to political entrepreneurs such as Richard Viguerie, who pioneered conservative use of direct mail. New conservative institutions such as the Heritage Foundation became important fixtures of U.S. politics. By 1979, there was a massive infrastructure in place to not just support Reagan's presidential campaign, but to staff the government after his election. There were furthermore a large number of conservative Republicans in Congress eager to pursue the Reagan agenda.

"Trumpism," if such a thing exists, followed a different path. Trump won the presidency on a right-wing populist platform largely on his own. After entering the White House, however, there was virtually no political infrastructure in place to support a right-wing populist agenda. If he wanted people with political experience to fill key roles in his administration, Trump had to look to establishment Republicans, including those that actively opposed him in the election and had no interest in pursuing a populist agenda. Furthermore, the Republican leadership in Congress did not change after the 2016 election. Ryan and McConnell had not changed their priorities and remained committed to the same policy agenda as before. For all his bluster about his skills as a dealmaker, Trump was no Lyndon Johnson when it came to relations with Congress.

The conservative policy victories of the last several years were not driven by massive public support for conservatism. As I have argued elsewhere, the percentage of the electorate that consistently shows strong support for all elements of the mainstream conservative policy agenda is remarkably small. The conservative movement's policy victories in the Trump era came largely because of the influential political institutions that have clout regardless of who happens to sit in the Oval Office.

The American Radical Right Has an Identity Crisis of Its Own

Roger Griffin, one of the most influential living scholars of fascism, defines fascism as "a genus of political ideology whose mythic core in its various permutations is a palingenetic form of populist ultra-nationalism."[16] "Palingenesis" means "rebirth." Griffin further argues that fascism is associated with racism, but not necessarily with biological theories of race. The Alt-Right matches this description. However, the Alt-Right's problem—and this has been a perennial problem for the radical Right—is that it is not always clear how the Alt-Right defines the nation it wishes to revive. What does it mean to be an American nationalist, given America's long history as a multiracial society? In the American context, what would palingenesis actually entail if you are a white nationalist? What is their vision for the future, one that would be sufficiently inspiring to warrant becoming a social pariah?

There are many possible ways for white nationalists in the United States to possibly resolve this problem. One solution has been to essentially agree with the Far Left, and double down on the narrative that the United States is, and always has been, a white supremacist nation, and that the Founding Fathers intended for the United States to be a nation of white Europeans. From this perspective, the formula for national revival is essentially reactionary: the country just needs to return to its white supremacist roots.

The southern element of the radical Right had its own solutions to these problems: either secession or a policy of "states' rights" so strong that southern states will be free to reassert older systems of racial hierarchy. Although hard numbers are not available, I saw little evidence that southern nationalists were ever a major element of the Alt-Right. Groups such as the League of the South did not have a leading role in the movement. Although the proposed removal of Confederate statues was the purported justification for the Unite the Right rally in Charlottesville, southern heritage had not previously been a dominant element of Alt-Right thought and activism. There are still southern nationalist organizations. The League of the South and the Council of Conservative Citizens still exist, but these were rarely referenced by the Alt-Right and did not have much influence.

Since the Alt-Right's implosion in the second half of 2017, a major faction of the Alt-Right has attempted to rebrand itself as an "American nationalist" movement. They wrap themselves in the flag, and adopt Trump's slogan, "Make America Great Again," as their own. They go a step further than Trump-style populist conservatives, however, and argue for a racial interpretation of the American identity. Many have also declared their strong Christian faith.

There is another element of the radical Right, however, that largely agrees with the egalitarian interpretation of U.S. history. For this reason they reject the American identity entirely. They agree that the nation's guiding ethos is contained in the Declaration of Independence. Even if the United States did not achieve its revolutionary ideal of equality in its early history, the trajectory has been toward greater freedom, tolerance, and equity. Unlike other Americans who have this interpretation of U.S. history and identity, however, elements of the radical Right find this loathsome, and consider the United States and its ideals a plague on the world—or at least the white race. This is also the branch of the extreme Right that typically maintains the hostility toward Christianity found among earlier white nationalist leaders, thinkers, and groups—twentieth-century figures such as William Pierce, Ben Klassen, William Simpson, and others who viewed Christianity as one of their movement's primary stumbling blocks. People proposing such views, however, must acknowledge the challenge of appealing to ordinary white Americans, most of whom remain patriotic and at least nominally Christian.

Some on the radical Right have sought to get around this seeming conundrum by calling for a movement that transcends traditional understandings of nationalism. That is, it is time to move beyond the nation-state to a new form of identity and social organization. In place of nation-states, Europeans, and whites in European diaspora countries, must develop a pan-European consciousness, and eventually work toward the creation of a new white empire. Spencer is a contemporary representative of this view, but his is not a novel argument. Francis Parker Yockey, one of the most influential postwar white nationalist thinkers, called for just this kind of white imperium. The notion of a single political unit, from Brest to Vladivostok, and perhaps including the European diaspora countries in North America and Australia, represents a much more ambitious vision than the Far Right pro-Trump American nationalists, who are essentially arguing for a more racist version of modern conservatism.

Both far-right approaches to politics have significant drawbacks. Further, they are ultimately not compatible. The two ideologies seem to share little beyond racism and disgust with mainstream conservatism and liberalism. This is obviously a significant overlap, but it has not proven sufficient to hold all sides together. Major figures representing both sides consistently attack each other. Even if all influential leaders from both wings of the radical Right were united, they would still represent a small percentage of the U.S. electorate. Divided, and even hostile to each other, they are mostly irrelevant to developments in mainstream politics.

The Alt-Right Tore Itself Apart over "Optics," but They Have Not Found a Workable Solution to the Problem

One of the longest running and most vitriolic debates within the Alt-Right is about the visual images they present to the world ("optics"). On one extreme, you find radicals who see no problem with embracing the most shocking visuals, including swastikas. On the other side, there were those calling for a more bourgeois, respectable sensibility. Both sides had arguments for their position. This debate has a long history within the racist Right.

At first glance, the argument in favor of extreme imagery seems quite weak. After all, why would a movement, ostensibly seeking real-world power, intentionally marginalize itself, presenting an image that ordinary middle-class patriotic white people (presumably the target audience for a right-wing racialist movement) would immediately reject? The idea that the Far Right needs to present itself in the least threatening way possible, wearing suits and avoiding the most bellicose language, was most recently presented by a young internet personality named Nick Fuentes, who was considered the leader of the "Groyper movement." The Groypers (named after a cartoon toad similar to the older Alt-Right mascot "Pepe") made waves in 2019 as they disrupted more mainstream conservatives when they went on college speaking tours.[17] This perspective had a few reasonable premises. According to this view, there was an essential nativist element to the 2016 Trump movement. Many Trump supporters, at least quietly, maybe just subconsciously, wanted Trump to be more radical when it came to implementing a right-wing populist agenda. Fuentes and his supporters thus argued that they, not the mainstream conservatives, represent the true core of "Trumpism." However, despite being fervent in their anti-immigration stance, they mostly avoided explicit support for white nationalism. In some ways they were similar to those ardent segregationists in the South who called for an alliance with the ascendant conservative movement, even though that movement disavowed explicit racial bigotry.

On the other side, among those calling for transparent radicalism, there is also a long historical precedent, going back to George Lincoln Rockwell of the American Nazi Party. Rockwell argued that radicalism was essential for any right-wing movement that genuinely wanted to shake up the status quo. A movement that just wanted to fit in with ordinary conservatives, perhaps having some quiet influence behind the scenes, is doomed to fail. Instead, radicals must make their case to the American people. To do this, however, you need the media to cover you. The swastika armbands and extreme theatricality (he was the son of vaudeville actors) made Rockwell irresistible to the media, who made him a household name. Rockwell described his strategy as follows:

> The first phase is to reach the masses: you can do nothing until you've reached the masses. In order to reach them—without money, without

status, without a public platform—you have to become a dramatic figure. Now, in order to achieve that, I've had to take a lot of garbage: being called a nut and a monster and everything else. But by hanging up the swastika, I reach the masses. The second phase is to disabuse them of the false picture they have gotten of me, to educate them about what my real program is. The third phase will be to organize the people I've educated into a political entity. And the fourth phase will be to use that political entity as a machine to win political power. That's the plan. They all overlap, of course. Right now we're about 50 percent involved in phase two; we're actually beginning to educate people—in interviews like this one, in speaking engagements at colleges and the like. The other 50 percent is still phase one—just raising hell to keep people aware that there's such a thing as the American Nazi Party, not caring what they call us, as long as they call us something.[18]

Rockwell eventually planned to drop the theatrical extremism and start making his argument in more reasoned terms. Whether he could have succeeded in the long run is, technically, impossible to know—he was murdered by a disgruntled former follower. I have my doubts that he could have ever made the transition to a mainstream political figure. I have these doubts because Rockwell had many successors who continued his legacy. William Pierce, who gave up a career as a physics professor to pursue a life as a racist extremist, died marginalized many decades later. His organization, the National Alliance, was similarly marginal. To the extent that Pierce is remembered at all, it is because his genocidal novel *The Turner Diaries* provided inspiration for Timothy McVeigh's bombing of the federal building in Oklahoma City, but racism does not appear to have been the central element of McVeigh's ideology, and he was never a member of the National Alliance. Nonetheless, the kind of bombing he committed was described in *The Turner Diaries*, and that book was once popular at gun shows and within McVeigh's social milieu—he was involved in the militia movement of the 1990s, which often, though not always, had white nationalist elements.

Other white nationalist extremists who wore their violent ideology on their sleeves died similarly marginalized. Harold Covington, who led the openly neo-Nazi Northwest Front and wrote novels envisioning a future race war in the Pacific Northwest, recently died penniless and mostly ignored. The same is true of Richard Butler of Aryan Nations, who had a related vision for a white ethnostate. The National Socialist Movement, now mostly defunct, for most of its history, also draped itself in Nazi regalia. It was similarly never more than an obscure and small group.

Given this history, it may seem strange that any group would go this route of obvious self-marginalization. If this strategy had a chance to succeed, surely we would see some evidence for this by now. However, there may be other reasons why small, unpopular groups choose to adopt extreme, unpopular symbols. Political scientist Rochelle Terman seeks to make sense of why already marginalized ideologies ("backlash movements"[19]) would engage in behavior that could only lead to their further stigmatization. She argues that there are practical reasons for such behavior. For people who feel like mainstream society treats them as deviants, and keeps them at the bottom end of the social order, rejecting dominant social mores in an outlandish fashion is important. From this perspective, social frustration is a subjective experience, and not necessarily connected to a person's objective social standing. Thus, a right-wing white male may *feel* that he is at the bottom of the societal order, even if many measures suggest otherwise. For people who believe societal values are limiting their social standing, breaking taboos is the point. They want those taboos destroyed. Furthermore, although all members of a social or ideological group may be stigmatized by the larger society, those that engage in the most outrageous attacks on dominant norms can enjoy higher levels of prestige within the group, in part making up for the other social costs. These expressions of defiance furthermore help to build a strong group identity, and the social consequences that follow the larger society's efforts to punish deviants only further reinforces the sense that they are an oppressed group fighting a great injustice. Although their objectives are very different, we might think of the Alt-Right as considering itself in a situation analogous to the gay liberation movement several decades ago. As Terman put it:

> Deviance and norm violation are far from aberrant features of backlash politics. They are central and foundational to them. Taboo-breaking will indeed invite stigma and condemnation—that is precisely the intended purpose. By provoking mainstream rebuke,

deviance advances the goals of backlash movements by cultivating a distinctive social identity, instilling collective feelings of status loss, and validating the political claims of backlash movements in popular discourse.[20]

In the case of the Alt-Right, doxing was the greatest fear of anonymous activists and content creators. Once their status as white nationalists was revealed, they carried a permanent stigma. Furthermore, the more involved in the movement a person was, the greater the probability became that they would be revealed. In recent years, as antiracists increased their efforts to weaken the Alt-Right, maintaining anonymity became almost impossible for the more high-profile people in the movement. Following a doxing, many people did suffer serious social consequences, but they did sometimes achieve higher status within the movement, in a few cases managing to raise money to offset their loss of employment.

Beyond the individual benefits of earning higher status within the Alt-Right by being especially "edgy," there was another reason for breaking some of society's ultimate taboos. For decades, the Nazi regime has been treated as the personification of evil in the modern world. This development has been used not just to stigmatize people who supported that particular historical regime and its ideology, but to attack the very idea of explicit white identity and exclusionary politics in Western countries. Even when it required some extreme logical leaps, every right-wing movement beyond the bounds of mainstream acceptability has been treated by their opponents as somehow analogous to Nazism and thus deserving of extraordinary stigmatization. At its peak on the internet, people on the Alt-Right were bombarding social media with Nazi imagery (swastikas, gas chambers, etc.). Often these images were presented in a humorous fashion, perhaps showing Pepe the cartoon frog in a Nazi SS uniform. Following World War II, all symbols of Nazism were treated as having no redeeming values, with the hope that most normal people would recoil in horror at the sight of them. When they become ubiquitous, and often presented as part of a joke, people may eventually become desensitized to them.

Although there is a logic to extreme transgressions of social norms, recent years have shown that this strategy has its limits. Or, at the very least, it is clear that there is not yet—and perhaps never will be—a critical mass of Americans, including Trump supporters, that wants anything to do with explicit neo-Nazism. Perhaps this suggests that the Alt-Right tried to transition to being a real-world movement too soon, before it has sufficiently laid the metapolitical groundwork. The more optimistic view is that the efforts of online Nazis and Twitter trolls will never break a taboo that is so deeply ingrained in the American psyche.

The COVID-19 Epidemic Further Demonstrates the Far Right's Weakness

The global COVID-19 pandemic sounds like the kind of event that could provide a massive boon to the Far Right. The deadly disease and its consequences in many ways seemed to confirm many of the Far Right's critiques of the modern liberal world order. The disease originated in a foreign country, and spread to the United States and other Western countries in part because it is so easy for people to cross national boundaries, and leaders were hesitant to close down borders even after the danger became apparent. After the disease began spreading in the United States, mainstream conservatives stood against aggressive state action out of fear that it would derail the economy. Furthermore, as the nation struggled to produce enough masks and other protective gear, the problems of economic globalization became obvious. Americans began to realize how little is actually manufactured in the United States, and how vulnerable the nation's supply chains are to these kinds of disruptions. Whether or not a radical right-wing government in the United States would have actually done a better job when faced with a problem like this is unknown. From a pure propaganda standpoint, however, COVID-19 seemed, to me, like a major gift to radical-right movements. At the very least, lockdowns meant people spent more time online, where radical-right materials are most prevalent.

As the crisis deepened throughout 2020, we began to see increasingly breathless reports in the media that the extreme Right was using the crisis to recruit.[21] Although these stories were factually correct, they often provided a misleading picture. Most notably, they implied that the Far Right was providing a more consistent and coordinated message than was actually the case. Some reports seem to conflate radical libertarians with white nationalists (groups that sometimes overlap, but they are not synonymous). In truth, the radical Right was all over the place when it came to COVID-19. Some, such as the writers at The Daily Stormer, engaged in the kind of conspiracy theories more common among radical libertarianism—calling the entire disease a "hoax." Some did express hateful remarks toward China and Asian people more broadly. Others, however, expressed their admiration for the Chinese government, noting how China was able to bring the virus under control relatively quickly. These far-right voices, rather than pushing an antigovernment message, used the virus as an excuse to praise Chinese authoritarianism, suggesting it represents a model for a postliberal nation. Some urged the Far Right to stay the course and continue to trust President Trump. Others suggested this was just more evidence that supporting Trump had been a mistake from the beginning. Perhaps more importantly, these various camps spent most of their time in the crisis sniping at each other rather than presenting a consistent message.

This is not to say that there was no movement among parts of the public toward different varieties of the extreme Right during COVID-19 crisis. At the time of this writing, I have seen no empirical evidence of this either way, but it is a possibility. However, if that occurred, it is because the pandemic provided a unique set of circumstances that—rightly or wrongly—seemed to validate a radical-right view of the world. Such a movement was not the result of a smart, coordinated propaganda effort by radical-right opinion leaders.

THE ALT-RIGHT WAS MOSTLY ABSENT FROM THE JANUARY 6 INSURRECTION

The Unite the Right rally provided some of the more striking images of the Trump era. That historical event, however, will likely be permanently overshadowed by the riot that occurred in the final days of Trump's time in the White House, the so-called insurrection of January 6, 2021. The details of this incident are now well known. On that day, some of President Trump's supporters sought to overturn the results of the 2020 presidential election by disrupting Congress. A mob attacked the Capitol, illegally breaking into the building and engaging in vandalism. The building was not cleared of rioters for several hours. Capitol police shot and killed one rioter.

That riot was never going to overthrow the government, but some of the attackers may have thought otherwise. The rioters had no means of doing so. No amount of vandalism or loitering would have resulted in any kind of substantive change in policy—and certainly could not have stopped Joe Biden from assuming office. Many rioters clearly had violent intentions. Voices in the mob repeatedly called to "hang [Vice President] Mike Pence" for failing to overturn the election, something he did not even have the authority to do.[22]

To be clear, I do not, and never would, condone the actions of the Capitol rioters. What they did was clearly criminal. But from my perspective, in the event's aftermath, both sides engaged in dishonest revisionism. President Biden's claim that the attack was "the worst attack on our democracy since the Civil War"[23] was preposterous hyperbole. On the other hand, the Republican member of Congress who said it looked like "a normal tourist visit"[24] was similarly dishonest. In a polarized climate, one should expect politicians and pundits to put a partisan spin on everything. Nonetheless, the lack of fair, dispassionate analysis about the event from leading analysts was disappointing.

From the perspective of my own research, the most interesting aspect of the January 6 riots was the relative dearth of Alt-Right figures. The people present at that event appeared to be mostly different from those at Unite the Right. There was some overlap. Fuentes was present at both, but he never entered the Capitol building. Fuentes, and I think it is fair to say he is still a white nationalist (or at least something close to it), had previously broken with major figures of the Alt-Right and attempted to rebrand as a more conventional "America First" Trump supporter. Tim Gionet, better known by his pseudonym "Baked Alaska," was also present at both events, and he actually did enter the Capitol and break into congressional offices. Few could honestly describe the erratic Gionet as a consistent ideologue or a person anyone looked to for leadership, however.[25] In between these two events, for example, he briefly totally disavowed white supremacy, warning people that right-wing memes were radicalizing people, suggesting that he was transitioning into becoming an antiracist activist.[26] Before January 6, he was already viewed as something as a joke within far-right circles, a figure who would do almost anything for internet clout and was not especially intelligent. The reappearance of Baked Alaska certainly did not presage the Alt-Right's revival.

The Proud Boys were probably the most well-known group with a presence at both Unite the Right and January 6. The organization is best known for battling with left-wing activists known as Antifa (short for "antifascists"). The Proud Boys are a group with an idiosyncratic, but still far-right, ideological orientation.[27] Well before January 6, the group's founder, Gavin McInnes, had publicly rejected the white nationalism of the Alt-Right[28] (but some antiracists questioned his sincerity), and not long after that he left the group entirely. The subsequent leader of the Proud Boys was Enrique Tarrio, a Black Cuban American. The presence of high-profile people of color within the group seems to undermine the idea that the organization is committed to white nationalism as an ideology, but again some on the left have argued that minority Proud Boys do not prove that the group is not white supremacist in at least some aspects.[29] For the purposes of this chapter, however, the important thing to note is that the Proud Boys, as of January 6, 2021, did not present themselves as part of the Alt-Right, and would prefer to build relationships with more mainstream conservatives.

None of this is to say that overt white nationalists were not at the riot. In fact, there were apparently people present who were already on government watch lists as potential white supremacist terrorists.[30] The significant presence of Confederate flags also seems to undermine the idea that there was not a racial element to the day's events. Nonetheless, the riots were ideologically and demographically dissimilar from the Alt-Right demonstrations that took place in 2017. The January 6 crowds appeared significantly older than those present at earlier Alt-Right gatherings. They were also, on average, clearly more influenced by the preposterous "QAnon" conspiracy theories than by Alt-Right propaganda. The riots on January 6 demonstrated that many Trump supporters were radicalized in recent years. Nonetheless, their radicalization has not been a direct boon to the Alt-Right.

CONCLUSION

In some ways, it would seem the history of the Alt-Right is at odds with other points I argue in this book. I claim that identity politics, in some form, is inevitable. I further claim that the conservative movement's failure to reckon with this inevitability is a problem, both for conservatism and for American life more broadly. And yet, with the Alt-Right, Americans were offered undistilled right-wing identity politics, and most Americans (including white conservatives) chose not to embrace it or even give it a serious hearing. Does this mean my argument is wrong? Perhaps. However, what I think it instead shows is that the Alt-Right was wrong about some key aspects of identity.

Richard Spencer's catchphrase during the Alt-Right's peak was "Race is real. Race matters. Race is the foundation of identity."[31] This was the opening line of the "Charlottesville Statement," which was to be the Alt-Right's equivalent to the conservative movement's "Sharon Statement" of 1960 and the New Left's "Port Huron Statement" of 1962. Those three sentences deserve more discussion than I can provide here, but they must be at least briefly considered. To say that "race is real" has many possible meanings, and many books and scholarly publications have focused entirely on that subject. That statement must be evaluated from a scientific, philosophical, linguistic, and sociological perspective. Even if scientists demonstrate that there are biological distinctions that mostly correspond to basic racial categories, it does not immediately follow that these distinctions are substantively important, or that the many ways in which race has been socially constructed were biologically determined. Furthermore, it is not clear against whom Spencer was arguing in the statement. Even if race is a social construction, social constructions are nonetheless "real."

Some in the Alt-Right would, perhaps reasonably, say that demanding such a rigorous approach to that statement is disingenuous. After all, for what other political questions do we insist upon such a discussion? But in this case, I do think it is appropriate, given the stakes involved. As for whether "race matters," I think most people across the political spectrum will agree with that statement, even if they disagree on whether race represents a valid biological category. Perhaps some conservatives represent an exception to this claim, those who hope that a postracial America really is close at hand and can be realized with a few changes to our political discourse.

We can challenge the statement that "race is the foundation of identity." There are too many counterexamples suggesting otherwise. Did identity not exist before the modern concept of race was fully developed? Do we not find identity politics in monoracial societies? The fact that white Americans did not rally behind the banner of white identity politics once it was raised seems to indicate that this statement is simply incorrect, but there are various ways we could interpret this development.

Perhaps the Alt-Right's failure does not prove that this point is mistaken; it may instead suggest that white Americans prefer that their racial identity politics to be just a little less explicit. That is, they want white identity politics, but they want a degree of plausible deniability. From this perspective, the Alt-Right was being just a bit too honest about what they were offering. Had they been a bit more dissembling, they might have had more success. If this is the correct interpretation, some might reasonably say it is evidence that white racism is just as powerful as ever, if just a little harder to detect. On the other hand, the fact that white Americans feel uncomfortable explicitly organizing as whites per se seems to be evidence of significant, if incomplete, success by antiracist movements. It means that most whites have accepted that, even if they quietly, and perhaps unconsciously, want a racial identity movement of their own, they nonetheless feel that such a movement would be in some way immoral. Progressives may find this an insufficient victory, and argue that more implicit forms of white identity politics are nonetheless insidious. It is a major victory nonetheless. If a majority, or even a large minority, of whites had openly embraced the Alt-Right, racial progressives would currently be in a much more difficult position.

Another possibility is that most whites really do not, at present, view race as the cornerstone of their identity. That is not to say that they have no sense of racial identity. Rather, their race is not more important than other attributes, such as party affiliation, religion, region, class, and educational attainment. When it comes to religion, the question gets a bit complicated, given that we now know that there was a racial element to the rise of the religious Right, but I think the antiracism of contemporary evangelical elites is sincere. Education and class, however, are also interesting. Over the last few decades, a new stereotype about race and class has developed. Explicit racism has increasingly been viewed as a "lowbrow" vice. That is, the stereotype of a racist is now typically a poorly educated hayseed. Holding (or at least expressing) racist views is a sign of being downscale, someone who will never be part of the elite. This sense of elite identity may be more important to these whites than their sense of racial identity and solidarity. As long as this understanding of racial attitudes remains the case, with racism associated with ignorance, violence, and bad taste, right-wing racial identity movements will have a difficult time attracting adherents.

NINE

Conclusion

Conservatism in the 2020s

In 1976, Irving Kristol, the godfather of neoconservatism, published one of his many valuable critiques of the modern conservative movement. Kristol argued that the standard conservative talking points about the welfare state were disconnected from political realities. This was a bold claim. Conservatives took pride in their political realism, condemning the Left for its utopian dreams. Nonetheless, Kristol argued that conservatives were hindered by their own ideological thinking. According to Kristol:

> The idea of a welfare state is in itself perfectly consistent with a con-servative political philosophy—as Bismarck knew, a hundred years ago. In our urbanized, industrialized, highly mobile society, people need government action of some kind if they are to cope with many of their problems: old age, illness, unemployment, etc. They need such assistance; they demand it; they will get it. The only interesting political question is: *How* will they get it?
>
> This is not a question the Republican Party has faced up to, be-cause it still feels, deep down, that a welfare state is inconsistent

with such traditional American virtues as self-reliance and individual liberty. Those virtues are real enough, and are a proper conservative concern. But the task is to create the kind of welfare state that is consistent, to the largest degree possible, with such virtues.[1]

Kristol argued that conservatives' commitment to an ideological dogma blinded them to basic facts about U.S. public opinion and the political realities that flowed from them. Thus, these conservatives violated an essential conservative principle (realism) in order to uphold another, less important conservative tenet (economic self-reliance). "Conservatism," in the political sense, has many possible definitions. Self-described conservatives have claimed many different values and philosophical foundations. Some of these values are at odds with each other. Conservative thinkers from many different conservative traditions, however, take pride in their realistic approach to what they typically call "human nature." That is, they take it as a given that human beings are flawed, that some of these flaws are easily predictable, and they are inevitable. Thus, a well-designed social order will take these flaws into account, mitigating them and, where possible, even channeling them in productive directions.

As one of the most well-known examples of this form of conservative argument, conservatives accept that individual greed is not a human failing that can be stamped out or wished away. The dangers of greed, however, can be partially softened by a capitalist system. For all their flaws, markets provide a socially beneficial means to satisfy greed. In a free market, at least in theory, all exchanges are voluntary, and thus none will occur unless all parties feel that they benefit from a trade. Although there may be asymmetries in these benefits, and all but a few radical libertarians accept the need for some regulations, markets are a better means to satisfy greed than their alternatives—banditry or violent conquest, to use extreme examples.

Conservatives are quick to reproach their opponents for their utopian efforts to fundamentally change human beings through social engineering. According to conservatives, there will never be a "New Soviet Man," perfectly socialized into an equitable, socialist society. Many leading conservatives have persuasively argued that attempts to reshape human nature in this way will fail. In the best-case scenario, massive sums of money will be wasted and the project will be abandoned. In the worst-case scenarios, the excesses of totalitarian communism, such as Gulags, are a foreseeable result. Whether the result of original sin or natural selection over millions of years, human nature is fixed, or at least not infinitely malleable. Russell Kirk, one of the twentieth century's most important conservative intellectuals, put it this way:

> Human nature suffers irremediably from certain grave faults, the conservatives know. Man being imperfect, no perfect social order ever can be created. Because of human restlessness, mankind would grow rebellious under any utopian domination and would break out once more in violent discontent—or else expire of boredom. To seek for utopia is to end in disaster, the conservative says: we are not made for perfect things. All that we reasonably can expect is a tolerably ordered, just, and free society, in which some evils, maladjustments, and suffering will continue to lurk. By proper attention to prudent reform, we may preserve and improve this tolerable order. But if the old institutional and moral safeguards of a nation are neglected, then the anarchic impulse in humankind breaks loose: "the ceremony of innocence is drowned." The ideologues who promise the perfection of man and society have converted a great part of the twentieth-century world into a terrestrial hell.[2]

Conservatives have not been consistent in their use of realism when it comes to human behavior, however. Kristol suggested one such inconsistency in the 1970s. In his view, conservatives needed to accept that a majority of citizens in modern democracies will demand some kind of welfare state and to focus their energies on designing a welfare state congruent with conservative values. In this book, I have argued that contemporary conservatives have a similar blind spot: identity politics. This is not to say that conservatives never talk about identity politics. They talk about identity politics all the time. Unfortunately, their discussions of the subject are often superficial, and their proposed solutions to the problems created by identity politics have proven ineffectual. This is not surprising, as their discussions of identity politics often amounts to little more than pleading with their fellow Americans to "stop the identity politics." This is insufficient. Such appeals feel disingenuous because they are incongruous with conservatism's own history—conservatives have never consistently opposed appeals to identity. They will also fail because identity politics in some form is likely inescapable, even if everyone would be better off without them.

Many conservative critiques of identity politics deserve a fair hearing. From a normative perspective, there are admirable aspects to the conservative vision of an enlightened electorate. Conservatives have nonetheless failed to develop a coherent response to the legitimate arguments identity politics practitioners make. At a time when identitarian concerns are an inescapable part of American politics, conservative talking points require an update. In this chapter, I consider some of the more recent conservative arguments about the causes of and solutions to contemporary problems, and offer a few parting thoughts of my own.

Although identity politics represents some special challenges, we can debate how concerned we should be about it. One could argue it represents a looming disaster, perhaps the end of the American experiment in ordered liberty. On the other hand, perhaps the rise of identity politics may be a sign that the United States remains strong and successful. Perhaps only in a wealthy and resilient society could we become so emotionally invested in battles that often have such limited stakes. This is of course especially true in some of the more famous examples of campus political correctness. Only in a pluralist society in which the most pressing material needs have been met could people get up in arms about insensitive Halloween costumes at private parties for young adults. If the country faced "real problems," perhaps "wokeness" about identity concerns would diminish.

Upheavals during the summer of 2020 seem to challenge that more optimistic perspective. Given the COVID-19 pandemic, the United States certainly faced a great challenge, one affecting every demographic group. Yet after George Floyd's murder, supporters of the Black Lives Matter movement protested across the nation. In some cases, this was followed by looting and rioting. For much of that year, racial discord in the United States seemed to be at its highest point since the Rodney King riots of the early 1990s. Perhaps a better comparison would be the late 1960s, when racial turmoil engulfed cities across the nation. Although it may seem reasonable to compare today's events to those of the late 1960s, given that today's protests are again across the nation, the overall death toll and scale of the property damage is not comparable at all. It is also possible that the violence and disorder of the summer of 2020 was a temporary phenomenon driven by anger at the Trump administration, a trend that will wither with a Democrat back in the White House.

Even if we experience a return to relative calm in the United States, American conservatives nonetheless need to think carefully about how their movement will approach the questions of identity politics that can no longer be dismissed. Even if we wish to diminish the importance of group identities and attachments to partisan politics, calls for individualism built on arguments about natural rights are unlikely to persuade Americans to abandon identitarian concerns.

CONSERVATIVES REVISIT WHERE THINGS WENT WRONG

As some conservatives have begun rethinking a few of the movement's key assumptions, several have sought to discern where the United States (and sometimes the West more broadly) got off track and set us on the path toward our current predicament. This is not a new trend among conservatives, of course. Conservatives have created various theories on this subject from the movement's earliest days. Over the last few years, however, conservative intellectuals have made some novel contributions to this genre, which are worth exploring in some detail.

In 2018, political theorist Patrick Deneen released *Why Liberalism Failed*.[3] As far as conservative books go, the title may not seem provocative. It seems like a title any number of conservative talk show hosts might have chosen for a book. Deneen was not talking about liberalism in the colloquial, partisan, contemporary sense, however. According to Deneen, the modern problems of the United States are rooted in the essential premises of classical liberalism, the very philosophy most conservatives claim to wholeheartedly support. Liberalism, in all of its forms, seeks to liberate individuals from "particular places, relationships, memberships, and even identities."[4] The inevitable result of liberalism is the loosening of social bonds, resulting in atomization. Echoing earlier work by conservatives such as Robert Nisbet, Deneen suggests that the quest for total individual autonomy weakens institutions that once stood between the individual and the state. The decline of these intermediary institutions leaves the state as the only safety net available to individuals in difficult times.

Although their disputes are unquestionably heated, Deneen argues that modern American conservatives and progressives are both members of the same liberal family, they simply disagree on which elements of individual liberation should be prioritized: conservative liberals emphasize economic individualism and autonomy; progressive liberals believe individual freedom is best realized when inequalities are reduced. Both sides, however, seek to broaden the scope of individual autonomy. Deneen even suggests that modern identity politics shares some essential premises with classical liberalism, noting that "both rose to dominance in the university in conformity with the modern notion of freedom."[5] Whereas the rationalism associated with classical liberalism is designed to tame nature and liberate human beings from natural limits, the postmodernist Left promotes "radical emancipatory theory focused on destroying all forms of hierarchy, tradition, and authority, liberating the individual through the tools of research and progress."[6] Both views reject the older conservative belief in custom and prescription.

If Deneen is correct, conservatives have been largely mistaken about the fault lines of modern politics. This position suggests that individualism and statism are not opponents:

> Thus, the insistent demand that we choose between protection of individual liberty and expansion of state activity masks the true relation between the state and the market: that they grow constantly and necessarily together. Statism enables individualism, individualism demands statism. For all the claims about electoral transformation—for "Hope and Change" or "Making America Great Again"—two facts are naggingly apparent: modern liberalism proceeds by making us both more individualist and more statist.[7]

Deneen argues that liberalism has had such a long, seemingly successful run in the West because, until recently, Western countries had not yet fully put liberalism into practice. The older social bonds, such as religion, community, and family, had not yet been dissolved. Liberalism's disastrous implications only became clear when liberalism became "true to itself."[8] In contrast to conservatives such as George Will who argue that the Progressive movement of the early twentieth century represented a betrayal of the Founding Fathers' vision, Deneen suggests that the Progressive Era and the Founding Era were "strikingly similar" in their beliefs about the purpose of government. Leading intellectuals from both eras sought to increase the nation's material wealth and thus "the Progressives were as much heirs as the Founders to the modern project of seeing politics as the means of mastering nature, expanding national power, and liberating the individual from interpersonal bonds and obligations, including those entailed by active democratic citizenship."[9]

If Deneen's view of the deleterious effects of classical liberalism becomes dominant among conservatives, the subsequent question is what this means for conservative politics. In the modern West, liberalism has faced two major ideological opponents: fascism and communism. Thinkers from both of these traditions critiqued liberalism, sometimes using language similar to Deneen's. Yet neither Deneen nor any of his conservative admirers are calling for anything analogous to those discredited ideologies. Indeed, as part of his solution to liberalism's problems, he asserts (like Kirk) that "we must outgrow the age of ideology."[10] For a more specific vision, Deneen praises Wendell Berry's localist worldview.[11] Berry has a number of salutary traits that may make him an increasingly attractive thinker to conservatives pursuing a new political paradigm. Berry has made compelling arguments against the growth of the state (including the welfare state), but has also critiqued the growth of multinational corporations disconnected from any local or regional loyalties. In many ways, his vision echoes that of the Southern Agrarians who achieved some notoriety in the early twentieth century, but he simultaneously rejects racism in all forms, even declaring that racism is antithetical to the community values he advocates.[12]

Deneen's is not the only voice on the mainstream Right to recently challenge some of classical liberalism's basic assumptions. Many conservatives have praised Ryszard Legutko, a contemporary Polish philosopher, for his critiques of modern democracy. Legutko has argued that liberal democracy shares many of communism's premises about human nature and the purpose of politics.[13] Legutko claims that, although they resulted in very different forms of government, modern liberal democracy has more similarities with totalitarian communism than most people realized during the Cold War. Both ideologies possess total confidence in their superiority to all other potential systems, and both possess an element of utopianism. They furthermore both "proved to be all-unifying entities compelling their followers how to think, what to do, how to evaluate events, what to dream, and what language to use. They both had their orthodoxies and their models of an ideal citizen."[14] Both are also driven by a view of human nature that is decidedly at odds with both the classical and the Christian perspective, and both are intolerant of competing visions. Although communism's totalitarianism was more vulgar and overt, in some ways liberalism is more insidious because many people do not recognize its radical nature.

In *The Age of Entitlement* (2020), one of the more provocative recent conservative books, Christopher Caldwell, a former senior editor at the *Weekly Standard* and now a contributing editor at the *Claremont Review of Books*, argues that many trends that conservatives decry have resulted from the civil rights movement. Caldwell does not defend racial segregation, but he suggests that the civil rights revolutions' opponents were largely correct in their predictions about what new civil rights legislation would mean for American life. By outlawing discrimination on the part of private businesses, the U.S. federal government dealt fatal blows to the right to private property and the right to freedom of association. Caldwell rejects the common conservative claim that there was a major distinction between the early civil rights movement, which conservatives now say was a good thing, and more contemporary identity politics, which they decry. Instead, the civil rights movement set the stage for all subsequent identity-based grievance movements: "Plainly the civil rights acts had wrought a change in the country's constitutional culture. The innovations of the 1960s had given progressives control over the most important levers of government, control that would exist as long as the public was afraid of being called racist. Not just excluded and exploited blacks but all aggrieved minorities now sought to press their claims under this new model of progressive governance."[15]

Conservative theories of political and cultural decay vary in the level of controversy they inspire. There is not a linear relationship between a conservative argument's radicalism and the amount of outrage it is likely to provoke. The least controversial conservatives are those making technocratic, utilitarian arguments about current policy debates, either accepting or not commenting on the philosophical foundations of modern, cosmopolitan liberal democracy. However, the most outlandish reactionaries attacking intellectual developments that occurred hundreds or even thousands of years ago, are also noncontroversial. Radical conservatives or libertarians who claim the Articles of Confederation were superior to the Constitution, reject the basics of Lockean liberalism, blame William of Ockham's nominalism for today's supposed social maladies, or think the Austro-Hungarian Empire represented an admirable social order are mostly given a pass or just ignored by mainstream critics. In some ways, conservative radicalism can reach a point where it is viewed as harmless, the musings of reactionary cranks that will go nowhere. Conservatives attacking the civil rights movement directly, however, are a genuine threat to the current social order if their arguments are taken seriously by a large number of people. This is unquestionably a key reason why Caldwell's book received furious denunciations from writers in the nation's most prestigious mainstream publications,[16] whereas other books, arguably more radically reactionary, were either unnoticed or given a more respectful hearing.

CONSERVATISM AND NATIONALISM?

The subject of nationalism has been salient in political discussions across the globe. It has not, however, been a common theme throughout the history of the conservative movement. In fact, conservatives have traditionally sought to distance themselves from nationalism as a concept. This may be changing. What a conservative embrace of nationalism means for the future of the United States will depend on how conservatives define nationalism, which can take many forms. In *The Philosophy of Nationalism* (1998), Paul Gilbert provides a helpful definition of the term that captures its meaning while remaining sufficiently flexible to contain many varieties of nationalism: "Nationalism is the principle that a nation is a group which has, ceteris paribus, a right to independent statehood by virtue of being the kind of group it is."[17] Working from this definition, nationalism as such is not an especially controversial idea. The challenge arises as we try to define what kind of groups deserve independence, how that independence is defined, and how that independence and cohesiveness is maintained into the future.

For much of U.S. history, progressives were arguably more nationalistic than conservatives. The Progressive movement of the early twentieth century was very keen on creating a new, more homogenous United
States, centrally administered by a rational national government. Many
conservatives have been hostile or ambivalent toward this idea, tending
to think about smaller loyalties than the nation. They wrote about small
communities and intermediate sources of authority that stood between
the individual and the central government, things such as churches,
community centers, and local government. Older generations of conservatives were skeptical of grand, national projects. The so-called Old
Right was concerned about too much flag-waving and praise for the
military, and tended toward isolationism in world affairs. This type of
conservatism became less pronounced in the latter decades of the twentieth century, as conservatives became the most pro-military faction of
the society. The ability of the United States to project power around the
globe is still a source of pride among many conservatives. Yet, in the
context of the Cold War, nationalism was less of a theme than the divide
between communist and noncommunist.

Nationalism also has traits that are at odds with other conservative
principles. For religious conservatives, especially those that subscribe to
a universalist religion such as Christianity, the community that most
interests them extends beyond national boundaries. They are presumably part of a community of believers that covers the entire globe. The
economic conservative can also have problems with nationalism. To
economic conservatives and libertarians, national sovereignty, which
extends to economic matters, can be a hindrance to the free flow of
goods across national borders. In this sense, nationalism can be a threat
to economic growth and efficiency. This is further confusing because
there is supposedly a distinction between patriotism and nationalism.
Conservatives tend to view themselves as patriotic, but will usually deny
that they are nationalistic. William F. Buckley Jr. once declared, "I'm as
patriotic as anyone from sea to shining sea, but there's not a molecule
of nationalism in me."[18]

But this is unsatisfying unless we can rhetorically disentangle the
two concepts. What makes a patriot different from a nationalist? George
Orwell thought they could be distinguished according to how they
approach power:

Nationalism is not to be confused with patriotism. Both words are normally used in so vague a way that any definition is liable to be challenged, but one must draw a distinction between them, since two different and even opposing ideas are involved. By "patriotism" I mean devotion to a particular place and a particular way of life, which one believes to be the best in the world but has no wish to force on other people. Patriotism is of its nature defensive, both militarily and culturally. Nationalism, on the other hand, is inseparable from the desire for power. The abiding purpose of every nationalist is to secure more power and more prestige, not for himself but for the nation or other unit in which he has chosen to sink his own individuality.[19]

Nationalism has had negative connotations for many decades. When we think of nationalism, we often immediately think of nationalism's worst excesses, such as the chauvinistic nationalists who dominated Europe in the first half of the twentieth century. If nationalism can lead to Nazism, many people would prefer that nationalism simply cease to exist.

Progressives often make this argument. Although the Left was a bit more sympathetic to nationalism during the period of decolonization of the Third World in the postwar period, overall most progressives would prefer that all the world be cosmopolitan, diverse, and tolerant. To avoid the excesses of nationalism, it may be better to simply get rid of the concept of nations. Ideas such as national sovereignty may even be dangerous because they are inherently exclusionary. The only way to save the world from war and its related atrocities is to simply abandon the idea of independent nations, perhaps creating a global government, or at least accepting the principle of open borders. Over the past several years, the antinationalist attitudes on the left have on only strengthened. In contrast, some conservatives are reconsidering the movement's ambivalence toward nationalism, suggesting that it should be integrated into conservative political thought and practice.

Philosopher Yoram Hazony, author of *The Virtue of Nationalism* (2019), is the most important conservative calling for a new embrace of nationalism. Like Deneen, Hazony has called for conservatives to reject important elements of the classical liberal intellectual tradition. He writes that Lockean liberalism is based on false premises about human nature, building theories of government on mistaken individualist

premises about human beings: "The *Second Treatise* . . . offers a rational-
ist view of human political life that has abstracted away every bond that
ties human beings to one another other than consent."[20] According to
Hazony, our loyalties to our families, tribes, and nations have never really
been the result of consent, and the notion that the state was brought into
being by individuals consenting to trade away some liberties in order to
safeguard certain interests is completely ahistorical: "In real life, nations
are communities bound together by bounds of mutual loyalty, carrying
forward particular traditions from one generation to the next."[21] However, Hazony is willing to embrace liberal thinkers when they share his
perspective: "My view resembles that of Mill, who saw the independence
of national states as an evident good and argued that such states should
be established where feasible."[22]

Much of Hazony's book is focused on defending nationalism from
its many critics. He was especially dismissive of the idea that World
War II shows us that nationalism is bad. In fact, he argues, World War II
demonstrated precisely why nationalism is important. In Hazony's
view, Adolf Hitler was not a nationalist. Instead, he argues, nationalism
means a united, culturally cohesive population living together within
geographical boundaries and sharing a state dedicated to that people's
interests. Hitler, in contrast, was an imperialist, seeking an empire.
Rather than exclusively pursuing the well-being of Germans, as a proper
nationalist would have done, he sought to dominate all of Europe. Furthermore, far from proving that nationalism is dangerous, the Holocaust
proved that nationalism is necessary. Hazony suggests that the Jewish
suffering was partly the result of the lack of a Jewish state that could
advocate for Jews on the world stage and provide a safe haven for Jewish
victims of persecution.

Despite his many arguments in defense of nationalism, Hazony is
careful to stop short of declaring that all cohesive peoples are entitled
to their own independent nations. Instead, he argues that this must be
considered on a case-by-case basis. He, for example, rejects the idea that
the southern states in the United States that sought their independence
in 1861 had a right to a separate independent state, and he applauds
President Lincoln for fighting to keep them in the Union.[23] His book
is also notable for a significant omission. Although Hazony complains
about how his own country of Israel is discussed on the world stage,

reasonably charging a great many of Israel's critics with hypocrisy, he never directly addresses the question of Palestinian independence in the book. One can reasonably assume that Palestinians do not meet his requirements.

Rich Lowry, editor of *National Review*, has also argued that conservatives must develop a new appreciation for nationalism.[24] Lowry argues that President Trump's variety of nationalism, as he understands it, does not deserve the indignation it has received from his opponents at home and abroad. According to Lowry, the basic contours of Trumpian nationalism—that the U.S. government and its leaders should give priority to the well-being of U.S. citizens—represent basic common sense. Furthermore, Lowry argues that efforts to equate nationalism with racism are misguided—the concepts are not invariably related. Indeed, in a highly diverse nation such as the United States, a strong national identity is necessary to unite various tribal interests. In other words, Lowry suggests that nationalism, as he envisions it, is not a manifestation of identity politics but is potentially the solution to identity politics.

A potential problem with Lowry's analysis is that, despite being an apparent attempt to reorient mainstream conservatism with the *Zeitgeist* of the Trump era, it essentially offers the same conservatism that *National Review* has long promoted. Aside from a few critiques of President George W. Bush's foreign policy mistakes and the overt anti-nationalism of radical libertarians, Lowry's nationalist program is not especially innovative.

CONSERVATISM AND POPULISM: CAN THEY BE RECONCILED?

Since 2016, mostly because of the successful Brexit vote in the UK and Trump's electoral victory, the Western intelligentsia has focused its attention on populism—usually to decry the phenomenon. The discussions of populism are tied with many of the themes of this book. Populism is often discussed as a form of backlash politics, a way in which majorities respond to demographic changes they never approved.[25] With right-wing populism apparently on the rise, it seems reasonable for conservatives to try to harness this "populist moment" and use it to its own ends. The problem with aligning explicitly with populism, however, is that conservatism and populism are seemingly incompatible, at least if conservatives wish to be consistent.

Within conservative thought, there has always been a wariness of "the masses." More so than the Left, the Right is concerned about the excesses of democracy and a turn toward mob rule. Among conservatives, the U.S. Constitution is revered largely because it places checks on the public's passions, ensuring order and stability. From this perspective, the Constitution's virtues result from its undemocratic nature. According to conservative intellectuals, excessive flattery of the common people, and vilification of the elite, can lead a nation down a path that ends with the guillotine and national devastation. The unchecked masses are more than a threat to the power of existing elites; unrestrained and led by a dema-gogue, they can threaten the basic stability that a society needs to flourish.

On the other hand, conservatism also seeks to be a mass move-ment. The nature of representative democracy precludes too much open elitism. To secure electoral victories, the Republican Party has to praise its base. For the most part, the conservative movement seems to under-stand this, and many prominent conservative journalists and intellectuals have embraced populist talking points. Trump was, rhetorically, the most populist Republican president in living memory, but he was not a total aberration. Conservatism has successfully branded itself as a common-sense ideology with plain-old-folks appeal. When framed in this way, conservatism has enjoyed tremendous electoral windfalls.

The relationship between conservatism and elitism has an addi-tional complication: ideological conservatives are woefully underrepre-sented among critical elite groups. For most of the twentieth century, and continuing to this day, much of the elite class has leaned to the left. This is especially true of academics, journalists, and entertainers. Thus, a successful conservative push for more elite control would actually strengthen conservatism's ideological opponents. So conservatives, the-oretically in favor of elitism, tend to demonize the nation's actual elites as out-of-touch "limousine liberals" who do not understand the common person. George W. Bush was presented as the candidate you "want to have a beer with," a man who spends his downtime clearing brush at his ranch, not hobnobbing with Hollywood celebrities or New York City socialites. Conservatives could presumably get around this problem by saying that contemporary elites do not deserve their status. They could say that the people in charge of shaping the country's politics and culture are not aristocrats in the proper ancient Greek sense—aristocracy defined as "rule of the best." However, no contemporary conservative has, to my knowledge, explained how a new elite class more to their liking could be realistically fostered and eventually usurp the existing elites.

Further, despite conservative praise for the undemocratic nature of the Constitution and republican government, they have also been frustrated by the checks that representative democracy places on their agenda. Today's conservatives tend to favor state-level initiatives and referenda in order to put their preferred policies into law. There are times when direct democracy is more efficacious for conservatives than representative democracy. It was largely through these channels that conservatives implemented bans on same-sex marriage during the George W. Bush years. This was also the means conservatives used to pass strong anti-immigration legislation in California during the 1990s. Even in 2020, conservatives managed to safeguard the ban on affirmative action in progressive California because the question was put to voters—if the California legislature had been able to decide this issue, the ban would have certainly been lifted.

The issue is additionally confusing because the term "populism" is often used by the media without explanation. Like conservatism, populism is a concept that most people intuitively grasp, but may not be able to define. Unlike, say, libertarianism, populism is not a coherent ideology based on a series of logical axioms. Nor is it tied to a particular set of policies. The fact that both Trump and Bernie Sanders were described as populists during their respective battles for presidential nominations demonstrates this. Yet populism is more than just a vague appeal to "the people." To be classified accurately as populist, a leader or movement should meet certain criteria. Cas Mudde describes "populism as an ideology that considers society to be ultimately separated into two homogeneous and antagonistic groups, 'the pure people' versus 'the corrupt elite,' and which argues that politics should be an expression of the volonté générale (general will) of the people."[26] Populism may often be associated with a charismatic leader or leaders, but populism does not require a particular leadership style.[27]

Although all populists are defined by their focus on the "people" verses the "elite," populism can manifest itself in multiple ways. For this reason, populism, in contrast to other political frameworks, is a "thin ideology,"[28] if it can be described as an ideology at all.[29] Although the populist stands for the pure people and their interests, these perceived interests will be dependent on the greater context. The most obvious example is how populism tends to manifest itself in economically developed countries compared to less developed countries. In poorer regions of the globe, such as Latin America, populism has been predominantly a phenomenon of the political Left, calling for greater social equity and a redistribution of resources. In more economically developed countries, populism tends to be found on the political Right, where populists defend "the people" from both globalist elites and Third World immigrants. There are exceptions to these generalizations, however; the political success of President Jair Bolsonaro in Brazil shows that developing nations are not immune to right-wing populism.

Unlike most center-right politicians and parties, the right-wing populist is (at least rhetorically) skeptical of big business, viewing its desire for cheap, immigrant labor a threat to the cultural integrity of the nation. Beyond attacking the official powerholders, the political and economic elites, the right-wing populist is also hostile to those institutions that shape and advance the elites' values, especially the media and academia.[30] We see examples of this variety of populism throughout Western Europe, with examples such as the National Rally in France and UKIP in the UK. We recently saw it most forcefully in the United States in the candidacy (though not necessarily in the presidency) of Donald Trump, but we saw earlier manifestations in the candidacies of George Wallace, Ross Perot, and Pat Buchanan. There was also a populist element to the Tea Party movement that achieved influence in the Republican Party during Obama's presidency.

The relationship between populism and democracy can be nebulous. On its face, it seems absurd to describe the populist as an antidemocrat, given that the populist explicitly calls for the rule of the majority. Indeed, the populist is more likely than other ideologues to favor decision-making via direct democracy: through referendums and popular initiatives. Given this trend, it seems odd that the democratic sensibilities of populists are ever called into question. Yet populism also has a transparent illiberal quality, and may threaten certain democratic values, such as minority rights. Today's most vigorous opponents of populism are found mostly on the center and the left, but there is also a strong and explicitly antipopulist tradition within American conservative thought.

Kirk was an early conservative critic of populism: "A populist, whose basic conviction is that the cure for democracy is more democracy, conserves nothing—even though he may wish to do so. Populism, in effect, is what Walter Bagehot called 'the ignorant democratic conservatism of the masses.'"[31] Kirk was not unique among the early conservatives in his distrust of both the common person and democracy. Richard Weaver also plainly stated: "Democracy cannot exist without aristocracy."[32] Other famous conservatives praised elitism, at least in theory. James Burnham viewed Machiavellian elites as "defenders of freedom."[33] While explaining why he felt the direct election of U.S. senators was a mistake, Peter Viereck declared:

> Democracy is housebroken, is tolerant, humane, civil-libertarian, only after being filtered, traditionalized, constitutionalized through indirect representation. Suppose America had retained the indirect election of Senators. . . . In that case, our Senate would today would contain more pompous asses and more stealers of graft but fewer thought-control demagogues, fewer stealers of our civil liberties. That gain would have been worth the price; a country so over-rich as ours can afford waste and graft. What it cannot afford is demagogues mauling our liberties and muddying our foreign policy.[34]

But, again, there is a problem with transparent elitism on the right. Conservative elitism only makes sense if a society's elites are also conservative. By the time the conservative movement was born, this was a questionable assumption. In fact, it was questionable before the conservative movement arrived. For the most part, the intelligentsia of the United States was fully on board with Roosevelt and his New Deal. In fact, support for actual communism was fashionable among many of the leading intellectuals during the prewar era. This tension in conservative thought was clear to anyone familiar with Albert Jay Nock's thinking. Although Nock died in 1945, he had a tremendous influence on many of the conservative movement's first important figures, including Buckley. In his most famous essay, "Isaiah's Job," Nock lamented the fate of any prophet telling the people what they need to hear.[35] According to

Nock, not only would the person advocating sound ideas be rejected by the masses, he would be equally dismissed by the elites, who stand to benefit from the entrenched system. A true prophet is thus doomed to forever preach to an ineffectual and unknown "Remnant," who will never succeed in changing a society's trajectory before reaching a point of total calamity.

If conservatism is content to be an insular ideology of curmudgeons, happy to speak to each other while waiting for society's dissolution, then disdaining both the elites and the masses is a fine strategy. But the conservative journalists and intellectuals who expended so much energy and creativity in the postwar years had greater ambitions. They ultimately wanted real power, which required both creating elites of their own and flattering the masses.

Buckley's contradictory ideological leanings in many ways personify the fraught relationship between conservatism and populism. Buckley was as close to an aristocrat as the United States produces. Throughout his long life he socialized with the leading literary and intellectual figures of the twentieth century, counting many great liberal luminaries among his friends. In no way was Buckley a "man of the people"; he was more comfortable among Manhattan socialites, sailing across the Atlantic, and enjoying the ski slopes of the Swiss Alps than mingling with the plebs of Peoria. Yet in spite of being an elitist in his everyday life, Buckley as a writer and speaker was prone to open hostility toward the intellectual class. He first entered the public arena with a book attacking his alma mater, *God and Man at Yale*. The book was especially critical of the Yale faculty's aggressive secularism and statism.

Buckley famously lashed out at the nation's leading intellectuals with his statement, "I am obliged to confess I should sooner live in a society governed by the first two thousand names in the Boston telephone directory than in a society governed by the two thousand faculty members of Harvard University." In his book defending Joseph McCarthy (coauthored with Brent Bozell), Buckley lambasted the intellectual elites that attacked McCarthyism, especially those that looked down on their fellow Americans and wished Americans were more like Europeans. Buckley praised the good sense of the American people, who, unlike American intellectuals and average Europeans, instinctively understood that McCarthy was correct on the major issues:

We are not accustomed, in most parts of America, to what you over here accept as a matter of course. The average American, unlike the average Frenchman, does not talk politics with his Communist barber in a friendly atmosphere of give-and-take, drink wine with his Communist neighbor, or have to inure himself to the antics of his Communist alderman. The American does not burn the midnight oil on election night because, like the Italian, he wonders whether the dawn will usher in a Communist government. The American does not, like the Englishman, have the slightest doubt in his mind as to who was responsible for the enslavement of Czechoslovakia, for the "revolution" in Greece, or for the war in IndoChina; nor is he inclined to view Stalin as a 20th-Century Luther, or Russia as a land where, unlike Hitler Germany, "horror" is not "calculated."

We believe, in short, that the average American is too balanced, too mature, too responsible to undulate in rhythm with the average European. America is simple.[36]

One interesting element of Buckley's career, given his dozens of books and thousands of articles, was his failure to make a meaningful contribution to political theory. Although some of his books are regularly featured in lists of texts conservatives should read, there is a clear qualitative difference between Buckley's books and the other major texts of the conservative canon. *God and Man at Yale* is less significant for the argument it contains than the fact that it launched Buckley into the national spotlight. *Up from Liberalism*, the other book often cited as Buckley's most important work, was a competent critique of the Left and a well-developed explanation of his own political philosophy. However, it lacked the originality and erudition apparent in many of the other important conservative books in that era.

Buckley recognized this particular shortcoming, and in the early 1960s expressed his desire to write a "big book," a major theoretical project that would cement his status as a genuine political philosopher.[37] The book he had in mind was to focus on liberalism's pathological commitment to democracy and universal equality. The book was tentatively titled *The Revolt against the Masses*, a nod to Ortega y Gasset's most famous work, *The Revolt of the Masses*.[38] The book was to be an expression

of Buckley's belief in the importance of elites and the dangers of dema-
goguery and even universal suffrage. Yet such an argument could not
be easily reconciled with Buckley's equally strong suspicion toward the
actually existing elites that directed policy in the United States at that
time. Buckley was well familiar with the political preferences and prejudices of the nation's academic and literary leaders—they were the ones
who were often so dismissive of *National Review*. He thus also recognized that deferring to those elites would only expedite the nation's turn
toward liberalism. As the 1960s progressed, it became increasingly clear
that "the masses" were not the primary catalyst for society's leftward
tilt. Buckley believed that worthy elites, rather than "mass men," should
direct society, but he never created a satisfactory answer for what con-
stituted a worthy elite class: he clearly did not think the faculty of Harvard qualified. Buckley biographer John P. Judis pointed out, "Buckley
seemed to be saying that those members of the elite who were liberals
were mass-men by virtue of their beliefs, in which case the category
had become meaningless."[39] Buckley never completed the book, and
upon that failure seemed to accept that he would never make his own
unique contribution to conservative political theory. Since that time, no
subsequent thinker has successfully resolved this seeming contradiction
within the conservative movement.

Trump's rise to power caused many conservatives to rethink their
opposition to nationalism, but we have not seen a similar explicit revisiting of the populism question. Andrew McCarthy, for example, writes
in *National Review* that he rejects the notion that populism explains
Trump's victory over Hillary Clinton: "No, Trump won because he ran
against a Democratic nominee whose support was tepid at best within
her own party, which itself is hemorrhaging supporters. Mrs. Clinton
was simply a very unappealing candidate—just as she had proven herself to be in 2008. It is likely that other, more committedly conservative Republican candidates with higher personal-approval ratings would
have beaten her more handily."[40]

Some conservatives suggested that the Trump administration should
lean into populism, but they had a unique form of populism in mind—
one disconnected from the usual social science definition of the term.
Thinkers such as Oren Cass of American Compass and Julius Krein of
American Affairs call for something described as "national populism," but

it is more technocratic than demagogic.[41] This element of conservative thought that emerged during the Trump era was generally uninterested in "culture war" issues, and instead focused on policy changes that would benefit the working and middle classes: the development of a coherent industrial policy at the national level, for example. Although these thinkers are often called populists, this is probably not an accurate description of their political program. R. R. Reno of *First Things* has also explicitly called for conservatives to embrace both nationalism and populism, stating that a proper conservative "is a populist because he resists the efforts of the richest Americans to define the nation's interests in terms of their own interests."[42] The problem with this argument is that it relies on a very loose definition of populism, suggesting that any set of policies not designed to specifically benefit the rich qualifies as populist.

To date, few important conservative thinkers defend populism as such. Nonetheless, conservative politicians will continue to employ populist rhetoric because it is a key to their electoral success. Conservative television and radio hosts will similarly speak like populists because it grows their audience. I look forward to reading a strong conservative argument in favor of populism per se. A conservative who could resolve this apparent contradiction would unquestionably make an important contribution to American political thought.

DOES THE INTELLECTUAL DARK WEB OFFER ANYTHING NEW?

The sudden and rapid growth of the so-called Intellectual Dark Web (IDW) was among the more curious developments on the right during the Trump era. The term first came to national attention in 2018, mostly because of Bari Weiss's *New York Times* article on the subject, but physicist and economist Eric Weinstein had coined it earlier.[43] As some of the movement's critics have pointed out, its name is something of a misnomer. The leading figures of the IDW all have massive platforms and audiences; it is thus unclear what makes them "dark." And although the members of the IDW are on the different points of the ideological spectrum, and disagree on specific policies, the key shared ideas promoted across the IDW are congruent with the mainstream conservative movement's message. According to Weiss: "Here are some things that you will hear when you sit down to dinner with the vanguard of the Intellectual Dark Web: There are fundamental biological differences between men and women. Free speech is under siege. Identity politics is a toxic ideology that is tearing American society apart."[44]

The IDW's marquee names are diverse in their approaches to these subjects, and many would probably not feel comfortable being categorized as part of the conservative movement. Although a precise roster of the IDW does not exist, Weiss's piece remains the best list of the IDW's leading figures. The IDW includes podcaster, speaker, and author Ben Shapiro; controversial Canadian psychologist Jordan Peterson; comedian, former mixed-martial arts commentator, and podcaster Joe Rogan; religious skeptics Sam Harris and Michael Shermer; iconoclastic feminists Christina Hoff Summers and Ayaan Hirsi Ali; and YouTube personality Dave Rubin. Rubin provides his own definition of the IDW: "We've committed ourselves to the open exchange of ideas and not silencing our opponents, no matter how many times they refuse to extend that same courtesy to us."[45]

Like many other groups on the right, the IDW is also united in its loathing of political correctness. The IDW has different approaches to the subject. Some treat the most extreme purveyors of political correctness with mockery, derisively describing their opponents as "snowflakes" who melt at the first sign of a challenging idea. Others treat political correctness as a proto-totalitarian ideology, just a few steps removed from Stalinism. Some seem to hold both positions at the same time, however incongruous that may seem.

Within the IDW, Shapiro is the figure most closely associated with the conservative movement. In fact, it is not clear to me why he is considered part of the IDW rather than simply a major voice of the conservative movement. Or, put another way, if Shapiro is part of the IDW, it is not obvious to me why countless other conservatives do not also bear the label.

To the extent that the IDW embraces a common ideological label, their preferred term is "classical liberal." That is, they promote their version of individualism and denounce various forms of collectivism, especially an identity politics that reduces people to their group memberships based on fixed traits. Support for free speech, especially in academia, is a shared concern, perhaps the IDW's preeminent issue. This hardly makes them stand out from the conservative movement. At least since

Buckley denounced his alma mater, the Right has viewed college campuses as enemy territory. Many of the IDW's leading figures engage in college speaking tours, including campuses notorious for their left-wing students and faculty. This is also not especially novel for conservatives. Buckley did the same throughout his career, and the same is true of some of the right's more bombastic personalities, such as Ann Coulter.

As a rejoinder to the charge that the IDW is a conservative or right-wing movement, its members and proponents point out that most of its members hold at least some positions that are typically associated with the Left. Blogger Daniel Miessler made the strongest case for this position in a 2019 piece that sought to discern the political positions of the IDW's most important names: Harris, Weinstein, Rogan, Rubin, Peterson, and Shapiro. He then showed the attitudes of each figure on a list of issues. Aside from Shapiro, all of the people on the list held the "liberal" position on each issue, and even Shapiro was not uniformly on the right.[46]

The list of issues was somewhat disingenuous, however. Whether deliberate or not, the list included several questions that are not accurate measures of where one falls on the ideological spectrum. For example, the table noted that the entire IDW supported "religion and state separation." Taken literally, one could take this to mean that none of them supported the creation of a theocracy, something that is true of most conservatives.

Other writers quickly pointed out various potential flaws in this line of reasoning. The most significant rejoinder came from Uri Harris, writing in the webzine *Quillette*.[47] Harris points out that, although it is true that on many specific issues of policy much of the IDW is aligned with liberals, these are not the issues they write and speak about, and their political allies are found almost exclusively on the political Right. Although the IDW may disagree with mainstream conservatives on issues such as climate change and abortion, they mostly maintain their focus on those points where they can make common cause with the Right, rather than the Left.

Whether or not the IDW considers itself on the right, most mainstream conservatives that discuss the subject seem grateful that the IDW exists. In a piece published by *The Intercollegiate Review*, a conservative website and publication associated with the Intercollegiate Studies Institute, Christian Alejandro Gonzalez argued that the IDW was this generation's equivalent to the neoconservative movement.[48]

The IDW has also been accused of being ideologically proximate to the Alt-Right, and perhaps even a gateway to far-right extremism. This accusation is most frequently leveled at Peterson and Shapiro, arguably the most right-wing voices in the IDW. The irony of this accusation is that both of these figures are reviled by most of the Alt-Right. Shapiro, in particular, has been the target of Alt-Right trolling and threats, especially during the 2016 presidential election, when Shapiro was one of Trump's most vocal critics on the right.

Although there are political and religious disagreements within the IDW, a key shared tenet is that it stands for individualism against collectivisms of the Left and Right. Another shared argument is that reason must prevail over emotion in political and policy debates, but the religious members of the IDW apparently make exceptions for positions built upon religious revelations presumably not subject to empirical inquiry. A consistent IDW critique of identity politics of the Left is that this variety of leftist politics favors emotion over logic and empiricism.

In 2020, two writers often associated with the IDW published what is, for now, the closest thing the movement has to a manifesto. *Cynical Theories*, by Helen Pluckrose and James Lindsay, critiques identity politics from a classical liberal perspective.[49] Pluckrose and Lindsay dedicate much of the text to the genealogy of contemporary identity politics, discussing the "postmodern turn" of the academic Left and its rejection of Enlightenment values.[50] They note the special influence of scholars such as Michel Foucault, who insisted upon the importance of discourses and their relationship to power. However, because the original postmodernists exhibited such radical skepticism toward claims about objective truth, their usefulness for activists who wished to transform the world was limited. Pluckrose and Lindsay argued that postmodernism really became toxic when it evolved into what they called "applied postmodernism" and "social justice scholarship." The authors accept many of the premises of modern progressives, including the existence of racism and sexism, but argue that the identity-politics approach is counterproductive and built on faulty reasoning. They instead insist that classical liberalism, with its commitment to empiricism and individualism, is the best approach to social inequalities.

The IDW is still developing as a movement, and it may never coalesce into a coherent set of beliefs. Indeed, such an end may not actually be the main goal, since the IDW is (apparently) more concerned with methodology than with the outcome of policy debates. That is, maintaining the classical liberal virtue of a free and open exchange of ideas is more important than reaching specific conclusions about which policies should be implemented by the U.S. government. They will likely maintain their audience of conservatives and other people frustrated with political correctness, but the IDW's primary arguments are similar to those made by conservatives for the last several decades.

IS CRITICAL RACE THEORY THE PROBLEM?

Shortly before the 2020 general election, President Trump sought to ban the use of critical race theory (CRT) in government trainings. Specifically, in a memo published on September 4, written at Trump's request, the director of the Office of Management and Budget stated, "All agencies are directed to begin to identify all contracts or other agency spending related to any training on 'critical race theory'" and "to identify all available avenues within the law to cancel any such contracts and/ or to divert Federal dollars away from these un-American propaganda training sessions."[51] This decision received relatively little attention; at that time, there were more significant political and policy developments dominating the news media. The order furthermore had relatively few long-term effects, given that, upon assuming office just months later, President Biden overturned it.[52]

Although Trump's attack on CRT had few direct consequences on public discourse, it proved to be a precursor to a much larger, longer fight about how Americans should talk about race. The specifics of this battle are new, but in many ways the current debate is a repetition of the ideological campus wars of the 1990s. As was the case in the earlier struggles about political correctness, the debate about CRT raises interesting and vexing questions about how educators should approach challenging subjects. Also like the older disputes, contemporary activists on both sides employ plenty of disingenuous claims.

Since Trump's departure, the conservative fight against CRT has largely been associated with a single figure. Christopher F. Rufo, a senior fellow at the conservative Manhattan Institute, is now the person leading this crusade—indeed, he was apparently the person, along with Tucker Carlson of Fox News, who brought the issue to the Trump administration's attention.[53] Whatever one thinks of Rufo's cause—and there are many reasons one might be critical—it is not hyperbole to describe him as one of the more successful conservative activists of his generation.

Rufo first began to gain widespread attention in 2020 when one or more people employed by the City of Seattle leaked aspects of a training session for white employees titled "Interrupting Internalized Racial Superiority and Whiteness."[54] As part of this training, participants were informed that some measures of workplace performance represented "internalized racial superiority." Included on this list was a preference for "individualism" and "perfectionism." When this list was leaked, it led to immediate conservative ridicule. Most expressed disdain for the fact that white employees were subjected to this kind of political training. Rufo subsequently received a steady stream of similar leaked materials, which made it easy for him to publish regular content on the subject for the Manhattan Institute's publication *City Journal*.

Opposition to CRT has since become common across the right. This is somewhat surprising, given that, until recently, the term was not in wide circulation. It is a well-established framework for scholarship in academia, and taken for granted as an accurate description of American life by many progressive activists, but it is not directly discussed frequently in the mainstream press, and certainly not well known among the broader public. CRT is associated with influential scholars such as Kimberle Crenshaw and Derrick A. Bell, who were responding to disappointment with the civil rights legislation of the 1960s. When new laws against discrimination failed to deliver full equality to African Americans on many important measures, some scholars began arguing that white supremacy was built into American life, and had been from the beginning. Thus, real equality would require more than small changes to law or white people showing more civility to Black people. Rather, radical changes that would tear down structures of white supremacy were necessary.

Given the history of CRT as a term, and the limited degree to which it was known and understood, it is curious that it has become such a lightning rod in recent years. Rufo, however, has explained the logic of focusing on this term and turning it toxic, arguing that "'critical race theory' is the perfect villain."[55] CRT has largely become a catchall for every progressive argument about race that conservatives do not like. In a way, it is comparable to the term "cultural Marxist," but has some advantages over that phrase. For one, although few people describe themselves as cultural Marxists, plenty of scholars and activists are happy to endorse CRT, and will aggressively defend it as a framework for understanding racial dynamics in the United States. Further, the term CRT does not contain the same historical baggage as cultural Marxism, a term now so associated with anti-Semitism that many conservatives have stopped using it.

With Democrats controlling the White House and both chambers of the U.S. Congress after the 2020 election cycle, the possibility of substantive action against CRT at the federal level seems to have disappeared. Rather than just drop the issue, however, conservatives have moved the battlefield to states and to local school districts, places where they have greater chances of success.

The focus on school districts is especially significant, as this is one arena where conservative grassroots activists are on equal footing with the Left, and may even have an advantage. On many issues, progressives have a stronger track record of sustained grassroots activism than conservatives. Some culture war issues, such as immigration, can get conservatives angry and fired up, but they do not typically lead to sustained protest movements or meaningful collective action.[56] Controversies in schools, however, have historically led the Right to continuous action: the effort to end busing as a means to achieve racial integration is a notable example. White parents who believe (rightly or wrongly) that their schools have become indoctrination factories, teaching their children to hate themselves, their parents, and their country's history, will engage in local activism to push back against this trend, as we saw over the last year.[57] Furthermore, regardless of who has the advantage at the national level, Republicans remain overwhelmingly dominant in many states, and at the time of this writing, more than a dozen states have banned, or are trying to ban, CRT from schools.

A problem with this entire debate is that it has led to many misleading arguments from both sides. I recognize that, in the world of partisan politics, the goal is to win, not to engage in high-brow, honest, and carefully constructed arguments. Nonetheless, this dispute seems to suffer a particular dearth of good faith discussion. Some on the left have argued that banning CRT means that students are not allowed to learn basic facts about American history, especially facts about slavery and Jim Crow laws and other forms of discrimination. In practice, this may be the case. Conservative legislators trying to ban CRT, who likely have little understanding of the concept, may end up banning discussions of important and unquestionable aspects of American history from the classroom. Opponents of the anti-CRT movement have reasonably claimed that the end results of these efforts, if successful, will be children who never learn about racism.[58] By insisting that CRT be banished from classrooms, we may end up in a situation where some undeniable truths are simply hidden from children, giving them the fantasy that the United States has always been a tolerant, equitable nation. The argument that banning CRT necessarily means banning any discussion of racism, however, is at odds with what leading theorists of CRT actually claim about the United States.

CRT does not just argue that racism is real, or that slavery and segregation were parts of the historical record. These things are indisputable, and no reasonable conservative would claim otherwise. However, some of the claims made by leading CRT theorists go far beyond that. CRT does not just claim that slavery was a moral abomination, or that contemporary racial prejudice is bad. Leading CRT theorists have long claimed that structural racism is built into capitalism itself, and basic elements of capitalism, such as property rights, are tools of white supremacy and must be abolished. This is not a fringe opinion among CRT scholars. Conservatives can reasonably say they do not want that claim taught in schools as though it is incontrovertibly true.

On the other hand, some left-wing critiques of CRT opponents are valid. What does it actually mean to ban CRT from the classroom? In public schools, it seems like a meaningless demand. K-12 students are not reading the seminal works of CRT scholars. In fact, it is quite easy to graduate from college without ever reading anything by Crenshaw, Bell, or the many other leading scholars associated with that particular framework, let alone the thousands of lesser-known academics working within that field. Even the contemporary authors most associated with the current antiracist movement, such as Ibram X. Kendi and Robin DiAngelo, who have written best-selling books on antiracism, are not considered CRT scholars. Thus, saying CRT is not welcome in public schools, if put into practice, would presumably change nothing. Yet it is also true that proponents of CRT have taken a very strong interest in education, and they do want their framework to be incorporated in schools, even if it is not named. The trickier questions are these: What exactly counts as teaching CRT? Is it just teaching that racial prejudice is bad? Is it teaching that America is structurally racist? If so, how do we define what is structural racism? These are questions not easily answered by blanket bans on CRT in schools.

A few on the left have suggested that the effort to ban ideas from public schools amounts to a modern-day "book burning," comparable to what occurred in Nazi Germany.[59] The problem with this perspective is that it suggests that K-12 education is, or should be, a period of total intellectual freedom, where students are introduced to every possible idea. This has never been true. Schools have established curricula, determined largely by school districts and states—that is, by government. The question of what students should be taught is a valid question for school boards and state legislatures to consider. This is, and should be, determined via democratic deliberation. If saying that schools should not teach CRT is the equivalent of book-burning, then so are bans on teaching creationism or gay conversion therapy. One may not like the outcome, but removing a subject from school curriculum is not the same as government censorship of ideas in general.

In my view, an interesting aspect of the CRT debate is that it has lasted so long already. When the CRT controversy began, there was little reason to assume the subject would receive sustained attention. Conservative outrage over purported progressive extremism is nothing new. Indeed, it now seems built into the news cycle. Fox News, conservative talk radio, and Republican politicians are incessantly complaining about "political correctness run amok." In recent years, we have witnessed conservatives worked into a frenzy about the Mr. Potato Head toy becoming gender neutral.[60] When Dr. Seuss Enterprises announced it was going to cease publishing certain books that were deemed racially insensitive, conservatives howled in outrage about "cancel culture": Senator Ted Cruz (R-Tex.) responded by selling signed copies of *Green Eggs and Ham* (which was not even one of the "canceled" books).[61] When New Zealand included a transgendered woman in its Olympic weightlifting team, conservatives argued that this was incredibly unfair to biological females.[62] The relevant thing to note about all of these cases, however, was that the conservative outrage machine in each case proved irrelevant.

Nothing changed as a result of their complaints, nor was there really even an attempt to do anything about it. In the case of Dr. Seuss, the conservative complaints may have even been counterproductive. If conservatives wanted to fight Dr. Seuss being "canceled" by buying his books, they were just giving money to the very people who had pulled some of his books out of circulation. In practice, these regular denunciations of the cultural Left seem to serve no other purpose than to make conservatives in the electorate angry, and sometimes to raise money for politicians. The fight against CRT in schools, in contrast, seems to be resulting in collective action. Whether these actions will have any long-term effects on American education remains to be seen.

WHAT IF THIS IS AS GOOD AS IT GETS?

Throughout this book, I have been critical of conservatives. I have noted the ways in which the conservative movement, and the Republican Party to which it is tied, has engaged in identity politics even while claiming to do otherwise. At times some were likely unaware that they were doing this. Others are likely unaware of their own movement's history on these matters. Many, unquestionably, know, and have always known, exactly what they were doing, and have been playing a cynical game. I unfortunately cannot at this time offer a clear solution to conservatism's conundrum. Many of the problems conservatives note about identity politics are real problems—if overstated. However, attempts to fully disentangle identity from democratic politics will almost certainly fail.

I therefore should give the conservative movement some credit. If identity politics really is as dangerous as many people argue, a claim seemingly vindicated by recent history, perhaps the conservative movement has actually done a reasonably good job of keeping its most dangerous elements at bay for so long. The conservative ascendancy in the late twentieth century was certainly built in part on the racial anxieties of white southerners who wanted to fight segregation and on the subsequent racial concerns of various white groups in the North opposed to the Democratic Party's racial progressivism. Yet neither Nixon nor Reagan ever did anything substantive to reverse the civil rights victories of the 1960s. When running for president, Nixon presented himself as a racial conservative, and then proceeded to expand affirmative action. Charles Wallace Collins thought building bridges with northern conservatives would lead to the permanent, legal entrenchment of white supremacy, to the point that nonwhites would be literally removed from the country. He was mistaken.

Contemporary white nationalists have long argued that supporting the Republican Party has been a disaster for the white supremacist cause. Progressives celebrate, and white nationalists lament, the sweeping demographic changes that have occurred over the last fifty years. It is worth noting that Republican presidents were at the helm for most of that period. Had they been committed to a racist vision, rather than just engaging in occasional dog whistling to activate the racist vote, they presumably would have more aggressively attempted to halt that trend. George W. Bush was personally committed to further liberalization of U.S. immigration policy. Reagan signed a law providing a pathway to citizenship for undocumented immigrants.

Even President Trump, described by so many of his opponents as a racist or even a fascist, was a disappointment to the racist Right. His immigration policies were unquestionably restrictionist, and his policy of family separation at the border provoked understandable criticism. Yet when it comes to restricting immigration, the Trump administration was more smoke than fire. He tweeted about an executive order ending birthright citizenship, exciting his anti-immigration supporters and enraging his opponents, but he never followed through. We witnessed paltry progress on the promised border wall across the U.S.-Mexico border.

As I read the conservative movement's talking points about identity politics, I conclude that they incorporate many lies. However, I wonder if, in a sense, they may be noble lies. Given the things I have noted throughout this book, I will not now exaggerate the influence that conservative thinkers have had on public opinion. However, for several decades now, conservatives have publicly attacked explicit racial bigotry, even as they took advantage of white racial anxieties. Conservatives, for various reasons, chose not to attack the egalitarian principles of their opponents directly, instead insisting that they were also committed to a color-blind society, built on egalitarian principles. This was not, in my view, preordained. Things could have worked out differently. Conservatives could have simply stated directly that the United States was a white man's country, and that there was nothing wrong with blatant identity politics among the white majority. There was certainly historical precedent for that.

WHAT NOW?

Few ideologues were satisfied with the 2020 election results. President Trump's supporters were frustrated by his defeat, and those who did not acknowledge that defeat as legitimate were of course furious. Progressives were delighted to see Trump leave office, but the Left does not find Joe Biden an inspiring figure. The election was also hardly a mandate for major progressive change. Despite all of the scandal and controversy of the Trump administration—including impeachment and a bungled response to the COVID-19 pandemic—President Trump came within striking distance in many key swing states. One could reasonably argue that, in the absence of COVID-19 and the corresponding economic contraction, Trump would have won reelection. Finally, although the Democrats took the White House, the Republican Party overall performed quite well. The GOP picked up seats in the House of Representatives, for example, and it maintained its advantage in state legislatures, which will prove incredibly important during the following round of redistricting. The progressive hope that the 2020 results would give the Democratic Party a free hand to implement a progressive agenda was not fulfilled. The next several years promise gridlock and mostly marginal policy changes.

Most Americans are not ideologues. The idea that the Biden administration might provide a new degree of normalcy certainly appealed to many of them. Perhaps, for at least a period, the endless cycle of offensive presidential tweeting followed by feigned media outrage might be short-circuited. The voting patterns along racial and ethnic lines furthermore suggested that U.S. politics did not become more racially polarized during the Trump era. In spite of all the talk of Trump as a white nationalist or a fascist, exit polls show that he improved his share of the vote among nonwhites. His new support among Hispanics in Florida and Texas was especially remarkable. Meanwhile, Biden's victory was largely possible because of a shift among white men toward the Democrats.

Narratives about a united white party engaged in zero-sum racial politics against a united coalition of Americans from other backgrounds received a blow at the end of 2020.

Nonetheless, the end of the Trump era does not signal the end of polarization or identity politics. As much as his election and presidency have been treated as some kind of aberration, it was marked more by continuity with previous trends than with drastic change. The heated rhetoric about identity issues is not simply going to go away, but I would not be surprised if it dissipates somewhat in the years ahead. The Alt-Right may be mostly gone, but some new variant of the white nationalist ideology will undoubtedly take its place. The rapid shift to the left among white liberals on identity issues over the last decade, dubbed by some critics as "the great awokening," is unlikely to reverse. The fact that a Democrat is in the White House is unlikely to satisfy the Black Lives Matter movement unless major police reforms and other issues related to social justice are enacted.

This book would probably be both more successful and controversial if I could offer some kind of plan for conservatives moving forward. Unfortunately, I remain as perplexed as I was at the start of this project. These are all very thorny problems without easy solutions. One thing I will say with confidence is that Americans' relationship with their political parties have become dysfunctional. The tribal nature of U.S. partisan politics is at odds with basic democratic theory. The fact that our political parties are increasingly a critical part of our social identities exacerbates polarization, for both elites and the general public. It is a problem that so many of us look at people as moral reprobates simply for supporting a different political party. I would favor electoral reforms that made third parties viable in the United States. Such a system may make our party identities more fluid and contingent. Third parties in this country are all but hopeless because our electoral system, with plurality-rule, single-member districts, makes anything other than a two-party system unlikely to survive beyond a single election cycle. Different systems could provide different results. For example, a party-list system, in which voters named their preferred party, and after the election parties were given seats according to how much support they received, would encourage more people to vote for third parties—in this situation, a third party could gain seats in the legislature even if it did not win an outright majority anywhere. A ranked-choice voting system, in which people are asked to rank a large number of candidates according to their preference, has also led to a proliferation of parties in other countries.

On the other hand, although I support such reforms, I hesitate to recommend them as a panacea. It bothers me that partisan hatred has become one of the last remaining forms of acceptable bigotry in American society. People who would never admit to prejudice along racial, ethnic, or religious lines have no problem openly stating that they *hate* people from the opposing party. What happens if strong partisan identities dissipate? Right now, Americans tend to launder other forms of identity through partisan politics, allowing them to plausibly deny that their group-based hostilities are driven by more primal identities. If we develop an electoral system that leads Americans to be less emotionally invested in their political parties, will some of these other identities become more salient? I do not know. I would like to think that they would not, but I must suggest it as a possibility. Furthermore, the lack of viable third parties in the United States has blocked the extreme Right and the extreme Left from gaining direct influence in government, as they are forced to work within the confines of one of the two major parties.

I also endorse the conservative argument that strengthening families may diminish the salience of identity politics. The empirical evidence for this claim is relatively weak, even if the logic of the argument seems sound. Nonetheless, policies that make life easier for people to form families are worth supporting even if they have zero direct effect on identitarian tendencies in the public. Policies as simple as a direct cash payment to new parents to help them offset the cost of having a child could gain support from conservatives (who could be persuaded such a policy is pro-family) and progressives (who may be sold on a policy designed to alleviate inequality). At the very least, a popular policy supported by both parties and implemented in a bipartisan manner would be a welcome change to our national politics. To critics who worry that a natalist policy is somehow racist or based on eugenic thinking, I would note that this claim is a non sequitur. Among women of childbearing age, women of color are overrepresented compared to the population overall. A baby boom that began today, assuming it had a comparable effect on all racial groups (and there is little reason to assume it would not), would actually expedite the process of demographic change, moving forward the date at which non-Hispanic whites cease to be an absolute majority in the United States.

To end on a hopeful note, however, those who claim that "America has never been more polarized" are mistaken. The United States has suffered upheavals far more violent than anything occurring today. The people predicting civil war or secession are, in my view, ridiculous. Identity politics represents a real challenge. But the polarization and violence occurring today is much less dramatic than we saw during the civil rights movement, to say nothing of the period preceding the Civil War. This is not necessarily an optimistic take. Those saying "America's best days are behind us" may be right, depending on how they define "best." We may have to accept that we cannot re-create the experience of (white) people in the 1950s—a period of optimism, upward mobility, the illusion of societal unity, and confidence that things will only get better from here. That was an unusual historical period, one largely possible because of the horrific two decades that preceded it. We may have to make peace with perpetual problems and conflict.

The smartest conservatives have never suggested they had a plan for utopia. A long-term period of people trying their best to get along, of seeking commonalities and compromise whenever possible, of trying to make incremental changes that make life better for everyone, is precisely what conservatism at its best seeks to achieve. But doing so requires taking a realistic approach to the nature of partisan politics, not condemning people for failing to live up to an impossible ideal.

NOTES

Introduction

1. For the strongest argument for this perspective from political scientists, see Matt Grossmann and David A. Hopkins, *Asymmetric Politics: Ideological Republicans and Group Interest Democrats* (New York: Oxford University Press, 2016).

2. Kwame Anthony Appiah, *The Ethics of Identity* (Princeton, NJ: Princeton University Press, 2005), xvi.

3. Jonah Goldberg, *Suicide of the West: How the Rebirth of Tribalism, Populism, Nationalism, and Identity Politics Is Destroying American Democracy* (New York: Crown Forum, 2018), 6.

4. I recognize that this is not always an approach aligned with reality. There have been cases of conservatives that make factually incorrect statements, were irrefutably corrected, but who nonetheless continued to spread the untruth. Dinesh D'Souza is one such example. See Adam Laats, "The Dangers of Dunking on Dinesh D'Souza," History News Network, November 25, 2018, https://historynewsnetwork.org/article/170521.

5. Gina Perry, *The Lost Boys: Inside Muzafer Sherif's Robbers Cave Experiment* (Melbourne, Australia: Scribe, 2018).

Chapter 1

1. There are far too many articles, and even too many books, to list that make this very argument. Here is just one: Daniel J. Flynn, *Why the Left Hates America* (New York: Crown Forum, 2004).

2. Again, this is a common argument, but here is just one recent example of someone on the left framing the issue in this way: Ed Kilgore, "Conservatives Want a 'Republic' to Protect Privileges," *New York Magazine,*

August 28, 2019, http://nymag.com/intelligencer/2019/08/conservatives
-want-a-republic-to-protect-privileges.html.

3. To take just one example, Dennis Prager, an influential writer and radio host, put it this way: "Which brings me to explaining Left–Right difference No. 5: How the Left and Right regard the role of the state (or government). This is such a significant difference that it might be said to be the defining difference between Left and Right. Without the belief in an ever-expanding state, there is no Left. Without a belief in limited government, there is no conservatism. Moreover, this difference is one that all people should comprehend in order to know whether they are on the right or the left"; see Prager, "Differences between Left and Right: It's All about Big Government," *National Review*, July 7, 2015, https://www.nationalreview.com/2015/07/differences
-liberal-conservative-big-government-greece/.

4. Thomas Sowell, *A Conflict of Visions: Ideological Origins of Political Struggles* (New York: Basic Books, 2007).

5. Arnold Kling, *The Three Languages of Politics: Talking across the Political Divides* (Washington, DC: The Cato Institute, 2017).

6. Ibid., 5.

7. Bryan Caplan, "My Simplistic Theory of Left and Right," *EconLog*, October 2, 2015, https://www.econlib.org/archives/2015/10/my_simplistic_t
.html.

8. Paleoconservatism is a branch of the conservative movement that emerged in the 1980s; it defined itself by its opposition to the neoconservative movement that was ascendant at that time. The most famous figure associated with it is Patrick Buchanan, who worked for both Richard Nixon and Ronald Reagan, and sought the Republican nomination for president in 1992 and 1996. Over the course of that struggle between these two conservative factions, the neoconservatives were the clear victors, and paleoconservatism has had little direct influence on the conservative movement or the Republican Party in recent decades.

9. "What Is Left? What Is Right?," *The American Conservative*, August 28, 2006, https://www.theamericanconservative.com/articles/what-is-left-what
-is-right/.

10. Norberto Bobbio, *Left and Right: The Significance of a Political Distinction* (Chicago: University of Chicago Press, 1993).

11. Corey Robin, *The Reactionary Mind: Conservatism from Edmund Burke to Donald Trump*, 2nd ed. (New York: Oxford University Press, 2018), 4.

12. Patrick J. Deneen, *Why Liberalism Failed* (New Haven, CT: Yale University Press, 2018), 43.

13. Vilfredo Pareto, *The Mind and Society*, ed. Arthur Livingston, trans. Andrew Bongiorno, Arthur Livingston, and James Harvey Rogers (New York: Harcourt, Brace, 1935), 2:735–36.

14. George Orwell, *Animal Farm* (London: Secker and Warburg, 1945).

15. James Burnham, "The Struggle for the World," in *Did You Ever See a Dream Walking? American Conservative Thought in the 20th Century*, ed. William F. Buckley Jr. (Indianapolis: Bobbs-Merrill, 1970), 269–302.

16. Amy Chua, *Political Tribes: Group Instinct and the Fate of Nations* (New York: Penguin Books, 2018).

17. Martin E. Spencer, "Multiculturalism, 'Political Correctness,' and the Politics of Identity," *Sociological Forum* 9 (1994): 556.

18. Patrick Allitt, *The Conservatives: Ideas and Personalities throughout American History* (New Haven, CT: Yale University Press, 2009), 2. NB: All emphasis in quoted material throughout the book is original.

19. George H. Nash, *The Conservative Intellectual Movement in America since 1945*, 30th anniversary ed. (New York: Basic Books, 2006), 151.

20. Frank S. Meyer, *In Defense of Freedom: A Conservative Credo* (Chicago: Henry Regnery, 1962).

21. Stephen J. Tonsor, "The Conservative Search for Identity," in *What Is Conservatism*, ed. Frank S. Meyer (New York: Holt, Rinehart and Winston, 1964), 150.

22. Russell Kirk, *The American Cause* (Wilmington, DE: ISI Press, 2002), 2.

23. Giovanni Sartori, "Politics, Ideology, and Belief Systems," *American Political Science Review* 63 (1969): 398–411.

24. Ibid., 402.

25. Ibid., 403.

26. Philip Converse, "The Nature of Belief Systems in Mass Publics," in *Ideology and Discontent*, ed. David Apter (New York: The Free Press, 1964), 206–61.

27. Samuel P. Huntington, "Conservatism as an Ideology," *American Political Science Review* 51 (1957): 454.

28. Robert Nisbet, *Conservatism: Dream and Reality*, 4th ed. (New York: Transaction, 2008), 15.

29. We can easily name many examples of this phenomenon, but the most recent prominent example can be found in Matt Lewis, *Too Dumb to Fail: How the GOP Betrayed the Reagan Revolution to Win Elections (and How We Can Reclaim Its Conservative Roots)* (New York: Hatchett, 2016).

30. Michael J. Lee, "The Conservative Canon and Its Uses," *Rhetoric and Public Affairs* 15 (2012): 1–40.

31. Ibid., 3.

32. F. A. Hayek, *The Road to Serfdom: Text and Documents—The Definitive Edition* (Chicago: University of Chicago Press, 2007), 148.

33. For a helpful introduction to this concept, I recommend Vivian L. Vignoles, Seth J. Schwartz, and Koen Luyckx, "Toward an Integrative Theory of Identity," in *Handbook of Identity Theory and Research*, ed. Seth J. Schwartz, Koen Luyckx, and Vivian L. Vignoles (New York: Springer, 2011), 1–27.

34. Scott Weiner and Dillon Stone Tatum, "Rethinking Identity in Political Science," *Political Science Review* 19 (2020): 464–81.

35. Ibid.

36. Howard J. Wiarda, *Political Culture, Political Science, and Identity Politics* (New York: Routledge, 2014), 150.

37. David Azerrad, "The Promise and Perils of Identity Politics," *The Heritage Foundation: First Principles* 72 (2019): 2.

38. Ibid., 3.

39. Peter Skerry, "What's Wrong with Identity Politics?," *Nexus: A Journal of Opinion* 6 (2001): 189–95.

40. Ibid., 192.

41. Linda Nicholson, *Identity before Identity Politics* (Cambridge: Cambridge University Press, 2008), 2.

42. Grant Farred, "Endgame Identity? Mapping the New Left Roots of Identity Politics," *New Literary History* 31, no. 4 (2000): 627–48.

43. Ibid., 631.

44. "The Combahee River Collective Statement," https://americanstudies.yale.edu/sites/default/files/files/Keyword%20Coalition_Readings.pdf.

45. Ibid.

46. Derrick A. Bell, *Race, Racism, and American Law* (New York: Little, Brown, and Co., 1973).

47. Charles Taylor, *Multiculturalism and "The Politics of Recognition"* (Princeton, NJ: Princeton University Press, 1992).

48. To quote Taylor directly: "The thesis is that our identity is partly shaped by recognition or its absence, often by the *mis*recognition of others, and so a person or group of people can suffer real damage, real distortion, if the people or society around them mirror back to them a confining or contemptible picture of themselves. Nonrecognition or misrecognition can inflict harm, can be a form of oppression, imprisoning someone in a false, distorted and reduced mode of being" (ibid., 25).

49. Ibid., 36.

50. Ibid., 43.

51. He put it this way: "Demanding respect for people *as blacks* and *as gays* can go along with notably rigid structures as to how one is to be an African American or a person with same-sex desires. In a particularly fraught and emphatic way, there will be proper modes of being black and gay: there will be demands that are made; expectations to be met; battle lines to be drawn. It is at this point that someone who takes autonomy seriously may worry whether we have replaced one kind of tyranny with another"; Kwame Anthony Appiah, *The Ethics of Identity* (Princeton, NJ: Princeton University Press, 2010), 110.

52. Shelby Steele, "Yo, Howard," *Wall Street Journal*, November 13, 2003, A18.

53. Ibid.

54. Francis Fukuyama, *Identity: The Demand for Dignity and the Politics of Resentment* (New York: Farrar, Straus, and Giroux, 2018), xv.

55. Ibid., 19.

56. Nancy Fraser, "From Redistribution to Recognition? Dilemmas of Justice in a 'Post-Socialist' Age," *New Left Review* (July 1995): 68–93.

57. Ibid., 76.

58. For example, see S. E. Cupp and Brett Joshpe, *Why You're Wrong about the Right: Behind the Myths: The Surprising Truth about Conservatives* (New York: Threshold Editions, 2008).

59. Iowa Legislature, Senate, "A bill for an act relating to consideration of political affiliation and balance in the employment of faculty at institutions of higher education governed by the state board of regents," Senate File 288, introduced February 20, 2017, https://www.legis.iowa.gov/legislation/BillBook ?ga=87&ba=SF%20288.

60. Renzo Downey, "'Intellectual Diversity' on College Campuses Measure Heads to Governor's Desk," Florida Politics, April 7, 2021, https:// floridapolitics.com/archives/418181-intellectual-diversity-on-college -campuses-measure-heads-to-governors-desk/.

61. Kimberle Crenshaw, "Demarginalizing the Intersection of Race and Sex: A Black Feminist Critique of Antidiscrimination Doctrine, Feminist Theory and Antiracist Politics," *University of Chicago Legal Forum* 8 (1989): 139–67.

62. Kimberle Crenshaw, "Mapping the Margins: Intersectionality, Identity Politics, and Violence against Women of Color," *Stanford Law Review* 6 (1991): 1241–1300.

63. Patricia Hill Collins, *Black Feminist Thought: Knowledge, Consciousness, and the Politics of Empowerment* (New York: Routledge, 1991).

64. For example, Ben Shapiro recently argued that Crenshaw developed her ideas specifically to "bully those who aren't members of these intersectional groups"; see Shapiro, *The Right Side of History: How Reason and Moral Purpose Made the West Great* (New York: Broadside Books, 2019), 200.

65. Nicholas Wolfinger, "I Know What Intersectionality Is, and I Wish It Were Less Important," *Quillette*, February 20, 2019, https://quillette.com/2019/02/20/i-know-what-intersectionality-is-and-i-wish-it-were-less-important/.

66. Crenshaw, "Mapping the Margins."

67. Setareh Rouhani, "Intersectionality-Informed Quantitative Research: A Primer," *American Journal of Public Health* 103 (2014): 1082–89.

68. Crenshaw, "Demarginalizing the Intersection of Race and Sex," 141–43.

69. Ibid., 142–43.

70. Keisha Lindsay, "God, Gays, and Progressive Politics: Reconceptualizing Intersectionality as a Normatively Malleable Analytical Framework," *Perspectives on Politics* 11 (2013): 447–60.

71. Ibid., 453.

72. "Planned Parenthood and Racism," Students for Life of America, https://studentsforlife.org/planned-parenthood-racism/.

73. Philip W. Gray, "'The Fire Rises': Identity, the Alt-Right, and Intersectionality," *Journal of Political Ideologies* 23 (2018): 141–56.

74. Ibid., 145.

75. Grover Norquist, *Leave Us Alone: Getting the Government's Hands off Our Money, Our Guns, Our Lives* (New York: HarperCollins, 2008).

76. Geoffrey Hughes, *Political Correctness: A History of Semantics and Culture* (Chichester, UK: Wiley-Blackwell, 2010), 62–63.

77. Ruth Perry, "A Short History of the Term *Politically Correct*," in *Beyond PC: Toward a Politics of Understanding*, ed. Patricia Aufderheide (Saint Paul, MN: Graywolf Press, 1992), 71.

78. Peter Wikström, "No One Is 'Pro-Politically Correct': Positive Construals of Political Correctness in Twitter Conversations," *Nordic Journal of English Studies* 15 (2016): 159–70.

79. Becky Ford, "Political Correctness," in *Oxford Research Encyclopedia of Communication*, August 2017, 1.

80. Zack Beauchamp, "The Controversy over Laws Punishing Israel Boycotts, Explained," Vox, January 9, 2019, https://www.vox.com/policy-and-politics/2019/1/9/18172826/bds-law-israel-boycott-states-explained.

81. Hughes, *Political Correctness*, 217.

82. Ibid., 224.

83. Dorris Lessing, *Time Bites: Views and Reviews* (New York: Harper-Collins, 2004), 76.

84. Ibid., 77.

85. Jim Nielson described this tactic as follows: "The effect of the great PC scare, then, has been to institutionalize a term that discredits even modest leftist concerns, presenting the left with one more obstacle, and moving the political 'center' to the right, thus further cementing the right's political and cultural hegemony"; see Nielson, "The Great PC Scare," in *PC Wars*, ed. Jeffrey Williams (New York: Routledge, 1995), 80.

86. Alan D. Sokal, "Transgressing the Boundaries: Toward a Transformative Hermeneutics of Quantum Gravity," *Social Text* 46/47 (1996): 216–52.

87. Alan D. Sokal, "A Physicist Experiments with Cultural Studies," *Lingua Franca*, June 5, 1996, https://physics.nyu.edu/faculty/sokal/lingua_franca_v4/lingua_franca_v4.html.

88. Ibid.

89. "Glenn Beck: Postmodern 'Arrogant Nonsense' Is the 'Cancer Being Taught to Our Children," The Blaze, September 26, 2018, https://www.theblaze.com/video/glenn-beck-postmodern-arrogant-nonsense-is-the-cancer-being-taught-to-our-children.

90. Sally Haslanger, "Ontology and Social Construction," *Philosophical Topics* 23 (1995): 95–125.

91. Ibid., 97.

92. Ibid.

93. Ibid., 98.

94. Ibid., 100.

95. In Haslanger's own words: "Consider, for the moment, causal construction. Is it plausible that the entire world—not just Earth, but everything there is—is a human artifact, even allowing that the mechanisms of construction might be highly complex and mediated? I don't think so" (ibid., 104).

96. Ibid., 107.

97. Ian Hacking, *The Social Construction of What?* (Cambridge, MA: Harvard University Press, 1999), 7.

98. Richard Weaver, *Ideas Have Consequences* (Chicago, University of Chicago Press, 1948), 3.

99. Harry V. Jaffa, *A New Birth of Freedom: Abraham Lincoln and the Coming of the Civil War* (Lanham, MD: Rowman and Littlefield, 2000), 104–6.

100. Hyrum Lewis, "The Conservative Capture of Anti-Relativist Discourse in Postwar America," *Canadian Journal of History* 43 (2016): 451–76.

101. Leo Strauss, "Relativism," in *Relativism and the Study of Man*, ed. Helmut Shoeck and James W. Wiggins (Princeton, NJ: D. Van Nostrand, 1961), 135–57.

102. Harry V. Jaffa, *The Rediscovery of America: Essays by Harry V. Jaffa on the New Birth of Politics* (Lanham, MD: Rowman and Littlefield, 2019).

103. John McCormack, "Paul Ryan: The Biggest Problem in America Isn't Debt, It's Moral Relativism," *The Weekly Standard*, November 18, 2011, https://www.washingtonexaminer.com/weekly-standard/paul-ryan-the -biggest-problem-in-america-isnt-debt-its-moral-relativism.

104. Jean-François Lyotard, *The Post-Modern Condition: A Report on Knowledge* (Minneapolis: University of Minnesota Press, 1984), xxiv.

105. For one influential example of this argument, see Natan Sharansky, *The Case for Democracy: The Power of Freedom to Overcome Tyranny and Terror* (New York: PublicAffairs, 2004).

106. George W. Bush, "President Bush's Second Inaugural Address," National Public Radio, January 20, 2005, https://www.npr.org/templates/story /story.php?storyId=4460172.

107. Steven R. Weisman, "Rice, in Alabama, Draws Parallels for Democracy Everywhere," *New York Times*, October 22, 2005, https://www.nytimes .com/2005/10/22/world/rice-in-alabama-draws-parallels-for-democracy -everywhere.html.

108. Joseph de Maistre, *Considerations on France*, trans. Richard A. Lebrun (Cambridge: Cambridge University Press, 1994), 235.

109. Ibid.

110. Jaffa, *A New Birth of Freedom*, 119.

111. Paul Gottfried, "Understanding the Phony American Right," *The Agonist*, July 1, 2019, http://www.theagonist.org/essays/2019/07/01/essays -gottfried.html.

112. Heather Mac Donald, "The Academy of Hatred," *The American Mind*, November 28, 2018, https://americanmind.org/features/the-reichstag -is-still-burning/the-academy-of-hatred-not-relativism/.

113. Jonah Goldberg, "The Wisdom of Youth," *National Review*, March 9, 2018, https://www.nationalreview.com/g-file/the-wisdom-of-youth/.

114. For a brief description of this group, see "New Black Panther Party," Southern Poverty Law Center, https://www.splcenter.org/fighting-hate /extremist-files/group/new-black-panther-party.

115. Geoffrey Layman, *The Great Divide: Religious and Cultural Conflict in American Party Politics* (New York: Columbia University Press, 2001), 55.

116. James L. Guth and John C. Green, "Salience: The Core Concept?," in *Rediscovering the Religious Factor in American Politics*, ed. David C. Leege and Lyman A. Kellstedt (Armonk, NY: M. E. Sharp, 1993), 157–76.

117. Will Herberg, *Catholic–Protestant–Jew: An Essay in American Religious Socialization* (Garden City, NY: Anchor Books, 1960).

118. Andrew L. Whitehead and Samuel L. Perry, *Taking American Back for God: Christian Nationalism in the United States* (New York: Oxford University Press, 2020).

Chapter 2

1. Meyer, *In Defense of Freedom*, 5.

2. Ibid., 8.

3. Quoted in Ben Weingarten, "William F. Buckley, Jr.'s Devastating Argument against Identity Politics," Encounter Books, November 9, 2015, https://www.encounterbooks.com/features/william-f-buckley-jr-s-devastating-argument-identity-politics/.

4. I discuss Will's views on religion and how they differ from other conservatives in George Hawley, *Right-Wing Critics of American Conservatism* (Lawrence: University Press of Kansas, 2016), 109–10.

5. George Will, *The Conservative Sensibility* (New York: Hachette, 2019), 379.

6. Ibid.

7. C. Bradley Thompson, "The Rise and Fall of the Pajama-Boy Nietzscheans," *The American Mind*, May 13, 2020, https://americanmind.org/essays/the-rise-and-fall-of-the-pajama-boy-nietzscheans/.

8. Hayek, *The Road to Serfdom*, 67–68.

9. F. A. Hayek, *The Constitution of Liberty* (Chicago: University of Chicago Press, 1960), 525.

10. Murray Rothbard, "Frank S. Meyer: The Fusionist as Libertarian Manqué," *Modern Age*, Fall 1981, 352–63.

11. Ibid., 363.

12. Thompson put it this way: "But the standard idea of the 'common good' as used by Ahmari is an abstraction that is greater than the sum of the individual men and women who make up a society. Thus the central problem with the anti-concept 'common good' is that has no basis in objective reality, which means that it's literally nothing other than a philosophic fantasy—a creation of the human imagination" (Thompson, "The Rise and Fall of the Pajama-Boy Nietzscheans").

13. Anthony Leonardi, "*Daily Wire* Founder: Conservatism Is about Saving 'Classical Liberalism,'" *Washington Examiner*, March 4, 2020, https://www.washingtonexaminer.com/news/daily-wire-founder-conservatism-is-about-saving-classical-liberalism.

14. Will, *Conservative Sensibility*, 95.

15. Goldberg, *Suicide of the West*, 224.

16. For a discussion of Mill's influence on Hayek, see Paul Gottfried, "*The Road to Serfdom* Revisited," *American Journal of Jurisprudence* 17 (1972): 38–45.

17. John Stuart Mill, *On Liberty*, in *The Basic Writings of John Stuart Mill* (New York: Random House, 2002), 60–61.

18. Will, *Conservative Sensibility*, 15.

19. Barry Alan Shane, *The Myth of American Individualism: The Protestant Origins of American Political Thought* (Princeton, NJ: Princeton University Press, 1994), 4.

20. Donald S. Lutz, "From Covenant to Constitution in American Political Thought," *Publius* 10 (1980): 101–33.

21. Harry Jaffa, *How to Think about the American Revolution* (Durham, NC: Carolina Academic Press, 1978), 41.

22. The following quote from Mill should suffice to demonstrate why Kirk thought Mill's ideas were incompatible with his conception of conservatism: "The despotism of custom is everywhere the standing hindrance on human advancement, being in unceasing antagonism to that disposition to aim at something better than customary, which is called, according to circumstances, the spirit of liberty, or the that of progress or improvement" (Mill, *On Liberty*, 72).

23. Russell Kirk, "Libertarians: The Chirping Sectaries," in *Redeeming the Time* (Wilmington, DE: ISI Books, 1996), 281.

24. Ben Shapiro, *The Right Side of History: How Reason and Moral Purpose Made the West Great* (New York: Broadside Books, 2019), 48.

25. Victor Davis Hanson, *The Other Greeks: The Family Farm and the Agrarian Roots of Western Civilization* (Los Angeles: University of California Press, 1995).

26. Mill, *On Liberty*, 18.

27. Ibid., 38.

28. Meyer, *In Defense of Freedom*, 168–69.

29. Madeleine Kerns, "Pornography Is a Public Health Problem," *National Review*, February 6, 2020, https://www.nationalreview.com/magazine/2020/02/24/pornography-is-a-public-health-problem/.

30. Douglas Murray, "Why Is No One Talking about the Violence of Popular Entertainment after Parkland?," *National Review*, March 22,

2018, https://www.nationalreview.com/2018/03/video-game-violence-mass
-shootings-nobody-discussing/.

31. William F. Buckley Jr. and L. Brent Bozell, *McCarthy and His Enemies: The Record and Its Meaning* (Washington, DC: Regnery, 1954).

32. James Burnham, *Suicide of the West: An Essay on the Meaning and Destiny of Liberalism* (Chicago: Regnery, 1985), 75–76.

33. Ibid., 229.

34. For one of the more extreme examples of this, see Ann Coulter, "McCarthyism: The Rosetta Stone of Liberal Lies," AnnCoulter.com, November 7, 2007, http://www.anncoulter.com/columns/2007-11-07.html. For a less histrionic example, see M. Stanton Evans, *Blacklisted by History: The Untold Story of Senator Joe McCarthy and His Fight against His Enemies* (New York: Crown Forum, 2007).

35. According to Kirk: "Loyalty cannot be forced, any more than love. The patriotism which is the product of fear or of self-interest is truly the last refuge of the scoundrel. We may prosecute for perjury on man who swears fidelity to the state, and then breaks his oath; but positive law cannot create loyalty"; Russell Kirk, "Conformity and Legislative Committees," *Confluence* 3 (1953): 342.

36. Will Herberg, "Government and Rabble-Rousing," *New Leader* 37 (1954): 16.

37. Willmoore Kendall, *John Locke and the Doctrine of Majority Rule* (Urbana: University of Illinois Press, 1941).

38. Willmoore Kendall, "The 'Open Society' and Its Fallacies," *American Political Science Review* 54 (1960): 976.

39. John Bloxham, *Ancient Greece and American Conservatism: Classical Influences on the Modern Right* (London: I. B. Taurus, 2018), 41.

40. Daniel Kelly, *James Burnham and the Struggle for the World* (Wilmington, DE: ISI Books, 2002), 187.

41. Ibid., 189.

42. Heather Mac Donald, "Double Standards and Distortions," *City Journal*, December 12, 2017, https://www.city-journal.org/html/double-standards-and-distortions-15602.html.

43. Rod Dreher, "The Racial Double Standard," *The American Conservative*, June 5, 2018, https://www.theamericanconservative.com/dreher/coleman-hughes-racial-double-standard/.

44. Ibn Warraq, "Why the West Is Best," *City Journal*, Winter 2008, https://www.city-journal.org/html/why-west-best-13075.html.

45. Burnham, *Suicide of the West*, 196.

46. Ibid., 198.

47. Ibid.

48. Ibid., 200.

49. For example, in recent years the rise of "deaths of despair" (deaths caused by suicide, drug overdoses, and alcoholism) among poor white people has received a great deal of news coverage. Many on the left have argued that this rise, which is mostly limited to whites, is due largely to racism. That is, white racism has been a hindrance to the kind of multiracial, working-class solidarity that would be needed to implement the policies that would keep these deaths from happening. For just one example of this kind of argument, see Keri Leigh Merritt, "Deaths of Despair and the Psychological Wages of Whiteness," *Common Dreams*, March 19, 2020, https://www.commondreams .org/views/2020/03/19/deaths-despair-and-psychological-wages-whiteness.

50. For the most thorough explanation of this argument, see Richard Sander and Stuart Taylor Jr., *Mismatch: How Affirmative Action Hurts Students It's Intended to Help, and Why Universities Won't Admit It* (New York: Basic Books, 2012). For a contrary argument, see William G. Bowen, Matthew M. Chingos, and Michael S. McPherson, *Crossing the Finish Line: Completing College at America's Public Universities* (Princeton, NJ: Princeton University Press, 2009). In the latter book, the authors argue that students are best served attending the best-ranked university that accepts them.

51. See, for example, Robert VerBruggen, "Harvard's Discrimination Problem," *National Review*, September 27, 2018, https://www.nationalreview .com/magazine/2018/10/15/harvards-discrimination-problem/.

52. Charles Murray, *Human Accomplishment: The Pursuit of Excellence in the Arts and Sciences* (New York: Harper, 2003).

53. See, for example, Nathan J. Robinson, "Why Charles Murray Is Odious," *Current Affairs*, July 17, 2017, https://www.currentaffairs.org/2017 /07/why-is-charles-murray-odious.

54. Weaver, *Ideas Have Consequences*, 87.

55. Ibid., 83.

56. Allan Bloom, *The Closing of the American Mind: How Higher Education Has Failed Democracy and Impoverished the Souls of Today's Students* (New York: Simon and Schuster, 1987).

57. Charles J. Sykes, *ProfScam: Professors and the Demise of Higher Education* (Washington, DC: Regnery, 1988).

58. Roger Kimball, *Tenured Radicals: How Politics Has Corrupted Our Higher Education* (New York: Harper and Row, 1990).

59. Dinesh D'Souza, *Illiberal Education: The Politics of Race and Sex on Campus* (New York: The Free Press, 1991).

60. Rush Limbaugh, *The Way Things Ought to Be* (New York: Pocket Books, 1992), 204.

61. "About Us," Professor Watchlist, https://professorwatchlist.org/index .php/about-us.

62. Jim Nielson, "The Great PC Scare: Tyrannies of the Left, Rhetoric of the Right," in *PC Wars: Politics and Theory in the Academy*, ed. Jeffrey Williams (New York: Routledge, 1995), 60–89.

63. Matthew Yglesias, "People Don't Like "PC Culture," *Vox*, October 12, 2018, https://www.vox.com/2018/10/12/17968336/pc-culture-no.

64. Milton Friedman, *Capitalism and Freedom*, 40th anniversary ed. (Chicago: University of Chicago Press, 2002), 109–10.

65. Sowell further argues that market competition can be critical to combatting racial discrimination, even in places such as South Africa: "Even in South Africa, where racial discrimination is required by law, white employers in competitive industries hired more blacks and in higher occupations than they were permitted to do by the government, and were often fined when caught doing so"; Thomas Sowell, *Basic Economics: A Citizen's Guide to the Economy* (New York: Basic Books, 2004), 154.

66. Thomas Sowell, "Victimizing Blacks," *Jewish World Review*, August 8, 2001, https://www.jewishworldreview.com/cols/sowell080801.asp.

67. Thomas Sowell, "Who Is Racist?," *Jewish World Review*, July 8, 2013, http://jewishworldreview.com/cols/sowell070913.php3#.Xo4EKHJO1PY.

68. Specifically, he suggests the result of the reparations pursuit would be the following: "The great majority of blacks will gain nothing. Among the things they will lose is the good will of the rest of the society—a society in which they are not even the largest minority any more. In that vulnerable position, blacks can ill afford to come across as people who are constantly trying to get something without earning it"; Thomas Sowell, August 8, 2001, *Jewish World Review*, http://www.jewishworldreview.com/cols/sowell080801.asp.

69. Richard Bernstein, *Dictatorship of Virtue: How the Battle over Multiculturalism Is Reshaping Our Schools, Our Country, Our Lives* (New York: Vintage, 1994).

70. Ibid., 11.

71. Robertson, Derek and Zack Stanton, "This List Is Why Trump Won," Politico, July 14, 2018, https://www.politico.com/magazine/story/2018 /07/14/this-list-is-why-trump-won-219009/.

72. Yascha Mounk, "Americans Strongly Dislike PC Culture," *The Atlantic*, October 10, 2018, https://www.theatlantic.com/ideas/archive/2018/10 /large-majorities-dislike-political-correctness/572581/.

73. Douglas Murray, *The Madness of Crowds: Gender, Race, and Identity* (London: Bloomsbury Continuum, 2019), 9.

74. Lucian Gideon Conway, Meredith A. Repke, and Shannon C. Houck, "Donald Trump as a Cultural Revolt against Perceived Communication Restriction: Priming Political Correctness Norms Causes More Trump Support," *Journal of Social and Political Psychology* 5 (2017): 244–59.

75. Specifically, they were presented with the following text: "First, we would like to get your opinions on societal norms. In our modern society, we have norms that dictate that we refrain from saying negative things—especially those things deemed as politically incorrect to say. These norms state that it is better to have rules that constrain us from anything that might sound too-negative or might be offensive to members of particular groups. These social norms that discourage too-negative conversation have many good benefits, and we first want to get your opinion on these norms before moving forward" (ibid., 248).

76. Lisa Legault, Jennifer N. Gutsell, and Michael Inzlicht, "Ironic Effects of Antiprejudice Messages: How Motivational Interventions Can Reduce (but Also Increase) Prejudice," *Psychological Science* 22 (2011): 1472–77.

77. John Sides, Michael Tesler, and Lynn Vavreck, *Identity Crisis: The 2016 Presidential Election and the Battle for the Meaning of America* (Princeton, NJ: Princeton University Press, 2018); George Hawley, *White Voters in 21st Century America* (New York: Routledge, 2014).

78. Darel Paul, *From Tolerance to Equality: How Elites Brought America to Same-Sex Marriage* (Waco, TX: Baylor University Press, 2018).

79. George Hawley, "Ambivalent Nativism: Trump Supporters' Attitudes toward Islam and Muslim Immigration," The Brookings Institution, July 24, 2019, https://www.brookings.edu/research/ambivalent-nativism-trump -supporters-attitudes-toward-islam-and-muslim-immigration/.

80. Daniel Martinez HoSang and Joseph E. Lowndes, *Producers, Parasites, Patriots: Race and the New Right-Wing Politics of Precarity* (Minneapolis: University of Minnesota Press, 2019), 26.

Chapter 3

1. For recent example of this argument, see Randy Barnett, *Our Republican Constitution: Securing the Liberty and Sovereignty of We the People* (New York: Broadside Books, 2016); Bruce P. Frohnen and George W. Carey, *Constitutional Morality and the Rise of Quasi-Law* (Cambridge, MA: Harvard University Press, 2016). For a critique of this variety of legal conservative thought, see Jesse Merriam, "Legal Conservatism and the Progressive Blame Game," *Humanitas* 33 (2020): 69–82.

2. Bloom, *Closing of the American Mind*, 27.

3. Charles R. Kesler, "America's Cold Civil War," *Arkansas Democrat Gazette*, December 2, 2018, https://www.arkansasonline.com/news/2018/dec/02/america-s-cold-civil-war-20181202/?opinion.

4. Theodore Roosevelt, "Address to the Knights of Columbus," speech delivered at Carnegie Hall, New York, October 12, 1915.

5. Specifically, Goldberg says, "During the war, all of the tribal impulses were given free reign. Woodrow Wilson demonized the 'others' in our midst: the so-called hyphenated Americans, i.e., German-Americans, Italian-Americans, and any other group that didn't want to commit to what many called '100 percent Americanism" (*Decline of the West*, 186).

6. Eric Kaufmann, *The Rise and Fall of Anglo-America* (Cambridge, MA: Harvard University Press, 2004).

7. Eric Kaufmann, *Whiteshift: Populism, Immigration, and the Future of White Majorities* (New York: Abrams Press, 2019), 49.

8. Ibid., 54.

9. Ibid.

10. Ludwig von Mises, *Socialism: An Economic and Sociological Analysis* (London: Jonathan Cape, 1969).

11. Patrick J. Buchanan, *The Death of the West: How Dying Populations and Immigrant Invasions Imperil Our Country and Civilization* (New York: Thomas Dunne Books, 2002).

12. Ibid., 80.

13. Jeet Heer, "Trump's Racism and the Myth of "Cultural Marxism," *New Republic*, August 15, 2017, https://newrepublic.com/article/144317/trumps-racism-myth-cultural-marxism.

14. William F. Buckley Jr., *In Search of Anti-Semitism* (New York: Continuum, 1992).

15. Jonah Goldberg, "Farce as Tragedy," *National Review*, August 9, 2018, https://www.nationalreview.com/magazine/2018/08/27/farce-as-tragedy/.

16. Mary Eberstadt, *Primal Screams: How the Sexual Revolution Created Identity Politics* (West Conshohocken, PA: Templeton Press, 2019).

17. Ibid., 38.

18. Ibid., 69.

19. George Hawley, "The Demography of the Alt-Right," The Institute for Family Studies, August 9, 2018, https://ifstudies.org/blog/the-demography-of-the-alt-right.

20. Eberstadt, *Primal Screams*, 35.

21. Alexis de Tocqueville, *Democracy in America*, trans. Henry Reeve (New York: Bantam Classic, 2002), 353.

22. For one conservative scholar who has persuasively made these arguments about family life in America, see Allan Carlson, *The American Way: Family and Community in the Shaping of American Identity* (Wilmington, DE: ISI Book, 2003).

23. Benjamin Franklin, "Observations Concerning the Increase of Mankind and the Peopling of Nations," in *The Papers of Benjamin Franklin*, ed. Leonard W. Labaree (New Haven, CT: Yale University Press, 1961), 4:225–34.

24. Angela Nagle, *Kill All Normies: Online Culture Wars from 4Chan and Tumblr to Trump and the Alt-Right* (Winchester, UK: Zero Books, 2017), 97.

25. Eberstadt, *Primal Screams*, 129.

26. Dora Gicheva, "In Debt and Alone? Examining the Causal Link between Student Loans and Marriage," 2012, unpublished manuscript.

27. Daniel Schneider and Adam Reich, "Marrying Ain't Hard When You Got a Union Card? Labor Union Membership and First Marriage," *Social Problems* 61 (2014): 625–43.

28. Jared Meyer, "Why Americans Love the Sharing Economy," *National Review*, June 7, 2016, https://www.nationalreview.com/2016/06/uber-lyft-ride-sharing-services-sharing-economy-are-future/.

29. Robert DeFina and Lance Hannon, "De-unionization and Drug Death Rates," *Social Currents*, 6 (2018): 4–13.

30. Ross Douthat, "In Defense of the Religious Right," *New York Times*, October 15, 2016, https://www.nytimes.com/2016/10/16/opinion/sunday/in-defense-of-the-religious-right.html?_r=0.

31. Hawley, *Making Sense of the Alt-Right*, 100–105.

32. For a helpful explanation of white nationalism's contentious relationship with Christianity, I recommend Damon T. Berry, *Blood and Faith: Christianity and American White Nationalism* (Syracuse, NY: Syracuse University Press, 2017).

33. Peter Beinart, "Breaking Faith," *The Atlantic*, April 2017, https://www.theatlantic.com/magazine/archive/2017/04/breaking-faith/517785/?utm_source=twb.

34. Ibid.

35. Paul H. Rubin, "Environmentalism as Religion," *Wall Street Journal*, April 22, 2010, https://www.wsj.com/articles/SB10001424052702304510004575186343555831322.

36. Bruce Thornton, "The Religion of Environmentalism," *Defining Ideas: A Hoover Institution Journal*, November 6, 2015, https://www.hoover.org/research/religion-environmentalism.

37. Andrew Sullivan, "America's New Religions," *New York*, December 7, 2018, http://nymag.com/intelligencer/2018/12/andrew-sullivan-americas -new-religions.html.

38. Ibid., 58–59.

39. Michael Brendan Dougherty, "The Church of Grievance," *National Review*, May 14, 2018, https://www.nationalreview.com/magazine/2018/05 /14/victim-mentality-identity-politics-dominate-modern-left/.

40. Ibid.

41. Ibid.

42. James Kurth, "The Protestant Deformation," *The American Interest*, December 1, 2005, https://www.the-american-interest.com/2005/12/01/the -protestant-deformation/.

43. Ibid.

44. Joshua Mitchell, "Dead Conservative Memes Can't Defeat the Identity Politics Clerisy," *The American Mind*, June 6, 2019, https://americanmind .org/essays/dead-conservative-memes-cant-defeat-the-identity-politics -clerisy/.

45. Spencer Klavan, "You Gotta Serve Somebody," *The American Mind*, December 27, 2019, https://americanmind.org/features/you-gotta-serve -somebody/.

46. James Lindsay, "Identity Politics Isn't about Meaning. It's about Control," *The American Mind*, December 27, 2019, https://americanmind.org /features/you-gotta-serve-somebody/identity-politics-isnt-about-meaning -its-about-control/.

47. "On Critical Race Theory and Intersectionality," The Southern Baptist Convention, 2019, https://www.sbc.net/resource-library/resolutions/on -critical-race-theory-and-intersectionality/.

48. David R. Swartz, "Identity Politics and the Fragmenting of the 1970s Evangelical Left," *Religion and American Culture: A Journal of Interpretation* 21 (2011): 81–120.

49. Ibid., 83.

Chapter 4

1. For an example of this form of argument, see Robert C. Smith, *Conservatism and Racism, and Why in America They Are the Same* (Albany: SUNY Press, 2010).

2. In one rare exception to this, in his mother's obituary, Buckley stated, "The cultural coordinates of our household were Southern." However, in

that same piece, he also noted that his family had never been enthusiastic supporters of segregation, and the question created moral anguish for his devout Catholic mother. See William F. Buckley Jr., "Saying Goodbye: Aloise Steiner Buckley, RIP," *National Review*, April 19, 1985, https://www.nationalreview.com/2008/03/saying-goodbye-aloise-steiner-buckley-rip-william-f-buckley-jr/.

3. John Judis, *William F. Buckley, Jr.: Patron Saint of the Conservatives* (New York: Simon and Schuster, 1988), 138.

4. Nicholas Buccolla, *The Fire Is upon Us: James Baldwin, William F. Buckley, Jr., and the Debate over Race in America* (Princeton, NJ: Princeton University Press, 2019), 70.

5. Judis, *William F. Buckley, Jr.*, 322.

6. Joseph Lowndes, *From the New Deal to the New Right: Race and the Southern Origins of Modern Conservatism* (New Haven, CT: Yale University Press, 2008).

7. Charles Wallace Collins, *Whither Solid South: A Study in Politics and Race Relations* (New Orleans: Pelican Press, 1947).

8. Ibid., 18.

9. After providing a brief description of the history of civilization in Africa, Collins concludes: "In the face of this record, can it be said that there is no innate difference between the white man and the Negro?" (ibid., 39).

10. Ibid., 8.

11. Ibid., 40.

12. Ibid., 76–77.

13. Ibid., 77.

14. Ibid., ix.

15. According to Collins, "Ever since the Civil War the attachment of the South to the Democratic Party has been axiomatic. No people have ever given to a political party such love, faith, and sustained devotion" (ibid., 240).

16. Collins described the situation as follows; note the many themes still embraced by contemporary conservatives he touched upon: "Within the last decade a new school of thought has arisen in American politics, but it cuts across the lines of both major parties. Members of this school call themselves 'liberals.' They would exalt the powers and responsibilities of the Federal Government at the expense of the states, counties, and municipalities. National planning in time of peace would proceed from Washington outward to govern the lives of every person in all walks of life throughout the country. A federal bureaucracy would be the controlling factor in education, health, housing, recreation, social security, employment, wages, and profits. It would use the taxing power to distribute the national wealth to deserve it" (ibid., 256).

17. Ibid., 257.

18. Ibid., 261–62.

19. Simon Topping, "'Never Argue with the Gallup Poll': Thomas Dewey, Civil Rights, and the Election of 1948," *Journal of American Studies* 38 (2004): 179–98.

20. Lowndes, *From the New Deal to the New Right*, 30.

21. Kevin P. Phillips, *The Emerging Republican Majority* (New Rochelle, NY: Arlington House, 1969).

22. Ibid., 280.

23. Ibid., 284.

24. Max Boot, "The GOP Is America's Party of White Nationalism," *Foreign Policy*, March 14, 2017, https://foreignpolicy.com/2017/03/14/the -gop-is-americas-party-of-white-nationalism/.

25. Collins wrote an entire chapter explaining how this could come about. To ensure a smooth transition, he suggested that the United States should annex a large tract of territory in sub-Saharan Africa. It would then declare this territory the forty-ninth state (at the time he was writing, there were still only forty-eight states). This state would, by constitutional amendment, be open only to Blacks, who would own all of the property and fill every government position. These Blacks in Africa would remain U.S. citizens, and enjoy the protection of the U.S. government, but be otherwise free to pursue their own destiny. Collins further expressed hope that the creation of such a state would lead to a mass voluntary exodus of Blacks from the mainland United States, and thus not require any expulsions by force (Collins, *Whither Solid South*, 303–20).

26. Carl T. Bogus, *Buckley: William F. Buckley and the Rise of American Conservatism* (New York: Bloomsbury Press, 2011), 153.

27. "Why the South Must Prevail," *National Review*, August 24, 1957.

28. Ibid.

29. Ibid.

30. Bogus, *Buckley*, 160.

31. L. Brent Bozell, "Open Letter: Mr. Bozell Dissents from Views Expressed in the Editorial, 'Why the South Must Prevail,'" *National Review*, September 7, 1957, 209.

32. Buckley, quoted in Judis, *William F. Buckley, Jr.*, 139.

33. In that book, Buckley wrote the following: "Yes, there are circumstances when the minority can lay claim to preeminent political authority, without bringing down upon its head the moral opprobrium of just men. In the South, the white community is entitled to put forward a claim to prevail politically because, for the time being anyway, the leaders of American

civilization are white—as one would expect given their preternatural advantages, of tradition, training, and economic status"; William F. Buckley Jr., *Up from Liberalism* (New York: McDowell-Obolensky, 1959), 127.

34. Buccolla, *The Fire Is upon Us*, 83.

35. Lowndes, *From the New Deal to the New Right*, 41.

36. James Jackson Kilpatrick, *The Sovereign States: Notes of a Citizen of Virginia* (Chicago: Henry Regnery and Sons, 1957).

37. James Jackson Kilpatrick, *The Southern Case for School Segregation* (New York: Crowell-Collier, 1962).

38. Frank Meyer, "The Negro Revolution," *National Review*, June 18, 1963, 496.

39. George H. Nash, "Ernest van den Haag (1914–2002)," *The University Bookman*, March 30, 2007, https://kirkcenter.org/essays/ernest-van-den-haag -19142002/.

40. Ernest van den Haag, "Negroes, Intelligence, and Prejudice," *National Review*, December 4, 1964.

41. Ernest van den Haag, "Negroes and Whites: Claims, Rights, and Prospects," *Modern Age*, 9(1965): 354–62.

42. Ernest van den Haag, "Race: Claims, Rights, and Prospects," in Buckley, ed., *Did You Ever See a Dream Walking?*, 303–18.

43. Ibid., 309.

44. Ibid., 316.

45. Ibid., 303.

46. Ibid.

47. Ibid., 303–4.

48. In Van den Haag's own words: "Whether social discriminations rest on misjudgments and prejudices, or in the correct assessments of one's preferences and those likely to meet them, the individual has a clear right to discriminate socially in however foolish a manner he wishes—though he might be wiser, and serve his interests better, by not exercising it" (ibid., 305).

49. Ibid., 306.

50. Ibid.

51. Chambers wrote the following in his discussion of Marian Anderson, an influential Black singer in the mid-twentieth century:

At Salzburg, backdropped by magical mountains, where Austria's great musical festivals were held before the war, and where he first heard Marian Anderson sing, Arturo Toscanini cried: "Yours is a voice such as one hears once in a hundred years." Toscanini was hailing a great artist, but that voice was more than a magnificent personal talent. It was the religious voice of a whole religious people—probably the most God-obsessed (and man-despised) people since the ancient Hebrews. White Americans had withheld from Negro Americans practically everything but God. In return the Negroes had enriched American culture with an incomparable religious poetry and music, and its only truly great religious art— the spiritual.

This religious and aesthetic achievement of Negro Americans has found profound expression in Marian Anderson. She is not only the world's greatest contralto and one of the very great voices of all time, she is also a dedicated character, devoutly simple, calm, religious. Manifest in the tranquil architecture of her face is her constant submission to the "Spirit, that dost prefer before all temples the upright heart and pure."

(Whittaker Chambers, *Ghosts on the Roof: Selected Journalism of Whittaker Chambers, 1931–1959* [Washington, DC: Regnery, 1989], 134.)

52. Kendall chose not to weigh in on whether the civil rights movement made reasonable demands. He did, however, believe that the subject of race was explosive and had the potential to create a constitutional crisis and massive social disorder. The Civil Rights Act, he thought, could diffuse the situation without conceding the movement's most radical demands. Furthermore, because Kendall always believed Congress should be the strongest branch of the U.S. federal government, the fact that the Civil Rights Act instituted these changes—as opposed to a presidential decree or a Supreme Court decision— was itself important from the standpoint of maintaining America's constitutional order. See Willmoore Kendall, "The Civil Rights Movement and the Coming Constitutional Crisis," *The Intercollegiate Review* 1(1965): 53–66.

53. Daniel Kelly, *James Burnham and the Struggle for the World* (Wilmington, DE: ISI Books, 2002), 311.

54. Ibid.

55. Nash, *The Conservative Intellectual Movement in America Since 1945*, 285.

56. Specifically, Meyer wrote: "If things continue in this way, the only hope of Constitutional government and a sound foreign policy will rest, as it rested under Truman and Roosevelt, in the coalition of traditional Republicans and Southern Democrats in the congress"; see Frank Meyer, "Where Is Eisenhower Going?" *American Mercury*, 78 (1954): 126.

57. Kevin J. Smant, *Principles and Heresies: Frank S. Meyer and the Shaping of the American Conservative Movement* (Wilmington, DE: ISI Books, 2002), 23.

58. Ibid., 211.

59. For a synopsis of the Southern Agrarian worldview, see Hawley, *Right-Wing Critics of American Conservatism*, 76–79. See also their manifesto: Twelve Southerners, *I'll Take My Stand: The South and the Agrarian Tradition*, 75th anniversary ed. (Baton Rouge: Louisiana State University Press, 2006).

60. Richard Weaver, *The Southern Tradition at Bay* (Washington, DC: Regnery, 1989).

61. Weaver said the following on this subject: "There was of course the curse of slavery. During the Civil War one ingenious Northern general pronounced the Negroes to be 'contrabands.' Contrabands they may well have been from the beginning, and I have often wondered why the sellers of this article were not held more responsible than the users, as is true of those who peddle cocaine. A large number of these hapless slaves were brought to America in New England bottoms, and more than one fortune in Newport and New Bedford owes its origin to profits in black flesh. The facts could be presented thus: New England sold the slaves to the South, then later declared their possession immoral and confiscated the holding"; Richard Weaver, *The Southern Essays of Richard Weaver* (Indianapolis: Liberty Fund, 1987), 241–42.

62. Richard Weaver, "Integration Is Communization," *National Review*, July 13, 1957, 67–68.

63. Ibid., 68.

64. William F. Buckley Jr., "The Week," *National Review*, April 23, 1963, 305.

65. Jesse Curtis, "'Will the Jungle Take Over?' *National Review* and the Defense of Western Civilization in the Era of Civil Rights and African Decolonization," *Journal of American Studies* 53(2019): 997–1023.

66. Smant, *Prophesies and Heresies*, 215.

67. For a thorough treatment of these broadcasters, their message, and their audience, see Paul Matzko, *The Radio Right: How a Band of Broadcasters Took on the Federal Government and Built the Modern Conservative Movement* (New York: Oxford University Press, 2020).

68. Nicole Hemmer, "How Conservative Media Learned to Play Politics," *Politico Magazine*, August 30, 2016, https://www.politico.com/magazine/story/2016/08/conservative-media-history-steve-bannon-clarence-manion-214199.

69. Matzko, *The Radio Right*, 59–60.

70. Ibid., 55.

71. Ibid., 57.

72. Ibid., 58.

73. Ibid., 56.

74. James Burnham, "The Struggle for the World," in Buckley, ed., *Did You Ever See a Dream Walking?*, 271.

75. Ibid.

76. Ibid., 275.

77. To put that statement into context, I am providing the full quote: "The most important issue of the day, we have to admit it, is survival. Here there is apparently some confusion among the ranks of conservatives, and hard thinking is in order for them. The thus-far invincible aggressiveness of the Soviet Union does or does not constitute a threat to the United States, and we have got to decide which. If it does, we shall have to rearrange, sensibly, our battle plans; and this means we have got to accept Big Government for the duration—for neither offensive nor defensive war can be waged, given our present government skills, except through the instrument of totalitarian bureaucracy within our shores"; William F. Buckley, "The Party and the Deep-Blue Sea," *Commonweal*, January 1952, 392–93.

78. William F. Buckley Jr., "Our Mission Statement," *National Review*, November 19, 1955, https://www.nationalreview.com/1955/11/our-mission -statement-william-f-buckley-jr/.

79. "The Sharon Statement" (1960), Young America's Foundation, https://www.yaf.org/news/the-sharon-statement/.

80. Bradford Evans, *Civil Rights Myths and Communist Realities* (New Orleans: The Conservative Society of America, 1965).

81. Ibid., 21.

82. According to Whalen, "The Negro, too, is a Southerner, deeply conservative and suspicious of change"; Richard Whalen, "Prince Edward: Law and Reality," *National Review*, September 12, 1959, 329–30.

83. Levison was one of King's friends and allies. He helped write some of King's speeches. He has also been accused of being a financial supporter of the Communist Party. Conservatives continue to bring up this connection. See, for example, Daniel J. Flynn, "The MLK Story No One Wants to Read," *The American Spectator*, May 31, 2019, https://spectator.org/the-mlk-story-no -one-wanted-to-read/.

84. John David Skrentny, "The Effect of the Cold War on African-American Civil Rights: American and the World Audience, 1945–1968," *Theory and Society* 2 (1998): 237–85.

85. Mary L. Dudziak, *Cold War Civil Rights: Race and the Image of American Democracy* (Princeton, NJ: Princeton University Press, 2000).

86. Edward G. Carmines and James A. Stimson, *Issue Evolution: Race and the Transformation of American Politics* (Princeton, NJ: Princeton University Press, 1989).

87. Antony S. Chen, Robert W. Mickey, and Robert P. Van Houweling, "Explaining the Contemporary Alignment of Race and Party: Evidence from California's 1946 Ballot Initiative on Fair Employment," *Studies in American Political Development* 22 (2008): 204–28.

88. Gary King, *A Solution to the Ecological Inference Problem* (Princeton, NJ: Princeton University Press, 1997).

89. Chen, Mickey, and Van Houweling, "Explaining the Contemporary Alignment of Race and Party," 225.

90. Lionel Trilling, *The Liberal Imagination* (New York: New York Review of Books Classic, 2008), xv.

91. In one of his early articles denouncing the John Birch Society, Buckley criticized the group for its conspiracy theories and its hateful rhetoric on the topic of civil rights. See William F. Buckley, "The Birch Society," *National Review*, August 5, 1965, 916.

92. Kendall, "The Civil Rights Movement and the Coming Constitutional Crisis," 53.

93. Buckley, quoted in Judis, *William F. Buckley, Jr.*, 140.

94. Reno put it this way: "Buckley was a public intellectual trying to persuade the American people to adopt the views he thought best served the commonweal. As early as *God and Man at Yale*, he intuited, at least in part, that he could engage in public life only if he adopted his arguments to the growing postwar consensus in favor of the open society"; see R. R. Reno, *Return of the Strong Gods: Nationalism, Populism, and the Future of the West* (Washington, DC: Regnery, 2019), 31.

95. Joshua Tait, "Conservatives Self-Delusion on Race," *Washington Post*, October 5, 2018, https://www.washingtonpost.com/outlook/2018/10/05/conservatives-self-delusion-race/.

96. Bloom, *Closing of the American Mind*, 33.

97. William Voegeli, "Civil Rights and the Conservative Movement," *Claremont Review of Books*, Summer 2008, https://claremontreviewofbooks.com/civil-rights-and-the-conservative-movement/.

98. Ibid.

Chapter 5

1. Daniel Kelly, *Living on Fire: The Life of L. Brent Bozell, Jr.* (Wilmington, DE: ISI Books, 2014), 167–68.

2. Ronnee Schreiber, *Righting Feminism: Conservative Women and American Politics* (New York: Oxford University Press, 2008), 18.

3. Mrs. Arthur Dodge, "Woman Suffrage Opposed to Woman's Rights," *American Academy of Political and Social Sciences* 56 (1914): 104.

4. Ibid., 101.

5. Ibid., 103.

6. Ibid., 99.

7. Weaver, *Ideas Have Consequences*, 179.

8. Kathleen M. Blee, *Women of the Klan: Racism and Gender in the 1920s* (Berkeley: University of California Press, 1991).

9. Schreiber, *Righting Feminism*, 20.

10. Michelle Nickerson, "Women, Domesticity, and Postwar Conservatism," *OAH Magazine of History* 17 (2003): 17.

11. Ibid., 17–18.

12. Nickerson puts it this way: "Out of the political limelight, housewife activists transformed the domestic sphere into the grassroots sphere. They revise our understanding of women, gender, and postwar conservatism in three ways. First, they show us that domesticity did not necessarily render women apolitical. These 'kitchen table activists,' to borrow an expression from historian Lisa McGirr, were not the cloistered, depressed, valium-popping housewives of Betty Friedan's *Feminine Mystique*. Second, they demonstrate how women can develop a militantly conservative worldview out of their *own* experiences. Housewife activists were not foot soldiers to their husbands or slaves to patriarchy. Lastly, women of the Old Right strike an important balance in the history of gender and postwar conservatism. Though the scholarly work on antifeminism is sophisticated and enlightening, it reinforces the misconception that conservative women are reactionary and backward looking. Antifeminism loses some of its 'backlash,' in other words, when we introduce women of the Old Right and women of the prewar Right. We see that in addition to the StopERA and right-to-life movements, a long tradition of women's conservatism has been brought to bear on United States' political history" (ibid., 20).

13. Catherine E. Rymph, *Republican Women: Feminism and Conservatism from Suffrage through the Rise of the New Right* (Chapel Hill, NC: University of North Carolina Press, 2006), 110.

14. Elizabeth Gillespie McRae, *Mothers of Massive Resistance: White Women and the Politics of White Supremacy* (New York: Oxford University Press, 2018), 183.

15. Ibid., 6

16. Ibid., 177.

17. Ibid., 168.

18. In 1972, the ERA was passed in the U.S. Senate and sent to the states for ratification.

19. The ERA at the time it came close to ratification read, "Section 1: Equality of rights under the law shall not be denied or abridged by the United States or by any state on account of sex. Section 2: The Congress shall have the power to enforce, by appropriate legislation, the provisions of this article. Section 3: This amendment shall take effect two years after the date of ratification."

20. Rymph, *Republican Women*, 175.

21. Donald T. Critchlow, *Phyllis Schlafly and Grassroots Conservatism: A Woman's Crusade* (Princeton, NJ: Princeton University Press, 2008), 128.

22. Rymph, *Republican Women*, 187.

23. Phyllis Schlafly, "What's Wrong with 'Equal Rights' for Women?," *The Phyllis Schlafly Report* 5 (1972).

24. Rick Perlstein, *Reaganland: America's Right Turn, 1976–1980* (New York: Simon and Schuster, 2020), 72.

25. Schlafly, "What's Wrong with 'Equal Rights.'"

26. Perlstein, *Reaganland*, 80.

27. Ruth Bader Ginsberg, "The Need for the Equal Rights Amendment," *American Bar Association Journal* 59 (1973): 1013.

28. Schlafly, "How the ERA Would Change Federal Laws," *The Schlafly Report* 15 (1981).

29. Phyllis Schlafly, *The Power of Positive Women* (New Rochelle, NY: Arlington House, 1977), 76.

30. Barbara Ehrenreich, "Defeating the ERA: A Right-Wing Mobilization of Women," *Journal of Sociology and Social Welfare* 9 (1982): 393.

31. Gillis J. Harp. *Protestants and American Conservatism: A Short History* (New York: Oxford University Press, 2019), 190.

32. Rymph, *Republican Women*, 240.

33. This idea was most fully developed by Rebecca Klatch, "Coalition and Conflict among Women of the New Right," *Signs: Journal of Women in Culture and Society* 13 (1988): 671–94.

34. Ibid., 677.

35. Ibid., 681.

36. Ibid., 686.

37. Ibid., 688.

38. Russell Kirk, *The Intelligent Woman's Guide to Conservatism* (New York: The Devin-Adair Company, 1957), 8.

39. Klatch, "Coalition and Conflict among Women of the New Right," 688.

40. Schreiber, *Righting Feminism*.

41. Specifically, Palin said, "I'm a feminist who believes in equal rights and I believe that women certainly today have every opportunity that a man has to succeed and to try to do it all anyway"; "Transcript: Palin and McCain Interview," CBS Evening News, September 30, 2008. https://www.cbsnews .com/news/transcript-palin-and-mccain-interview/.

42. Meghan Daum, "Sarah Palin: Feminist," *Los Angeles Times*, May 20, 2010, https://www.latimes.com/archives/la-xpm-2010-may-20-la-oe-0520 -daum-fword-20100520-story.html.

43. Katie L. Gibson and Amy L. Heyse, "Depoliticizing Feminism: Frontier Mythology and Sarah Palin's 'The Rise of the Mama Grizzlies,'" *Western Journal of Communication* 78 (2014): 87–114.

44. Sarah Palin, *America by Heart: Reflections on Faith, Family, and the Flag* (New York: HarperCollins, 2010).

45. Ibid., 140.

46. Kathryn Jean Lopez, "Sarah Palin: A Feminist in the Pro-Life Tradition," *National Review*, May 24, 2010, https://www.nationalreview.com/2010 /05/sarah-palin-feminist-pro-life-tradition-kathryn-jean-lopez/.

47. Jessica Valenti, "Opinion: The Fake Feminism of Sarah Palin," *Washington Post*, May 30, 2010, https://www.washingtonpost.com/wp-dyn/content /article/2010/05/28/AR2010052802263.html?sid=ST2010052804193.

48. Kate Harding, "5 Ways of Looking at 'Sarah Palin Feminism,'" *Jezebel*, May 26, 2010, https://jezebel.com/5-ways-of-looking-at-sarah-palin -feminism-5548464.

49. Meghan Daum, "Sarah Palin, Feminist," *Los Angeles Times*, May 20, 2010, https://www.latimes.com/archives/la-xpm-2010-may-20-la-oe-0520 -daum-fword-20100520-story.html.

50. Christina Hoff Sommers, *Who Stole Feminism? How Women Have Betrayed Women* (New York: Simon and Schuster, 1995).

51. Ibid., 22.

52. For a thorough discussion of this subject, see David M. Whitford, *The Curse of Ham in the Early Modern Era: The Bible and the Justifications for Slavery* (Burlington, VT: Ashgate, 2009).

53. For one example of this kind of recent argument, see Courtney Ariel, "For Our White Friends Desiring to Be Allies," *Sojourners*, August 16, 2017, https://sojo.net/articles/our-white-friends-desiring-be-allies.

54. "Feminism," *Firing Line* broadcast records, Hoover Institution, March 31, 1975, https://digitalcollections.hoover.org/objects/6354/feminism ?ctx=b4b62c67-1cc8-4d14-8c14-41f3bde7a37d&idx=5.

55. Ian Hacking, *The Social Construction of What?* (Cambridge, MA: Harvard University Press, 1999), 7–9.

56. For the most well-known argument in favor of this position, see Judith Butler, *Gender Trouble: Feminism and the Subversion of Identity* (New York: Routledge, 1990).

57. Andrew Sullivan, "The Nature of Sex," *New York Magazine*, February 1, 2019, https://nymag.com/intelligencer/2019/02/andrew-sullivan-the -nature-of-sex.html.

58. Norquist, for example, urged his fellow Republicans to be supportive of Caitlyn Jenner during her gender transition. See David Weigel, "Rick Santorum and the GOP's Transgender Tolerance Movement," *Bloomberg*, May 2, 2015, https://www.bloomberg.com/news/articles/2015-05-02/rick-santorum -and-the-gop-s-transgender-tolerance-movement.

59. Rush Limbaugh, "Why Transgenders Get So Much Press," *The Rush Limbaugh Show*, August 29, 2018, https://www.rushlimbaugh.com/daily/2018 /08/29/why-transgenders-get-so-much-press/.

60. "The Inequality of the Equality Act: Concerns from the Left," The Heritage Foundation, Washington, DC, January 28, 2019, https://www .heritage.org/event/the-inequality-the-equality-act-concerns-the-left.

61. Zoe Williams, "Are You Too White, Rich, Able-Bodied and Straight to Be a Feminist?" *The Guardian*, April 18, 2013, https://www.theguardian.com /commentisfree/2013/apr/18/are-you-too-white-rich-straight-to-be-feminist.

62. Jamillah Bowman Williams, "Maximizing #MeToo: Intersectionality and the Movement," working paper (2020).

63. Abby Vesoulis, "Women First Marched to Challenge Trump. Now They Are Challenging Each Other," *Time*, January 19, 2019, https://time.com /5505787/womens-march-washington-controversy/.

Chapter 6

1. See, for example, Ann Coulter, *In Trump We Trust: E Pluribus Awesome!* (New York: Penguin Random House, 2016).

2. Madison Grant, *The Passing of the Great Race: Or, The Racial Basis of European History* (New York: Charles Scribner's Sons, 1916).

3. Daniel Tichenor, *Dividing Lines: The Politics of Immigration Control in America* (Princeton, NJ: Princeton University Press, 2002), 176–218.

4. D. J. Mulloy, *Years of Rage: From the Klan to the Alt-Right* (Lanham, MD: Rowman and Littlefield, 2021).

5. Judis, *William F. Buckley, Jr.*, 186–87.

6. Kelly, *James Burnham*, 366.

7. Smant, *Principles and Heresies*, 341.

8. Gillis J. Harp, *Protestants and American Conservatism: A Short History* (New York: Oxford University Press, 2019), 164.

9. Kelly, *Living on Fire*, 192.

10. For an early example of this, see L. Brent Bozell, "National Trends," *National Review*, January 12, 1957, 104–5.

11. James Burnham, "The Right to Leave," *National Review*, March 23, 1971, 306.

12. William F. Buckley Jr., "The Jackson Amendment," *National Review*, July 29, 1974, 438–39.

13. James Burnham, "The Right to Leave," *National Review*, March 23, 1971, 306.

14. Howard E. Hunt, "Castro's Worms," *National Review*, June 13, 1980, 722–24.

15. Ernest van den Haag, "More Immigration?," *National Review*, September 21, 1965, 821–42.

16. Tichenor, *Dividing Lines*, 202.

17. Perlstein, *Reaganland*.

18. For a comprehensive history of *National Review*'s approach to immigration, see Savannah Eccles Johnston, "The Rise of Illiberal Conservatism: Immigration and Nationhood at *National Review*," *American Political Thought* 10 (2): 190–216.

19. Lawrence Auster, *The Path to National Suicide* (Monterey, VA: The American Immigration Control Federation, 1990).

20. Ibid., 8–9.

21. Peter Brimelow, *Alien Nation: Common Sense about America's Immigration Disaster* (New York: Random House, 1995).

22. "VDare," Southern Poverty Law Center, https://www.splcenter.org/fighting-hate/extremist-files/group/vdare.

23. Matt Gertz, "*The Daily Caller* Has Published White Supremacists, Anti-Semites, and Bigots. Here Are the Ones We Know About," Media Matters for America, September 5, 2018, https://www.mediamatters.org/maga-trolls/daily-caller-has-published-white-supremacists-anti-semites-and-bigots-here-are-ones-we.

24. Even so, VDare has certainly published work that would not be accepted by mainstream conservative publications even in the 1990s. For example, the site has published open white nationalists, such as Jared Taylor, and anti-Semites, such as Kevin MacDonald.

25. Peter Brimelow, "Time to Rethink Immigration?" *National Review*, June 22, 1992, 30–42.

26. Elaine Kamarck and Christine Stenglein, "How Many Undocumented Immigrants Are in the United States and Who Are They?," The Brookings Institute, November 12, 2019, https://www.brookings.edu/policy2020/votervital/how-many-undocumented-immigrants-are-in-the-united-states-and-who-are-they/.

27. Nick Miroff, "July Was Busiest Month for Illegal Border Crossings in 21 Years, CBP Data Shows," *Washington Post*, August 12, 2021, https://www.washingtonpost.com/national/record-numbers-illegal-border-crossings/2021/08/12/e3d305e2-facd-11eb-b8dd-0e376fba55f2_story.html.

28. Mark Krikorian, *The New Case against Immigration: Both Legal and Illegal* (New York: Sentinel, 2008).

29. Ibid., 25–28.

30. George J. Borjas, *Heaven's Door: Immigration Policy and the American Economy* (Princeton, NJ: Princeton University Press, 1999).

31. Victor Davis Hanson, "On Assimilation," *National Review*, January 30, 2019, https://www.nationalreview.com/corner/on-assimilation/.

32. Hansi Lo Wang, "No Middle Eastern or North African Category on 2020 Census, Bureau Says," National Public Radio, January 29, 2018, https://www.npr.org/2018/01/29/581541111/no-middle-eastern-or-north-african-category-on-2020-census-bureau-says.

33. Tichenor, *Dividing Lines*.

34. Robert A Dahl, *Who Governs? Democracy and Power in an American City* (New Haven, CT: Yale University Press, 1961), 59.

35. Richard D. Alba and Reid M. Golden, "Patterns of Ethnic Marriage in the United States," *Social Forces* 65 (1986): 202–23.

36. Stanley Lieberson, "Unhyphenated Whites in the United States," *Ethnic and Racial Studies* 8 (1985): 159.

37. Brian K. Arbour and Jeremy M. Teigen, "Barack Obama's 'American' Problem: Unhyphenated Americans in the 2008 Election," *Social Science Quarterly* 92 (2011): 563–87.

38. Arnold R. Hirsch, *Making the Second Ghetto: Race and Housing in Chicago* (Chicago: University of Chicago Press, 1983), 81.

39. Perhaps the most influential work in this regard was Noel Ignatiev, *How the Irish Became White* (New York: Routledge, 1995).

40. Richard D. Alba, "The Twilight of Ethnicity among American Catholics of European Ancestry," *Annals of the American Academy of Political and Social Science* 454 (1981): 96.

41. Herbert J. Gans, "Symbolic Ethnicity: The Future of Ethnic Groups and Cultures in America," *Ethnic and Racial Studies* 2 (1979): 9.

42. Matthew Fry Jacobson, *Roots Too: White Ethnic Revival in Post-Civil Rights America* (Cambridge, MA: Harvard University Press, 2006).

43. Hawley, *White Voters in 21st Century America*, 58–59.

44. Per Urlaub and David Huenlich, "Why Are the German-Americans Trump's Most Loyal Supporters?," in *US Election Analysis 2016: Media, Voters and the Campaign*, ed. Darren Lilleker, Daniel Jackson, Einar Thorsen, and Anastasia Veneti (Poole, UK: Centre for the Study of Journalism, Culture and Community), http://www.electionanalysis2016.us/.

45. John B. Judis and Ruy Teixiera, *The Emerging Democratic Majority* (New York: Scribner, 2004).

46. For a more recent analysis making a similar argument, see James Gimpel, "Immigration, Political Realignment, and the Demise of Republican Political Prospects," Center for Immigration Studies, 2010, https://cis .org/Report/Immigration-Political-Realignment-and-Demise-Republican -Political-Prospects.

47. George Hawley, *Demography, Culture, and the Decline of America's Christian Denominations* (Lanham, MD: Lexington Books, 2017).

48. "Exit Polls," CNN, https://www.cnn.com/election/2020/exit-polls /president/national-results.

49. Rene R. Rocha and Tetsuya Matsubayashi, "The Politics of Race and Voter ID Laws in the States: The Return of Jim Crow?," *Political Research Quarterly* 67 (2013): 666–79; Benjamin Highton, "Voter Identification Laws and Turnout in the United States," *Annual Review of Political Science* 20 (2017): 158; Zoltan Hajnal, Nazita Lajevardi, and Lindsay Nielson, "Voter Identification Laws and the Suppression of Minority Voters," *Journal of Politics* 79 (2017): 363–79.

50. M. V. Hood III and Scott E. Buchanan, "Palmetto Postmortem: Examining the Effects of the South Carolina Voter Identification Statute" *Political Research Quarterly* 73 (2020): 492–505; Enrico Cantoni and Vincent Pons, "Strict ID Laws Don't Stop Voters: Evidence from a U.S. Nationwide Panel, 2008–2016," *Quarterly Journal of Economics* 136 (2021): 2615–60; M. V. Hood III and Charles S. Bullock III, "Much Ado about Nothing? An Empirical Assessment of the Georgia Voter Identification Statute," *State Politics and Policy Quarterly* 12 (2012): 394–414; Justin Grimmer, Eitan Hersh, Marc Meredith, Jonathan Mummolo, and Clayton Nall, "Obstacles to Estimating Voter ID Laws' Effect on Turnout," *Journal of Politics* 80 (2018): 1045–51.

51. "Exit Polls," CNN, November 23, 2016, https://www.cnn.com /election/2016/results/exit-polls.

52. "Exit Polls," CNN, December 10, 2012, https://www.cnn.com /election/2012/results/race/president/.

53. Gordon Allport, *The Nature of Prejudice* (New York: Doubleday, 1954).

54. Myron Rothbart and Oliver P. John, "Intergroup Relations and Stereotype Change: A Social-Cognitive Analysis and Some Longitudinal Findings," in *Prejudice, Politics, and the American Dilemma*, ed. Paul M. Sniderman, Philip E. Tetlock, and Edward G. Carmines (Stanford, CA: Stanford University Press, 1993).

55. V. O. Key, *Southern Politics in State and Nation* (New York: Alfred A. Knopf, 1949).

56. Robert A. Levine and Donald T. Campbell, *Ethnocentrism: Theories of Conflict, Ethnic Attitudes, and Group Behaviors* (New York: Wiley, 1972).

57. Thomas F. Pettigrew, Linda R. Tropp, Ulrich Wagner, and Oliver Christ, "Recent Advances in Intergroup Contact," *International Journal of Intercultural Relations* 35 (2011): 271–80.

58. Hubert M. Blalock, *Toward a Theory of Minority-Group Relations* (New York: John Wiley and Sons, 1967).

59. Michael R. Alvarez and Tara L. Butterfield, "The Resurgence of Nativism in California: The Case of Proposition 187 and Illegal Immigration," *Social Science Quarterly* 81 (2000): 167–79; Caroline Tolbert and Rodney Hero, "Dealing with Diversity: Racial/Ethnic Context and Social Policy Change," *Political Research Quarterly* 54 (2001): 571–604; Andrea Louise Campbell, Cara Wong, and Jack Citrin, "'Racial Threat,' Partisan Climate, and Direct Democracy: Contextual Effects in Three California Initiatives," *Political Behavior* 28 (2006): 129–50.

60. Yolande Pottie-Sherman and Rima Wilkes, "Does Size Really Matter? On the Relationship between Immigrant Group Size and Anti-Immigrant Prejudice," *International Migration Review* 51 (2017): 218–50.

61. Marisa Abrajano and Zoltan L. Hajnal, *White Backlash: Immigration, Race, and American Politics* (Princeton, NJ: Princeton University Press, 2015).

62. "Exit Polls," CNN, November 23, 2018, https://www.cnn.com /election/2016/results/exit-polls/california/president.

63. John Sides, Michael Tesler, and Lynn Vavreck, *Identity Crisis: The 2016 Presidential Campaign and the Battle for the Meaning of America* (Princeton, NJ: Princeton University Press, 2018).

64. George Borjas, "Does Immigration Grease the Wheels of the Labor Market?," *Brookings Papers on Economic Activity* 1 (2001): 69–133; Borjas, "The Labor Demand Curve Is Downward Sloping: Reexamining the Impact of

Immigration on the Labor Market," *Quarterly Journal of Economics* 118 (2003): 1335–74.

65. Rafaela Dancygier and Michael Donnelly, "Sectoral Economies, Economic Contexts, and Attitudes toward Immigration," *Journal of Politics* 75, no. 1 (2013): 17–35.

66. Kenneth Scheve and Matthew Slaughter, "Labor Market Competition and Individual Preferences over Immigration Policy," *Review of Economics and Statistics* 83 (2001): 133–45.

67. Judith L. Goldstein and Margaret E. Peters, "Nativism or Economic Threat: Attitudes toward Immigrants during the Great Recession," *International Interactions* 40 (2014): 376–401.

68. Jens Hainmueller and Michael J. Hiscox, "Attitudes toward Highly Skilled and Low-skilled Immigration: Evidence from a Survey Experiment," *American Political Science Review* 104 (2010): 61–84.

69. Peter Burns and James G. Gimpel, "Economic Insecurity, Prejudicial Stereotypes, and Public Opinion on Immigration Policy," *Political Science Quarterly* 115 (2000): 201–25.

70. Antoine Banks, "Are Group Cues Necessary? How Anger Makes Ethnocentrism among Whites a Stronger Predictor of Racial and Immigration Policy Opinions," *Political Psychology* 38 (2016): 635–57; Donald Kinder and Cindy Kam, *Us against Them: Ethnocentric Foundations of American Opinion* (Chicago: University of Chicago Press, 2009).

71. Felicia Pratto, James Sidanius, Lisa M. Stallworth, and Bertram F. Malle, "Social Dominance Orientation: A Personality Variable Predicting Social and Political Attitudes," *Journal of Personality and Social Psychology* 67 (1994): 741–63.

72. Lotte Thomsen, Eva Green, and Jim Sidanius, "We Will Hunt Them Down: How Social Dominance Orientation and Right-Wing Authoritarianism Fuel Ethnic Persecution of Immigrants in Fundamentally Different Ways," *Journal of Experimental Social Psychology* 44 (2008): 1455–64; Maureen Craig and Jennifer Richeson, "Not in My Backyard! Authoritarianism, Social Dominance Orientation, and Support for Strict Immigration Policies at Home and Abroad," *Political Psychology* 35 (2013): 417–29.

73. Jardina, *White Identity Politics* (New York: Cambridge University Press, 2019).

74. Mara Ostfeld, "The Backyard Politics of Attitudes toward Immigration," *Political Psychology* 38 (2015): 21–37.

75. Brenda Major, Alison Blodorn, and Gregory Major Blascovich, "The Threat of Increasing Diversity: Why Many White Americans Support Trump

in the 2016 Presidential Election." *Group Processes and Intergroup Relations* 21 (2018): 931–40.

76. Eric Leon McDaniel, Irfan Nooruddin, Allyson Faith Shortle, "Divine Boundaries: How Religion Shapes Citizens' Attitudes toward Immigrants," *American Politics Research* 39 (2011): 205–33.

77. Pazit Ben-Nun Bloom, Gizem Arikan, and Marie Courtemanch, "Religious Social Identity, Religious Belief, and Anti-Immigration Sentiment," *American Political Science Review* 109 (2015): 203–21.

78. Benjamin R. Kroll, "'And Who Is My Neighbor?' Religion and Immigration Policy Attitudes," *Journal for the Scientific Study of Religion* 48 (2009): 313–31.

79. Tatishe M. Nteta and Kevin J. Wallsten, "Preaching to the Choir? Religious Leaders and American Opinion on Immigration Reform," *Social Science Quarterly* 93, no. 4 (2012): 891–910; Michelle Margolis, "How Far Does Social Group Influence Reach? Identities, Elites, and Immigration Attitudes," *Journal of Politics* 80 (2018): 772–85.

80. Shanto Iyengar and Sean J. Westwood, "Fear and Loathing across Party Lines: New Evidence on Group Polarization," *American Journal of Political Science* 59 (2014): 690–707.

81. Lilliana Mason, *Uncivil Agreement* (Chicago: University of Chicago Press, 2018).

82. George Hawley, "Immigration Status, Immigrant Family Ties, and Support for the Democratic Party," *Social Science Quarterly* 100 (2019): 1171–81.

83. George Hawley, "Political Threat and Immigration: Party Identification, Demographic Context, and Immigration Policy Preference," *Social Science Quarterly* 92 (2011): 404–22.

84. George Hawley and Richard Hanania, "Cui Bono? Partisanship and Attitudes towards Refugees," working paper.

85. Rudolfo de la Garza and Jeronimo Cortina, "Are Latinos Republicans but Just Don't Know It? The Latino Vote in the 2000 and 2004 Presidential Elections," *American Politics Research* 40 (2007): 450–75.

86. Angus Campbell, Philip E. Converse, Warren E. Miller, and Donald Stokes, *The American Voter* (New York: Wiley, 1960).

87. Sergio Wals, "Made in the USA? Immigrants Imported Ideology and Political Engagement," *Electoral Studies* 32 (2013): 756–67.

88. See, for example, Linda Chavez, "Supporting Family Values," *Jewish World Review*, April 17, 2009, http://www.jewishworldreview.com/cols /chavez041709.php3.

89. Jeb Bush and Clint Bolick, *Immigration Wars: Forging an American Solution* (New York: Simon and Schuster, 2013).

90. Linda Chavez, "Welcome to America," *Jewish World Review*, November 21, 2008, http://jewishworldreview.com/cols/chavez112108.php3.

91. Matt Barretto, "New Poll: Immigration Policy Stance Directly Tied to Winning the Latino Vote," Latino Decisions, 2013, https://latinodecisions.com/blog/new-poll-immigration-policy-stance-directly-tied-to-winning-the-latino-vote/.

92. Iris Hui and David O. Sears, "Reexamining the Effects of Racial Propositions on Latino's Partisanship in California," *Political Behavior* 40 (2018): 149–74.

93. Tichenor, *Dividing Lines*, 203.

94. Carol Swain, "The Congressional Black Caucus and the Impact of Immigration on African American Unemployment," in *Debating Immigration*, ed. Carol Swain (New York: Cambridge University Press, 2007), 175–88.

95. Tichenor, *Dividing Lines*, 233.

96. Ibid., 236–37.

97. Hop Hopkins, "How the Sierra Club's History with Immigrant Rights Is Shaping Our Future," Sierra Club, November 2, 2018, https://www.sierraclub.org/articles/2018/11/how-sierra-club-s-history-immigrant-rights-shaping-our-future.

98. Jonathan Tilove, "Strange Bedfellows, Unintended Consequences, and the Curious Contours of the Immigration Debate," in *Debating Immigration*, ed. Carol Swain (New York: Cambridge University Press, 2007), 206–17.

99. "On Immigration," Southern Baptist Convention, 2018, https://www.sbc.net/resource-library/resolutions/on-immigration/.

100. David Frum, *Dead Right* (New York: Perseus Books, 1994), 130.

101. Abigail Fisher Williamson, *Welcoming New Americans? Local Governments and Immigrant Incorporation* (Chicago: University of Chicago Press, 2018).

102. Peter H. Schuck, "The Disconnect between Public Attitudes and Policy Outcomes in Immigration," in *Debating Immigration*, ed. Carol Swain (New York: Cambridge University Press, 2007) , 17–31.

103. For an outstanding explanation for why this is the case, see Christopher Baylor, *First to the Party: The Group Origins of Political Transformation* (Philadelphia: University of Pennsylvania Press, 2018).

104. Toni Caushi, "Opinion: Shapiro? Why Not Listen?," Boston University News Service, October 9, 2019, https://bunewsservice.com/opinion-shapiros-landing/.

105. Ben Shapiro, "Are Conservative Immigration Restrictionists Racist?," *Pittsburgh Post-Gazette*, November 16, 2019, https://www.post-gazette.com /opinion/Op-Ed/2019/11/16/Ben-Shapiro-Are-conservative-immigration -restrictionists-racist/stories/201911160005.

106. Stephen Welch, *The Concept of Political Culture* (New York: Macmillan, 1993).

107. Lucien W. Pye, "Political Culture," in *International Encyclopedia of the Social Sciences*, ed. David W. Sills (New York: Macmillan, 1968), 12:218.

108. Wilbur Zelinsky, *The Cultural Geography of the United States* (Eaglewood Cliffs, NJ: Prentice-Hall, 1973).

109. Raymond D. Gastil, *Cultural Regions of the United States* (Seattle: University of Washington Press, 1975), 26.

110. Daniel Elazar, *Cities of the Prairie* (New York: Basic Books, 1970).

111. David Hackett Fischer, *Albion's Seed: Four British Folkways in America* (New York: Oxford University Press, 1989).

112. Collin Woodard, *American Nations: A History of the Eleven Rival Regional Cultures of North America* (New York: Viking, 2011).

113. Samuel Huntington, *Who Are We? The Challengers to America's National Identity* (New York: Simon and Schuster, 2004).

114. Ibid., 40.

115. Ibid., 41.

116. Ibid., 18.

117. Ibid., 143.

118. Samuel Huntington, "The Hispanic Challenge," *Foreign Policy*, October 28, 2009, https://foreignpolicy.com/2009/10/28/the-hispanic -challenge/.

119. Ibid.

120. Gillian Brockell, "Controversial Lincoln Statue Is Removed in Boston, but Remains in D.C.," *Washington Post*, December 29, 2020, https:// www.washingtonpost.com/history/2020/12/29/lincoln-statue-removed -boston-dc/.

121. Specifically, I wrote the following: "On this point, many of today's white nationalists and contemporary progressives agree. Conservatives frequently argue that America's founders had a sincere vision of equality and that they pointed the way toward a peaceful, diverse, and egalitarian society. But this narrative is commonly rejected by both white nationalists and progressives. Jared Taylor, of the 'race realist' group American Renaissance, probably agrees with Bernie Sanders on very little, but his own writings on the subject ('Since early colonial times, and until just a few decades ago, virtually all Whites believed race was a fundamental aspect of individual and group

identity') clearly echo Sanders' claim that the United States was created 'on racist principles.' Although they reach different conclusions, both men argue that the United States was viewed by its founders as a country for people of European ancestry" (Hawley, *Making Sense of the Alt-Right*, 23).

122. "The 1619 Project," *New York Times Magazine*, August 14, 2019, https://www.nytimes.com/interactive/2019/08/14/magazine/1619-america -slavery.html.

123. Tom Mackaman, "An Interview with Historian Gordon Wood on the *New York Times'* 1619 Project," World Socialist Web Site, November 28, 2019, https://www.wsws.org/en/articles/2019/11/28/wood-n28.html.

Chapter 7

1. Ramesh Ponnuru, "A Conservative No More," *National Review*, October 11, 1996, 36.

2. Anthony Downs, *An Economic Theory of Democracy* (New York: Harper and Row, 1957).

3. James Davison Hunter, *Culture Wars: The Struggle to Control the Family, Art, Education, Law, and Politics in America* (New York: Basic Books, 1992).

4. Stephen Ansolabehere and M. Socorro Puy, "Identity Voting," *Public Choice* 169 (2016): 91.

5. Ibid.

6. Morris Fiorina, *Retrospective Voting in American Elections* (New Haven, CT: Yale University Press, 1981).

7. Angus Campbell, Philip E. Converse, Warren E. Miller, and Donald Stokes, *The American Voter* (New York: Wiley, 1960).

8. Donald Green, Bradley Palmquist, and Eric Schickler, *Partisan Hearts and Minds: Political Parties and the Social Identities of Voters* (New Haven, CT: Yale University Press, 2002).

9. Henri Tajfel and John Turner, "An Integrative Theory of Intergroup Conflict," in *The Social Psychology of Intergroup Relations*, ed. W. G. Austin and S. Worchel (Monterey, CA: Brooks/Cole, 1979), 33–47.

10. Ibid., 23.

11. Geoffrey L. Cohen, "Party over Policy: The Dominating Impact of Group Influence of Group Influence on Political Beliefs," *Journal of Personality and Social Psychology* 85 (2003): 819.

12. Dan M. Kahan, "Ideology, Motivated Reasoning, and Cognitive Reflection," *Judgment and Decision Making* 8 (2013): 407–24.

13. Gabriel S. Lenz, *Follow the Leader? How Voters Respond to Politicians' Policies and Performance* (Chicago: University of Chicago Press, 2012).

14. Michael Barber, "Does Party Trump Ideology? Disentangling Party and Ideology in America," *American Political Science Review* 113 (2019): 38–54.

15. Ibid., 52.

16. Sean Theriault, *Party Polarization in Congress* (New York: Cambridge University Press, 2008).

17. Matthew Levendusky, *The Partisan Sort: How Liberals Became Democrats and Conservatives Became Republicans* (Chicago: University of Chicago Press, 2009), 2.

18. Morris P. Fiorina, Samuel J. Abrams, and Jeremy C. Pope, *Culture War: The Myth of a Polarized America* (New York: Pearson, 2005), 7.

19. Alan Abramowitz, *The Disappearing Center: Engaged Citizens, Polarization, and American Democracy* (New Haven, CT: Yale University Press, 2011).

20. Alan Abramowitz and Kyle Saunders, "Is Polarization a Myth?," *Journal of Politics* 70 (2008): 542–55.

21. George Hawley, "Republican Voters and Conservative Ideology," in *The Vanishing Tradition: Perspectives on American Conservatism*, ed. Paul Gottfried (Ithaca, NY: Cornell University Press, 2020), 134–51.

22. Liliana Mason, "The Rise of Uncivil Agreement: Issue versus Behavioral Polarization in the American Electorate," *American Behavioral Scientist* 57 (2013): 140–59.

23. Ibid., 156.

24. Lilliana Mason, *Uncivil Agreement: How Politics Became Our Identity* (Chicago: University of Chicago Press, 2018), 18.

25. Hawley, *White Voters in 21st Century America*.

26. Despite the stereotype of liberal mainline Protestants and conservative evangelicals, there is actually a good deal of political diversity within the pews of most mainline denominations. The leadership of the mainline denominations is unquestionably more liberal than the leadership of evangelical denominations, but this has not trickled down to general adherents to the extent that many people have assumed. For example, Republicans actually outnumber Democrats in the mainline United Methodist Church and the Presbyterian Church (USA). See George Hawley, *Demography, Culture, and the Decline of America's Christian Denominations* (Lanham, MD: Lexington Books, 2017), 112.

27. Robert D. Putnam and David E. Campbell, *American Grace: How Religion Unites and Divides Us* (New York: Simon and Schuster, 2010), 91–133.

28. Michael Hout and Claude S. Fischer, "Why Americans Have No Religious Preference: Politics and Generations," *American Sociological Review* 67 (2002): 165–90.

29. Hawley, *Demography, Culture, and the Decline of America's Christian Denominations*, 78.

30. Nicholas Vargas, "Retrospective Accounts of Religious Disaffiliation in the United States: Stressors, Skepticism, and Political Factors," *Sociology of Religion* 73 (2010): 200–223.

31. Paul Djupe, Jacob Neiheisel, and Anand Sokhey, "Reconsidering the Role of Politics in Leaving Religion: The Importance of Affiliation," *American Journal of Political Science* 62 (2018): 161–75.

32. Paul A. Djupe, Jacob R. Neiheisel, and Kimberly H. Conger, "Are the Politics of the Christian Right Linked to State Rates of the Nonreligious? The Importance of Salient Controversy," *Political Research Quarterly* 71 (2018): 910–22.

33. Michelle Margolis, *From Politics to the Pews: How Partisanship and the Political Environment Shape Religious Identity* (Chicago: University of Chicago Press, 2018).

34. "Links between Childhood Religious Upbringing and Current Religious Identity," Pew Research Center, October 26, 2016, https://www.pewforum.org/2016/10/26/links-between-childhood-religious-upbringing-and-current-religious-identity/.

35. Alexander Agadjanian and Dean Lacy, "Linking Politics to Racial Identity: Race Change and Vote Switching in the 2012–2016 Presidential Elections," working paper.

36. Ibid., 7.

37. Martin Gilens, *Why Americans Hate Welfare: Race, Media and the Politics of Anti-Poverty Policy* (Chicago: University of Chicago Press, 1999).

38. Alberto Alesina, Edward Glaeser, and Bruce Sacerdote, "Why Doesn't the US Have a European-style Welfare System?" (No. w8524), National Bureau of Economic Research, 2001, https://www.nber.org/papers/w8524.

39. For just a few of the prominent examples, see Edward G. Carmines and James Stimson, *Issue Evolution: Race and the Transformation of American Politics* (Princeton, NJ: Princeton University Press, 1989); Donald R. Kinder and Lynn M. Sanders, *Divided by Color: Racial Politics and Democratic Ideals* (Princeton, NJ: Princeton University Press, 1996); Donald R. Kinder and Cindy D. Kam, *Us against Them: Ethnocentric Foundations of American Opinion* (Chicago: University of Chicago Press, 2010); Vincent L. Hutchings and Nicholas A. Valentino, "The Centrality of Race in American Politics," *Annual Review of Political Science* 7 (2004): 383–408.

40. Tali Mendelberg, *The Race Card: Campaign Strategy, Implicit Messages, and the Norm of Equality* (Princeton, NJ: Princeton University Press, 2001).

41. For further discussion of this, beyond the literature cited above related to partisanship and religious identity, see Gabriel S. Lenz, *Follow the Leader? How Voters Respond to Politicians Policies and Performance* (Chicago: University of Chicago Press, 2012).

42. Andrew M. Englehardt, "Racial Attitudes through a Partisan Lens," *British Journal of Political Science* 51 (2021): 1062–79.

43. John Sides, Michael Tesler, and Lynn Vavreck, *Identity Crisis: The 2016 Presidential Campaign and the Battle for the Meaning of America* (Princeton, NJ: Princeton University Press, 2018).

44. Daniel J. Hopkins and Samantha Washington, "The Rise of Trump, the Fall of Prejudice? Tracking White Americans' Racial Attitudes via a Panel Survey, 2008–2018," *Public Opinion Quarterly* 84 (2020): 119–40.

45. Eric Groenendyk, *Competing Motives in the Partisan Mind: How Loyalty and Responsiveness Shape Party Identification and Democracy* (New York: Oxford University Press, 2013).

46. Eric Groenendyk, "Competing Motives in a Polarized Electorate: Political Responsiveness, Identity Defensiveness, and the Rise of Partisan Antipathy," *Political Psychology* 39 (2018): 159–71.

47. A. W. Geiger, "For Many Voters, It's Not Which Presidential Candidate They're for but Which They're Against," Pew Research Center, September 2, 2016, https://www.pewresearch.org/fact-tank/2016/09/02/for-many-voters-its -not-which-presidential-candidate-theyre-for-but-which-theyre-against/.

48. Ibid., 170.

49. Wolfgang Donsbach, "Exposure to Political Content in Newspapers: The Impact of Cognitive Dissonance on Readers' Selectivity," *European Journal of Communication* 6 (1991): 155–86; Natalie Jomini Stroud, "Media Use and Political Predispositions: Revisiting the Concept of Selective Exposure," *Political Behavior* 30 (2008): 341–66.

Chapter 8

1. Paul Gottfried, "The Decline and Rise of the Alternative Right," *Taki's Magazine*, December 1, 2008, https://www.takimag.com/article/the_decline _and_rise_of_the_alternative_right/

2. Jesse Washington, "Gunman May Reflect Growing Racial Turmoil," NBC News, June 11, 2009, https://www.nbcnews.com/id/wbna31271698# .Xb9K-S2ZPOR.

3. For a thorough discussion of this history, see Tim Alberta, *American Carnage: On the Front Lines of the Republican Civil War and the Rise of President Trump* (New York: Harper, 2019).

4. Chris Kenning, "Review Faults Police Response to Charlottesville Far-Right Rally," Reuters, December 1, 2017, https://www.reuters.com/article/us-usa-protests-charlottesville/review-faults-police-response-to-charlottesville-far-right-rally-idUSKBN1DV5DZ.

5. For a recent analysis of public views on the Alt-Right, see Jack Thompson and George Hawley, "Does the Alt-Right Still Matter? An Examination of Alt-Right Influence between 2016 and 2018," in *Nations and Nationalism* 27 (2021): 1165–80.

6. In that book, I wrote: "The Alt-Right was able to inject itself into the conversation by entering spaces predominantly occupied by people outside the movement. If they are denied access to these spaces, the far right may find itself back where it was when white nationalists congregated at places like Stormfront, where they engaged with each other but otherwise could be ignored. The Alt-Right could presumably create its own social-network sites (in fact, the new social-media site Gab seems to have been invented for this purpose), but it is difficult to see what this would accomplish if they fail to attract people outside the movement—they would just end up trolling each other" (Hawley, *Making Sense of the Alt-Right*, 163).

7. Ibid., 166.

8. Ian Haney-Lopez, *Dog Whistle Politics: How Coded Racial Appeals Have Reinvented Racism and Wrecked the Middle Class* (Oxford: Oxford University Press, 2014).

9. Atwater, in a 1981 interview, explained the GOP's changing racial rhetoric in an interview, in which he was assured anonymity, with a political scientist. His identity as the person who made these remarks was not revealed until 2012. He said the following during that interview:

> Y'all don't quote me on this. You start out in 1954 by saying, "N-----, n------, n------". By 1968 you can't say "n------"—that hurts you. Backfires. So you say stuff like forced busing, states' rights and all that stuff. You're getting so abstract now [that] you're talking about cutting taxes, and all these things you're talking about are totally economic things and a byproduct of them is [that] blacks get hurt worse than whites.
>
> And subconsciously maybe that is part of it. I'm not saying that. But I'm saying that if it is getting that abstract, and that coded, that we are doing away with the racial problem one way or the other. You follow me—because obviously sitting around saying, "We want to cut this," is much more abstract than even the busing thing, and a hell of a lot more abstract than "N-----, n-----." So, any way you look at it, race is coming

on the backbone. (Alexander P. Lamis, *The Two-Party South* [New York: Oxford University Press, 1990], 26.)

10. Adrian Sol, "'It's Okay to Be White' Flyers Still Sending Universities into Chaos," *The Daily Stormer*, November 4, 2019, https://dailystormer.su/its -okay-to-be-white-flyers-still-sending-universities-into-chaos/.

11. Katlyn Patton, "Ohio Universities Involve FBI in Investigation of 'It's Okay to Be White' and White Nationalist Group's Postings on Campus," *The Fire*, November 14, 2019, https://www.thefire.org/ohio-universities-involve -fbi-in-investigation-of-its-okay-to-be-white-and-white-nationalist-groups -postings-on-campus/.

12. Nuria Martinez-Keel, "Suspended Student Expelled after Posting 'IT'S OKAY TO BE WHITE' Flyers at OCU," *The Oklahoman*, December 10, 2019, https://oklahoman.com/article/5649422/suspended-student -expelled-after-posting-its-okay-to-be-white-flyers-at-ocu.

13. Brandon Morse, "'It's Okay to Be White' Sign Appears above Massachusetts Highway," *RedState*, November 9, 2019, https://www.redstate .com/brandon_morse/2019/11/04/okay-white-sign-appears-massachusettes -highway/.

14. Tucker Carlson quoted in Michael Edison Hayden, "It's Okay to Be White: How Fox News Is Helping to Spread Neo-Nazi Propaganda," *Newsweek*, November 19, 2017, https://www.newsweek.com/neo-nazi-david-duke -backed-meme-was-reported-tucker-carlson-without-context-714655.

15. See chapter 5 of Hawley, *Making Sense of the Alt-Right*.

16. Roger Griffin, *The Nature of Fascism* (New York: Routledge, 2013), 26.

17. For a longer discussion of the Groyper movement, see George Hawley, "The 'Groyper' Movement in the US: New Strategies in the Post-Alt-Right," in *Far Right Thinkers and the Future of Liberal Democracy*, ed. A. James McAdams and Alejandro Castrillon (New York: Routledge, 2021), 225–41.

18. Alex Haley, "Playboy Interview: George Lincoln Rockwell," *Playboy*, April 1966, 80.

19. Karen J. Alter and Michael Zürn, "Conceptualizing Backlash Politics," *British Journal of Politics and International Relations* 22 (2020): 563–84.

20. Ibid., 8.

21. For a sample of these stories, see Hannah Allam, "'A Perfect Storm': Extremists Look for Ways to Exploit Coronavirus Pandemic," *National Public Radio*, April 16, 2020, https://www.npr.org/2020/04/16/835343965/-a -perfect-storm-extremists-look-for-ways-to-exploit-coronavirus-pandemic; Jason Wilson, "US Far Right Seeks Ways to Exploit Coronavirus and Cause

Social Collapse," *The Guardian*, April 5, 2020, https://www.theguardian.com /world/2020/apr/05/us-far-right-seeks-ways-to-exploit-coronavirus-and -cause-social-collapse; Neil MacFarquhar, "The Coronavirus Becomes a Battle Cry for U.S. Extremists," *New York Times*, May 3, 2020, https://www.nytimes .com/2020/05/03/us/coronavirus-extremists.html/.

22. Christian Britschgi, "Trump Tweets about Mike Pence's Betrayal While His Supporters Force the V.P. to Evacuate the Capitol," *Reason*, January 6, 2021, https://reason.com/2021/01/06/trump-tweets-about-mike -pences-betrayal-while-his-supporters-force-the-v-p-to-evacuate-the -capitol/.

23. Lee Brown, "Biden Ripped for Calling Capitol Riots 'Worst Attack on Our Democracy since the Civil War,'" *New York Post*, April 29, 2021, https://nypost.com/2021/04/29/biden-calls-capitol-riots-worst-attack-on -our-democracy-since-the-civil-war/.

24. Chris Cillizza, "A Republican House Member Just Described January 6 as a 'Normal Tourist Visit,'" *CNN*, May 13, 2021, https://www.cnn .com/2021/05/13/politics/andrew-clyde-january-6-riot/index.html.

25. I briefly describe Baked Alaska in Hawley, *Making Sense of the Alt-Right*, 153.

26. Will Sommer, "Right Richter," *The Daily Beast*, March 27, 2019, https://elink.thedailybeast.com/view/5bae99853f92a46ecbcf5b739rlr3.15s /0f27da77.

27. I discuss this group in detail in Hawley, *The Alt-Right: What Everyone Should Know*, 194–97.

28. Luke Barnes, "Proud Boys Founder Disavows Violence at Char-lottesville but One of Its Members Organized the Event," *Think Progress*, August 24, 2017, https://archive.thinkprogress.org/proud-boys-founder-tries -and-fails-to-distance-itself-from-charlottesville-6862fb8b3ae9/.

29. For the most thorough left-wing scholarly consideration of the Proud Boys, see Daniel Martinez HoSang and Joseph E. Lowndes, *Producers, Parasites, Patriots: Race and the New Right-Wing Politics of Precarity* (Minneapolis: University of Minnesota Press, 2019).

30. Devlin Barrett, Spencer S. Hsu, and Marissa J. Lang, "Dozens of People on FBI Terrorist Watch List Came to D.C. the Day of Capitol Riot," *Washington Post*, January 14, 2021, https://www.washingtonpost.com/national -security/terror-watchlist-capitol-riot-fbi/2021/01/14/07412814-55f7-11eb -a931-5b162d0d033d_story.html.

31. Richard Spencer, "The Charlottesville Statement," AltRight.com, August 11, 2017, https://web.archive.org/web/20210217082056/https:// altright.com/2017/08/11/what-it-means-to-be-alt-right/.

Chapter 9

1. Irving Kristol, *Neoconservatism: The Autobiography of an Idea* (New York: Free Press, 1995), 346.

2. Russell Kirk, "Ten Conservative Principles," The Russell Kirk Center for Cultural Renewal, https://kirkcenter.org/conservatism/ten-conservative -principles/.

3. Patrick Deneen, *Why Liberalism Failed* (New Haven, CT: Yale University Press, 2018).

4. Ibid., 16.

5. Ibid., 122.

6. Ibid.

7. Ibid., 17.

8. Ibid., 3.

9. Ibid., 172.

10. Ibid., 183.

11. For a brief introduction to Berry's perspective, see Hawley, *Right-Wing Critics*, 80–82.

12. Wendell Berry, *The Art of the Commonplace: The Agrarian Essays of Wendell Berry* (Berkeley, CA: Counterpoint, 2002), 178.

13. Ryszard Legutko, *The Demon in Democracy: Totalitarian Temptations in Free Societies* (New York: Encounter Books, 2016).

14. Ibid., 3.

15. Christopher Caldwell, *The Age of Entitlement: America since the Sixties* (New York: Simon and Schuster, 2020).

16. Jonathan Rauch, "Did the Civil Rights Movement Go Wrong?," *New York Times*, January 17, 2020, https://www.nytimes.com/2020/01/17/books /review/christopher-caldwell-age-of-entitlement.html; Benjamin C. Water-house, "Blaming All of America's Problems on the Civil Rights Movement," *Washington Post*, March 5, 2020, https://www.washingtonpost.com/outlook /blaming-all-of-americas-problems-on-the-civil-rights-movement/2020/03 /05/b1f6de8a-526e-11ea-b119-4faabac6674f_story.html.

17. Paul Gilbert, *The Philosophy of Nationalism* (Boulder, CO: Westview, 1998), 19.

18. Quoted in John Fonte, "American Patriotism and Nationalism: One and Indivisible," *National Review*, May 1, 2017, https://www.nationalreview .com/2017/05/nationalism-patriotism-american-history-conservatives -progressives/.

19. George Orwell, "Notes on Nationalism (1945)," The Orwell Foundation, https://www.orwellfoundation.com/the-orwell-foundation/orwell/essays-and-other-works/notes-on-nationalism/.

20. Yoram Hazony, *The Virtue of Nationalism* (New York: Basic Books, 2019), 31.

21. Ibid., 32.

22. Ibid., 167.

23. Ibid., 171.

24. Rich Lowry, *The Case for Nationalism: How It Made Us Powerful, United, and Free* (New York: Broadside Books, 2019).

25. For a scholarly, but generally sympathetic review of national populist movements, see Roger Eatwell and Matthew Goodwin, *National Populism: The Revolt against Liberal Democracy* (London: Pelican, 2018).

26. Cas Mudde, "The Populist Zeitgeist," *Government and Opposition* 39 (2004): 543.

27. Ibid., 545.

28. Ben Stanley, "The Thin Ideology of Populism," *Journal of Political Ideologies* 13 (2008): 95–110.

29. For a refutation of the claim that populism can be properly classified as an ideology in any sense, see Paris Aslanidis, "Is Populism an Ideology? A Refutation and a New Perspective," *Political Studies* 64 (2016): 88–104.

30. Margaret Canovan, "Trust the People! Populism and the Two-Faces of Democracy," *Political Studies* 47 (1999): 3.

31. Russell Kirk, *The Politics of Prudence*, 2nd ed. (Wilmington, DE: Intercollegiate Studies Institute, 2004), 143.

32. Ibid., 49.

33. James Burnham, *The Machiavellians: Defenders of Freedom* (Chicago: Henry Regnery, 1943).

34. Peter Viereck, *Unadjusted Man in the Age of Overadjustment: Where History and Literature Intersect* (New Brunswick, NJ: Transaction, 2004), 134.

35. Albert Jay Nock, "Isaiah's Job," in Buckley, ed., *Did You Ever See a Dream Walking?*, 509–22.

36. Buckley and Bozell, *McCarthy and His Enemies*, 338–39.

37. Judis, *William F. Buckley, Jr.*, 201–19.

38. Ibid., 213.

39. Ibid., 217.

40. Andrew McCarthy, "No, Conservatism Should Not Embrace Populism," *National Review*, November 26, 2016, https://www.nationalreview.com/2016/11/donald-trump-election-populism-new-fad-conservatism/.

41. For a longer discussion of this group, including its political weaknesses, see George Hawley and Richard Hanania, "The National Populist Illusion: Why Culture, Not Economics, Drives American Politics," The Center for the Study of Ideology and Partisanship, November 30, 2020, https://cspicenter.org/the-national-populist-illusion-why-culture-not-economics-drives-american-politics/.

42. R. R. Reno, "Nationalism and Populism Are the GOP's Future," *Newsweek*, December 9, 2020, https://www.newsweek.com/nationalism-populism-are-gops-future-opinion-1553161.

43. Bari Weiss, "Meet the Renegades of the Intellectual Dark Web," *New York Times*, May 8, 2018, https://www.nytimes.com/2018/05/08/opinion/intellectual-dark-web.html.

44. Ibid.

45. The Rubin Report, "What Is the Intellectual Dark Web," YouTube, January 30, 2018, https://www.youtube.com/watch?v=n5HN-KT9rj0.

46. Daniel Miessler, "A Visual Breakdown of the Intellectual Dark Web (IDW) Political Positions," *Daniel Miessler*, April 12, 2019, https://danielmiessler.com/blog/a-visual-breakdown-of-intellectual-dark-web-idw-political-positions/.

47. Uri Harris, "Is the 'Intellectual Dark Web' Politically Diverse?," *Quillette*, April 17, 2019, https://quillette.com/2019/04/17/is-the-intellectual-dark-web-politically-diverse/.

48. Christian Alejandro Gonzalez, "The New Neocons," *The Intercollegiate Review*, June 6, 2019, https://isi.org/intercollegiate-review/new-neocons/.

49. Helen Pluckrose and James Lindsay, *Cynical Theories: How Activist Scholarship Made Everything about Race, Gender, and Identity—and Why This Harms Everybody* (Durham, NC: Pitchstone Publishing, 2020).

50. Ibid., 30.

51. Russell Vought, "Training in the Federal Government," official memorandum, Washington, DC, Executive Office of the President Office of Management and Budget, 2020, https://www.whitehouse.gov/wp-content/uploads/2020/09/M-20-34.pdf.

52. Jessica Guynn, "President Joe Biden Rescinds Donald Trump Ban on Diversity Training about Systemic Racism," *USA Today*, January 20, 2021, https://www.usatoday.com/story/money/2021/01/20/biden-executive-order-overturns-trump-diversity-training-ban/4236891001/.

53. Benjamin Wallace-Wells, "How a Conservative Activist Invented the Conflict over Critical Race Theory," *The New Yorker*, June 18, 2021, https://www.newyorker.com/news/annals-of-inquiry/how-a-conservative-activist-invented-the-conflict-over-critical-race-theory.

54. Christopher F. Rufo, "City of Seattle 'Interrupting Internalized Racial Superiority and Whiteness' Training," christopherrufo.com, July 8, 2020, https://christopherrufo.com/city-of-seattle-interrupting-internalized-racial-superiority-and-whiteness-training/.

55. Wallace-Wells, "How a Conservative Activist Invented the Conflict over Critical Race Theory."

56. For a thorough discussion of how conservatives and progressives differ in their activism on immigration at the local level, I recommend Abigail Fisher Williamson, *Welcoming New Americans: Local Government and Immigrant Incorporation* (Chicago: University of Chicago Press, 2018).

57. Hannah Natanson, "How and Why Loudon County became the Face of the Nation's Culture Wars," *Washington Post*, July 5, 2021, https://www.washingtonpost.com/local/education/loudoun-critical-race-theory-transgender-rights/2021/07/05/3dab01b8-d4eb-11eb-ae54-515e2f63d37d_story.html.

58. Jania Hoover, "Critical Race Theory Hysteria Overshadows the Importance of Teaching Kids about Racism," *Vox*, July 9, 2021, https://www.vox.com/first-person/22568672/critical-race-theory-crt-education-racism-teachers.

59. Travis Fain, "NC House Divided over How, Whether to Teach America's Racist Past," WRAL, May 12, 2021, https://www.wral.com/nc-house-divided-over-how-whether-to-teach-america-s-racist-past/19674912/.

60. Allison Morrow, "Mr. Potato Head Tries to be More Gender Neutral," CNN, February 6, 2021, https://www.cnn.com/2021/02/25/business/mr-potato-head-hasbro-gender-neutral/index.html.

61. Kevin Shalvey, "Ted Cruz Has Been Selling Signed Copies of the Dr. Seuss Book 'Green Eggs and Ham,' and Raised $125,000 in 24 Hours," *Business Insider*, March 13, 2021, https://www.businessinsider.com/sen-cruz-sells-signed-dr-seuss-books-green-eggs-and-ham-2021-3.

62. Steve McMorran, "Expert: Transgender Olympic Athlete Could Polarize Opinion," *Seattle Times*, June 23, 2021, https://www.seattletimes.com/sports/olympics/expert-transgender-olympic-athlete-could-polarize-opinion/.

INDEX

abortion, 41, 101, 156, 211, 216, 277
Abrajano, Marisa, 185
Abramowitz, Alan, 211
Adorno, Theodor, 92
affirmative action: in college admissions, 74, 75, 77; for conservatives in academia, 38; discriminatory nature of, 77; in government hiring, 138; intersectional arguments on, 41; state bans on, 269
AFL-CIO, 193
African Americans. *See* Black community
Agadjanian, Alexander, 219
Age of Entitlement, The (Caldwell), 262–63
Ahmari, Sohrab, 64, 299n12
Alba, Richard, 179
Alien Nation (Brimelow), 171, 172
Allitt, Patrick, 19
Allport, Gordon, 183–84
Alt-Right, 227–54; absence from Capitol insurrection, 251–52; anti-Semitism of, 228–30, 233; barriers to success, 11, 227; Christianity opposed by, 99; doxings and, 227, 248; Intellectual Dark Web and, 278; intersectionality as used by, 42; lessons learned from, 235–50; online deplatforming of, 234–36; optics debate

within, 244–45, 248; propaganda used by, 237–39; on race as biological category, 42–43; rebranding efforts of, 243; rise and fall of, 228–35; Unite the Right rally by, 232–34, 243, 250; victim politics used by, 42; white identity politics and, 4, 95–97, 228, 252–54. *See also* white nationalism
amendments to U.S. Constitution. *See specific amendments*
American Dilemma, An (Myrdal), 115–17
American Federation of Labor (AFL), 193
American nationalism, 243, 244
American Revolution, 67–68, 200
American Voter, The (Campbell et al.), 208
Anderson, Marian, 310–11n51
Andrews, Louis, 229
Ansolabehere, Stephen, 207
anticolonial movements, 33
anticommunism, 20–21, 26, 29, 119, 129, 146
antifeminism, 9–10, 144, 148–52, 156, 161, 315n12
anti-immigrant sentiment: Catholic roots of, 165–67; in conservative intellectual movement, 166–67; in

government (*continued*)
　in separation of church and state,
　119; white supremacy undermined
　by, 117, 138
Gramsci, Antonio, 92
Grant, Madison, 164, 165
Gray, Philip W., 42–43
Great Depression, 165, 177
Greek philosophy, 62, 68–69
Green, Donald, 208
Griffin, Roger, 242
Groenendyk, Eric, 223–24
group contact theory, 183–84, 187
group threat theory, 184, 187
Groyper movement, 245

Hacking, Ian, 50
Hainmueller, Jens, 186
Hajnal, Zoltan L., 185
Hanania, Richard, 188
Hanson, Victor Davis, 69, 176
Harding, Kate, 156
Hargis, Billy James, 129
Harp, Gillis, 151
Harris, Uri, 277
Haslanger, Sally, 49–50, 297n95
Hayek, F. A., 26–29, 64–66, 166
Hazony, Yoram, 265–67
Hemmer, Nicole, 128
Herberg, Will, 59, 72–73
Heritage Foundation, 27, 161, 241
Heyse, Amy, 155
higher education. *See* college education
Hirsch, Arnold, 178
Hiscox, Michael, 186
Hispanics. *See* Latinos/Latinas
Hiss, Alger, 21
Hitler, Adolf, 57, 101, 266
homosexuality. *See* LGBT community
Horkheimer, Max, 92
horseshoe theory of political spectrum,
　57

HoSang, Daniel Martinez, 85–86
Houck, Shanno, 84
Hout, Michael, 214–15
Huenlich, David, 180
Hughes, Geoffrey, 47
Hui, Iris, 192
Hunter, James Davison, 206
Huntington, Samuel, 25, 198, 199, 202

Ibn Warraq, 75
Ideas Have Consequences (Weaver), 26,
　52, 113, 166
identity politics: of antifeminism, 10,
　150; complexity of, 2–3, 258; defi-
　nitions of, 1–2, 30–32; demand for
　recognition in, 34–39; in democracy,
　7, 30; double standards and, 74–77;
　family structure change as driver of,
　94–99; freedom of speech and, 46,
　70–74; history of, 32–34; individu-
　alism as alternative to, 62–69; as
　innate behavior, 5; Intellectual Dark
　Web on, 276, 278; intersectionality
　in, 30, 39; natural rights in opposition
　to, 9, 88; patterns within, 56–57; in
　Progressive Era, 9, 87–91; religion in,
　58–60, 104–6; utilitarian arguments
　against, 81–83. *See also* left-wing
　identity politics; right-wing identity
　politics; white identity politics
ideology, definitions of, 23–25
IDW (Intellectual Dark Web), 275–79
immigration, 163–202; assimilation
　and, 174–78, 195–96, 198; Cold
　War and, 167–69; Democratic Party
　and, 168, 181, 187–92; demographic
　change from, 168, 170–73, 195;
　Ellis Island and, 174, 179; as for-
　eign policy tool, 167–68; in formative
　years of conservatism, 164–65; legal,
　171, 173–75; open-border policies,
　170, 174; political coalitions and,

GEORGE HAWLEY
is associate professor of political science
at the University of Alabama. He is the author of a number
of books, including *Making Sense of the Alt-Right,*
Right-Wing Critics of American Conservatism, and
White Voters in Twenty-First Century America.

CPSIA information can be obtained
at www.ICGtesting.com
Printed in the USA
LVHW082225170123
737383LV00003B/101